British Paramountcy in

JAIPUR STATE

(1818-1905)

British Paramountcy in JAIPUR STATE

(1818-1905)

ANJU SURI

MANAK
PUBLICATIONS PVT. LTD

Publisher

MANAK

PUBLICATIONS PVT. LTD

B-7, Saraswati Complex, Subhash Chowk,
Laxmi Nagar, New Delhi 110092
Phone: 22453894, 22042529
E-mail : manak_publications@hotmail.com
manak.publications@gmail.com

USA Office
8145 KOLB AVE, ALLEN PARK, M.I. 48101 USA
E-mail: rahul_upma@yahoo.com

First Edition 2010 (Nov.)

ISBN 978-81-7831-251-4

Laser Typeset by: T. ALI, Hamdard Nagar, New Delhi
Printed in India by: Nice Printing Press, New Delhi

Contents

Preface

A large number of books have been written and published on the history of Rajasthan and some exclusively on Jaipur State. But no serious and systematic research work based on original documents on the British paramountcy has been attempted heretofore. The present work is an intensive and indepth case study of the evolution of British paramountcy in this premier State of erstwhile Rajputana.

To begin with, an account of the dynastic profile of the early rulers of Jaipur State, based on secondary sources, has been given which is intended to serve as historical background. The year 1818, when the State came under British protection, marks the beginning of British paramountcy. In the following four decades of the East India Company's rule the British authorities intervened almost continuously through the British Political Agencies in the internal affairs of the State which forms the subject-matter of the second chapter. The roots of British paramountcy in the State could be perceived during this period. After the Revolt of 1857-58 a new era dawned in the evolution of British paramountcy under the Crown. It was declared in the Queen's Proclamation of 1858 that there would be no further extension of British dominions in India, that all the treaties concluded with the States earlier would be scrupulously maintained and that rights and dignity of the Princes would be duly respected. But these promises were honoured more in breach than in observance. In the following decades of the Crown's regime the British paramountcy assumed wide dimensions in response to growing requirements of the Imperial Government which exercised ever-increasing intervention in the internal affairs of Jaipur, as also of other States. Such a manifold intervention exercised in gross violation of the treaty of 1818 was manifested in the questions of succession, border disputes between the States and their isolation from one another, fiscal and economic matters (salt, coinage, opium-trade, etc.), transport and communications (railways, roads, post and telegraph), military establishment in the State and British intervention in, and influence on, almost every department of internal administration. All these matters have been discussed comprehensively and critically in various chapters. The concluding chapter sums up findings in retrospect.

The British policy towards the Jaipur State in all the aforesaid matters has not been viewed in isolation. It has been examined, as far as possible, in the context of general policy adopted by the British statesmen towards numerous Princely States of India as a whole. At the same time, peculiarities in respect of Jaipur State have been highlighted.

All the Viceroys of the period from 1858 to 1905 had made their respective contribution in the growth of various and manifold facets of British paramountcy according to their personality and propensity, but they had all been guided predominantly by imperial consideration. The process reached its culmination during the viceroyalty of Curzon (1899-1905). The year 1905 has, therefore, been regarded as befitting for the close of our study.

The work has been based largely upon the original and primary sources which have been listed in the bibliography. Mention may be made here of the Proceedings of the Government of India in the Foreign Department (Political, Internal, General, Secret, Financial, Revenue, Judicial and Military branches); Despatches to and from the Secretary of State for India; Private Papers of the Viceroys (Microfilms); Jaipur Agency/Residency Record; Annual Reports on the Political Administration of Rajputana States and of Jaipur State; Reports of Public Works Department of Jaipur State; Speeches of the Viceroys; *Imperial Gazetteers of India* (relevant volumes); and Contemporary Vernacular Newspapers Reports. Secondary sources have also been made use of.

Grateful thanks are due to the authorities of the following institutions for allowing me free access to the documents, records and books in their possession as well as for the co-operation generously extended by them in this regard : National Archives of India, Nehru Memorial Museum and Library, Library of Indian Council of Historical Research, all located in New Delhi; Central Library, University of Rajasthan, Jaipur; Maharaja Sawai Man Singh II Museum and Library, Jaipur; Maharaja Divisional Public Library, Jaipur; Jaipur Archives and Library, Secretariat; Rajasthan State Archives, Bikaner; Punjab State Archives, Patiala; Haryana State Archives, Panchkula; A.C. Joshi Library, Panjab University, Chandigarh; Dwarka Dass Library, Chandigarh; Maharana Pratap Library, Chandigarh; and Punjabi University Library (Dr. Ganda Singh Collection), Patiala.

I should express my deep sense of gratitude and indebtedness to my father, Dr.A.C. Arora, former Professor and Head, Department of History, Punjabi University, Patiala for going through the manuscript thoroughly and giving his valuable suggestions and critical comments which were immensely helpful in the finalisation of this work.

I am thankful to Dr. B.L. Gupta, former Professor and Head, Department of History, University of Rajasthan, Jaipur who helped me in ways more than one during my stay at the University Guest House for a number of days. Dr. V.K. Vashishtha, former Professor and Head of the same Department, gave useful information about the source-material available at various institutions of Jaipur for which I feel obliged to him. I am also grateful to him for permitting me to use the Map of Jaipur from his book. My thanks are due to Dr. K.S. Gupta, former Professor and Head, M.L.S. University, Udaipur who evinced keen interest in the preparation of this work.

I am beholden to Professor Rajiv Lochan, present Head of History Department, Panjab University, Chandigarh and to my dear colleague, Dr. Devi Sirohi for their spontaneous co-operation and help in the completion of this project.

I should inscribe my genuine appreciation for all my family members (husband, Er. Anil Suri, son Karan, father-in-law, Dr. K.K. Suri and mother-in-law, Dr. Vinod Suri) for the most willing co-operation extended by them. They voluntarily shouldered all the family responsibilities and spared enough time for me to complete this project to my satisfaction.

Lastly, I owe my sincere thanks to Shri M.P. Yadav, Director, Manak Publications, who took a keen personal interest in the publication of this book so promptly.

ANJU SURI
Department of History
Panjab University, Chandigarh

Abbreviations

AGG	...	Agent to Governor-General, Rajputana States
Capt.	...	Captain
Col.	...	Colonel
Comp.	...	Compiler
Cons.	...	Consultations
D.O.	...	Demi-Official
ed.	...	edited
Enc.(s)	...	Enclosure(s)
FD	...	Foreign Department
GOI	...	Government of India
Govt.	...	Government
I.G.	...	Inspector General
IGI	...	*Imperial Gazetteer of India*
Ibid.	...	*Ibidem*
K.W.	...	Keep With
Lieut.	...	Lieutenant
n.d.	...	no date
No.(s)	...	Number(s)
N.W.P.	...	North-Western Province
Offg.	...	Officiating
op. cit.	...	*opere citato*

Progs.	...	Proceedings
P.W.D.	...	Public Works Department
RPARS	...	Report on Political Administration of Rajputana States
S. No.	...	Serial Number
Vol.	...	Volume

CHAPTER 1

Historical Background and Review of Literature

Rajputana[1] comprised a vast tract which included eighteen Native States, viz. Jaisalmer, Jodhpur (Marwar), Bikaner, Alwar, Jaipur, Bharatpur, Dholpur, Karauli, Bundi, Kotah, Jhalawar, Partabgarh, Banswara, Dungarpur, Udaipur (Mewar), Sirohi, Kishangarh and Tonk, two Chiefships of Shahpura and Lawa, and the British province of Ajmer-Merwara. This tract lay between 23° 3' and 30° 12' N. and 69° 30' and 78° 17' E., with a total area of about 130,462 square miles. It was bounded on the west by the province of Sind; on the north-west by the Punjab State of Bahawalpur; on the north and north-east by the Punjab; on the east by the United Provinces of Agra and Oudh and the Gwalior State; and on the south by the central region of India.[2] The Aravallis divide Rajputana into two main divisions, namely, the north-west and the south-east, the former being largely sandy, ill-watered and unproductive and the latter comparatively much more fertile.

Between the seventh and the beginning of the eleventh century, several Rajput dynasties arose and fell in this tract till the said eighteen Princely States and two Chiefships were established. Setting aside the two Jat States of Bharatpur and Dholpur and the Muhammadan principality of Tonk, Rajputana might be described as a region within which the pure-blooded Rajput clans had maintained their independence under their own Chieftains for a long time.[3]

The Jaipur State was located in the north-east and east of Rajputana, lying between 25° 41′ and 28° 34′ N. and 74° 41′ and 77° 13′ E. Its area was 15,579 square miles, and was consequently the fourth largest of the Rajputana States. It was bounded on the north by Bikaner, Loharu, and Patiala, while its detached district of Kot Kasim adjoined the Rewari *tahsil* of Gurgaon District and the State of Nabha; on the west by Bikaner, Jodhpur, Kishangarh, and the British District of Ajmer; on the south by Udaipur, Bundi, Tonk, Kota and Gwalior; and on the east by Karauli, Bharatpur, and Alwar.[4] Thus surrounded by the States of Rajputana and Punjab, and contiguous to some British districts, the geographical location of Jaipur State explains in some measure the working of various aspects of British paramountcy in this State.

Around Jaipur there were a good number of semi-autonomous estates owned by the *Thakurs* or feudatory chiefs who owed allegiance to the Raja/Maharaja of Jaipur. They either paid regular tribute to the latter or prepared soldiers for him. Of these, particular mention may be made of Samod, Chomu, Jhelli, Uniara, Diggi and Shekhawati comprising a cluster of estates such as Manoharpur, Khandela, Sikar, Khetri, etc.[5] Some of the *Thakurs* of these estates played an important role in the administration of Jaipur as members of the Jaipur Council.

Dynastic Profile of Jaipur State

A brief account of the dynastic profile of Jaipur State may be given so as to serve as historical background for our study.

Rise of Kachhawahas and Early Rulers

The Jaipur State which was known as Dhundhar in ancient and medieval times, was ruled by the Rajputs of Kachhawaha clan. The origin and early history of the Kachhawaha Rajputs, despite a number of genealogical tables of considerable antiquity, bardic accounts, and a few epigraphic records, is shrouded in obscurity.[6] The Kachhawahas of Jaipur claim to belong to the solar dynasty, tracing their descent from Kusha, the second son of Lord Rama of Ayodhya. Kusha, or some of his immediate offspring, is said to have migrated from the parental abode and constructed the celebrated castle of Rohtas on the bank of river Sone. After the lapse of several generations, another distinguished scion, named Raja Nal, migrated westward, and in 295 A.D., founded the kingdom of Narwar or Naishadha near Gwalior.[7] Dhola, the son of Raja Nal is said to have fallen in love with the daughter of the prince of Ajmer whose name was Maruni and whom he subsequently married.[8] In the tenth century, the Kachhawahas expanded their territory in the present Madhya Pradesh stretching along the Chambal river with Gwalior, Dubkhund and Narwar as their seats. According to popular tradition and bardic chronicles, Dulha Rai[9] one of the rulers of this clan left Gwalior and laid the foundation of Dhundhar[10] in 966 or 967 A.D.[11] The Kachhawahas then conquered many territories. They subdued the Badgujars and the Minas and settled at Dausa, 50 km east of Jaipur. Dulha Rai got help from the Chauhan Chief of Lalsot, named Ralhan-si who gave half of the township of Dausa in the dowry of his daughter. Soon after Dulha Rai expelled the Badgujars from Dausa. Thus Dausa became the first capital of the Kachhawahas in Dhundhar. With Dausa as the base of operations he subjugated more territories, expelled the Minas from Machi (18 miles north-west of Jaipur) and Khoh (6 miles east of Jaipur). Machi was renamed as Jamwa Ramgarh after the name of the deity, *Jamwa Mata.* A temple dedicated to this goddess was also built to commemorate the victory over Minas.[12] Subsequently Getor (2 miles north-east of Sanganer) and Jhotwara (3 miles west of Jaipur) were also conquered from Jaita Mina and Jhota Mina respectively. Thus Dulha Rai established his authority over a territory about 50 miles in length and 30 miles in width, and to keep the newly conquered territory under his control he shifted his capital from Dausa to Khoh[13] which became the second capital of the Kachhawahas.

After the death of Dulha Rai in 1036, his son Kakil Deo succeeded him. An ambitious and gallant ruler like his father, Kakil attacked Amber[14] and after defeating the Mina Chief, Rao

Bhatto succeeded in conquering it. He shifted his capital from Khoh to Amber. He constructed a temple and dedicated it to Ambikeshwar Mahadeva. He also built a fort in Bairath known as Kakilgarh. Another fort raised by him at Amber began to be known as the Amber fort, after the name of the town. Amber thus became the third capital of the Kachhawahas and continued to remain as such for about seven centuries.

Pajvan, the great-grandson of Kakil Deo is believed to be the most chivalrous among the Kachhawaha kings before the advent of the Mughals. After his marriage with a cousin of Prithvi Raj Chauhan, the celebrated ruler of Ajmer-Delhi, he became a conspicuous companion of the latter and participated successfully in many of his campaigns. According to Chand Bardai, the author of *Prithvi Raj Raso,* "Prithviraj fought many big battles and he had many valiant warriors under him, but Pajvan was the bravest among them". Displaying his extraordinary courage and valour Pajvan defeated not only Bhimdeva, the Solanki king of Gujarat but also Parmal, the Chandela ruler of Bundelkhand from whom he wrested Mahoba. He participated heroically in the first battle of Tarain (1191) by the side of Prithvi Raj Chauhan who succeeded in defeating the Turkish invader, Mohammad Ghori. But he did not live to take part in the second battle of Tarain as he had died while fighting against Jaichand's forces in the course of the Chauhan Prince's elopement with the Kanauj Princess.[15]

After the demise of Pajvan, his eldest son, Malesi became the Kachhawaha Chief. He raised his State to great heights, greater than ever before.[16] Two of his notable successors, Kilhan and Kuntil founded Kilhanpur and Kuntilgarh respectively. The alleged invasion of Mohammad-bin-Tughlaq in 1327-28 might have not only checked the expansion of Amber, but also cost independence of Kachhawahas.[17] This was followed by a long period of political stagnation in the history of Kachhawahas which lasted till the beginning of the 16th century. In his endeavour to establish his supremacy over the whole of Rajputana, Rana Kumbha of Mewar swept the Kachhawaha territory and probably exacted tribute from Amber.[18] Prithvi Raj, the ruler of Amber (1503-1527) is believed to have joined the Rajput Confederacy organised under the leadership of the famous Rana Sanga of Mewar. Prithvi Raj played an important role in the campaigns of the Rana. He is said to have been present in the battle of Bayana with the Rana fought on 16 February 1527. He also fought on the side of the Rana in the famous battle of Khanwa (17 March 1527). When Rana Sanga was wounded and fell unconscious in the course of this battle, Prithvi Raj along with others escorted the Rana to a safe place (Baswa). Prithvi Raj died on 19 November 1527, about two months before Rana Sanga's death (30 January 1528).[19]

Prithvi Raj had nine wives by whom he had twentyone children, eighteen sons and three daughters. Before his death he had assigned to eight of his sons and four collaterals appanages in perpetuity which are styled the *bara kotri* or 'twelve chambers' of the Kachhawaha house. Their holders formed the highest nobility in Amber State. "The portion of each was necessarily very limited; some of the descendants of this hereditary aristocracy now hold estates equal in magnitude to the principality itself at that period."[20]

For the next two decades after the death of Prithvi Raj (1527) his two sons, Puranmal and Bhim followed by Bhim's sons named Ratan Singh and Askaran, ruled over the State of Amber.

Raja Bharmal, 1547-1573

On 25 June 1547 Bharmal also known as Biharimal ascended the throne. With his accession "a completely new chapter opens in the history of Jaipur as well as that of Rajputana."[21] After becoming the ruler Bharmal had to face serious troubles from within and without. Shiya, the son of Puranmal (elder brother of Bharmal) coveted the throne for himself and was looking for an opportunity to dispossess his uncle. From without he had to face troubles due to aggressive designs of Mirza Mohammad Sharifuddin Hussain, the Mughal Governor of Mewat. The Mirza led a large army to attack Amber and he was joined by Shiya in his expedition against Bharmal. Finding himself helpless to face the enemies, he came to terms with the Mirza by promising to pay a fixed tribute to him, and handed over his son Jagannath and two nephews (Raj Singh and Khangar Singh) as hostages.[22] Not satisfied with these terms, the Mirza made preparation for renewing his expedition to Amber the following year (1562). At this time Chaghtai Khan, a friend of Raja Bharmal at the Mughal court, came to the rescue of the latter. He informed the Mughal Emperor Akbar about the plight of Raja Bharmal due to aggressive designs of Mirza Mohammad Sharifuddin. Praising the qualities of the Raja he said, "The Raja is eminent for wisdom and valour and has always been loyal to the imperial family and rendered excellent service."[23] He urged the Emperor to own the Raja as he would prove to be 'a tower of strength to him'. Accepting his suggestion, the Emperor sent a message to Raja Bharmal to present himself in the imperial camp when the royal party was near Amber on the way to Ajmer to pay obeissance to the shrine of Khwaja Muin-ud-din Chisti. Instead of going himself the Raja sent his brother Rupsi and the latter's son Jaimal to meet the Emperor to know his reaction. Akbar, however, was not satisfied with the visit of these two Kachhawaha princes and desired the personal attendance of Raja Bharmal. Thereupon the Raja visited the Emperor in person at Sanganer. According to Abul Fazl, "His Majesty with his discerning glance read devotion and sincerity in the behaviour of the Raja and his relatives."[24] The Raja on his part felt elated with the kind gesture of the Emperor and offered the hand of his daughter in marriage to him. Akbar consented and on his return journey from Ajmer when Akbar reached Sambhar, Raja Bharmal arrived there along with his daughter. Here the marriage ceremony between the Emperor and the Rajput princess was performed in March 1562 amidst proper festivity. To win over the friendship of the Raja, Akbar ordered Mirza Sharifuddin Hussain to surrender his hostages as well as the booty to the Raja. Not only that, the Emperor also conferred a *mansab* of 5000 on the Raja. Further he admitted Kanwar Bhagwant Das and Kanwar Man Singh (son and grandson respectively of the Raja) into the imperial service who joined the royal camp and proceeded towards the capital.

Akbar's marriage with the Amber princess is a highly

significant event in the political history of Mughal India as well as that of Rajputana. This marriage was followed a few years after by the Emperor's marriages with the princesses of Bikaner and Jaisalmer. Consequently a good number of Rajput Chiefs and their sons and close relatives joined the Mughal service. In the words of Beni Prasad, "It (this marriage) symbolised the dawn of a new era in Indian politics; it gave the country a line of remarkable sovereigns; it secured to four generations of Mughal Emperor the services of some of the greatest captains and diplomats that medieval India produced."[25] For the Rajput Chiefs of Amber also this matrimonial alliance proved highly useful. To quote M.L. Sharma, "The policy initiated by Beharimal and pursued by his worthy successors was responsible for the high prestige the princely house of the Kachhawas enjoyed in the Mughal Court, the brilliant military career which the Kachhawa sardars obtained in Mughal service, and the continuous peace and prosperity which about two million subjects of Amber enjoyed for about two centuries before the Marathas appeared on the horizon."[26] The Rajput princes who joined the Mughal service got the opportunities to display their courage and valour as a result of which they could win name and fame for themselves; otherwise they might have died as obscure and unknown figures.

Raja Bharmal displayed unflinching loyalty towards the Mughal Emperor and the latter also reposed complete trust in the former; so much so that when the Emperor left the capital, he often entrusted the charge of administration to this trusted Rajput Chief.[27] Raja Bharmal ruled over the Amber State for about twenty-five years from 1547 to 1573.

Raja Bhagwant Das, 1573-1589

After the death Raja Bharmal, his eldest son Bhagwant Das ascended the throne in February 1573. Bhagwant Das was an intrepid military general who, like his father, was very loyal and faithful to the Mughal Emperor. The Emperor bestowed upon him the title of *Amir-ul-Umara*. He made his mark by showing extraordinary bravery in several Mughal campaigns. He sided with Akbar during the siege operations of Chittor and

Ranthambhor in 1568 and 1569 respectively. It was Bhagwant Das who along with Man Singh negotiated terms of peace with Surjan Hara, the ruler of Ranthambhor.[28]

On his return journey from Ranthambhor to Agra, Akbar stayed at Amber in 1569 and enjoyed the hospitality of Raja Bhagwant Das and his son Man Singh. The Raja is believed to have constructed a mosque at Amber known as Akbari Mosque on the eve of Akbar's visit in order to enable the Emperor and his Muslim nobles to recite their prayers there.[29] He was present at Nagaur at the time when the rulers of Bikaner and Jaisalmer offered submission before the Mughal Emperor in 1570. He is believed to have played a significant role in the young Emperor's marriage with the Jaisalmer princess; he was sent to Jaisalmer to bring the princess to the royal camp.[30] He also played an important part in Akbar's Gujarat campaign for which he was honoured with the award of a standard or banner and a kettledrum, never before bestowed on a Hindu.[31] Being a trustworthy noble, he was sent by the Emperor on a mission to Rana Pratap. Although he was received cordially and also seen off courteously by the Rana, he did not succeed in his mission to win over the Rana to the Emperor's side. After the battle of Haldighati, Akbar sent Bhagwant Das and Man Singh to accompany the Mughal generals Qutb-ud-din Khan and thereafter Shahbaz Khan in expeditions launched for the annihilation of Rana Pratap but these expeditions failed to achieve the desired object.[32] In 1581 when Akbar founded Din-i-Ilahi, both Bhagwant Das and his son Man Singh refused to accept the new sect. Bhagwant Das is said to have remarked, "I would willingly believe that Hindus and Musalmans have each a bad religion, but only tell us what the new sect is, and what opinion they hold, so that I may believe.[33]

In 1581-82, Raja Bhagwant Das was appointed as joint governor of Lahore along with Saeed Khan. It is said that on the Raja's request the Emperor, in the course of his visit to the Punjab, went to the residence of the Raja at Lahore — a signal honour shown by the Emperor towards the Rajput Chief.[34] In 1583, Raja Bhagwant Das was appointed as the sole governor of Lahore, and this office he held till his death in 1589.

Early in 1585 Bhagwant Das offered the hand of his daughter, Man Bai for marriage with prince Salim (later Jahangir). The marriage was solemnised at Bhagwant Das's residence on 13 February 1585 according to Hindu and Muslim rites. Bhagwant Das gave a rich dowry to his daughter which included a large number of horses, hundred elephants, many male and female servants, various kinds of golden vessels set with jewels, all sorts of stuff, jewels and other precious articles.[35] In the words of a Muslim historian, it "is the first indication of the growing prosperity of the Kachhwas."[36] The Prince gave her the name of Sultan Nisa; later on she became famous by the name of Shah Begum after she had given birth to Khusro in 1587. Soon after this marriage Bhagwant Das was honoured with the mansab of 5000 on the occasion of *Nauroz* in March 1585.

In the same year (1585) Bhagwant Das was directed to accompany Mirza Shahrukh in expedition against Sultan Yusuf Khan of Kashmir. After defeating Yusuf Khan, Bhagwant Das concluded an agreement with him on 22 February 1586 by which the Sultan recognised the suzerainty of the Mughal Emperor and Bhagwant Das pledged the safety of his person. However, when Bhagwant Das returned to Akbar's camp at Attock with the deposed Sultan of Kashmir (March 1586), the Emperor did not approve of the said agreement. He expressed his annoyance with the Raja by forbidding him temporarily to attend the Mughal court and also ordered the imprisonment of Yusuf Khan.[37] The Raja felt greatly embarrased and stabbed himself with a dagger in order to save his honour. Akbar at once ordered the court surgeons to treat him and the Raja recovered quickly. According to V.A.Smith, this charge, so discreditable to Akbar may be safely rejected as untrue.[38] Another expedition was sent to Kashmir which resulted in the defeat of Yakub Khan (son of Yusuf Khan) and annexation of Kashmir to the Mughal Empire. Raja Bhagwant Singh died in November 1589 at Lahore; at that time he was a 'Commander of 5000' and bore the lofty title of *Amir-ul-Umara*, or Premier Noble.

It is obvious from the above account that Bhagwant Das was a constant and conspicuous companion of Akbar ever since he joined the Mughal service in 1562. He had taken a significant part in all the important Mughal campaigns from Gujarat in the west to Kabul and Kashmir in the north-west. He possessed some admirable qualities due to which he rose to be a prominent ruler of Amber. In the words of Abul Fazl, "Raja Bhagwant Das was endowed with uprightness, weight of counsel and courage." Seeds for the future greatness of Kachhawa house were sown during the reign of Raja Bhagwant Das.[39]

Raja Man Singh, 1589-1614

Bhagwant Das was succeeded by his eldest son Man Singh who ruled over the State of Amber from 1589 to 1614. He had acquired military training in his boyhood and grew into a courageous and brave youth. He joined the Mughal service along with his father immediately after the marriage of Amber Princess with Akbar in March 1562. He distinguished himself as a valiant soldier and an intrepid warrior in the numerous Mughal campaigns and earned the reputation of being one of the greatest generals of the Mughal Empire. He had started participating in the military exploits of Mughals during the time of his grandfather and continued to fight in the service of the Mughals during the time of his father, and very often in collaboration with him. A succinct account of his activities and achievements during this long period (1562-1589) may be given as under :

Man Singh participated in the imperial campaign of Ranthambhor (1569) led by Akbar and along with his father he played an important part in negotiating a peace treaty with Rana Surjan Hara of Ranthambhor.[40] In 1573 Man Singh joined the Emperor when he led an expedition to Surat undertaken to suppress the Mirzas.[41] In the same year Man Singh invaded Dungarpur with a large army and succeeded in defeating Askaran, its ruler. Consequently he conquered and looted the territories of Dungarpur. Thereafter he proceeded to Udaipur where he was warmly received but curtly treated. Man Singh and his accomplices were sent by Akbar to the eastern provinces for suppressing the rebellion of Daud Khan. In the list of nineteen persons sent to this expedition the names of Bhagwant

Das and Man Singh figure at the first and the second place respectively. The father and the son played an important part in suppressing the turbulent Afghans, compelling Daud Khan to flee towards Bengal.[42]

In 1576 Man Singh was given the sole command of the imperial army to proceed against Rana Pratap of Mewar. It was the first great honour which had been shown to him and as such it brought him into prominence. Man Singh set out of Ajmer towards Gogunda early in April 1576. He encamped at Mandalgarh (75 miles south of Ajmer and 25 miles north of Chittor) for about two months so that other Mughal generals might join him there. Both Man Singh and Rana Pratap prepared themselves for the battle which took place on 18 June 1576 at Haldighati (so called because of yellow colour of its soil). In the beginning the Mewar Rajputs took offensive and appeared to have bright prospects of their victory. With the arrival of imperial reinforcement, however, the tables were turned against Rana Pratap who lost the battle.[43] Although the Mughals came out victorious in this battle, Man Singh failed to capture or kill the Rana, and his men could not get sufficient provisions to eat. The failure of Man Singh annoyed the Emperor and Man Singh was called back. On reaching Ajmer he, along with Asaf Khan, was forbidden entry to the Mughal court for some time. Akbar, however, soon realised that Man Singh was not at fault[44] and in October 1577 he was again deputed to accompany the Mughal army against the Rana sent under the command of Qutb-ud-din Khan.

The year 1581 was a critical year in the career of Akbar when his "life and throne seemed to be in imminent danger."[45] There were revolts against him in Bihar and Bengal in the east and troubles were created in the north-west by his step-brother, Mirza Muhammad Hakim. The Mirza marched towards the Punjab with his force. At this time Man Singh was directed by the Emperor to proceed against the Mirza. He was put in charge of the territory of Indus. Akbar himself came to Punjab. It is said that on hearing the news of Akbar's arrival, the Mirza fled to Kabul. In June 1581, when Akbar marched against Kabul, Man Singh was appointed Commander of the vanguard of the

Mughal army. The Mirza was defeated but he was pardoned. On return from Kabul, Akbar appointed Man Singh as the Commander of the Indus region in September 1581. On the death of Mirza Muhammad Hakim in July 1585, Man Singh was directed to proceed rapidly to Kabul with troops to maintain peace and order there and to bring the people to the imperial subjection. He succeeded in his object and as a reward for his meritorious services, he was appointed as governor of Kabul with the instructions to suppress the turbulent tribes of the north-west frontier. Man Singh took stern action against the Raushaniyas, Yusufzais and Afridis.[46]

In March 1587, Man Singh was transferred from Kabul to Bihar where his presence was required to deal with the recalcitrant Afghan Chiefs. Man Singh remained the governor of Bihar from 1587 to 1594. In the mean time he assumed the charge of kingship of Amber after the death of his father in 1589. He succeeded in crushing the rebellions of Afghans and other Hindu Chiefs and maintain peace and order in Bihar. On the orders of the Emperor, Man Singh launched his campaign against the Afghans of Orissa in March-April 1590. He made repeated endeavours to crush the power of the Afghans for about two years and by 1592 the Mughal suzerainty over Orissa was fully established. It became a regular province of the Empire. It is significant to note that Man Singh had constructed a temple consecrated to the main deity of Jagannath.[47]

For his meritorious services to the Emperor during his governorship of Bihar, he was rewarded with the governorship of the Suba of Bengal in March 1594 in place of Said Khan. "Due to the mischievous activities and the machinations of the Afghans, the province of Bengal had become Afghanistan in Hindustan." In order to take effective action against rebellious Afghans, Man Singh thought it prudent to change the capital of the province of Bengal from Tanda to Akmahal which was situated on the bank of the river Ganges and was protected by hills on one side. He renamed Akmahal as Akbarnagar. As a result of persistent efforts, Man Singh succeeded in extirpating the rebellious Afghans of the eastern Bengal. In 1596 Man Singh brought the state of Cooch-Bihar under the Mughal suzerainty.

Raja Lakshmi Narayan of Cooch-Bihar offered formal submission to the Mughal Emperor and this was accepted by Man Singh gracefully. Thus a new vassal state was created on the north-eastern frontier of Bengal.[48] The friendship between Man Singh and Raja of Cooch-Bihar was cemented by a matrimonial alliance; Man Singh married Abla Devi, the sister of Raja Lakshmi Narayan. Akbar was highly pleased to learn about the glorious feats of Man Singh in Bengal. In August 1605, Man Singh paid homage to the Emperor at the imperial court. He was rewarded by the Emperor with a grant of a mansab of 7000 *zat* and 6000 *sowar* — a mansab which was never granted to any Mughal noble except the royal princes. Akbar also conferred upon him the titles of *Farzand* (son) and *Mirza Raja*. He veritably became 'the most dominant and powerful grandee of the imperial court'.[49] "He was one of the most conspicuous of the Imperial generals."[50]

After the death of Akbar (October, 1605), Raja Man Singh was reduced to the position of a second rate commander of the Mughal Empire. The new Emperor Jahangir was not favourably inclined towards the Raja. One reason for this was that Raja Man Singh and Aziz Koka (Khan-i-Azam) had conspired to put forward the claim of Khusrau, a grandson of Akbar, in place of Prince Salim for the Mughal throne after Akbar; Khusrau was the son of Raja Man Singh's sister and son-in-law of Khan-i-Azam. After becoming the Emperor, Jahangir had, however, reconciled with the Raja who was sent back to Bengal as governor. But his mansab was reduced to 5000. The Raja did not have a peaceful time in Bengal because he had to face a serious rebellion of the Afghans under Usman Khan. The Raja's governorship of Bengal lasted only eight months. In June 1606, he was transferred to Rohtas in order to chastise the rebels there. After suppressing the rebellion he remained there till the end of that year. Thereafter he went to his home State, Amber where he stayed for about two and a half years.[51] On the orders of Emperor Jahangir he was sent to participate in Deccan campaign in July 1609. Man Singh did not fare well in this expedition against Malik Amber, the brilliant *Wazir* of Ahmadnagar. An important reason for this was that he was not given an independent command in the south and, therefore, he had no opportunity to show his initiative and drive in this campaign.[52] He had thus played only secondary role in this Mughal expedition to the south though he remained there till his death at Elaichpur on 6 July 1614.

Summing up it may be said that Man Singh was one of the bravest warriors and most successful military generals of the Mughal Empire in the times of Akbar and Jahangir. He, undoubtedly, played a momentous role in the consolidation and expansion of Mughal Empire. He was an able administrator which is evident from the fact that he had set up an efficient administration as governor in the provinces of Kabul, Bihar and Bengal. A lover of art and architecture, he raised a large number of imposing buildings such as palaces, forts, temples and mosques. He is accredited to have commenced the beautiful palace at Amber which was later on completed by Jai Singh I. He built Jagatsiromany temple at Amber which is one of the brilliant specimens of Rajput architecture. He is no less known for constructing a temple at Brindaban, a sacred place of pilgrimage of the Hindus. Besides, he constructed a large number of temples and mosques in the eastern provinces, while he was governor of Bihar and Bengal. Himself a man of letters, who was held in high esteem by both Hindus and Muslims, he patronised a large number of poets and scholars.[53] Though Man Singh occupies an important place in the history of Mughal India for his brilliant achievements, he was 'an absentee ruler' so far as his hereditary kingdom of Amber is concerned. For most of the years before and even after occupying the throne of Amber he had been engaged in campaigns practically in the whole of India, from Kabul in the north-west to east Bengal and Orissa in the east, and to the territory of Ahmadnagar in the south. Nevertheless his outstanding achievements for the cause of the Mughal Empire added considerably to his prestige and dignity as the ruler of Amber State which also witnessed geometrical expansion.

Mirza Raja Jai Singh (1621-1667)

After the death of Raja Man Singh, his only son Bhau Singh

became the ruler of Amber. His claim to the *gaddi* was contested by his nephew Maha Singh, the son of his late brother Jagat Singh. Emperor Jahangir, however, recognised Bhau Singh as the legitimate ruler in July 1614 with the title of *Mirza Raja.* Bhau Singh's mansab was also raised to 4000 *zat* and 3000 *sowar.* Bhau Singh did not play any significant role in the service of the Mughals nor had he made his mark in any of the Mughal campaigns. He had been sent to Deccan in 1619 where he died in December 1621 without achieving any substantial success.

Mirza Raja Jai Singh, the son of Maha Singh succeeded to the Chiefship of Amber in 1621 as Bhau Singh had died without any male heir. "The accession of Jai Singh", writes M.L. Sharma "heralded a new age of fame and prosperity for the House of Amber".[54] The political career of Mirza Raja Jai Singh is prominently associated with the history of Shah Jahan's reign and that of the first decade of Aurangzeb's. After his accession Shah Jahan raised the mansab of Mirza Raja Jai Singh to 4000 *zat* and 3000 *sowar.* In 1629 when Khan Jahan Lodhi revolted against the Emperor, Jai Singh was directed to proceed against him along with other Mughal generals. Khan Jahan had fled to Ahmadnagar where he was welcomed by the Nizam Shahi Sultan. The situation had become so menacing that Shah Jahan had to march personally to the Deccan in December 1629. Jai Singh rendered valuable assistance to the Emperor in suppressing Khan Jahan Lodhi and displayed extra-ordinary valour in the campaign against the rebel. In 1630-31, Jai Singh won laurels in the conquests of Balaghat, Gulbarga and Bijapur in the Deccan for which he was liberally rewarded by the Emperor.[55] In the prolonged siege of Parenda (January-March 1634) launched under Khan-i-Khanan Mahabat Khan, Jai Singh commanded the vanguard and displayed exemplary courage. Again in the retreat to Burhanpur, the Kachhawaha general bore the chief burden. In November 1634, Jai Singh took leading part in a long chase of Shahji Bhonsala and looted a sizeable portion of his belongings. Next year when the Emperor came to the Deccan in person in order to take action against the Sultans of Bijapur and Golkonda, Jai Singh and other Rajputs as his vanguard in the army under Khan-i-Dauran played an important part in invading and plundering Bijapur. From the Deccan, Jai Singh accompanied Khan-i-Dauran to invade the Gond country and played a conspicuous role in the capture of the fort of Nagpur. For all these services, Jai Singh was promoted to the rank of *panj-hazari* mansab and rewarded with the grant of the pargana of Chatsu (in the Suba of Ajmer), a khillat, a jewelled dagger, a horse with gold saddle from the Emperor's stable, an elephant and the royal robe.[56]

In 1638 Jai Singh was sent along with other generals under Prince Shuja and Khan-i-Dauran to take charge of the fort of Qandhar which the Persian governor Ali Mardan Khan had offered to hand over to the Mughals. On 20 April 1639 the Emperor conferred the title of *Mirza Raja* on Jai Singh which his great-grandfather Man Singh had received from Emperor Akbar. In 1641 the Mirza Raja was ordered to proceed to Kabul along with Prince Murad. He joined the prince in his expedition against Mau (in the hilly tract north of Sialkot). After a long siege the fort was stormed on 14 December 1641. Jai Singh was among the first to enter the fort. In October 1644 Jai Singh, then at Amber, was directed to proceed to the Deccan to take charge of that province as a result of the murder of Khan-i-Dauran. For about two years (1644-1646) Jai Singh performed the functions of governor successfully. As a Subedar, he "ruled the Deccan with justice and moderation, but with firmness and impressed the king with his administrative ability."[57]

In the beginning of 1647 Jai Singh was asked by the Emperor to reach Afghanistan. When he arrived at Kabul along with his troops, he was ordered by the Emperor to join the Mughal army under Prince Aurangzeb in the expedition against the Uzbeghs in Balkh and Badakhshan. Though the Prince conquered and occupied Balkh he had to face tough opposition from the Uzbeghs in his further advance towards the Oxus river. The snowing up of the Hindukush passes added to his difficulties. Under the circumstances he had to abandon his conquest and began his retreat towards Kabul. Jai Singh led his right wing during this 'perilous movement', with the Uzbeghs surrounding him from three sides. As a result of the failure of

Central Asian campaign the Shah of Persia reconquered Qandhar.

Three sieges of Qandhar (1649, 1652 and 1653), the first two under the command of Prince Aurangzeb and the third under that of Prince Dara, were undertaken to re-conquer the fort and in all these Raja Jai Singh joined the imperial army. During the first siege, Jai Singh commanded left wing of the army; he led the vanguard during the second siege; and at the time of the third siege, he had the charge of trenches facing the Mashuri Gate. However, the Mughals failed to re-occupy Qandhar, but Jai Singh's performance in all the three sieges was 'brave and creditable'. Thus, Jai Singh "fought under the Imperial banner in every part of the empire, from Balkh in Central Asia to Bijapur in the Deccan, from Qandhar in the west to Monghyr in the east. Hardly a year passed during the long reign of Shah Jahan when this Rajput chief did not see active service somewhere and receive some promotion for conspicuous merit."[58]

In the war of succession which took place among the four sons of Shah Jahan in 1658, Jai Singh played a highly significant role. He behaved like a shrewd politician in the course of this war, who was neither steadfastly loyal to the Mughal Emperor nor to any of the Princes, though in the later stages of the war, he whole-heartedly supported Aurangzeb. In the initial stage he was on the side of Dara and under the nominal command of Sulaiman Shikoh (Dara's son), he played a decisive role in the battle of Bahadurgarh (24 February 1658) in which Shah Shuja was defeated. After this victory he chased Shuja upto Monghyr and subjugated Patna on the way. As a reward for his service, Emperor Shah Jahan had raised his mansab to 7000 *zat* and 7000 *sowar*. Mirza Raja Jai Singh, however, no longer remained loyal to Dara or Sulaiman Shikoh. After the victory of Aurangzeb and Murad in the battle of Dharmat (15 April 1658) against Dara's forces, he joined on the side of Aurangzeb and actively supported him. He proceeded to Delhi and waited for the arrival of Aurangzeb there. Aurangzeb was pleased to have his support and as a mark of gratitude, the Prince conferred upon him the *jagir* of Sambhar as well as governorship of Delhi. He was directed by Aurangzeb to proceed to Amber with his force to keep watch on the movements of Dara who then was at Bhakkar. On the basis of Aurangzeb's *Farman* to Jai Singh dated 22 August 1659, it is asserted that it was Jai Singh who captured Dara Shikoh during his flight.[59]

After becoming Emperor, Aurangzeb confirmed Jai Singh's mansab of 7000 *zat* and 7000 *sowar* of which 5000 were *du-aspa sih-aspa*. Aurangzeb was impressed by Jai Singh's qualities of military generalship and diplomacy. In 1664 he was sent with a force to chastise Shivaji who had inflicted a defeat upon the Mughal general Shayista Khan and had also sacked Surat. On reaching the Deccan Mirza Raja Jai Singh realised that it would be prudent to enter into an alliance with Shivaji against the Shia State of Bijapur. After the conquest of Bijapur it would be easier for the Mughals to deal with Shivaji effectively.[60] Aurangzeb and some of his generals like Dilir Khan, however, did not agree with this plan of Mirza Raja. Be that as it may, Jai Singh's forces besieged Purandar and at the same time launched vigorous attacks on Vajragarh (east of Purandar). The siege continued for about two months in the course of which a gallant commander of Shivaji, Murar Baji Prabhu lost his life along with 300 of his men. Under these circumstances, Shivaji was compelled to negotiate terms of peace with Jai Singh. This resulted in the conclusion of Treaty of Purandar on 13 June 1665 by which Shivaji recognised the sovereignty of the Mughal Emperor and surrendered 23 of his fortresses, retaining only 12 forts with him. He also agreed to support the Mughals against the Sultan of Bijapur. Jai Singh also succeeded in persuading Shivaji to visit Agra. This was the crowning achievement of Mirza Raja's career. His letters to Emperor Aurangzeb in which he urged him to ratify the treaty and to permit him to proceed against Bijapur, 'show him to be a masterful personality'.[61]

Shivaji appeared in the Mughal court sometime in May 1666 after Jai Singh's solemn personal pledge assuring his safety. Shivaji was not accorded good treatment by the Emperor who made him stand among the *panj-hazari mansabdars*. Shivaji felt insulted and walked out of the court. The efforts of Ram Singh, the son of Mirza Raja Jai Singh, to make him return to the imperial court failed. Thereafter the Emperor agreed that Shivaji be kept under surveillance in the house of Ram Singh. Shivaji cleverly escaped from Agra on 18 August 1666 at which the Mughal Emperor was much annoyed. He strongly suspected the complicity of Mirza Raja's son Ram Singh and also began to suspect the loyalty of Mirza Raja. The latter was also held responsible for the failure of the Mughals in the Bijapur campaign. He was not even reimbursed the money which he had spent in the Bijapur campaign from his personal coffers. In the words of Jadunath Sarkar :

> Not a pice of the *krore* of rupees of his own money that he had spent in the Bijapur war would be repaid by his master. Broken-hearted from disgrace and disappointment, and labouring under disease and old age, Jai Singh sank in death at Burhanpur, on 28 August, 1667. Like Walsingham of Elizabeth's Court, he died bankrupt after serving too faithfully an exacting but thankless master.[62]

Mirza Raja Jai Singh was, undoubtedly, one of the outstanding personalities of the times of Shah Jahan and Aurangzeb. As a military general and a diplomat he was incomparably superior to the Mughal dignitories who served the throne of Delhi. He was a learned man himself and was a patron of scholars. The reputed poets of the eminence like Bihari and Kulpati Mitra enjoyed his patronage.[63] In the words of a famous historian of medieval India, "Raja Jay Singh was in a sense the ablest among the Mughal commanders, for he combined with military talents high diplomatic acumen. His knowledge of Turki, Persian, Urdu and Rajasthani added to his habitual urbanity stood him in great stead in dominating friends and foes alike."[64]

Sawai Jai Singh (1700-1743)

During the interlude between the death of Mirza Raja Jai Singh (1667) and accession of Sawai Jai Singh, Ram Singh I and Bishan Singh ruled over the Amber State. The former, as already mentioned, had been serving the Mughal Empire during the time of his father, and after his accession, he continued to render service to the Mughal Emperor, Aurangzeb. In 1668 he was ordered to proceed to Bengal in order to take action against turbulent elements of Assam. His operations against Assamese continued for about nine years (1669-1676) and in appreciation of his services the Emperor raised his mansab to 5000. Thereafter he served in Afghanistan in 1677-78 and again from 1681 to 1688. Ram Singh was a prolific writer who had a number of books to his credit. He set up the nucleus of a book-collection, the famous *pothikhana* called 'great library'[65] which is his noteworthy contribution to the cultural development of Jaipur.

Ram Singh I was succeeded by his grandson, Bishan Singh (since his only son Kishan Singh had died in 1682) who ruled from 1689 to 1700. He was ordered to suppress the rising of Jat rebels under Raja Ram around Mathura, and was granted the *faujdari* of Islamabad (Mathura). His successful operations against the Jats were appreciated by Aurangzeb who granted him the zamindari of some parganas. Thereafter Bishan Singh was sent to the north-west frontier and he died at Kohat in 1700.

The accession of Sawai Jai Singh II in 1700 marks a new era in the history of Amber and Jaipur. He is well-known by his title of *Sawai*, i.e., one and a quarter which signified that he was a quarter more intelligent than his great grand-father Mirza Raja Jai Singh.[66] Soon after his accession he received orders from the Mughal Emperor Aurangzeb to proceed to the Deccan with his troops. On reaching there he was attached to Prince Bidar Bakht (grandson of Aurangzeb). Bidar Bakht accompanied by the Raja of Amber attacked the Khelna fort. The fort was captured on 27 April 1702 as a result of a gallant assault led by the Amber contingent under Jai Singh. As a reward for this valuable service an increase of 500 *zat* was made in the rank of Jai Singh. It was a satisfactory start for a lad of fourteen years in the Imperial service. Thereafter he continued to serve Bidar Bakht who sent Jai Singh along with other generals in November to guard Khandesh against Maratha incursions. In February 1703, Nima Sindhia invaded Khandesh and plundered many places around the capital Burhanpur. Jai Singh failed to check the invader and due to this negligence the Emperor reduced his mansab by 500 *zat*. In the winter of 1703, when Nima Sindhia burst into Berar and Malwa, Jai Singh resisted him successfully supported by the forces sent by Bidar Bakht from Aurangabad. As a result of this success, Jai Singh was rewarded by the restoration of his mansab of 500 *zat* in January 1704. Due to the incompetence displayed by the Malwa governor Shaiysta Khan II, he was removed and Bidar Bakht was made the governor of that province in August 1704. During his illness in December 1704 Bidar Bakht appointed Jai Singh as deputy governor of Malwa but the Emperor did not sanction the appointment and ordered that no Rajput would be appointed as *subahdar* or even as *faujdar*. Jai Singh's desire was, however, realised in June 1705 when Bidar Bakht while leaving for Burhanpur appointed him as the deputy governor with the formal assent of the Emperor received soon after.[67]

After the death of Aurangzeb in February 1707, a war of succession took place in which Prince Azam was pitted against Prince Muazzam (Bahadur Shah). A fierce battle took place between the Princes near Jajau (20 miles south of Agra). In this battle Jai Singh sided with Bidar Bakht and his father Azam whereas Jai Singh's younger brother Bijay Singh and brother-in-law Budh Singh supported Muazzam. In the course of battle Jai Singh had been wounded in his arm by an arrow but when he saw that the tide in the battle had decidedly turned against Azam, he deserted his masters. Both Azam and Bidar Bakht perished in the battle-field and Jai Singh saved himself from 'death and disaster'. V.S. Bhatnagar aptly remarks in justification of Jai Singh's stand, "In this predicament, he preferred, in the interest of Amber, his own safety to death, though the latter would have been in conformity with the accepted notions of Rajput conduct and ideals."[68] After his victory in the war of succession when Bahadur Shah arrived at Amber (10 January 1708), he deprived Sawai Jai Singh of his hereditary *watan* of Amber and entrusted the kingdom to Bijay Singh. This sowed the seed of internecine feud between Jai Singh and Bijay Singh.

Bahadur Shah's stern attitude towards Jai Singh and Ajit Singh (of Jodhpur) not only brought them closer to each other but Maharana Amar Singh of Mewar also joined them. The alliance between Jai Singh and Ajit Singh was cemented by the marriage of Rathor princess with Jai Singh on 26 July 1708. Both the Rajput Princes pooled up their military resources. Their joint armies led by them as well as Durga Das attacked a large Mughal contingent of about 20,000 headed by some famous Mughal generals at Sambhar. In the fierce battle which ensued (October 1708), the Mughals were defeated with heavy losses. As a result of this victory, Jai Singh was proclaimed as the ruler of Amber at Sambhar, and Ajit Singh and Jai Singh became the joint rulers of Sambhar. The defeat of the Mughals in the battle of Sambhar brought about a change in Bahadur Shah's attitude towards Jai Singh and Ajit Singh. He opened negotiations with the Rajput Rajas through Asad Khan and Zulfiqar Khan. Consequently the Emperor restored the mansabs to both the Rajas.[69] In the meantime Bijay Singh, the brother and rival of Jai Singh, had left the Mughal court in disgust as he had been dissatisfied with the attitude of the Emperor. He decided to win over his brother and wrote a letter expressing his desire to meet him. Jai Singh, responded favourably to his overtures and also sent Rs. 10,000 to his brother.[70] Bahadur Shah died in February 1712. "With his death the stormy period of Sawai Jai Singh's life was also over."

Bahadur Shah was succeeded by Jahandar Shah who ruled for a very short period, from March to December, 1712. He was favourably inclined towards Jai Singh and restored to him the State of Amber including Dewasa and Chatsu. The title of Mirza Raja with a mansab of 7000 *zat* and 7000 *sowar* was also conferred upon him. Despite all these favours, Jai Singh refused to extend help to Jahandar Shah against Farrukhsiyar in the battle of Agra. Jahandar Shah was defeated in this battle and Farrukhsiyar became the Emperor in February 1713.

Farrukhsiyar was convinced of the loyalty as well as brilliant military generalship of Sawai Jai Singh. He, therefore, appointed him as the governor of Malwa early in 1714 to check the Maratha incursions effectively. It was felt that no general other than one of Jai Singh's calibre had the capability to prevent Maratha menace.[71] The Marathas had been posing a threat to Mughal supremacy not only in the Deccan but also in Malwa-Gujarat region. Jai Singh followed a vigorous policy and in May

1715 he successfully repulsed the advance of a Maratha contingent which was proceeding towards Malwa under the command of Kanhoji Bhonsle and Khande Rao Dhabre.[72]

In 1716 Jai Singh was summoned to the Imperial Court and he was ordered to lead an expedition against the Jat leader Churaman. Having collected a large force and accompanied by some valiant Rajput generals he proceeded against the Jats. On 9 November 1716 he commenced the siege of the Jat fort of Thun which was protected by lofty walls, a deep wet ditch and a thick thorny jungle around it. Despite Jai Singh's best efforts the progress of the siege was slow due to certain difficulties faced by the imperial forces. The operations continued for about twenty months. Sayyid Abdullah who was secretly hostile to Jai Singh used his kinsman Khan Jahan to bring discredit to Jai Singh. Khan Jahan, as directed by the Sayyid Wazir, arranged for Churaman's nominal submission and visit to the Emperor. The Emperor was prevailed upon to write to Jai Singh for making peace with the Jat leader. Consequently, on 10 April 1718, Churaman and his nephew Rupa were presented to the Emperor at Delhi through Khan Jahan and "thus the credit of victory was snatched away from Jai Singh's hands."[73]

In 1719, the Mughal Emperor Farrukhsiyar was succeeded by Mohammad Shah who ruled till 1748. Sawai Jai Singh enjoyed the goodwill of the new Emperor which helped increase his influence in the Mughal Court. During his reign Jai Singh had to first deal with the Jats of Thun.

Churaman was no longer loyal to the Mughal Emperor. He even sent his troops for helping rebels like Ajit Singh and Chhatrasal. In 1721 Churaman's eldest son Muhakam assassinated the deputy Subedar of Agra. Under these circumstances, the Mughal Emperor appointed Jai Singh as Subedar of Agra in August 1722 and instructed him to take strong action against the rebellious Jats. By this time Churaman had died and his son Muhakam had become the leader of the Jats. Jai Singh marched with a large army and besieged the fort of Thun which he was able to conquer with the help of Muhakam's rival cousin, Badan Singh. Muhakam was driven into exile and Badan Singh was recognised as the leader of the

Jats. For this triumph he was rewarded by the Mughal Emperor with the titles of *Raj Rajeshwar, Shri Rajadhiraj, Maharaj Maharaja Sawai.*[74]

Due to the failure of the Malwa Subedar Bhawani Ram in checking the incessant raids of the Marathas, the Emperor appointed Jai Singh as the Subedar of Malwa for the second time in 1729. After taking over the governorship of the province, Jai Singh decided to follow the policy of conciliation and appeasement towards the Marathas which alone could establish peace and order in the province. In pursuance of this policy, he recommended that a *jagir* worth ten lakhs of rupees per annum be granted to the son of Chhatrapati Shahu on the condition that Marathas would stop their incursions on the Malwa suba. The Emperor Muhammad Shah I accepted the recommendation. Sawai Jai Singh sent his envoy Dip Singh to the court of Shahu. Soon after, the Emperor under the influence of other nobles who were opposed to Jai Singh, changed his mind. Jai Singh's policy was reversed and he was charged with 'slothfulness and treachery'. Therefore, in September 1730, Jai Singh was relieved of the subedari of Malwa. The only achievement of Jai Singh's second subedari of Malwa which lasted for a few months was the recovery of the fort of Mandu from the Marathas.

Muhammad Khan Bangash was appointed as the new Subedar of Malwa in place of Sawai Jai Singh. He miserably failed to check the increasing raids of the Marathas in Malwa. He tried to secure help from Nizam-ul-Mulk and by so doing he incurred the displeasure of the Emperor. Khan-i-Dauran, the Mir Bakshi got support from other nobles of the court and prevailed upon the Emperor to remove Muhammad Khan Bangash from the governorship of Malwa. The governorship of Malwa was entrusted to the charge of Jai Singh for the third time in September 1732. He arrived at Ujjain (capital of Malwa) in December 1732. Early next month the Marathas under the leadership of Malhar Rao Holkar, Ranoji Sindhia supported by other Maratha leaders attacked Malwa. In February-March 1733 Jai Singh was engaged in a fight with the invaders at Mandsaur. When he was overpowered by the Marathas, Jai Singh had to sue for peace offering six lakhs of rupees in cash to Holkar. He also agreed to cede 28 *parganas* to the Peshwa in lieu of *chauth.* After accepting these terms, the Marathas left the province. Thereafter Jai Singh was too involved in the affairs of Rajputana to pay any personal attention to Malwa though the province continued to be under his charge for the following four years.[75]

Jai Singh decided to create a common front of the Rajput Rajas to check the inroads of the Marathas. With that object, he convened a conference of leading Rajput Chiefs at Hurda on 17 July 1734. The pact arrived at the conference could not be enforced owing to the personal and tribal differences among the participants. During the absence of Jai Singh from Malwa, the Marathas resumed their pillaging activities in that province. The Emperor sent two armies to confront the Marathas, one under the command of Mir Bakshi, Khan-i-Dauran and the other under that of Wazir Qamaruddin. Khan-i-Dauran was joined by Sawai Jai Singh and some other Rajput Chiefs in November 1734. The Marathas launched a vigorous attack on the Mughal army early in February 1735 and surrounded it from all the four sides. During eight days' fight they captured a large number of camels and horses, and on the ninth day, they proceeded towards Rajputana for extending their raids in that region. Leaving the Imperial forces behind they quickly marched to Kota, Bundi and thence into the defenceless territories of Jaipur and Jodhpur. They plundered the rich city of Sambhar on 28 February. At this critical juncture Khan-i-Dauran, accepting the advice of Jai Singh, made peace with Sindhia and Holkar. An offer of 22 lakhs of rupees per year as *chauth* of Malwa was made to the Maratha leaders. Having accepted this offer, the Marathas retired beyond the Narmada.[76]

On 14 March 1736 Sawai Jai Singh had a meeting with Peshwa Baji Rao which was within the knowledge of the Mughal court. Jai Singh made efforts to bring about an agreement between the Mughal Emperor Muhammad Shah and the Maratha Peshwa Baji Rao. "Central to it was the notion of sustaining the empire with the Mughal emperor as its nominal head, and adequate scope for the Marathas to take part in administration". The Peshwa was somewhat inclined to accept this idea. It was "an idea that might have changed the entire future history of South Asia" but it could not somehow materialise and remained a "utopian dream".[77] In June 1736 the Peshwa returned to the Deccan. Not long after he led an expedition to the Doab, around Delhi which frightened the Emperor who summoned Nizam-ul-Mulk to come to his rescue. In August 1737 the eldest son of the Nizam was appointed as Subedar of Malwa. Thus ended Jai Singh's third governorship of Malwa. The Nizam too, did not achieve any success against the Marathas. On the other hand, he was defeated by the Marathas in the battle of Bhopal fought in December 1737. Sawai Jai Singh's eldest son Ishwari Singh also participated in this battle. The Nizam had to settle peace terms with the Marathas by which the subedari of Malwa was granted to the Peshwa and rupees 50 lakhs were to be paid as war expenses. Thus the Mughals virtually lost Malwa to the Marathas.

From 1737 to 1740 Jai Singh mostly resided at Jaipur, his new capital. "Though Jai Singh had not rendered any assistance to the Emperor at the time of Nadir Shah's invasion, he retained his high position at the Court and continued to influence the Government's attitude towards various political problems, especially the problems of the Marathas."[78] In 1740 Jai Singh was appointed as the Subedar of Agra. He, however, took less interest in the affairs of Agra province and applied his energy and efforts in developing his new capital. At the same time he involved himself more and more in the affairs of other Rajputana States. His activities in respect of States of Bundi, Bikaner, Marwar and Kota made his position supreme and unchallengeable in Rajputana. He inflicted defeats on some Rajput Chiefs with whom he was involved in warfare including Prince Bakht Singh of Nagaur and brother of Abhay Singh, the Maharaja of Marwar. He had friendly relations with Mewar whose Maharana attached great importance to his advice. He successfully manipulated affairs in Bundi and Kota. He had played a decisive role in the ouster of the Bundi ruler, Rao Budh Singh and succeeded in installing his son-in-law Dalel Singh as the ruler of Bundi. In 1740 he extended valuable help to Zorawar Singh, the ruler of Bikaner in retaining his kingdom which was threatened by Abhay Singh of Marwar. The ruler of Bikaner felt grateful to him for this favour. Durjansal, the ruler of Kota, also recognised the supremacy of Jai Singh and participated in several campaigns under the leadership of Jai Singh. Badan Singh, the Jat leader who became the chief of Bharatpur also acknowledged overlordship of Jai Singh. "Thus Sawai Jai Singh was indubitably the leading ruler of Rajasthan. Though the province did not belong to him, his diplomatic and military leadership was universally recognised."[79]

From what has been discussed above, it is obvious that Sawai Jai Singh was one of the most powerful grandees of the Mughal Empire during the reigns of five successive Emperors —Aurangzeb, Bahadur Shah, Jahandar Shah, Farrukhsiyar and Muhammad Shah. A brave soldier, a brilliant military general and a shrewd diplomat, he played a highly significant role in the Mughal campaigns he was associated with. According to Tod, "his talents for civil government and court intrigue, in which he was the Machiavelli of his day, were at that period far more notable auxiliaries" than his courage and bravery characteristic of the Rajputs.[80] Be that as it may, his performance had, more often than not, been appreciated by his superior commanders and no less by the Mughal Emperors themselves. It is a measure of his commendable work that he had been appointed as the governor of Malwa thrice and that of Agra once. There is no doubt that he had experienced many vicissitudes in his fortunes while in the Mughal service. It was due to the fact that the Mughal court during the period under review had become a hot-bed of intrigues which inevitably exercised influence on the ups and downs of his political career.

Great as was the role of Sawai Jai Singh in the service of the Mughal Empire, his achievements in building the Amber State were far greater indeed. Despite his prolonged absence from Amber, he made keen and consistently zealous efforts for making his State pre-eminent and prosperous. In the words of Tod, "...amidst revolution, the destruction of the empire, and the meteoric rise of the Mahrathas, he not only steered through the dangers, but elevated Amber above all the principalities around."[81]

In the first instance, Jai Singh made Amber one of the

largest tributary States in the country. When he ascended the throne its area was not more than 3,000 square miles and it comprised of only three *parganas* of Amber, Dausa and Baswa. But at the time of his death in 1743, it had a vast area exceeding 20,000 square miles. He had acquired additional territories for his State as a result of annexing the territories, by legitimate or illegitimate means, of the neighbouring Rajput States, as well as, of the Mughals. At any rate Amber, now called Jaipur, became a premier State in the whole of Rajputana, and its ruler Jai Singh a pre-eminent figure — a *primus inter pares.* The population of the State had also increased considerably. According to Tod, the total population of Jaipur State in 1832 was 18,56,700 but V.S. Bhatnagar puts the population of the State during the closing years of Jai Singh's reign at about 16,00,000 which was owing to the secession of some territories from the State.[82] The resources of the State also seem to have been greater than those of all other States of Rajputana.

An ever-lasting achievement of Jai Singh is that he founded a new city near Amber in 1727 which became famous as Jaipur after his name. It became new capital of the State. Initially the official name of the city was Sawai Jaipur but later on the title 'Sawai' fell into disuse. Uptil the end of the eighteenth century and in the early decades of the nineteenth century, Jaipur was also called Jainagar.[83] The city was built according to a definite plan. The original plan of the city of Jaipur was prepared by Jai Singh himself. It is believed that he not only collected plans of many contemporaneous European cities but also examined those of many cities in the country built on the basis of traditional architecture. In the planning as well as execution of plan, he was assisted by some of his ministers and officers, notably Vidhyadhar, an Amber-based Bengali Brahmin. Vidhyadhar appears to have been the chief architect and the engineer for the buildings of the city, both State and private. The city was designed with streets and lanes that intersect each other at right angles. Civic buildings, temples, *havelis,* gardens, etc. were built according to the laid out plan. A protective wall was constructed around the city. Jaipur with its vast plains and picturesque surroundings gradually developed into one of the most beautiful cities in northern India. He also raised many forts and temples some of which are excellent specimens of architecture.

Jai Singh was a profoundly learned scholar who was keenly interested in astronomy and mathematics. He is accredited to have built five observatories at Delhi, Jaipur, Benaras (Varanasi), Ujjain and Mathura. Of these the Jantar Mantar at Delhi was the first to be built which was followed by the Jantar Mantar at his new capital, Jaipur. Himself having a deep knowledge of astronomy, he constructed at least thirteen different types of instruments which were used for his calculations in the observatories. Jai Singh employed twenty astronomers at the Jaipur observatory alone which is testified by the Jaipur State records. He was also a liberal patron of literary figures. He was verily a versatile genius. "He was hailed in his own life time and by posterity as one of the most remarkable men of his time, excelling in diverse fields, and richly endowed with many diverse faculties."[84]

Sawai Jai Singh may be regarded as a real builder of the Jaipur State. He had transformed the Amber State into a large and far-flung kingdom which was second to none in the whole of Rajputana. Emulating the example of the great sovereigns of ancient India, he had performed the *Ashvamedha yajna* in consultation with, and under the supervision of, Brahmins of the court. He also set up a well-organised administration in the State which functioned efficiently. In the words of V.S. Bhatnagar, "It is doubtful if any region of India at that time was better administered than the state of Sawai Jai Singh."[85]

Raja Ishwari Singh, 1743-1750

The death of Sawai Jai Singh in 1743 marked end of the era of peace and prosperity which was followed by a period of court intrigues, rivalry and personal jealousies. His eldest son, Ishwari Singh succeeded to the Chiefship but he had to face serious troubles from his step brother Madho Singh who made persistent efforts to put forth his claim to the Jaipur throne. Jai Singh had married the daughter of Maharana of Mewar (Udaipur) in 1708 on the condition that a son born to her would be the heir to the throne of Amber. This provided the basic cause of a prolonged conflict between the two brothers, Ishwari Singh and Madho Singh, the latter being the son born to the Mewar princess. In support of his claim to the *gaddi*, Ishwari Singh asserted the right of primogeniture. His succession was recognised by the Mughal Emperor as well as various rulers of the neighbouring Rajput States. Maharana Jagat Singh II of Mewar supported by Rao Durjansal of Kota proceeded with their forces to support the claim of Madho Singh and encamped at Jamoli. Ishwari Singh also set out with a large force to resist the enemies and encamped at Pander. For forty days, the rival armies faced each other. Eventually a compromise was made by which Ishwari Singh agreed to grant the tracts of Toda and Tonk along with three other *parganas* to Madho Singh. The Maharana of Mewar sought help from the Maratha Chief, Malhar Rao Holkar who agreed to send forces under his son Khande Rao in support of Madho Singh in return for two lakhs of rupees. When Ishwari Singh learnt about the advance of allied forces against Jaipur, he marched out of his capital with a large army. In the battle which was fought at Rajmahal in March 1747, he won a victory.

After the battle of Rajmahal, Malhar Rao Holkar continued to support Madho Singh's cause. The Maharana of Mewar also sent an envoy to Poona in order to solicit Peshwa's intervention in procuring from Ishwari Singh an appanage worth 24 lakhs a year for Madho Singh. Ishwari Singh was indignant at the Peshwa's partisanship of his rival. In May 1748, Peshwa Balaji Rao entered the Jaipur kingdom. He was joined by Madho Singh and other Rajput Chiefs. The Maratha hordes began to cause devastation in the territories of Jaipur. Under these circumstances Ishwari Singh sent his minister Keshav Das to the Peshwa to sue for peace but the Marathas made unreasonably high demands and the negotiations broke down. The conflict between the two rival parties continued, each trying to enlist the support of the Marathas.

Madho Singh supported by the Maharana of Mewar, Durjansal of Kota and Ummed Singh of Bundi marched against Ishwari Singh. The allied forces were also joined by a Maratha contingent led by Gangadhar Tatya. A battle was fought between the two rivals at Bagru (23 miles east of Sambhar) sometime in August 1748 in which Ishwari Singh was defeated. Keshav Das negotiated terms of peace on behalf of Ishwari Singh. The peace terms agreed upon included yielding of five *parganas* to Madho Singh, giving a large sum of money to the Marathas, and returning Bundi to Ummed Singh. Ishwari Singh, however, failed to honour these terms. In 1750 Malhar Rao Holkar with his large forces encamped near the city of Jaipur and demanded from Ishwari Singh the payment of the promised sum. Ishwari Singh found himself unable to meet the demand of the Maratha Chief as his treasury was depleted as a result of the continuous civil war. He also could not get co-operation from his courtiers and rich bankers and merchants of Jaipur. The Maratha soldiers surrounded the city of Jaipur. Finding himself helpless to resist the formidable enemy and prevent the sack of city of Jaipur, he took poison and committed suicide. Three of his queens and a favourite concubine took poison along with him and all of them died in the palace chamber.[86] According to Tod, "The consequence of this barbarous intervention (of the Marathas) in the international quarrels of the Rajputs annihilated the certain prospect they had of national independence, on the breaking up of the empire."[87]

Raja Madho Singh, 1750-1768

After the death of Ishwari Singh, Madho Singh ascended the throne of Jaipur and he ruled till 1768. Unlike his predecessor, who was a weak and vacillating ruler, Madho Singh displayed greater vigour of mind and action. Malhar Rao Holkar took a leading part in the accession of Madho Singh and he demanded from him a large sum of money as the price of his support. At about the same time Jayappa Sindhia also arrived at Jaipur and demanded his share for his assistance to the new Chief. The depleted treasury of Madho Singh did not enable him to satisfy the demands of the two Maratha Chiefs. He was convinced that the Marathas coveted to seize about one-third territories of the Jaipur State and, therefore, he turned against them. In January 1751 about four thousand Maratha mercenaries suddenly penetrated into the city of Jaipur and began to loot and plunder the city. The inhabitants of Jaipur had already turned against the Marathas due to their aggressive designs and they offered stout resistance to the Maratha intruders for about eight hours. No less than 1500 Maratha soldiers were wounded or killed in the encounter.

Hereafter Madho Singh applied both diplomacy and force to deal with the Marathas. Whenever the Marathas raided the State he offered to pay them *chauth* in order to prevent their depradations. Sometimes he would ward off their danger by making tall promises also. When his diplomacy seemed to be failing, he threatened to use force against them. He used all these tactics when the Maratha Chiefs Raghunath Rao, Jankoji Sindhia and Holkar put forth extravagant demands during 1756-59.

While Madho Singh was embroiled in struggle against the Marathas, he had to face a more serious menace from the Jats of Bharatpur due to the ambitious and aggressive designs of their ruler Jawahar Singh. He hastily made peace terms with Malhar Rao Holkar and the Peshwa by agreeing to pay the long-standing arrears of subsidy and giving the current instalment of five lakhs of rupees. In order to resist the designs of Jawahar Singh he prepared a large army. Jawahar Singh (the son and successor of Suraj Mal who had been loyal to the ruler of Jaipur) had organised a powerful army consisting of 15,000 cavalry, 25,000 infantry and 300 pieces of cannon. Proud of his army, "Jawahir Singh found it galling to owe allegiance to the house of Jaipur." In November 1767 he had won over the friendship of Rathor Chief of Marwar which was not to the relish of Sawai Madho Singh. Before Jawahar Singh attacked the coveted territories of Jaipur, Madho Singh took initiative and with a large army launched a vigorous attack on the Jat forces at Maonda (23 miles south-west of Narnaul). A fierce and hard contesting battle ensued in which the Jats were defeated. Jawahar Singh himself escaped unhurt from the battle-field but he left behind 70 pieces of cannon, tents and baggage including his royal umbrella on the battle-field. There were huge casualties on both the sides. Jawahar Singh, however, claimed his escape as his victory. As a matter of fact, the Jats had been shaken as a result of this defeat. Madho Singh with his force of 16,000 men pursued the Jats in their country. Near Kama, Jai Singh inflicted another defeat on the Jats on 29 February 1768. About four hundred Jat soldiers were killed in this battle and their greatest general Dan Shah was wouded. This was the last battle fought by Madho Singh, for he died a few days after, on 5 March 1768.[88]

Like his father, Madho Singh was keenly interested in architecture. He founded a new city in January 1763 which was named Sawai Madhopur. To him are also attributed some notable buildings such as Jaipur's Madho-Vilas and Moti Doongri. Himself a great scholar and author of a number of books, he patronised many scholars.

Raja Prithvi Singh, 1768-1778

"With Madho Singh departed, for a time, the military glory of the House of Jaipur. Then followed minority after minority, faction fights among the nobility, and inroads by Marathas and Afghans, which brought the home of Man Singh and Jai Singh to the lowest depth of misery and humiliation."[89]

Madho Singh was succeeded by his elder son, Prithvi Singh who was a minor of only five years at the time of his accession. He ruled from 1768 to 1778. During his minority, a Regency Council headed by the senior queen, who belonged to Chundawat clan, was formed. The Council consisted of three ministers — Khushali Ram Bohra, Raj Singh and Firuz. Jaswant Singh Chundawat, the father of the queen also came to Jaipur and started exercising the powers of regency in consultation with the three ministers. Soon after, the members of the Council began to be opposed by other nobles mainly because of illicit relations of the queen mother with Firuz, originally an elephant-driver. The nobles conspired to overthrow the Regency Council. Taking advantage of the situation, Pratap Singh Naruka used his power to oust the queen and her father, got Firuz arrested and also confined Khushali Ram Bohra. Thus, he practically assumed the powers of regent for the minor Raja. He also became unpopular among the people because of his unscrupulous actions and secretly fled from Jaipur. During the decade of Prithvi Singh's reign, the Jaipur State, however, remained free from Maratha incursions and Mughal intervention. Prithvi Singh died in April 1778 due to a fall from his horse.[90]

Sawai Pratap Singh, 1778-1803

After the sudden death of Prithvi Singh, his half brother, Pratap Singh succeeded to the Chiefship, whose reign extended from 1778 to 1803. The new Chief was a minor of thirteen years at the time of his accession. During his minority, his mother acted as the head of Regency Council. The two prominent members of the Council, Khushali Ram and Firuz intrigued against each other and even sought help from outsiders. Besides these internal dissensions, the State had to face frequent predatory hordes of the Marathas, as Tod, aptly remarks, "Throughout the twenty-five years' rule of Pratap, he and his country underwent many vicissitudes. He was a gallant prince, and not deficient in judgement, but neither gallantry nor prudence could successfully apply the resources of his petty State against its numerous predatory foes and its internal dissensions."[91]

Mahadji Sindhia, who had become *Vakil-i-Mutlaq* and commander-in-chief of Mughal forces in 1784, marched towards Jaipur in order to wrest the amount due to the Mughal Emperor. In order to confront the enemy, Sawai Pratap Singh formed an alliance with Maharaja Bijay Singh of Marwar (Jodhpur). In July 1787, battle of Tunga was fought between the Maratha-cum-Mughal forces and the allied forces of Jaipur and Marwar. In this battle, neither of the two parties won a decisive victory. Thereafter Sindhia made greater military preparations and he defeated first the Marwar army and then the Jaipur army separately. He started plundering the Jaipur territories which compelled the ruler of Jaipur to purchase peace with Sindhia by paying rupees seventeen lakhs. He had also to cede the *pargana* of Rampur to Holkar, another Maratha Chief who threatened to follow Sindhia's example. A few years after, an agreement was concluded at Dausa between the Maratha commander Tukoji Holkar and Pratap Singh (January 1792) by which the former agreed to assist the latter in recovering territories from the recalcitrant feudal chiefs in return for half of the share of recovered areas.

This was not the end of Maratha inroads into the Jaipur State. A few years later, Vaman Rao was deputed by the Commander of the Maratha forces to collect arrears of *chauth* from the Raja of Jaipur. He got help from George Thomas (a European adventurer who had carved out a small principality for himself at Hansi in modern Haryana) by promising him a substantial amount of money. The combined forces of the two marched against the Jaipur ruler in 1799. On the other side, Pratap Singh collected a huge army supported by his feudatories to face the enemy. A fierce battle took place at Fatehpur (in Shekhawati). Realising his vulnerable position against the stronger forces of the enemies, Pratap Singh sued for peace offering a huge amount to the Maratha Chiefs. As a result of this, Vaman Rao and George Thomas withdrew their forces.[92]

The continuous troubles which Pratap Singh had to face from within and without throughout his reign, did not deter him from taking measures for the development of art and literature in his State. He constructed a magnificent building known as Hawa Mahal at Jaipur. An extraordinary development in the fine arts of painting and music was witnessed during his period which was entirely due to his liberal patronage of the artists. Pratap Singh, himself, was a celebrated poet who composed several volumes of poetry. He had gathered a number of scholars and poets in his court who under his patronage produced valuable literary works.

It may be useful to refer here briefly to the friendly correspondence which took place between the Jaipur Raja and the British Governor-General of Bengal. To be sure, the predecessor of Pratap Singh, Prithvi Singh had written a friendly letter in October 1776 to the Governor-General Warren Hastings and the latter had given a good response in January 1777. In July 1778 Warren Hastings wrote a letter to Raja Pratap Singh expressing his condolence on the death of his brother Prithvi Singh. Thereafter, ceremonial presents were exchanged between the two in 1778-79. The friendship between the Governor-

General and the Raja was strengthened when in 1783 Pratap Singh sent Bal Krishna to Calcutta on a friendly mission who was received cordially.

In 1787, when Pratap Singh was confronted with the danger of impending attack of Jaipur by Mahadji Sindhia, he communicated with the new Governor-General, Cornwallis through his minister requesting him for help by sending English troops in the defence of Jaipur. But Cornwallis, who was following the policy of strict non-intervention in respect of the Native States, did not respond favourably. Moreover, he did not think it prudent to antagonise Mahadji Sindhia whose help might be required in the possible war of the British with Tipu Sultan.[93]

In 1798, Wellesley became the Governor-General who adopted a vigorous and spirited policy in dealing with the Princely States and Chiefs. He had to take action against the Maratha Chiefs who posed a serious danger to the British supremacy in India. He won over the Peshwa by the treaty of Bassein and thereafter made preparation for war against the Maratha Chiefs, Bhosala, Sindhia and Holkar. Under these circumstances he decided to conclude friendly treaties with Rajputana States, notably Jaipur and Jodhpur. Accordingly, he made a proposal to the Jaipur Vakil at Calcutta and sent a letter to the Maharaja of Jaipur along with draft of a treaty to be concluded. Before the draft treaty was received by Pratap Singh he suddenly breathed his last on 1 August, 1803 when he was only thirty-nine years old.

Raja Jagat Singh, 1803-1818

After the death of Pratap Singh, his son Jagat Singh succeeded as the ruler of Jaipur. The period of fifteen years of his rule (1803-1818) is highly significant due to his relationship with East India Company. In the very first year of his accession, a treaty of 'firm and permanent friendship and alliance' was concluded between the East India Company and the Jaipur State (12 December 1803). This treaty concluded during the governor-generalship of Wellesley was, however, repudiated in March 1806 by the Governor-General, George Barlow. After a few years, Jagat Singh was involved in war with the ruler of Jodhpur over the issue of his marriage with Krishna Kumari which was followed by incursions of Jaipur State by the Maratha Chief, Sindhia and the Pathan Chief, Amir Khan. This together with some other developments led to the conclusion of a momentous treaty between the East India Company and the Jaipur State during the Governor-Generalship of Marquess of Hastings (1813-1823) in 1818.[94] Incidentally this year marked the close of Jagat Singh's reign due to his sudden demise.

The treaty of 1818 provided the basis of East India Company's relations with the Jaipur State. It also marked the beginning of British paramountcy in the State. The period from 1818 to 1905 witnessed the growth of various facets of British paramountcy in the State which will be discussed in detail in the following chapters.

Review of Literature

Sir William Lee-Warner and Sir Charles Lewis Tupper, the two high-ranking British officials, were among the first who wrote comprehensive accounts of British relations with the Princely States of India. Lee-Warner was an eminent member of the Indian Civil Service who had worked for sometime as Under-Secretary in the Foreign Department of the Government of India. He was much impressed by the analogy of Roman Imperialism and "pushed it to the length of claiming for the Paramount Power unlimited right of authority over the States." He remarks in his work, *The Protected Princes of India* that there were three sources from which the rules governing the British relations with the Native States could be drawn — treaties, engagements and *sanads*, the decisions taken by the Paramount Power from time to time which would become precedents, and the prevalent customs and usages. "Each of these factors acts and reacts upon the other with which it is intimately connected."[95] Charles Lewis Tupper, in his work, *Our Indian Protectorate*, too, has asserted the supreme sovereign authority of the Paramount Power in respect of Native States. According to him, "These native states of the continent of India are the feudatory states of which the British Government is the

Suzerain." He sees in the relationship of the Paramount Power and the States all the important elements of feudalism.[96] Both these works were officially inspired and aimed at interpreting and justifying the various aspects of the British policies in respect of the Princely States. One can find, in these books, only a general survey of the British relations with all the States with reference to the principal States and events of some consequence. C.L. Tupper's *Indian Political Practice* in three volumes (Calcutta, 1895), if inspired by similar motivation, is much more useful. It is a compilation work containing leading cases and precedents from the Princely States of all the regions, including Rajputana. Originally intended to serve as 'confidential' instructions for the guidance of Political Officers and for reference of the Foreign Department, it gives first hand information about the principles of British policy meant to be adopted and enforced by the officials concerned.[97]

As a reaction against the ever-growing British Paramountcy which inevitably involved encroachments on most cherished rights of the Princes and Chiefs, appeared a number of books, pamphlets and articles to represent the view-point of the aggrieved Royalties. Of these, particular mention may be made of *The British Crown and the Indian States : An Outline Sketch Presented to the Indian States Committee on behalf of the Chamber of Princes* (1929) and K.M. Panikkar's *The Indian States and the Government of India* (London, 1932) which is a revised edition of his work, *An Introduction to the Study of the Relations of Indian States with the Government of India* (1927). These works ably trace the evolution of British policies towards the Princely States and highlight the several rights of the Princes appropriated by the Paramount Power arbitrarily, in violation of the existing treaties, engagements and *sanads.* Though throwing a very useful light on the British policies from an angle different from 'official', these works, too, betray a lack of objectivity; nor can these be said to be comprehensive in view of the large number of Princely States which have been left unrepresented.

Lieutenant-Colonel James Tod (1782-1835) was the first writer who wrote a detailed account of the history of Rajputana

States, entitled *Annals and Antiquities of Rajasthan,* 2 Vols. published in 1829 and 1832. An official of the East India Company, Tod was appointed in 1818 as Political Agent for the States of Western Rajputana. He laboured hard to collect materials from all the available sources about the contemporary geography and history of Rajputana and Central India along with the history of the Rajput clans who ruled over most of the area at that time. His voluminous work is the most comprehensive study of the history of various Rajputana States. In this work, he not only gives minutest details of historical facts but also includes numerous myths and traditions prevalent about these States. His book till date is regarded as the most informative work about the Rajputana States, especially about the East India Company's relations with these States in the first quarter of the eighteenth century of which he had most intimate knowledge.

After independence of the country and formation of Rajasthan province, a large number of books were written and published about the history of Rajasthan and British relations with the erstwhile Rajputana States. A.C. Banerjee's book, *The Rajput States and the East India Company* (Calcutta, 1951) is a comprehensive and scholarly work based largely on the proceedings of Foreign Department of the Government of India (Secret Consultations and Political Consultations) available in the National Archives of India. It throws light on the relations of Rajput States, especially Jaipur, with the British East India Company.

G.N. Sharma's work, *Rajasthan Through the Ages, Vol.II, from 1300 to 1761 A.D.* (Bikaner, 1990) discusses the history of medieval Rajasthan. It gives a comprehensive and chronological account of the various kings of the Rajput States, their relations with the Mughal emperors, their role during the decline of the Mughal empire, their relations with the Marathas and their polity and administrative organisation. The study is based largely on primary sources, both literary and archaeological. Its companion volume, *Rajasthan Through the Ages, Vol. III, from 1761 to 1949 A.D.* (Bikaner, 1996), authored by M.S. Jain, continues the history of Rajasthan in the modern period, from the Third Battle of Panipat (1761) till the formation of Rajasthan in 1949. The author has given a detailed account of the British intervention in the affairs of Rajputana States after they were brought under British protection in 1818 in order to assert their supremacy and promote their economic interests in the States. During the revolt of 1857-58 the Rajput rulers and nobles, by and large, remained loyal to the British Government. The most significant development in the post-1858 period was the exposition of the doctrine of paramountcy and British civilizing mission which witnessed culmination during the period 1870-1890. The British authorities asserted their economic interests effectively in the matters of salt, opium, custom duties, roads, railways, etc., and sought to integrate the economy of the States with that of the Imperial economy. The land revenue system was re-organised and land settlements were introduced in the States on the pattern of those of British India, resulting in the oppression of peasantry. Judicial and administrative changes were also brought about in some States. During the early decades of the twentieth century there was a substantial change in the tone of the British high-ups which led to the formation of Chamber of Princes in 1921. The last two decades of British rule witnessed the emergence of political awakening in the States and the consequent States people's movement spearheaded by the educated minority. All these developments have been analysed and examined critically by the author, basing his study largely on the original sources available in the Rajasthan State Archives, Bikaner and the National Archives of India. The omission of bibliography may be viewed as a shortcoming of this comprehensive work.

Sukumar Bhattacharyya's book, *Rajput States and the East India Company from the close of 18th century to 1820* (New Delhi, 1972), is a comprehensive and critical study of the first phase of East India Company's relations with Rajput States. After discussing the political disintegration of Rajputana in the closing years of 18th century, the author has examined the policies of British Governors-General, Wellesley, Cornwallis, Barlow, Minto and Marquess of Hastings, in the context of existing circumstances in Rajputana States. He has discussed at length the momentous role played by Charles Metcalfe, British Resident at Delhi, in the conclusion of treaty with the Maharaja of Jaipur in 1818 after protracted negotiations, using all weapons in his armoury including threats of sending forces. After this he has mentioned his role in conclusion of treaties with other Rajputana States. The terms of all these treaties have been examined comparatively, pointing out common provisions as well as dissimilarities. A brief account of the developments during 1818-1820 has been given in the form of epilogue. The work is based on the original records of the Foreign Department of Government of India (Secret Consultations and Political Consultations) and Letters to and from the Court of Directors, and also on Rajputana Agency Office Records, Vols. 1-62.

Vijay Kumar Vashishtha's work, *Rajputana Agency 1832-1858* (Jaipur, 1978), originally a doctoral thesis, examines the role of Rajputana Agency in the formation and execution of British policy towards the Rajputana States. Apart from discussing the role of Agents to Governor-General at Ajmer during the period 1832-1858, the author has also given details about the performance of Political Agents posted in various States, including the Political Agent at Jaipur. The study is based largely on the original records of the Foreign Department (Political Consultations) and correspondence with the Court of Directors available in the National Archives of India.

F.K. Kapil's book, *Rajputana States, 1817-1950* (Jodhpur, 1999) gives a very brief account of the working of British paramountcy in Rajputana States. In 1818 when the Rajput States came under 'British protective umbrella' a new era began in Rajputana in which the British exercised power without responsibility while the Princes were saddled with responsibility without power. Alluding to some aspects of the growth of British paramountcy after 1858, he has referred to its reaction and consequent resentment in the premier States of Rajputana. He has then discussed at length the issue of Indian federation and the reaction and response of the Princes some of whom favoured and the others disfavoured the scheme contemplated by the British authorities. A chapter has been devoted to the emergence of freedom movement and Praja Mandal movement in the Rajputana States, pointing out the attitude of the rulers and their British masters in regard to these movements. The integration of the Rajputana States in the post-independence years leading to the formation of Rajasthan together with the tussle for power, has been examined in the concluding chapter. The study is based on the primary as well as secondary sources.

Rima Hooja's book, *A History of Rajasthan* (New Delhi, 2006), is a comprehensive and complete study of the history of Rajputana States from 500 B.C. to 1947 A.D. The author has taken pains to collect relevant material from almost all readily available published sources, and compiled the account in a well-planned and systematic manner. She has discussed all the important events of the times of all the rulers of Rajput States of medieval and modern times chronologically and clearly. She has not ignored administrative, socio-cultural, economic and subaltern aspects, and one can find in the work highly useful information about the elite, merchants, traders, religious sects, etc. in the various periods of annals of Rajasthan. She has devoted considerable space to the discussion of British relations with the Rajputana States. Starting from the treaties of 1818 when these States came under British protection, she has described the establishment of Rajputana Agency in 1832, and examined the role of Agents to Governor-General and the Political Agents posted at various States in conducting relations with the Native Royalties. After describing the role of the Princes and their *Thakurs* in the revolt of 1857-58, she has discussed various aspects of British paramountcy in the post-1858 period of nineteenth century and the first half of the twentieth century, pointing out the reaction and response of Princes of various Rajputana States. She has also discussed the rise of people's movements in the form of Praja-Mandal and Kisan movements in various States till the independence of the country. In a study of this nature, it is not possible to go through all, even major part of, original unpublished records of the Foreign Department of the Government of India available in the National Archives of India. Despite this limitation, the author has produced a commendable voluminous work covering the entire history of Rajasthan. It may be regarded as an extremely useful single book for students and general readers who are interested to acquire knowledge about the history and culture of Rajasthan.

Apart from the above-mentioned books dealing with the history of Rajput States of Rajasthan as a whole, a number of books have been published specifically about the history of Jaipur State. In the first instance, there are many research-oriented books pertaining to the origin and early rulers of the State and even on individual rulers of the State who played a conspicuous role in the service of the Mughal empire. Of these, particular mention may be made of R.N. Prasad's *Raja Man Singh of Amber* (Calcutta, 1966), V.S. Bhatnagar's *Life and Times of Sawai Jai Singh 1688-1743* (Delhi, second edition, 2002) and V.S. Bhargava's *Rise of the Kachhawas in Dhundhar* (Jaipur) (Ajmer, 1979). These books deal with the historical events and eminent personalities of medieval times.

H.C. Batra's book, *The Relations of Jaipur State with East India Company, 1803-1858* (Delhi, 1958) is the first notable research-work on modern times of Jaipur history. Originally a doctoral thesis, it discusses in details the relations of Jaipur State with the British from 1803, when the first treaty was concluded between the Company and the State, till the end of the Company's rule in 1858. It describes analytically the circumstances leading to the annulment of the treaty of 1803 and the conclusion of new treaty in 1818. This is followed by a comprehensive and critical account of the British intervention in the internal affairs of the State through the British Political Agent of Jaipur (since 1821) and the Agent to Governor-General at Ajmer (since 1832) leading ultimately to the establishment of Council of Regency during the minority of Maharaja Ram Singh which functioned under the dominating control of the Political Agent. The author has not omitted any event of importance in the Company's relations with the State, and has particularly pointed out the unjust and high-handed measures of the British authorities to promote their Imperial interests in the State. The reaction and resentment of the two Regent Ranis against the British measures taken during the two cases of minority rule has been expressed emphatically. Even after 1851 when the Maharaja had assumed the reins of administration in his hands as a major, the Agent to Governor-General and the Political Agent at Jaipur continued to exercise their decisive influence in the affairs of the State, and some of their recommendations were over-ruled by the Supreme Government. In the end, valuable services rendered by the Maharaja to the British Government during the 'Mutiny' (1857) have been described briefly. The author laboured hard to consult all the original and authentic documents under the head, Foreign and Political Proceedings available in the National Archives of India, and has presented the subject matter in a well-planned manner and lucid style.

M.L. Sharma's book, *History of the Jaipur State* (Jaipur, 1969), is a concise and compact narrative of the history of the State from the earliest times till the end of Sawai Madho Singh II's reign (1922). Starting with the description of geographical location, area and population of the Jaipur State, together with its importance as one of the premier States of Rajasthan, the author gives a chronological account of the main events and achievements of the reign of every ruler of Amber and Jaipur. He has highlighted the role of Jaipur rulers, Baharimal, Bhagwandas, Man Singh and Mirza Raja Jai Singh, in the building and extension of the Mughal empire, and then examined the role of the British Government since 1818 in ensuring peace and prosperity in the State. Under the influence of the British authorities the administration of the State was thoroughly re-organised and extraordinary development on modern lines was witnessed in education, public works, railways, revenue, police and judicial departments during the reigns of Ram Singh II and Sawai Madho Singh. The commendable measures of reforms introduced on modern lines by these two rulers of progressive outlook were appreciated by the British authorities who granted a number of titles of English style upon both of them, keeping in view their steadfast loyalty to the Paramount Power. The work is based on the source-material then available in the Jaipur State Archives, the accounts of contemporary Persian historians and the Maratha documents. The value of the work would have greatly increased, had the author taken care to give references in the form of footnotes and added select bibliography at the end of the book.

Jadunath Sarkar's book, *A History of Jaipur, c. 1503-1938,* revised and edited by Raghubir Sinh (Reprint New Delhi, 1994, first published 1984), is a comprehensive and complete history of the Jaipur State from the beginning of 16th century till 1938. The idea of writing a history of his dynasty and State was conceived by Maharaja Sawai Man Singh II, the last ruler of Jaipur State. He entrusted this arduous task to eminent historian, Sir Jadunath Sarkar who completed the manuscript in 1939-40 which, however, took about fortyfive years to see the light of the day. After describing briefly the geographical features of the State, including the land and people of various sects and castes, the author has given an account of the rise of Kachhwas, and then dwelt at length on the exploits and achievements of the Kachhwa kings, Bihar Mal, Bhagwan Das, Man Singh and Jai Singh I, in the service of the Mughal empire. The outstanding role of Sawai Jai Singh in the service of the Mughal Empire, expansion of the Jaipur State and building of the well-planned and beautiful city of Jaipur, has been highlighted by the author. The period of successors of Sawai Jai Singh, covering the second half of the eighteenth century, was marked by internal dissensions and Maratha incursions from without till the Jaipur State came under the British protection. The doyen of Indian historians of later medieval India, Sarkar has given a brilliant and masterly account of all these events of the medieval history of Jaipur State. He has devoted the last seven chapters (out of thirty chapters) to the modern history of the State covering the period of the rule of Jagat Singh, Ram Singh II, Madho Singh II and Sawai Man Singh II. He has discussed the important events of the British relations with the Jaipur State under the East India Company (1818-1857) and the British Crown (1858-1938), and has highlighted the achievements of Maharaja Ram Singh II and Maharaja Madho Singh II in the modernisation of the State by describing numerous measures of administrative changes and reforms undertaken by them under the influence of the British authorities. He has attributed these commendable attainments to the extraordinary capability and conduct of the two Chiefs who were consistently loyal to the Paramount Power. The study is based on the material preserved intact in the ancient archives of the Royal House of Jaipur for about three and a half centuries. The original unpublished records of the Foreign Department of the Government of India available in the National Archives of India could not, for obvious reason, be consulted. A conspicuous omission is bibliography which, if given at the end of the book, would have enhanced the value of the work considerably. This is, however, not to deny that, taken as a whole, it is a scholarly work of high merit.

Ashim Kumar Roy's book, *History of the Jaipur City* (New Delhi, 1978), as the title suggests, is a study of the evolution of Jaipur as one of the most prosperous cities of northern India. The author has given a detailed account of the work and achievements of Jai Singh II, a versatile genius, who founded the city in 1727 A.D. and made it his capital. He has discussed at length how the city was planned by Jai Singh with the valuable help and assistance of his minister, Vidhyadhar, a person of profound 'wisdom and knowledge'. The Maharaja built a magnificent Observatory at Jaipur which was one of the five Observatories raised by him. As an administrative centre, Jaipur witnessed great development in education, public works, health, water-works, metalled streets and painting of buildings around in pink colour during the reign of Maharaja Ram Singh II, and its population increased substantially in proportion to its prosperity. It was, however, during the period 1922-1940 that the city was thoroughly modernised as a result of earnest efforts made by the State Council of Jaipur. The city has acquired importance as a centre of jewellery industry and gemstone cutting industry. In the religious sphere it became a centre of Vaishnava temples, and Jainas of Digambara sect flourished; some of the Jain scholars having made a significant contribution to the growth of Hindi prose. After the formation of Rajasthan in 1949 Jaipur became the capital of the new state. The book is confined to the study of Jaipur city and gives very little information, tantamount to nothing, about the history of Jaipur State which, in fact, does not fall within the purview of this study.

The overview of the above-mentioned literature tends to suggest that no substantial and systematic research work has been done so far on the working of British paramountcy in the Jaipur State under the British Crown. The proffered work is intended to be an intensive and indepth case-study of the working of British paramountcy in Jaipur, one of the premier States of Rajasthan. After giving a succinct account of the evolution of paramountcy in the State under the East India Company during 1818-1857, the study seeks to examine in detail various facets of British paramountcy in the post-1858 period which was the most crucial period in the growth of paramountcy. During this period the Paramount Power asserted its authority to intervene most frequently in the internal affairs of the States, not only in spite of, but very often in violation of, the existing treaties, engagements and *sanads* in response to the growing requirements of the Imperial Government. Earnest endeavours were made by the Supreme Government to bring all important economic and fiscal matters and the means of transport and communication of British India and Indian India under a 'single charge'. The process reached its culmination during the viceroyalty of Curzon (1898-1905), and, therefore, it has been considered proper to close the study in the year 1905.

The work is based largely on the original records of the Foreign Department of Government of India (Political, Secret, Internal, General, Financial, Judicial and Military branches), Despatches to and from the Secretary of State for India, Private Papers of the Viceroys and Secretaries of State, and Jaipur Agency Record — all available in the National Archives of India, New Delhi. The Reports on the Political Administration of the Rajputana States lying in the Abu Collection (A.C.) of the Jaipur University Library and relevant records in the Rajasthan State Archives, Bikaner, have also been made use of. Taken together, all these sources provide ample first hand information about all aspects of the working of British Paramountcy in Jaipur State. It may, however, be observed that all these sources are 'official' and as such they explain the policies and measures of the Imperial Government from British point of view. The sources other than 'official' have also been tapped so as to attempt an objective analysis of the British policy in the multi-dimensional aspects of paramountcy.

References and Notes

1. The name 'Rajputana' was used for the first time by George Thomas. Vide William Franklin, *Military Memoirs of Mr. George Thomas* (London, 1805), p. 347. Later on, in 1829, Col. Tod, the author of the famous work *Annals and Antiquities of Rajasthan,* used the word Rajasthan for this tract of the country.
2. *The Imperial Gazetteer of India* (hereafter given as *IGI), Vol. XXI* (Oxford, 1908), pp. 82-83.
3. *Ibid.*, pp. 94-95.
4. *IGI, Vol. XIII* (Oxford, 1908), p. 382.
5. For details, see H.C. Batra, *The Relations of Jaipur State with East India Company 1803-1858* (Delhi, 1958), pp. 8-10.
6. V.S. Bhatnagar, *Life and Times of Sawai Jai Singh, 1688-1743* (Delhi, 2002), p. 1.
7. James Tod, *Annals and Antiquities of Rajasthan, Vol. III,* edited by William Crooke (Reprint Delhi, 1994), p. 1328.
8. *Ibid.*, p. 1331; Jadunath Sarkar, *A History of Jaipur, 1503-1938,* revised and edited by Raghubir Sinh (Reprint New Delhi, 1994), p. 21.
9. Since he was a youth of remarkable beauty and valour, he was called Dulha Rai meaning 'the Bridegroom Prince'; Sarkar, *op. cit.*, p. 22.
10. The word Dhundhar is derived from the name of a demon king named Dhundhu. A cave at Galta is ascribed to Dhundhu and a small stream rising north of Amber and flowing southward flanking the Jaipur hills is called Dhundhu river. (cited in V.S. Bhargava, *Rise of the Kachhawas in Dhundhar,* Ajmer, 1979, p. 1 n). (James Tod, however, does not subscribe to this view. According to him, the etymology of Dhundhar is from a once celebrated sacrificial mount (*dhundh*) on the western frontier near Kalakh Jobner. (Tod, *op. cit.*, p. 1328)
11. Tod, *op. cit.*, p. 1329; Bhatnagar, *op. cit.*, p. 4; G.N. Sharma, *Rajasthan through the Ages, Vol. II* (Bikaner, 1990), p. 104.
12. The statue of goddess *Jamva Mata* in this temple is still worshipped by the royal family of Jaipur to this day.
13. M.L. Sharma, *History of the Jaipur State* (Jaipur, 1969), p. 23.

14. The word 'Amber' is said to have been derived from Ambikeswara (a title of Lord Shiva) or from Ambarisha, son of Mandhata and king of Ayodhya. Its original name is said to have been Ambarikshaner, that is 'town of Ambarisha'. *IGI, Vol. V,* p. 290, cited in Tod, *op. cit.,* p. 1332 n.
15. Tod, *op. cit.,* pp. 1334-35; Sarkar, *op. cit.,* pp. 25-26. Some scholars, however, contend that there is no reliable evidence to prove that Pajvan had taken any prominent part in Chauhan-Chandel and Chauhan-Chalukya wars; see Dashratha Sharma, *Early Chauhan Dynasties* (Delhi, 1959), pp. 75-77; A.K. Majumdar, *Chaulukyas of Gujarat* (Bombay, 1956), pp. 140-41.
16. Sarkar, *op. cit.,* p. 26.
17. Bhargava, *op. cit.,* p. 8.
18. Sarkar, *op. cit.,* p. 31.
19. G.N. Sharma, *op. cit.,* p. 104; Bhatnagar, *op. cit.,* p. 6; Akshya Nath, Ms. *Mewar-ka-Sankshipta Itihas,* cited in Bhargava, *op. cit.,* p. 8 n; Sarkar, *op. cit.,* pp. 31-32.
20. Tod, *op. cit.,* p. 1336.
21. Sarkar, *op. cit.,* p. 34.
22. R.N. Prasad, *Raja Man Singh of Amber* (Calcutta, 1966), pp. 5-6; Sarkar, *op. cit.,* p. 35.
23. Abul Fazl, *Akbarnama,* translated by H. Beveridge, *Vol. II,* p. 241.
24. *Ibid.,* p. 242; Prasad, *op. cit.,* pp. 7-8.
25. Beni Prasad, *History of Jahangir* (Allahabad, 1940), p. 26.
26. M.L. Sharma, *op. cit.,* pp. 43-44.
27. For further details, see Abul Fazl, *op. cit., Vol. II,* pp. 18-20, 240 44; A.L. Srivastava, 'Alliance with Akbar', *Rajasthan History Congress Proceedings,* 1967, pp. 49-55; G.N. Sharma, *op. cit.,* p. 104.
28. A.L. Srivastava, *Akbar the Great, Vol. I* (Agra, 1972), p. 114.
29. Prasad, *op. cit.,* p. 26.
30. Bhargava, *op. cit.,* pp. 16-17; Srivastava, *op. cit.,* p. 117.
31. V.A. Smith, *Akbar the Great Mogul* (Reprint Delhi, 1966), p. 80; Srivastava, *op. cit.,* p. 127.
32. Bhargava, *op. cit.,* pp. 18-20; Srivastava, *op. cit.,* pp. 199-200.
33. Quoted by Smith, *op. cit.,* p. 153; also Srivastava, *op. cit.,* p. 284.
34. Srivastava, *op. cit.,* p. 269.
35. Sarkar, *op. cit.,* p. 304.
36. Refaqat Ali, *The Kachhawas under Akbar and Jahangir* (New Delhi, 1976), p. 46.
37. M.L. Sharma, *op. cit.,* p. 68; Srivastava, *op. cit.,* pp. 324-25.
38. Smith, *op. cit.,* pp. 172-73.

39. Bhargava, *op. cit.*, pp. 23-24.
40. R.N. Prasad, however, opines that the credit of negotiating peace treaty with Hara Chief goes to Hussain Quli Khan and not to Kunwar Man Singh; Prasad, *op. cit.*, p. 26.
41. *Ibid.*, p. 31.
42. Abul Fazl, *op. cit., Vol. III*, pp. 123, 141; Prasad, *op. cit.*, pp. 32-33.
43. For details of the battle, see Prasad, *op. cit.*, pp. 34-53; Sarkar, *op. cit.*, pp. 48-55; Srivastava, *op. cit.*, pp. 186-197; Smith, *op. cit.*, pp. 8-9.
44. Srivastava, *op. cit.*, pp. 196-197.
45. Smith, *op. cit.*, p. 144.
46. For details, see Sarkar, *op. cit.*, pp. 63-73.
47. *Ibid.*, pp. 76-80; Prasad, *op. cit.*, pp. 79-89.
48. Sarkar, *op. cit.*, pp. 80-82; Prasad, *op. cit.*, pp. 90-104.
49. Prasad, *op. cit.*, pp. 104-05.
50. *IGI, Vol. XIII*, p. 385.
51. According to M.L. Sharma, the Raja stayed at Amber for less than a year, from 12 Sept. 1608 to 28 July 1609; see M.L. Sharma, *op. cit.*, p. 84.
52. Prasad, *op. cit.*, p. 128.
53. For details, see *ibid.*, pp. 141-43, 146-170.
54. M.L. Sharma, *op. cit.*, p. 92.
55. Bhargava, *op. cit.*, p. 46.
56. Sarkar, *op. cit.*, pp. 102-04.
57. M.L. Sharma, *op. cit.*, p. 103.
58. Sarkar, *op. cit.*, p. 99.
59. Bhargava, *op. cit.*, pp. 50-53.
60. According to Satish Chandra, "this policy might appear to be machiavellian but it was based on... the reality of the situation"; for details see Satish Chandra, 'Deccan Policy of Mirza Raja Jai Singh : A Reappraisal' in *Rajasthan History Congress Proceedings* (Jodhpur Session, 1967), pp. 76-84.
61. Bhatnagar, *op. cit.*, p. 10.
62. Sarkar, *op. cit.*, p. 142.
63. G.N. Sharma, *op. cit.*, p. 106.
64. A.B. Pandey, *Later Medieval India* (Allahabad, 1967), p. 207.
65. Rima Hooja, *A History of Rajasthan* (New Delhi, 2006), p. 579.
66. This title was given to Jai Singh by Aurangzeb in April 1696. But it is clear from the contemporary letters that he officially received the title of *Sawai* only in July 1713 from Emperor Farrukhsiyar; see Bhatnagar, *op. cit.*, p. 16.
67. *Ibid.*, pp. 22-25; Sarkar, *op. cit.*, pp. 158-59.
68. Bhatnagar, *op. cit.*, p. 36.

69. Bhargava, *op. cit.*, pp. 73-79.
70. When Bijay Singh, after a considerable hesitation, came to Sanganer in May 1713 to meet Jai Singh, he was arrested by strategam and sent to Amber as a prisoner. Many years later Budh Singh hatched a conspiracy to secure Bijay Singh's release and to install him as king in Jaipur. When Jai Singh learnt about this conspiracy, he got Bijay Singh killed. See Bhatnagar, *op. cit.*, pp. 86-87, 217-18.
71. Sarkar, *op. cit.*, p. 163.
72. Hooja, *op. cit.*, p. 668.
73. Sarkar, *op. cit.*, pp. 168-70; Bhatnagar, *op. cit.*, pp. 124-28.
74. G.N. Sharma, *op. cit.*, p. 107.
75. Sarkar, *op. cit.*, p. 180.
76. Bhatnagar, *op. cit.*, pp. 222-28; Bhargava, *op. cit.*, pp. 100-110.
77. Hooja, *op. cit.*, p. 670.
78. Bhatnagar, *op. cit.*, p. 256.
79. *Ibid.*, pp. 256-267; Hooja, *op. cit.*, p. 671; M.L. Sharma, *op. cit.*, p. 154; G.N. Sharma, *op. cit.*, pp. 107-08.
80. Tod, *op. cit.*, p. 1342.
81. *Ibid.*, p. 1350; *IGI, Vol. XIII*, p. 386.
82. Bhatnagar, *op. cit.*, pp. 269-70.
83. Ashim Kumar Roy, *History of the Jaipur City* (New Delhi, 1978), p. 49.
84. Bhatnagar, *op. cit.*, p. 268.
85. *Ibid.*, p. 313.
86. Sarkar, *op. cit.*, pp. 229-41; Hooja, *op. cit.*, pp. 676-79.
87. Tod, *op. cit.*, p. 1357.
88. Sarkar, *op. cit.*, pp. 246-56.
89. *Ibid.*, p. 257.
90. Tod, *op. cit.*, pp. 1361-62.
91. *Ibid.*, pp. 1363-64.
92. Hooja, *op. cit.*, pp. 682-83.
93. Sarkar, *op. cit.*, pp. 315-16.
94. For details, see *infra*, pp.
95. William Lee-Warner, *The Protected Princes of India* (London, 1894), p. 29.
96. Charles Lewis Tupper, *Our Indian Protectorate* (London, 1893), pp. 3, 239.
97. These three volumes along with the fourth index-volume have since independence been made available to research scholars for consultation in the Library of the National Archives of India, New Delhi.

CHAPTER 2

Paramountcy under East India Company (1818-1857)

According to William Lee-Warner, the English East India Company during the period from 1757 to 1813 followed the policy of non-intervention or 'the policy of ring-fence' but from 1813 to 1857 it followed the policy of 'subordinate isolation'.[1] This categorisation of the British Company's policy into two clear-cut labelled periods appears to be a faulty generalisation which is not fully borne out by a close and candid scrutiny of historical facts. During the Governor-Generalship of Wellesley (1798-1805), for instance, the British authorities did not adhere scrupulously to the policy of 'ring-fence' or non-intervention. There is no doubt that the officially declared policy of the British Government was that of non-intervention, for it was laid down in Pitt's India Act (1784) in clear and unambiguous terms : "...to pursue schemes of conquest and extension of dominions in India are measures repugnant to the wish, the honour and the policy of this nation."[2] But in practice this clause was honoured more in breach than in observance. As a matter of fact, the British policy during the century of the Company's rule varied from Governor-General to Governor-General and from State to State; for the British relations with the Indian States were not conducted by doctrinnaire theorists but by practical politicians.[3]

Every Governor-General had his own personality and propensity, and in the context of the given situation he would determine his policy on the basis of his diplomatic calculations and merits of each case. There was also "the interplay of diverse pulls and pressures operating through the Parliament, the Cabinet, the Board of Control, the Court of Directors and the Indian authorities" which exercised influence on the policy from time to time. Besides, the British Resident or Political Agent — the man on the spot, as it were — played no less significant role in the conduct of relations with the Princely State or States under his charge. These remarks are truly applicable to East India Company's relations with the Jaipur State.

During the times of Warren Hastings and Cornwallis, as already mentioned[4], overtures for friendly alliance between the Jaipur State and the British had been made by Raja Jagat Singh of Jaipur which, however, did not evoke favourable response. It was during the Governor Generalship of Wellesley (1798-1805) that the East India Company entered into treaty-relationship with the Jaipur State. When Wellesley assumed office in 1798 the Company's position, as he himself described, was 'extremely critical' though 'by no means alarming'.[5] The Nizam of Hyderabad had turned against the British because the latter due to Sir John Shore's policy of non-intervention had not helped him in his war against the Marathas, and he had engaged French officers to reorganise his army. The Marathas under the leadership of the Peshwa, the Bhonsla, the Sindhia and the Holkar had greatly increased their power and influence due to the 'weak and vacillating' policy of the two predecessors of Wellesley. Of these Sindhia was potentially most dangerous who had reorganised his army under two brilliant French generals, De Boigne and Perron, and had established his supremacy both in southern and northern India. Perron had assumed the supreme command of Sindhia's army after De Boigne had become most powerful due to Sindhia's prolonged stay in the south of India. All the administrative powers had fallen into his hands which made his status almost that of a reigning sovereign. He received tributes from the Rajput States of Jaipur and Jodhpur. He was granted the monopoly of salt and custom duties in Hindustan. He allocated to himself the regal privileges of coining money and his annual revenue was estimated at £ 1,632,000. He possessed the important fortress of Agra, imperial Delhi and the person of the 'Great Mughal' (Shah Alam). He also occupied the richest province of the Doab.[6] Tipu Sultan was intriguing on all sides not only to recover his former dominions but also to expel the English from India, and, worse still for the British, was in negotiation with the French.[7]

Under these circumstances the task before Wellesley was both to secure and consolidate the Company's dominions in India; he believed that security lay in boldness and that if the Company was to stay in India, it must attain the position of the paramount power.[8] Wellesley sought to achieve his objective by a comprehensive system of alliances known as 'Subsidiary Alliance System' which was 'a potent system for the infiltration of British supremacy'[9]; it was to be supplemented by war and annexation, if required. Having concluded subsidiary treaty with the Nizam of Hyderabad (1798) and crushed the power of Tipu Sultan of Mysore (1799), he succeeded in winning over Peshwa Baji Rao II by entering into treaty of Bassein (Dec. 1802) with him by which he accepted the terms of the subsidiary alliance. As Bhonsla and Sindhia proved defiant he declared war against them — the Second Anglo-Maratha war — on August 3, 1803; Wellesley had also the avowed intention of destroying the power and influence of Perron. The fortunes of Rajputana came to be vitally linked up with the vicissitudes of the war which created a situation that was really favourable to the establishment of alliance and treaty-relations between the Company and the Rajput States. "Hence this war may be regarded as a landmark in Anglo-Rajput relations."[10]

Wellesley believed that an alliance with the Rajput States, especially Jaipur and Jodhpur, would be an asset of inestimable value. Their revenues and resources were adequate to support a British subsidiary force. He had also developed a conviction that the Rajput Princes were smarting under the galling tutelage of Sindhia and General Perron, and the British protection, if offered, would be earnestly and eagerly welcomed by them.[11] Wellesley in view of the imminence of war with the Marathas, made a direct approach to the rulers of Jaipur and Jodhpur through their *Vakils* in Calcutta. Thereafter the Governor-General addressed a letter to Raja Pratap Singh of Jaipur, enclosing the draft of a treaty to be concluded with him. Before the draft-treaty could reach Jaipur, Pratap Singh suddenly died on 1st August 1803 but his son and successor, Jagat Singh assured Wellesley of his loyalty to the British and his earnest desire to identify his interests with those of the Company. It is a tribute to the military genius of Lake that his campaign against Sindhia in the North proved 'short, swift and successful'. Perron submitted on 7 September 1803 and Sindhia's forces were defeated at the battle of Delhi on 11 September. The historic fort of Agra was captured by Lake on 18 October.

These brilliant victories of the British against Sindhia and close proximity of Agra to Rajputana convinced Wellesley that Jaipur and other States would shortly be induced to connect their interests with the British Government and they would be now willing to co-operate with the British troops against the enemy. Alarmed by the victories of the British against Sindhia, his rival Holkar sent his *Vakil* Khandeh Rao to Jaipur on 18 November 1803. He provoked the Raja by warning him against the aggressive designs of the British and telling him further that the British domination of Jaipur would cause grievous injuries to Hindu religion. Most of the ministers of Jaipur were convinced by the arguments of the Maratha emissary and prevailed upon the Raja not to conclude alliance with the British. To keep up pretension of friendship with the British the Raja, however, wrote a letter to the Governor-General suggesting the conclusion of "formal engagements with the Company similar to those which were about to be contracted by the late Raja". Due to the dilly-dallying attitude of Jagat Singh the British authorities decided to resort to coercion. Lake threatened to send forces towards Jaipur. This movement of forces had the desired effect. The treaty of firm friendship and alliance was signed on 12 December, after 'a lot of reluctance on the part of the one and bluff and bluster on the part of the other'.[12] It was ratified by the Governor-General on 15 January 1804.

The terms of this 'Treaty of Amity and Alliance' tended to

secure the interests of both the Company and the Maharaja of Jaipur. It was stipulated that the friends and enemies of one of the parties would be considered friends and enemies of both. The Company undertook not to interfere in the government (administration) of the State and would not demand any tribute from the State. In case of an attack on the dominions of the Company by the enemies, the Maharaja was bound to send the whole of his forces to the assistance of the Company's army. The Company, on its part, guaranteed the security of Maharaja's State against external enemies, and in case any misunderstanding should arise between him and any other State, the Maharaja would submit the cause of dispute to the Company's Government for its settlement. Whereas the Company recognised the Maharaja as the master of his own army, he was bound to act during the time of war in accordance with the advice and opinion of the Commander of the English army. Lastly, the Maharaja would not entertain in his service or give admission to, any English or French subjects or any other European person without the consent of the Company's Government.[13]

A few months after the signing of the treaty with the Maharaja of Jaipur, the Company was involved in war against Jaswant Rao Holkar declared on 16 April 1804. A force under Colonel Monson was sent ahead of the main army to Jaipur and having reached the vicinity of Jaipur on 21 April he requested the Maharaja to take 'effective and vigorous' measures in conjunction with the British forces for frustrating the designs of Holkar. The Maharaja gave all possible help. However, despite his help Monson suffered humiliating reverse at the hands of Holkar. General Lake blamed the Maharaja for having failed to prevent the advance of Holkar through his territories and charged him with violation of fourth article of the treaty of 1803. Later on Lake admitted that the Maharaja's conduct was 'not perfidious' and that subsequently he did render faithful assistance to the British against Holkar. While Holkar was in the north, his capital Indore was captured by Colonel Murray. A part of his army was destroyed at Dig on 13 November 1804 and he himself was defeated at Farrukhabad four days after. Holkar escaped towards Punjab to get help from Ranjit Singh and other Sikh Chiefs. In the meanwhile Lake failed to capture Bharatpur whose Jat ruler had left the British and joined Holkar. This adversely affected the prestige of Wellesley who was recalled immediately by the ministry at home while war with the Marathas was still inconclusive. As a matter of fact, Wellesley's policy of war and aggrandisement which was at variance with Pitt's India Act of 1784, and lately his protracted war with the Marathas, alarmed the authorities in England. They not only objected to the extension of dominion, but also to that of the subsidiary treaties which in case of disputes among the Indian States would render British interference inevitable and might drag the Company to war.[14] "To augmented responsibilities were added impoverished finances."[15]

Cornwallis, who was earlier known for his policy of 'peace and reforms', was appointed again as Governor-General in place of Wellesley in July 1805. He was considered "the fittest instrument for reversing Wellesley's policy and restoring political and financial balance in the Company's affairs."[16] He came to India with instructions from the Court of Directors to terminate the war with the Marathas, to refrain from assuming new political responsibilities, to observe strict abstention as regards Indian States beyond the British frontiers, and even to avail of proper occasion for the dissolution of alliances already formed between the Company and Chieftains of Jaipur, Alwar, etc.[17]

Cornwallis earnestly desired to patch up differences with the Marathas and put an end to the war with them.[18] At the same time he decided to abandon the defensive alliance with the State of Jaipur on the excuse that the Maharaja had so far not only failed in the performance of his duties towards the British Government under the treaty but had also supported the cause of the enemy.[19] Before the Governor-General could accomplish all this he died on 5 October 1805 after serious illness for a few days. He was succeeded by Sir George Barlow as acting Governor-General who was the senior-most member of the Council of Bengal. Evidently the task before the new Governor-General was to give a practical shape to the unfulfilled plan of his deceased predecessor — conclusion of peace with the Marathas and revival of the policy of non-intervention with regard to the Princely States. As a result of negotiations conducted by Lt.-Col. Malcolm on behalf of the Company treaty of peace was signed with Sindhia on 22 November 1805 and that with Holkar on 24 December. Thereafter the Governor-General decided that the dissolution of the treaty with the Jaipur State should be immediately declared and he did not even listen to the request of Lord Lake (Commander-in-Chief) that the renunciation of the alliance should be deferred for some time. Consequently on 8 March 1806 Captain Sturrock, the British Resident at Jaipur informed the Maharaja that he was directed by the Governor-General to declare the dissolution of the alliance between him and the British Government, for the Maharaja had failed to fulfil his engagements.[20] Maharaja Jagat Singh remonstrated against this decision of the British Government in these words :

> I had indulged in the flattering hope of realising all my aims and aspirations, but the ink with which the Treaty of Alliance was written however was hardly dry, when you announced to me this resolution to the utter disappointment of those expectations.[21]

The conduct of the British Government towards the Jaipur State in dissolving arbitrarily the Treaty of 1803 was strongly condemned by the contemporary statesmen and historians. Grant Duff dubbed this measure of Barlow as 'short-sighted', 'selfish' and 'indiscriminating'.[22] Referring to the impolicy and impracticability of the principles by which the measures of the Government were regulated, Sir John Malcolm specifically condemned the dissolution of the treaty with Jaipur and expressed his bitter reaction in these words, "This is the first measure of the kind that the English have ever taken in India, and I trust in God it will be the last."[23] He warned that the British statesmen should have had enough of political vision to foresee that the abandonment of Jaipur, under pressure of immediate circumstances, would produce disastrous repercussions in the distant future because "if we endeavour to fly from the political embarrassments and complex relations, which have been in all ages the condition of extended power and dominion, we always meet with much greater evils than those from which we try to escape."[24] His warning proved prophetic. It may be observed that the treaty with Jaipur was dissolved, not when that state had given indications of disloyalty, but after it had rendered useful services to the Company. James Tod, who had an intimate personal knowledge of British relations with the Rajput Princes, remarks, "...we vainly attempted to throw the blame of violating the treaty upon our ally."[25] It was evidently a breach of faith on the part of the Company's Government. Therefore Jaipur *Vakil's* complaint was not unreasonable that the British Government had made "its faith subservient to its convenience".[26] The action of Barlow's government seems to be inexpedient as well, for it produced a "general distrust of its principles" and a "doubt of its strength".[27] It was really ungenerous on the part of the Company to deny protection to, and deliberately abandon, the weak Rajput States to the mercy of the unscrupulous Marathas, particularly at a time when the Rajputs badly needed and sought for British help.[28] It is significant to remark that the differences of opinion between the Governor-General and Commander-in-Chief (Lake) on the policy matters including the treatment meted out to Jaipur and other States and Barlow's disregard of Lake's suggestion in this regard led to the resignation of the latter early in 1807.

Barlow was succeeded by Lord Minto who held the office of Governor-Generalship from 1807 to 1813. The new Governor-General made no change in the policy of the Company with regard to the Rajputana States and the policy of non-intervention was adhered to as in the times of his predecessors. In the early years of his tenure fierce struggle took place between Maharaja Jagat Singh of Jaipur and Maharaja Man Singh of Jodhpur. The basic cause of this conflict centred on Krishna Kumari, the beautiful princess of Udaipur whose marriage had been arranged with Jagat Singh and whose hand in marriage was claimed by Man Singh also. With the support of Dhonkal Singh (Chief of Jodhpur) and the Pathan Chief, Amir Khan, the Maharaja of Jaipur invaded the territory of Jodhpur and their forces resorted to loot and plunder of Jodhpur city. Amir Khan who was an opportunist and a free-booter took advantage of the conflict between the two Rajput Chiefs. Leaving his ally in the lurch, "he commenced his historic incursions into the State of Jaipur, which completely undermined the peace and prosperity of this once celebrated principality."[29] In this situation Jagat Singh had to raise the siege of Jodhpur and return to his capital only to find his country surrounded by a host of enemies. During this struggle both Man Singh and Jagat Singh appealed to the British for assistance but their request was declined on the plea of British policy of non-intervention which was being followed strictly and scrupulously. At this time, Daulat Rao Sindhia fished into troubled waters and he sent a force under the command of Bapuji Rao Sindhia against Jaipur which besieged the town of Todri. The Maharaja of Jaipur once more failed to procure help from the British Resident, Seton.[30] Under the circumstances, the Maharaja had to compromise with Sindhia by paying him a big amount. Realising their mistake of fighting with each other over a woman which caused great losses to both of them, the Chiefs of Jaipur and Jodhpur resolved their differences and concluded a treaty of friendship and alliance which was cemented by the marriage of Maharaja of Jaipur with a daughter of Maharaja of Jodhpur and that of Maharaja of Jodhpur with the sister of the former.[31] In the beginning of 1811, Amir Khan again invaded and devastated the territory of Jaipur. In the absence of expected help from the British, the Maharaja had to pay an amount of seventeen lakhs of rupees to get rid of troublesome invader.[32] Soon after this, the Maharaja of Jaipur had to face troubles caused by the incursions of Rao Raja of Macheri who was under the protection of the British. He invaded the territories of Jaipur and succeeded in occupying the fortresses of Sikrawa and Dubi. This time the Maharaja was successful in getting help from the British. Metcalfe, the new British Resident, was sympathetic towards the appalling situation of Jaipur. He dispensed warning to the Rao Raja to withdraw his forces, failing which the British forces were despatched and the Rao Raja had to surrender the said districts. Besides he had to pay to the British Company the cost incurred in mobilisation of their forces.[33]

In 1812, as a result of encroachment on and plunder of British territories of Behil, Parsrampur and others by one Thakur Sham Singh, a chief of Shekhawati and a vassal of Jaipur State, the British Government asked Maharaja Jagat Singh to take strong action against him, failing which the British threatened to send a force against the feudatory chief. At last, on the persuasion of the Jaipur ruler, Sham Singh restored the property he had plundered to the British Resident in July 1812. Both the Maharaja and Sham Singh gave a written guarantee of the latter's good conduct in future.[34] Metcalfe did not insist on the payment of rupees thirty thousand which was the cost of preparation of an expedition against Sham Singh. "Thus ended a historic drama, which was apprehended to cause grave repercussions, due to a display of energy and statesmanship by Maharaja Jagat Singh and an admirable goodwill and generosity by Sir Charles Metcalfe."[35]

As a whole the British authorities from 1806 to 1813 covering the Governor-Generalship of Cornwallis, Barlow and Minto, followed the policy of non-intervention in the Princely States including Jaipur. This period has been styled as 'hands off' in the history of rise and expansion of British dominions in India.

II

In 1813 the Earl of Moira (afterwards Marquess of Hastings) took over as Governor-General who once more followed a 'forward' and aggressive policy in dealing with Indian Chiefs and States. P.E. Roberts has aptly remarked, "The Earl of Moira had been an opponent of Lord Wellesley's policy, and yet he was destined to complete the fabric of British dominion in India almost exactly as his great predecessor had planned it."[36] After his arrival in India, Hastings "found himself called upon by circumstances to carry the same policy to completion."[37] Between the departure of Wellesley and advent of Hastings the enemies of the Company had become very active and aggressive, and created a precarious situation for the East India Company. Particularly the Maratha Chiefs, the Peshwa, the Bhonsla, the Gaekwar, the Sindhia and the Holkar along with the Pathans and the Pindaris, posed a great danger to the supremacy of the Company in India. Hastings himself stated :

> Our object in India ought to be to render the British Government paramount in effect, if not declaredly so, to hold the other states as vassals, though not in name, and to oblige them, in return for our guarantee and protection, to perform the two great feudatory duties of supporting our rule with all their forces, and submitting their mutual differences to our arbitration.[38]

In order to achieve this object he planned to apply both diplomacy and force. He collected a large force of 1,16,000 men and 300 guns from all the presidencies which he divided into two parts — northern force which was to be commanded personally by him and the Deccan force which was to be under the command of Sir Thomas Hishop. While using this force against the enemies he resorted to diplomatic manoeuvres so as to avoid a junction of his enemies by treating them singly and separately. But before Hastings could execute his plan, he was involved in a war with Gorkhas of Nepal which continued for about a couple of years (1814-16). Thereafter he applied his energy and efforts in subduing the Pindaris and Maratha Chiefs. At the same time he decided to win over Jaipur and other States of Rajputana in order to detach them from their formidable enemies. Shocked at the miserable plight of the Jaipur State, he wrote on 15 January 1815 that an alliance with Jaipur was "equally counselled by generous humanity and by unquestionable interests."[39] The Home authorities expressed a considered opinion that the renewal of connection with that State would be of great benefit to the Company's affairs with the hope that the 'former departure from Equity' would be healed up by taking Jaipur once again under the protection of the Company. Hastings himself concurred in this view. British honour, he felt, would be gratified by undoing what had been done in regard to the treaty of 1803, in the dissolution of which "our (the Company's) supposed convenience had perhaps too much share."[40]

Charles Metcalfe, who had become the Resident at Delhi in 1811, like Lake, Malcolm and Elphinstone, was a severe critic of the policy of non-intervention adopted by the successors of Wellesley. He considered this policy as impolitic, inexpedient and unjust.[41] He opined that the States of Rajputana should be taken under British protection and for this he had been pressing the Government for a considerably long time. He argued that apart from depriving the predatory hordes of their main source of income, it would prove to be of great financial advantage to the British Government. Apart from this, humanitarian considerations had prompted Metcalfe to save these States from the misery inflicted on them by the Marathas, the Pathans and the Pindaris.[42] Metcalfe held that in case protection was not afforded when it was solicited, it might not be accepted when offered.[43] He suggested that an alliance could be concluded with Jaipur State as the first step. The views of Metcalfe were accepted by the Governor-General without reservation. As a matter of fact, the Memorandum of Metcalfe on Central India provided the basis for the elaborate minute presented by the Governor-General to the Council later on. "The policy it inculcated was indeed emphatically Metcalfe's policy."[44] In a brilliant note Metcalfe rebutted the arguments of those who were against a treaty with Jaipur and maintained that treaties with Sindhia and Holkar did not preclude the possibility of alliance with the States of Rajputana. He opined that Jaipur would not be a liability to the Company as it would be required to pay a handsome tribute when as a result of British protection peace would be established in its territories. While agreeing with the proposal that Jaipur should be included in a general plan of bringing all the States of Rajputana under British protection, he urged that an alliance with that State should mark the beginning of a series of treaties with other powers in that region, for it would be too much to expect that all the States would seek an alliance simultaneously and at a time convenient to the British Government alone. He concluded with a note of warning : "if we refuse now to conclude an alliance with Jeypore, it may happen that Jeypore will be reluctant to conclude one at the precise period, when we deem it advantageous for ourselves."[45]

The decision to conclude treaty with Jaipur, however, could not be taken by the Governor-General without opposition or difference of opinion in his Council. Two members of the Council, Edmonstone and Dowdeswell were not in favour of concluding this treaty but other members of the Council notably Seton, who was formerly Company's Resident in Delhi, strongly supported the proposal. Seton put forward an elaborate list of the 'benefits' which could be expected from the proposed alliance : it would prevent Jaipur from falling into the hands of Amir Khan; Jaipur as an ally would assist in the expansion of the 'useful political influence' of the Company towards the west; as a subordinate ally, Jaipur would virtually become an advanced military cantonment in that quarter; the alliance would have a pleasing consequence by removing, 'somewhat unfavourable impression' caused by the dissolution of the former treaty in 1806 which was 'a harsh and hasty measure'.[46] Having finally decided to make a treaty with the Jaipur State, the Governor-General issued necessary instructions to Metcalfe regarding the terms of negotiations for the proposed treaty. The negotiations were, however, prolonged for some time because Jaipur's new Prime Minister Bakshi Manji Das, wished to maintain the integrity and independence of the State against all foreign influences, including those of the Pindaris, the Marathas and the British. Moreover, Amir Khan again invaded Jaipur, and after devastating the countryside (he) laid siege to the capital itself. Manji Das wanted to keep alive the negotiations with the British Government, as a stick with which to beat Amir Khan and he sent a diplomatic mission headed by Shankar Das to Delhi. Negotiations came to a stand-still, because, though all other clauses of a proposed treaty were settled, the clause concerning the annual tribute proved a stumbling block.[47]

The Maharaja of Jaipur began to indulge in procrastinations. Modifications after modifications were suggested and incapacity to payment of tribute was urged time and again. The opposition of a faction of the *Thakurs* hostile to the British Government, the incapacity of the State to pay the stipulated amount and pressure from Holkar, Sindhia and Amir Khan, led to the abandonment of negotiations.[48]

However, three factors helped in the finalisation of the treaty. First, the British authorities had been successful in concluding treaties with Amir Khan and Sindhia in May 1817 and November 1817 respectively as a result of which both these erstwhile enemies of the British could no longer stand in the way of the proposed treaty with Jaipur. Secondly, an army was despatched under the command of David Ochterlony from Rewari towards Jaipur which would serve as implied threat of military operations for the purpose of coercing Jagat Singh into submission. Thirdly, Metcalfe also expected that Ochterlony's advance would invite overtures from the chiefs dependent on the Raja of Jaipur — overtures which would urge upon the Maharaja the need of an expeditious treaty.[49] Metcalfe actually opened negotiations with the feudatory chiefs of Khetri and Uniara. The Maharaja was alarmed and he sent his representatives to implore the Resident to suspend negotiations with the chiefs till the arrival of another envoy from Jaipur.[50] At last, after extraordinarily protracted negotiations with some breaks, the treaty was concluded on 2 April 1818.[51]

Article 1 of the Treaty provided that there would be 'perpetual friendship, alliance and unity of interest' between the East India Company and Maharaja Jagat Singh and his heirs and successors and that friends and enemies of one party would be friends and enemies of both. By Article 2, the British Government undertook to protect the territory of Jaipur against its enemies. Article 3 laid down that the ruler of Jaipur and his successors would act in subordinate cooperation with the British Government and acknowledge its supremacy and would not have any connection with other Chiefs and States. It was stipulated in Article 4 that the Maharaja, his heirs and successors would not enter into negotiations with any Chief or State without the knowledge and sanction of the British Government. It was laid down in Article 5 that all disputes between Jaipur and other States would be submitted to the arbitration and award of the British Government. Article 6 provided that no tribute was to be charged from Jaipur during the first year after the conclusion of the Treaty. But during the second, third, fourth, fifth and sixth year; four, five, six, seven and eight lakhs of rupees respectively were to be paid by Jaipur. Thereafter eight lakhs of Delhi rupees annually were to be paid by Jaipur, but when its revenues exceeded rupees forty lakhs a year, it was required to surrender to the British Government five-sixteenth of the excess, in addition to the eight lakhs above mentioned. By Article 7 of the Treaty, the Maharaja of Jaipur was bound to furnish troops according to its means at the requisition of the British Government. According to Article 8 of the Treaty, the Maharaja and his heirs and successors would remain absolute rulers of their territory and their dependents according to long established usage and British civil and criminal jurisdiction would not be introduced into that principality. It was laid down in Article 9 that the prosperity of the State would be favourably considered and attended to if the Maharaja would remain faithful to the British Government.[52]

The British Government had also concluded similar treaties with 18 other Rajputana States at about the same time. A comparative study of the provisions of all these treaties shows that all the Articles of the treaty with Jaipur, except Article 6 pertaining to tribute, were common with Articles of treaties concluded with the principal States like Jodhpur and Udaipur and lesser States like Kota, Bundi, Bikaner, Karauli, Dungarpur, Banswara and Kishangarh.

III

After the conclusion of treaties with Jaipur and other Rajputana States, David Ochterlony was appointed Resident and Commissioner-General for conducting the affairs of Rajputana States. Since the danger from the Marathas and the Pindaris had been successfully eliminated for the British, the new relations between the East India Company and the Rajput States began to take shape in the context of the internal situation.[53] It was, indeed, a baffling task to restore internal authority and order within the States. The internal situation in Jaipur, as in Mewar and Marwar States, was marked by anarchy and disorder. "Its political life was characterized by the defects of its incompetent and dissolute prince, the inefficiency of its ministers and officers, and the conflict between the prince and the nobles."[54] Under such conditions the British authorities had to intervene even in violation of the treaty of 1818 to improve upon the existing state of affairs. In May 1818 Ochterlony personally visited Jaipur in order to regulate the relations of the Maharaja with the *Thakurs* on a sound footing. On 21 June he convened a special meeting of the *Thakurs* in the presence of the Maharaja in which the feudatory chiefs were asked to execute a paper laying down the fundamental rules regarding their relations with the Maharaja. The chiefs were compelled to sign this document though they did so reluctantly. According to the terms of the said agreement all the 'recent' usurpations of the *Thakurs* were to be disposed of according to the will of the Darbar; the chiefs promised not to give shelter to thieves and robbers; they were required to protect the merchants in their respective estates and not to molest them in any way. They agreed to render service at home and abroad as per the usages of the Darbar. Their brothers, sons and dependents would also render the required service to the Darbar. The *Thakurs* pledged not to oppress the *ryots*. The Maharaja, on his part, also assured that the chiefs would enjoy their ancient rights and domains subject to their being obedient and loyal to the former. Some of the *Thakurs*, however, declined the proposition of restoring the *Khalsa* lands but they were compelled to do so, thereby, establishing the Maharaja's just authority throughout his territory.[55]

As the Jaipur Darbar found it difficult to pay the annual tribute to the British under article 6 of the treaty of 1818, they had to place before the British Agent all the facts about 'financial and territorial arrangements'. In the words of Tod :

> ... the 'absolute rulers' of Jaipur have been compelled to unfold to the resident Agent the whole of their financial and territorial arrangements, to prove that the revenues did not exceed the sum of forty lakhs, as, of the sum in excess (besides the stipulated tributary fifth), our share was to be three-sixteenths.[56]

The British authorities had also to intervene in the affairs of the State due to succession troubles following the death of Raja Jagat

Singh on 21 December 1818. The deceased Chief had left behind no natural or adopted heir. On the following day a minor of 9 years named Mohan Singh, a distant relative of the ruling family was placed on the *gaddi* by Mohan Nazir, the chief eunuch who then had the reins of power in his hands. He declared that the succession of Mohan Singh was in accordance with the wish of the late Maharaja but there was no evidence in support of this declaration. "There was no previous consultation or concert amongst the military vassals, or the queens." It was only after the installation of Mohan Singh that the Nazir tried to secure the approval of the nobles and the British Government. The nobles refused to make any commitment in this regard but on 7 February 1819 the British Government after preliminary enquiry through their *Munshi* confirmed publicly the succession of Mohan Singh. Even after the approval of the Paramount Power the queens and nobles rejected the claim of Mohan Singh as a legitimate successor. The chief queen of Sawai Jagat Singh "breathed nothing but open defiance of the Nazir and his junta" and she had all the support of the nobles in her stand. Meanwhile in March 1819 Rajawat chief of Jhalai resorted to arms in favour of his claim to the *gaddi*. At about the same time another party put forth the claim of Man Singh, the posthumous son of Prithvi Singh. The Nazir also made preparations for moving troops against the nobles and relatives of the deceased Raja who opposed him. Civil war seemed imminent but it was averted on account of the timely discovery that one of the queens of Sawai Jagat Singh — the Bhattiani queen — was pregnant. On 25 April 1819 she gave birth to a son. Ochterlony immediately proceeded to Jaipur, removed Mohan Singh from the *gaddi* and installed the newly born child who was named Jai Singh III. He was recognised as the legitimate ruler both by the Jaipur nobles and the British Government and his mother at the same time was recognised as his Regent.[57] But the British Resident Ochterlony continued to meddle in the internal affairs of Jaipur and, worse still, he took the side of Mohan Nazir, the Prime Minister who was opposed to the Regent Rani.

Ochterlony's policy was full of harmful results for future, because it drove the Regent Rani into a state of opposition to the British, a conduct which she ceaselessly followed till the end of her life. This struggle for supremacy between the Resident and the Regent Rani ended in triumph for the latter, who dismissed Mohan Nazir and appointed Rawal Bairisal as *Mukhtiar* or Prime Minister.[58] She informed Ochterlony that all other appointments would be made on the advice of Rawal Bairisal, and expressed hope that the Resident would support him wholeheartedly.

During the Regency of the Rani (1819-33) "Jaipur was a scene of corruption and misgovernment, and the British Government found it necessary to appoint an officer to reside at Jaipur and to authorise him to interfere in the internal administration of the State, with the view of guarding the interests of Government and securing the payment of the tribute."[59] The Governor-General approved of the proposal because he realised that it was difficult for the Resident at Delhi with his multifarious duties to pay exclusive attention to the affairs at Jaipur.[60] Thus was appointed Political Agent at Jaipur in 1821 on behalf of the British Government. Captain J. Stewart was the first British officer to be appointed on this important post. The news of the appointment of British Political Agent caused a stir at Jaipur. All parties, including that of Rawal Bairisal were united in their resolve to oppose such an appointment, fearing that a Political Agent would inevitably interfere in the day-to-day administration and undermine the power and prestige of both the Regent Rani and the Rawal. Despite their opposition Captain Stewart took over his duties at Jaipur, though he was accorded a cold reception.[61]

During 1821-24 the newly appointed British Political Agent, Captain Stewart backed by the Resident Ochterlony began to interfere continuously and ceaselessly in the affairs of Jaipur, and such an intervention was resented by the Regent Rani. The Resident supported Stewart's plea rejecting the suggestion of the Regent Rani to place Jhota Ram and Amar Chand at the helm of revenue affairs, and appointed Misr Ganesh Narain to assist the Rawal and Captain Stewart in the working of Department of Revenue so as to improve the finances of the State.[62] This was resented by Rani Mother. Due to her persistent opposition to Ganesh Narain's appointment the Governor-General, after the matter was reported to him, cancelled his appointment as the *defacto* head of the Revenue Department but allowed him to be employed on the staff of Stewart.[63] In June 1821 the Governor-General accorded sanction for dual interference in the administration of the revenue and the expenditure of the State but priority was to be given to the improvement of revenue as the Jaipur Darbar had failed to pay the fixed tribute. On receiving the orders of the Governor-General Rawal Bairisal and Jhota Ram waited upon Stewart and promised to furnish him with all the details of Revenue Department. It was agreed that the share of the British Government in the revenues of Jaipur would be calculated on the basis of *Khalsa* and *Tunkha* lands and such *jagir* lands as were granted after the treaty of 1818.[64] The British policy of interference in Jaipur's internal administration widened the gulf that already existed between the Regent Rani and Rawal Bairisal. In September 1821 the Rawal expressed his apprehension that the Regent Rani instigated by her favourites like Rawal Chand Singh and Jhota Ram, would thwart his plans for revenue reforms and suggested that she should be deprived of Regency, but as Stewart did not favour such an extreme step, his suggestion was declined.[65]

At about this time Maharaja Kishore Singh of Kota who wanted to wrest power from his usurping minister Rana Zalim Singh escaped from his State and entered the boundaries of Jaipur. On the orders of Stewart, Bairisal issued command to all the *Thakurs* to cooperate with British troops in expelling the Maharaja of Kota. Consequently Kishore Singh was completely routed by joint forces of Zalim Singh and Captain Tod with the assistance of Jaipur troops in October 1821.[66]

Soon after this a British Military Officer was stopped and insulted by local inhabitants at Madhopur. On the insistence of Stewart, two culprits involved in the incident, named Har Charan and Parbatti Das, were handed over by Bairisal to the British Political Agent but they were soon released after a suitable warning by the orders of Governor-General.[67]

Meanwhile the chasm between the Regent Rani and Rawal

Bairisal (who was backed by Stewart) was becoming deeper and wider. The Rawal demanded the dismissal of Rao Chand Singh and *Thakur* Megh Singh of Diggi, the *Darogha* and the *Naib Darogha* of the palace respectively both of whom were considered the main supporters of the Rani. Incensed at this suggestion, she decided to replace the Rawal by a new minister. When she sounded Stewart about her intention to do so, the latter asserted that though her right of appointing a minister could not be denied, she could not do so without a reference to the Governor-General. Thereupon the Rani dropped the idea of appointing Megh Singh of Diggy as Prime Minister. Very tactfully and boldly and bypassing Stewart, she won over Rawal Bairisal and entered into a working agreement with him. Bairisal continued as *Mukhtiar* but he renounced his insistence on the removal of Chand Singh and Megh Singh.[68]

In February 1823 the British Resident Ochterlony paid a visit to Jaipur. Bairisal tried to poison the ears of Ochterlony by telling him that all the misfortunes and troubles of the State were due to the Rani and her inefficient and corrupt advisers. Thereupon Octerlony reprimanded the Rani for her incompetence and advised her to hand over all the powers of government to Bairisal. After the departure of the Resident the Rani, making use of her prerogative, removed Bairisal from the office and appointed Megh Singh of Diggi as Prime Minister. At the intervention of the British Agent Stewart and Resident Ochterlony who got necessary orders from the Governor-General, Bairisal was reinstated as Prime Minister. Megh Singh was removed from the office and he was also deprived of the fort of Lamba which was handed over to the charge of British officers temporarily. Jhota Ram, the great favourite of the Regent Rani was compelled to leave Jaipur in April 1823 with the warning that he would be arrested immediately if he set his foot again in Jaipur.[69]

After the departure of Captain Stewart from Jaipur as Political Agent on 23 April 1824, Major Raper took over as the British Political Agent at Jaipur. Raper was asked to effect reconciliation between the Regent Rani and Rawal Bairisal but he failed in his attempt. Due to incompetence of the Rawal and his assistant Fateh Lal in the Revenue Department, several battalions could not receive their salaries for many months. At last four battalions mutinied and having placed their officers in confinement they marched towards Jaipur to realise their arrears. British troops were requisitioned from Nasirabad to meet the crisis. Raper believed that the troops had revolted as a result of incitement from the Rani who also convened a conference of *Thakurs* at her palace. This caused alarm and concern among the British authorities. The rebels were, however, persuaded to retire to their posts with an assurance on behalf of the Rani, Resident and Misr Ganesh Narain to the soldiers that their arrears would be cleared as per old rules. Raper was not happy with the conduct and measures taken by the Regent Rani and when the Rani appointed Thakur Bairisal of Bachoon without his concurrence, he decided to quit the city. He encamped at Bakrota (nine miles from Jaipur) where he began to await arrival of reinforcements from Nasirabad. He refused to return despite repeated requests made to him by the Regent Rani. He said that he would not return until assembly of the *Thakurs* summoned by the Rani was revoked and assurance was given of the restoration of the Rawal as Prime Minister. The Rani finally agreed to receive back Rawal Bairisal as her nominal Prime Minister as *Mukhtiar*. Raper returned to Jaipur on 10 November 1824.[70] On the visit of the Resident Ochterlony to Jaipur in the last week of November, sharp differences arose between him and the Political Agent Raper, for the latter was ignored completely in the course of a month-long negotiations between the Resident and the Regent Rani regarding reforms in the administration of Jaipur. Megh Singh of Diggi was now appointed as *Mukhtiar* and Misr Ganesh Narain and his kinsman Misr Govind Narain were placed at the helm of affairs in the Revenue Department. The Governor-General approved of new administrative arrangements of Jaipur settled between Ochterlony and the Regent Rani but directed that the Rawal's possessions should not be disturbed and that the Regent Rani would not allow the return of Jhota Ram to the State.[71] Much annoyed with the conduct of the Rani, Raper tried to lower her position in his reports which contained "distorted and occasionally perverted accounts of happenings at Jaipur" to the higher authorities. He reported that the Rani was seriously considering to bring Jhota Ram back and that she was strongly under the influence of her favourite slave girl, Rupa Bhandarin who administered intoxication drugs and spirits to the Rani.[72]

In August 1825 she asked for recall of Jhota Ram and also removal of a *Vakil* of Rawal Bairisal attached to Political Agency at Jaipur but her request was turned down by Raper. However, just before relinquishing his office as Political Agent, Raper accepted the Rani's request for the recall of Jhota Ram to the State which caused nervousness in the mind of Bairisal who asked for the return to him of village Anandpura from the Political Agent. But the Rani opposed his demand, pleading that the village should lapse to the State. Captain Low, who succeeded Raper as Political Agent at Jaipur, declined to intercede with the Regent Rani for the restoration of Anandpura to Bairisal and the new British Resident Metcalfe agreed with him. On 17 February 1826 the Governor-General Amherst issued instructions, permitting recall of Jhota Ram and adding that the British Government would never hesitate to interfere "to prevent any measure of persecution and oppression against that chief (Rawal Bairisal)."[73]

Like his predecessors, Captain Low also placed himself in opposition to the Regent Rani. In order to prevent the possibility of intrigues on his part with the rival faction, no person of rank or influence was allowed to meet him and all roads leading to the Agency were put under surveillance by the orders of the Rani. Annoyed with the Rani's attitude and conduct, he complained about it to the Resident, Charles Metcalfe. The Resident wished to abstain from interference in the internal affairs of the State but he did not rule out the right of British Government to interfere, in case the interests of the State and the minor Raja were jeopardised by the maladministration of the Jaipur ministry. He, however, wanted to restrict it to the sphere of advice and renonstrance, if possible.[74] Captain Low, who was in agreement with Metcalfe, regarding the general policy of non-interference, believed that the pecuniary interest of the British Government necessitated minute interference in the revenue administration of the State. It was, therefore, decided to reserve the right of interference in order to ascertain the revenue collection of the State and to secure the due share of the British Government, but to waive the 'obnoxious interference' founded on that right until it became evident that some 'adequate benefit' would accrue from a rigid scrutiny.[75] It is evident that non-interference was motivated not by principles but by considerations of benefits.[76] Metcalfe directed Captain Low to abstain from scrutinizing the revenue accounts as was the practice earlier and also instructed him not to visit and entertain complaints from the people against the Rani.[77]

Meanwhile there was deterioration of administrative efficiency mainly because the Rani disregarded the advice of high functionaries and nobles of the State and fell under the influence of Jhota Ram and some persons of low origin and disreputable character such as Rupa Bhandarin, Hukam Chand, etc. Captain Low suggested that the public appearance of the minor Maharaja might help improve the situation, for the Maharaja could then be placed under the supervision of a reputed *Thakur* who could also act as the *Mukhtiar.* Some nobles led by the chiefs of Uniara, Rawal Bairisal and Megh Singh who were jealous of Jhota Ram, were also keenly desirous of change in the administration from which they had been excluded.[78] Metcalfe agreed with the Political Agent that an assembly of *Thakurs* should be held in the presence of the Maharaja but he desired that such an assembly should be convened by the Rani and not at the instance of the British Government. When approached by the Political Agent to convene the assembly of *Thakurs,* the Rani did not evince any enthusiasm about it nor about the public appearance of the Maharaja. By September 1826 *Thakurs* from various parts of the State gathered in Jaipur. The supporters of the Rani encamped inside the city, whereas Bhairisal and others who were opposed to the Rani encamped near the Agency House. This was not to the relish of the Rani and she prohibited communication between the *Thakurs* of hostile camps.[79] After getting necessary orders from the Supreme Government the assembly was held at the residence of the Political Agent on 14 October. It was decided by a majority of *Thakurs* to remove the Rani from the regency, with 31 votes for and 23 against, after the public appearance of the young Maharaja.[80] The implementation of this decision was suspended by Captain Low in view of the forthcoming visit of Resident Charles Metcalfe to Jaipur.

On his arrival at Jaipur and after examining the situation personally Metcalfe became critical of the biased role which the Political Agent played in the recent developments in the State. He noticed that the general impression current at that time was that the British Government was supporting Rawal Bairisal and his faction against the Rani. He was convinced that the Political Agent had exercised his influence against the Rani at the time of voting; the *Thakurs* who were opposed to the Rani were "few in number and bore the appearance of a small body".[81] He perceived that an influential section of the *Thakurs* evinced a feeling in favour of the continuance of the Rani as the Regent and felt convinced that the British Government had so far been acting on false notions and wrong assumptions.[82] He, therefore, decided to convene another assembly which should make the verdict impartially. Though the Governor-General was not enthusiastic about a second assembly, he had already given discretionary powers to Metcalfe to act according to his judgement.[83] Accordingly the second assembly of the *Thakurs* was held on 8 November 1826. In this assembly the votes were recorded in the presence of two chiefs of each party in order to prevent any appearance of interference on the part of the British Government. The verdict of this assembly went in favour of the Rani by a majority of 28 votes for and 22 votes against.[84] Metcalfe immediately gave assurance to the Rani that she would exercise full authority as Regent to select and appoint ministers and officials without any interference from the British side. "Thus the British interference in Jaipur, partial in principle but complete in practice, initiated by Ochterlony, was at the end reversed by Metcalfe."[85]

With the decision of the *Thakurs* made in her favour the Rani now announced sweeping changes in the ministry and replaced Thakur Megh Singh of Diggi by Rao Chand Singh as the *Mukhtiar* of the State. The relations between the Political

Agent and the Regent Rani deteriorated.

In view of financial constraints and heavy tributary obligations of Jaipur to the Paramount Power, the Regent Rani thought of a scheme of seizing money from all who possessed it whether they owed any debt to the State or not. The British Agent Captain Low refused to sanction this scheme. After this British authorities adopted a harsh attitude, and on 25 August 1827 Low was required to make a satisfactory arrangement for the liquidation of British arrears of tribute with the Jaipur Darbar failing which some *parganas* of the *Khalsa* yielding the amount required would be brought under British management. Fearing such an action, the Jaipur Darbar hastily raised loans and on 7 October 1827 fourteen *Hundies* amounting to eight lakhs of rupees were handed over to Captain Low. In February 1828 the Rani made a request to reduce the exorbitant amount of tribute to four lakhs of rupees which was rejected by the British Political Agent. The Rani sought the Agent's permission to appoint Jhota Ram as *Mukhtiar* who alone was capable to raise money and pay tribute regularly. Though Captain Low was opposed to his appointment, the Resident Colebrooke and the Governor-General accorded permission to the Rani to appoint him as Prime Minister provided the tribute in future was paid unfailingly without falling into arrear.[86]

Jhota Ram after assuming office took a number of measures to improve the administration and finances of the State. One such measure was the reduction of garrisons in the *Khalsa* forts. Many disbanded troops consisted of men furnished by the feudal chiefs who enjoyed extensive *jagirs* for their maintenance; with the result many *jagirs* were resumed. This measure of Jhota Ram led to outbreak of insurrection at Ranthambhor as the fortress had a mixed garrison including *Khalsa* troops and a number of contingents of chieftains (*Thakurs*) who were enjoying British guarantee. The Minister sent a large army which besieged the fort but as the siege continued for a long time it caused a heavy strain on resources of the State. The British aurhorities deliberately kept aloof and announced in November 1830 that the British Agency at Jaipur would be closed and the British Agent at Ajmer would perform the duties in place of Political Agent at Jaipur. Accordingly British Agency at Jaipur was closed by Major Low on 17 November 1830. The Governor-General, William Bentinck (who believed in the policy of non-intervention in the internal affairs of the States) declined to lend British troops and he even forbade British officers to mediate between the Jaipur Darbar and the rebel *Thakurs* of Ranthambhor. Both the British Political Agent at Ajmer and the Resident at Delhi discouraged the proposal of the discontented *Thakurs* to convene a conference of the chiefs which aimed at undermining the authority of the Rani and her Minister Jhota Ram. The British authorities also deprived the rebellious *Thakurs* of the benefits of British guarantees.[87] At last the rebellion at Ranthambhor ended due to tactful handling of the situation by Jhota Ram who was aided and encouraged by the Rani.

In the meanwhile in 1828-29 many border disputes of Jaipur with the States of Jodhpur, Bikaner, Karauli and Tonk occurred. In these disputes not only the civilians were involved but occasionally armed forces of these States also clashed with each other. The British Government intervened decisively to settle all these disputes.[88] These disputes involved lot of expenditure which depleted the treasury of Jaipur. Economic distress was further aggravated during 1832-33 due to drought and attacks of swarms of locusts resulting in the destruction of crops. The Jaipur Darbar requested the British Government to reduce tribute at least for the current year but this request was declined by Lt.-Colonel Lockett, the then Political Agent at Ajmer. The Governor-General agreed with the view of the Agent, adding that the tribute of Jaipur was "fixed with reference to its average capacity and not on an estimate of peculiarly favourable seasons."[89] Despite repeated requests of the Jaipur Darbar for reduction in tribute, the Governor-General refused to change his decision.[90]

Under these circumstances Jhota Ram failed to improve the finances of the State. He had also lost the goodwill of many *Thakurs* whose estates were threatened by him but he could not succeed in his plan as the British Government supported these nobles whose possessions had been guaranteed. The position of Jhota Ram was further weakened due to the death of the Regent Rani whose greatest favourite he was.

British relations with the Jaipur State were strained due to decided, and to a great extent unjust, intervention of the British authorities in the districts of Shekhawati and Torawati. When lawlessness was created in Shekhawati by the predatory elements, Jhota Ram sent an expedition under Bakshi Munna Lal who succeeded in suppressing and expelling several robbers, including the notorious Laxman Singh of Khandela. But due to shelter offered to robbers by the courts of Bikaner and Jodhpur, complete peace and order could not be restored. Despite the request of the Jaipur Maharaja and the Minister, the British authorities neither took any action against the Bikaner and Jodhpur Darbars nor extended any help to the army of Jaipur in suppressing lawless elements in Shekhawati. On the other hand, the British aurhorities decided to intervene directly in Shekhawati and Torawati. Misconstruing the hesitation of the Jaipur Darbar in handing over two groups of three and eleven robbers respectively held in Jaipur jails to the British Government as a hostile action, British forces were sent which occupied Shekhawati and Torawati. Not only that, the charge of the Lake and district of Sambhar was also assumed by a British Superintendent on 27 January 1835.[91] "The British acquisition of Shekhawati and Sambhar was the first decided interference of great magnitude in the internal affairs of Jaipur and was neither dictated by political requirements nor by any strategic urgency."[92]

IV

Soon after this, the young Maharaja Jai Singh III died on 5 February 1835 due to serious ailment caused by diabetes.[93] It was a bolt from the blue for Jhota Ram who expressed his desire to be relieved of his office of Minister with immediate effect. Rani Chandrawat and the step-mothers and grand-mothers of the new Maharaja appealed to the Governor-General in Council that Jhota Ram should be permitted to continue to serve the State during the minority of the new ruler, Maharaja Ram Singh.

But as it was strongly suspected by the British authorities that the late Maharaja had been poisoned to death by Jhota Ram, the Governor-General ordered that he should be asked to quit the office of Minister immediately and should also reside beyond the territorial jurisdiction of the State.[94] Jhota Ram began to reside in the town of Dausa.

With the permission of the Governor-General Bairisal was appointed as *Mukhtiar* of the State[95] with unfettered powers in the administration. This measure "marked the beginning of the process of depriving the Regent Rani of her ascendancy in the State."[96] As a result of the ill-treatment of Jhota Ram and his departure from the State, a tragic incident took place in Jaipur on 4 June 1835 in which Jhota Ram and his supporters were strongly suspected to be involved. "By raising a popular disturbance on the very day of the Agent's arrival, and by hiring assassins to murder the English officers, he (Jhota Ram) hoped to embroil the *Thakurs* with the Government, so that he might be brought back to power through their being discredited." When Major Alves (British Agent to Governor-General at Ajmer), accompanied by Martin Blake, John Ludlow, Cornet Macnaghten and others came out of the palace after some discussion with Maji Chandrawat (mother of the minor Maharaja) and the *Thakurs,* he was suddenly attacked with a sword by one Fateh Singh. He received serious injuries but he was rescued by Blake and Ludlow. Thereafter Blake was attacked by an excited crowd of the people and he was killed. The Minister ordered the execution of five persons who were considered guilty of the murder of Blake and other suspected culprits were detained and imprisoned for further enquiry.[97] A court was constituted to give its verdict on the charges levelled against Jhota Ram and his party. The court awarded death punishment to Diwan Umar Chand, Hidayat Ullah and some other culprits, life imprisonment to others and five years' rigorous imprisonment to Fateh Lal (a nephew of Jhota Ram). Jhota Ram and his brother were also awarded capital punishment but the British authorities commuted their death-punishment to confinement for life in Chunar fortress.[98]

Meanwhile Shekhawati and Torawati were handed back

to Jaipur Darbar which apparently had been taken over by the British authorities to damage the reputation of Jhota Ram who was considered inimical to the British. A local force called Shekhawati Brigade was, however, retained in Shekhawati under a British officer which could not be employed elsewhere by the Jaipur Darbar without prior approval of the Agent to Governor-General.

In July 1838 Rawal Bairisal died and his son Rawal Shiva Singh succeeded him. His appointment was made at the initiative of the Regent Rani herself without seeking prior approval of the Governor-General. Though the latter had given his approval, the general impression was that the Rani had asserted her prerogative as a Regent by appointing Shiva Singh as Minister. In the following month on the repeated requests of Alves (AGG) the Governor-General Auckland announced the appointment of Major Ross as the Political Agent at Jaipur.[99] He assumed the charge on 29 September 1838. He was to work under the directions of the AGG, Alves who urged him to play an active role in the affairs of Jaipur, though the Governor-General advised him to keep aloof from all interference. Following the advice of the former, he began to ignore the Regent Rani. In order to undermine the position of Ross in the State, the Rani had tried to prevail upon Shiva Singh to accept her 'implicit obedience' and to have no direct contact with Ross. But the Minister considering the Political Agent as the real source of his strength, refused to pledge obedience to her and showed his determination to consult Ross on all matters of the State.[100] Ross refused to receive any *Vakil* from her and communicated with her only through the minister Rawal Shiva Singh, thus unnecessarily provoking the Rani and causing feelings of mistrust and suspicion in her mind about his own bonafides.[101]

Both Alves and Ross made concerted efforts to undermine the authority and influence of the Rani. The Minister began to play into their hands and worked under their guidance in every matter. He had also appointed his brother, Thakur Laxman Singh as Commander of the Jaipur army in place of Munna Lal who was removed with the tacit acquiescence of Ross. In the beginning of 1839, Lt.-Colonel Sutherland was appointed as the Agent to Governor-General at Ajmer in place of Alves. Sutherland visited Jaipur towards the end of February 1839 and held detailed discussion with Major Ross and Rawal Shiva Singh regarding new and fool-proof administrative arrangements at Jaipur during the minority of Maharaja Ram Singh. He told the Regent Rani bluntly that whereas all respect and courtesy would be shown to her, she would not be permitted to exercise any control over the administration of the State. After considering various proposals, Sutherland in consultation with Ross and Rawal Shiva Singh recommended to the Governor-General that a Council of Regency of the chiefs of the State under the presidentship of the Political Agent should be constituted which should administer the affairs of the State during the minority of the young Maharaja.[102] The British Agency at Jaipur was made permanent on 18 April 1839.

Accordingly Council of Regency consisting of 'Five Sirdars' was constituted — Rawal Shiva Singh, Thakur Laxman Singh, Thakur Bhopal Singh, Thakur Sur Singh and Thakur Sumer Singh. The British Agent was to be the President of the Regency Council. All the five members were to be of equal status. Rawal Shiva Singh was recognised as Prime Minister. Thus the Regent Rani was deprived of the right to exercise any control over the Council. In spite of her unwillingness the Rani had to accept her exclusion from the Council of Regency as a fait accompli.[103] In order to gratify the British Government the Regency Council decided to appoint officials at each of the stages on the roads from Delhi and Agra to Jaipur, Nasirabad and Neemuch to meet the requirements of the British personnel passing through the State. Another significant measure taken by the Council was to appoint competent officials on each frontier of the State for settling border disputes promptly. The Shekhawati Brigade was placed under the control of the Regency Council. Soon a sharp difference arose between the Regency Council and the British Political Agent on the matter of control over Major Forster, the Commander of Shekhawati Brigade. The Council asserted that all orders issued to Major Forster should proceed from the 'Five' (Members of Council of Regency) and all his reports should also be addressed to the 'Five' as he was a servant of the State and paid by the State. Sutherland (AGG at Ajmer) strongly opposed this action of the Council of the 'Five'. He refused to recognise the 'Five' and held that the Regency Council could not take any measure without the concurrence of the Political Agent at Jaipur. A Proclamation was issued in this regard to the chiefs and people of Jaipur in the name of the British Government defining clearly the respective position of the Rani, the Members of Council of Regency and the British Political Agent at Jaipur. Though the Rani was to be shown all the respect due to her rank as mother of the minor Maharaja, she was not to be permitted to interfere in the management of administration of the State except in the matters connected with her palace. The Council of Regency would consist of, as hitherto, five principal *Thakurs* with Major Ross at the head who had the powers to remove any of the members for incompetence or disagreeable conduct, and associate any other *Thakur* in addition to five members in the Council. If due to factional animosities the *Thakurs* failed to work satisfactorily, the British authorities, on the recommendation of the Political Agent, might take over the entire management of the State, to the complete exclusion of the *Thakurs*.[104] "The Proclamation was so unequivocal and mandatory that it hushed all opposition against the authority of Major Ross, and established his absolute hegemony in the Council of Regency."[105]

Due to his sickness, Ross proceeded on a long leave and he was succeeded by Major Thoresby on 14 August 1839.[106] Soon after this the British Government felt the necessity of armed intervention in the affairs of Jodhpur State. With the willing consent of the Jaipur Council of Regency, the Shekhawati Brigade under the command of Forster was sent to reinforce the British expeditionary force. The Regency Council also offered to send its own regiments of infantry and cavalry, if necessary. The Governor-General expressed his happiness over the measures adopted by the Regency Council.[107] On the whole the administration of Jaipur, under the guidance of Thoresby worked satisfactorily. In February 1840 when Sutherland visited Jaipur, he reported very favourably about the administration and the general contentment that prevailed in the State.

In July 1841 an objectionable action on the part of Thoresby came to the fore. An envelop addressed to Rani Chandrawat (mother of the young Maharaja) arrived at Jaipur by Calcutta Mail which was intercepted by Thoresby. The latter sent the letter to Calcutta before it was delivered to the addressee. In fact, Thoresby suspected the designs of the Maharani on the basis of reports current about her attempts at Calcutta to secure her lost authority at Jaipur. Sutherland was critical of Thoresby's conduct and the Governor-General reprimanded him, warning him that "unless a valid case of political plotting was established, it was desirable to follow the strict principle of abstaining from all interference of the Government with packets and letters in the course of transmission by the post office."[108]

In 1839-41 when the British were involved in war with Afghanistan the Jaipur Darbar placed all the forces of the State unreservedly at the disposal of the Paramount Power. The Supreme Government directed Sutherland to arrange for the despatch of as many troops of the Shekhawati Brigade as could be spared for duty at Delhi Cantonment. The Council of Regency after customary assurance of loyalty and co-operation to the British authorities readily accepted the suggestion of Major Thoresby and allowed the despatch of as many troops of the Shekhawati Brigade and the army of Jaipur as were required at Delhi.[109]

Major Thoresby felt concerned about the "colossal financial burden under which Jaipur was groaning." He realised that it was mainly due to the heavy tribute which Jaipur Darbar had to pay to the British Government. In January 1841 he strongly recommended to the Government of India to reduce the amount of tribute charged from Jaipur. He opined that in 1818 the annual payment of rupees eight lakhs was fixed on the basis of the misleading report about the revenues of the State. Rawal Bairisal had agreed to the extravagant demand of eight lakhs of rupees per annum in order to retain his position as Prime Minister. With all its meagre resources the Jaipur Darbar had paid by 1842 to the British Government a 'staggering sum' of rupees 1,35,71,000 as tribute. The taking over of the Sambar Lake by the British Government in January 1835 had deprived the State of an annual income of about one and a half lakhs of rupees. The State had also to incur annual recurring expenditure of about two and a half lakhs of rupees on the maintenance of the Shekhawati Brigade. The State also owed heavy debts to bankers amounting to rupees one million or so for which interest amounting to rupees one lakh had to be paid annually. By April 1842 the arrears of the tribute alone had gone up to the 'incredible sum of rupees 46,28,999. Realising fully that injustice had been done to the State, Thoresby strongly pleaded for reduction of tribute in order to improve finances of the State. On his recommendation the Supreme Government reduced the tribute of Jaipur State from rupees eight lakhs to a fixed annual tribute of rupees four lakhs with retrospective effect from November 1, 1840; the arrears of tribute were no longer to be taken and the management and revenues of Sambhar Lake were restored to the Jaipur Darbar.[110] Later on it was decided that the approximate expenditure of rupees 2,50,000 on the maintenance of the Shekhawati Brigade was to be deducted from the tribute of rupees four lakhs payable by the Jaipur Darbar.[111]

Having improved the financial condition of the State considerably, Thoresby left Jaipur in January 1844 to take over his new assignment as Officiating Agent to Governor-General at Ajmer in place of Sutherland. In his place Major John Ludlow was appointed as the Political Agent at Jaipur on 24 January 1844.[112] Under the guidance of Major Ludlow suitable measures were taken for the education and administrative training of the young Maharaja. A Brahman graduate from Agra College, named Sheodeen was appointed for imparting instruction to him. By the time Ram Singh became fifteen years old in September 1847, he had cultivated his interest in Urdu, Hindi, Persian and English. He was also taught History of the World, Botany and Philosophy. He was also kept informed about the administrative matters of the State. Ludlow hoped that as a result of his education and training the Maharaja would become 'a merciful and benign ruler'.[113] Ludlow also took measures for the education of the masses. In 1844 he opened a 'Free School' which later became Maharaja's College. He revived the schools established earlier by Maharaja Sawai Jai Singh II. He brought into operation 118 village schools which were placed under the superintendence of local officers.[114] By the efforts of Ludlow, commendable public works were undertaken and social reforms were brought about. In May 1844, a dispensary and hospital was established in the city of Jaipur which attracted the attention of the people not only in the Jaipur State but also in the neighbouring States.[115] A dam was constructed across a rivulet and arrangement was made for the supply of water to the capital. Under the supervision of a newly appointed English engineer, Lt. Morton, roads in and in the neighbourhood of Jaipur were repaired and some new roads and passes were constructed for the benefit of travellers and traders.[116] Necessary measures were taken for the abolition of inhuman practices of *Sati*[117] and female infanticide.[118] Slavery was abolished and even the use of the term *gola* and *goli* (for slave boys and girls) was declared illegal.[119] Ludlow had earned the reputation of being an English Political Agent of 'unbiased and progressive views'. Thus the minority of Ram Singh ushered in 'an era of peace and prosperity for Jaipur'.[120]

On 2 February 1848 Captain W.H. Rickards took charge of the Political Agency at Jaipur when Ludlow had gone to Europe on furlough.[121] He continued to guide the Council of Regency in the work of reforms and improvement in the administration of the State. His main achievement was that with his energetic efforts he succeeded in improving the finances of the State.

The Jaipur State owned a piece of land measuring about 14 acres at Allahabad which was required by the British military authorities. The Council of Regency was reluctant to accept its price but showed willingness to surrender the land in lieu of a piece of land in British province of Ajmer to which the British authorities objected. At last under the influence of the Political Agent the Jaipur Darbar gave the required land free of any charge.[122]

By the beginning of 1851 the administration of the State had greatly improved and it was reported by Captain Rickards that financial condition of the State had also become quite sound; the treasury of the State was likely to show a surplus of rupees 2.5 lakhs and the character and conduct of the Maharaja was very satisfactory.[123] On the basis of his report, Colonel Low, the then Agent to the Governor-General, recommended that Maharaja Ram Singh should be invested with full ruling powers in the coming September when he would attain the age of eighteen years. Accepting his recommendation, the Supreme Government ordered that suitable arrangements should be made for the investiture of the young Maharaja in September 1851.[124] The Governor-General, Dalhousie himself participated in the investiture ceremony held on 23 September, presenting a *khillat* of rupees 10,250 to the Maharaja on the occasion.[125] The Council of Regency was abolished but the British Political Agent at Jaipur continued to guide the Maharaja in the administrative affairs of the State.

The Political Agent Rickards continued to dominate in the administrative affairs of Jaipur. He lived with pomp and show in a regal style at the cost of the State. He was also found guilty of gross corruption and malpractices by a judge of the Diwani Adalat, named A.B. Harrington, who was appointed to investigate the charges levelled against him. As a punishment he was transferred to Bhopal on a reduced salary,[126] which was, of course, a very meagre punishment in view of the serious charges proved against him.

During the rule of Maharaja Ram Singh the British authorities intervened authoritatively in 1852-54 to settle the boundary conflict between the feudatory estate of Uniara (under the suzerainty of Maharaja of Jaipur) and the State of Tonk. The people of Uniara and Jaipur were held guilty by the British official Lt. R. Jenkins who was appointed to settle the dispute. A fine of rupees 2,000 and subsequently of rupees 5,000 was imposed on the Jaipur State which was paid reluctantly by the Maharaja as he considered the award to be unfair. The British authorities also intervened to effect the marriage of Maharaja Ram Singh with the daughter of Maharaja Takht Singh of Jodhpur on 9 June 1853 before the former could proceed to Rewa to marry a princess of that State.[127] Due to frequent robberies committed in the territories of Jaipur and the neighbouring States in 1855-56, Agent to Governor-General Henry Lawrence recommended strongly that Captain Hardcastle (who had led successful campaign against the robbers and lawless elements) should be appointed as Superintendent in Shekhawati and the governments of Sikar and Khetri should be assumed directly by the British officers as long as necessary but the Supreme Government declined to accept these recommendations which would erode the authority of the Maharaja.[128]

In 1856, at the behest of Major Burton, officiating Political Agent at Jaipur, the Maharaja of Jaipur undertook the construction of a road from Jaipur to Bharatpur frontier which, it was thought by the British Agent, would not only add to the prosperity of the State but would also be useful for the British as providing a good military road in a strategic area. The contract for the construction of the road was given to an English contractor named Harcourt from Agra who, it was found afterwards, worked dishonestly and inefficiently to the disadvantage of the Jaipur State. Major Burton was reprimanded by the Governor-General and the contract was cancelled. On the recommendation of Captain W.F. Eden, the new Political Agent at Jaipur, an interest-free loan was advanced by the British Government to the Jaipur Darbar for the construction of this road.[129]

V

A perusal of the East India Company's relations with the Jaipur State, as discussed above, leads us to the conclusion that the British authorities intervened very frequently in the internal affairs of the State even in gross violation of the terms of the treaty of 1818 on which these relations were based. The opportunities for such intervention were provided by the minority of the two successive Maharajas, Jai Singh III and Ram Singh, which together extended over a period of more than three decades (1819-1851). The former had been installed on the *gaddi* immediately after his birth and his mother, the Bhattiani queen was recognised as his Regent. Corruption, misgovernment and factionalism prevalent in the State during the Regency of the Rani called for intervention of the British Government to safeguard the interests of the Jaipur government and to ensure the payment of regular tribute to the British. For this purpose it was considered essential by the British authorities to appoint a British Political Agent at Jaipur in 1821 who might exercise day-to-day control and supervision over the affairs of Jaipur — a measure which was strongly opposed by the Regent Rani and the Prime Minister, Rawal Bairisal. The newly appointed British Political Agent, Captain Stewart backed by the British Resident at Delhi, David Ochterlony began to interfere continuously in the affairs of Jaipur to the annoyance of the Regent Rani. Both the Resident and the Political Agent actively supported the Rawal who had, in fact, become their stooge (or a 'stalking horse', to use the words of Ochterlony), and tried to undermine the legitimate authority and influence of the Rani. She was not even permitted to wield her prerogative of replacing Rawal Bairisal by another Prime Minister. Major Raper, who was appointed as Political Agent at Jaipur in 1824 in place of Stewart, opposed the Rani tooth and nail, and endeavoured to lower her position by presenting distorted and often perverted accounts of happenings at Jaipur to the higher authorities. The next Political Agent, Captain Low also placed himself in opposition to the Rani and even made efforts to remove her from the office of Regent but his efforts were set at naught by the new Resident, Charles Metcalfe.

After the death of the young Maharaja Jai Singh III in February 1835, Ram Singh, who was a minor of about two years at that time, succeeded to the Chiefship and his mother Rani Chandrawat began to act as the Regent. At the intervention of the British authorities the Minister Jhota Ram was removed from his office and Bairisal was appointed as *Mukhtiar* in Jaipur. Due to ill-treatment of Jhota Ram and his departure from the State, a tragic incident took place in June 1835. Major Alves (Agent to Governor-General at Ajmer), when coming out of the palace of the Regent Rani after some discussion, was suddenly attacked and injured by a Jaipur resident and thereafter his companion

Blake was attacked and killed by an excited crowd; punishment varying from death sentence to life imprisonment was awarded to the culprits by the court. After the death of Rawal Bairisal in July 1838 his son Rawal Shiva Singh succeeded him as Minister. Major Ross was appointed as the new Political Agent at Jaipur in September 1838. He gave full support to Rawal Shiva Singh who was in turn guided by the former in every important matter of administration, thereby undermining the authority of the Rani as Regent. In 1839 it was decided by the British authorities that the Rani should be excluded from the administrative affairs of the State and a Council Regency of the chiefs of the State under the presidentship of the Political Agent should be constituted to administer the affairs of the State during the minority of the young Maharaja. Accordingly Council of Regency consisting of 'Five Sirdars' (*Thakurs*) of the State was constituted and the British Political Agent assumed the charge of President of the Regency Council. It was virtually the rule of the Political Agent and the Regency Council played a second fiddle to him in all administrative matters. The Political Agent could remove any member of the Regency Council on the ground of misconduct or incompetence and could also associate additional members.[130] The two successive Political Agents — Major Thoresby (1839-1844) and Captain Ludlow (1844-1847) — took commendable measures for the improvement of administration of the State. They maintained peace and order in the State, suppressed the refractory elements in Jaipur and the neighbouring territories. As a result of the efforts of Thoresby, the Supreme Government agreed to reduce the annual tribute of the State from rupees eight lakhs to rupees four lakhs. During the tenure of Ludlow dams and roads were constructed; a large number of schools were established for the education of the people; creditable measures were taken for the abolition of evil practices of *Sati*, female infanticide and slavery. The next Political Agent, Captain W.H. Rickards (1847-1851) continued to guide the Council of Regency in the work of reforms and improvement in the administration of the State.

The administration of the State during the minority of the two Chiefs was also made use of by the British authorities, through their Political Agents, to safeguard and promote fiscal and other Imperial interests of the British Government. They took care to see that the full amount of annual tribute was paid regularly by the State to the British Government under all circumstances even of financial stringency. In 1827 the Political Agent, Captain Low had warned the Jaipur government that the arrears of tribute due to the British Government should be paid in time failing which some *parganas* of the *Khalsa* land yielding the amount required would be taken over under the British management. Thereupon Jaipur Darbar hastily raised loans, and on 7 October 1827 fourteen *Hundies* amounting to eight lakhs of rupees were handed over to Low. Again in 1832-33 when due to drought and destruction of crops caused by attacks of swarms of locusts the Jaipur Darbar requested the British Government to reduce the tribute at least for the current year, the request was rejected by the Supreme Government on the recommendation of the Political Agent. Later on, when the then Political Agent Thoresby was convinced of the genuine financial predicaments of the State due to heavy annual tribute and other liabilities,the Supreme Government accepting his recommendations, agreed in 1842 to reduce the annual tribute from rupees eight lakhs to rupees four lakhs.

Under the influence of the Political Agent, one of the early measures taken by the Council of Regency in 1839 was to appoint officials at each of the stages on the roads from Delhi and Agra to Jaipur, Nasirabad and Neemuch to meet the requirements of the British personnel passing through the State.

In order to check endemic lawlessness and robberies in Shekhawati and neighbouring territories Shekhawati Brigade was organised under the command of Major Forster. The Council of Regency opined that all orders issued to Forster should emanate from the Council and all his reports should also be sent to the Council of 'five'. But the British authorities asserted that no orders could be issued by the Council without the concurrence of the Political Agent. In fact, the Shekhawati Brigade remained practically under the exclusive control of the Political Agent and the services of this Brigade could be utilised by the Imperial Government at any time, even out of Jaipur.

During the first Anglo-Afghan war, for example, the Jaipur Darbar, accepting the suggestion of the Political Agent Thoresby, despatched as many troops of the Shekhawati Brigade as were required for service at Delhi Cantonment.

In 1851 a piece of land measuring over 14 acres which was owned by the Jaipur State at Allahabad, was ceded by the Council of Regency to the British free of charge as it was required by the British military authorities of that place. This was done under the influence of the Political Agent.

In September 1851 when Maharaja Ram Singh became eighteen years old he was invested with ruling powers and the Council of Regency was abolished. But the Political Agent Rickards and then his successor Major Burton continued to dominate in the affairs of Jaipur. During 1854-56 daring dacoities occurred in Jaipur and the neighbouring States of Jodhpur, Udaipur, Bikaner and the British province of Ajmer. Henry Lawrence, Agent to Governor-General, deputed Captain Hardcastle to punish the dacoits and he succeeded to a great extent in restoring peace and tranquillity. Lawrence desired the appointment of Hardcastle as Superintendent in Shekhawati, and sometime later recommended the assumption of the governments of Sikar and Khetri by the British officers, but fortunately for the Maharaja of Jaipur these recommendations were not accepted by the Supreme Government who did not wish to erode the sovereign authority of the Maharaja. The Maharaja, however, conducted the administration of the State efficiently with the assistance of his Chief Minister, Laxman Singh and Chief Adviser, Pandit Sheodeen. He remained steadfastly loyal to the British Paramount of which he gave an ample proof during the revolt of 1857-58.

References and Notes

1. For details, see William Lee-Warner, *The Protected Princes of India* (London, 1894), Chapters III and IV, pp. 50-121.
2. Clause (34) of Pitt's India Act, 1784 cited in A.C. Banerjee (ed.), *Indian Constitutional Documents, Vol. I* (Calcutta, 1948), p. 79.

3. Sri Nandan Prasad, *Paramountcy under Dalhousie* (Delhi, 1964), p. 15.
4. *Supra*, pp. 35-36.
5. Montgomery Martin (ed.), *The Despatches, Minutes and Correspondence of the Marquess of Wellesley, Vol. I* (London, 1836), p. 192.
6. P.E. Roberts, *India under Wellesley*, (Reprint Gorakhpur, 1961, first published London, 1929), p. 223.
7. Martin, cited in Sukumar Bhattacharyya, *The Rajput States and the East India Company from the close of 18th century to 1820* (New Delhi, 1972), p. 27.
8. Ramsay Muir, *The Making of British India, 1756-1858* (Manchester, 1915), p. 201.
9. Roberts, *op. cit.*, p. 45.
10. Bhattacharyya, *op. cit.*, p. 44.
11. H.C. Batra, *The Relations of Jaipur State with East India Company, 1803-1858*, (Delhi, 1958), p. 15.
12. *Ibid.*, p. 20.
13. C.U. Aitchison, Comp., *A Collection of Treaties, Engagements and Sanads, Vol. III* (Calcutta, 1932), pp. 66-67.
14. Ross-of-Bladensburg, *The Marquess of Hastings* (Oxford 1893, p. 530; James Grant Duff, *A History of the Marhattas, Vol. III* (Calcutta, 1918), pp. 316-17.
15. The Company's deficit which was £ 118,746 in 1798 increased to £ 2,268,608 in 1805 when Wellesley was obliged to tender his resignation. Vide James Mill, *History of British India, Vol. VI* (London, 1848), p. 473.
16. Bhattacharyya, *op. cit.*, pp. 61-62.
17. Ross, *op. cit., Vol. III*, p. 530; Mill, *op. cit., Vol. VI*, p. 449; Muir, *op. cit.*, p. 247.
18. FD, Secret Cons., 12 Sept. 1805, No. 122.
19. FD, Secret Cons., 12 Sept. 1805, No. 120; also Sir John Malcolm, *Political History of India*, 1784-1803, *Vol. I* (London, 1826) pp. 348-49.
20. FD, Secret Cons., 10 April 1806, No. 4 and 22 May 1806, No. 37.
21. Translation of a Persian letter from Maharaja Jagat Singh to Governor-General, Letters received, No. 129 dated 31 March, 1806, P.C., cited in Batra, *op. cit.*, p. 26.
22. Duff, *op. cit., Vol. III*, p. 317.
23. John William Kaye, *The Life and Correspondence of Major-General Sir John Malcolm, Vol. I* (London, 1856), p. 358.
24. Malcolm, *op. cit.*, p. 438.

25. James Tod, *Annal and Antiquities of Rajasthan*, edited by W. Crooke, *Vol. III* (London, 1920, Reprint Delhi, 1994), p. 1367.
26. Malcolm, *op.cit.*, p. 373.
27. Mill, *op. cit.*, p.470.
28. Bhattacharyya, *op. cit.*, p. 82.
29. Batra, *op. cit.*, p. 33.
30. FD, Political Cons., 12 Sept. 1808, No. 28.
31. FD, Political Cons., 21 June 1810, No. 42.
32. FD, Political Cons., 17 May 1811, No. 52.
33. John William Kaye, *The Life and Correspondence of Charles Lord Metcalfe, Vol. I* (London, 1858), p. 381.
34. FD, Political Cons., 21 August 1812, No. 21.
35. Batra, *op. cit.*, p. 42.
36. P.E. Roberts, *History of British India* (Reprint London, 1958), p. 279.
37. Ross, *op. cit.*, pp. 216-18; Muir, *op. cit.*, p. 249.
38. *The Private Journal of the Marquess of Hastings, Vol. I* (London, 1858), pp. 54-55.
39. *Ibid.*, p. 301.
40. FD, Secret Cons., 20 April, 1816, No. 1.
41. Metcalfe to Edmonstone, 20 June 1811, FD, Political Cons., 12 July 1811, No. 1.
42. Metcalfe's Memorandum on Central India, Kaye, *op. cit., Vol. I*, pp. 314, 317; FD, Political Cons., 12 July 1811, No. 1, para 14; also see K.N. Panikkar, *British Diplomacy in North India : A Study of Delhi Residency, 1803-1857* (New Delhi, 1968), pp. 49-50, 52.
43. Kaye, *Vol. I, op. cit.*, p. 320.
44. *Ibid.*, p. 300.
45. John Kaye, *op. cit.*, pp. 435-38; also see Batra, *op. cit.*, p. 45.
46. FD, Secret Cons., 20 April 1816, No. 3; also Bhattacharyya, *op. cit.*, pp. 174-76.
47. Batra, *op. cit.*, p. 46.
48. Metcalfe to Adam, 3 July 1816, FD, Secret Cons., 3 Aug. 1816, No. 3; 11 Aug. and 19 Aug. 1816, *ibid.*, 7 Sept. 1816, Nos. 6-7. Also see Panikkar, *op. cit.*, p. 56.
49. FD, Secret Cons., 19 Dec. 1817, No. 112.
50. Metcalfe to Adam, 29 Jan. 1818, FD, Secret Cons., 20 Feb. 1818, No. 26.
51. FD, Secret Cons., 17 April 1818, No. 74.
52. Aitchison, *op. cit., Vol. III*, pp. 68-69.
53. Bhattacharyya, *op. cit.*, p. 240.
54. *Ibid.*, p. 250.

55. Tod, *op. cit., Vol. III,* pp. 1364-65; H.T. Prinsep, *History of the Political and Military Transactions in India during the Administration of the Marquess of Hastings 1813-23, Vol. II* (London, 1825), pp. 373-74; Bhattacharyya, *op. cit.*, pp. 250-51.
56. Tod, *op. cit.*, Vol. III, pp. 1371-72.
57. *Ibid.*, pp. 1375-78; A.C. Banerjee, *The Rajput States and the East India Company* (Calcutta, 1951), pp. 389-90; Bhattacharyya, *op. cit.*, pp. 251-53.
58. Batra, *op. cit.*, pp. 58-59.
59. Aitchison, *op. cit., Vol. III,* p. 91.
60. FD, Political Cons., 10 Feb. 1821, Nos. 7,12.
61. Batra, *op. cit.*, p. 64.
62. FD, Political Cons., 23 June 1821, Nos. 14, 18.
63. FD, Political Cons., 22 Sept., 1821, No. 10.
64. FD, Political Cons., 22 Sept. 1821, No. 7.
65. FD, Political Cons., 22 Sept. 1821, No. 9.
66. FD, Political Cons., 6 Oct. 1821, Nos. 10-11.
67. FD, Political Cons., 4 May 1822, No. 35; FD, Secret Cons., 10 May 1822, Nos. 36-37.
68. FD, Political Cons., 21 March 1823, No. 29.
69. FD, Political Cons., 21 March 1823, Nos. 32-37; and 2 May 1823, Nos. 21-22.
70. FD, Political Cons., 3 Dec. 1824, Nos. 29-32.
71. FD, Political Cons., 15 April 1825, Nos. 23-27, 38.
72. FD, Political Cons., 15 July 1825, Nos. 64-66, 70.
73. FD, Political Cons., 17 Feb. 1826, Nos. 16-17, 27.
74. FD, Secret Cons., 16 Sept. 1826, Nos. 20-21.
75. FD, Political Cons., 17 Feb. 1826, No. 27.
76. Panikkar, *op. cit.*, p. 92.
77. FD, Political Cons., 17 Feb. 1826, No. 2.
78. FD, Political Cons., 19 May 1826, No. 12.
79. FD, Political Cons., 6 Oct. 1826, No. 61.
80. FD, Political Cons., 24 Nov. 1826, No. 11.
81. Metcalfe to Amherst, 23 Nov. 1826, FD, Political Cons., 2 Feb. 1827, No. 19.
82. *Ibid.*
83. Amherst to Metcalfe, 7 Nov. 1826, FD, Political Cons., 24 Nov. 1826, No. 13.
84. FD, Political Cons., 2 Feb. 1827, No. 19.
85. Panikkar, *op. cit.*, p. 97.
86. FD, Political Cons., 25 April 1828, Nos. 31-33.
87. FD, Political Cons., 31 Jan. 1831, No. 6, and 17 June 1831, No. 20.

88. For details, see Batra, *op. cit.*, pp. 117-22.
89. FD, Political Cons., 31 Oct. 1833, Nos. 29, 34.
90. FD, Political Cons., 5 Dec. 1833, No. 7 and 27 Dec. 1833, No. 24.
91. FD, Political Cons., 19 Feb. 1835, Nos. 20, 34.
92. Batra, *op. cit.*, p. 127.
93. FD, Political Cons., 5 March 1835, No. 54.
94. FD, Political Cons., 1 June 1835, No. 21.
95. FD, Political Cons., 6 July 1835, Nos. 10-12.
96. Vijay Kumar Vashishtha, *Rajputana Agency, 1832-1858* (Jaipur, 1978), p. 154.
97. FD, Political Cons., 13 July 1835, Nos. 22-26.
98. FD, Political Cons., 1 Aug. 1836, No. 20; 19 Dec. 1836, Nos. 22-24; also see D.C. Boulger, *Lord William Bentinck* (Oxford, 1892), pp. 140-44.
99. FD, Political Cons., 14 Nov. 1838, Nos. 23-25.
100. FD, Political Cons., 5 Dec. 1838, No. 56.
101. FD, Political Cons., 19 Dec. 1838, Nos. 50-52.
102. FD, Political Cons., 26 June 1839, Nos. 29-30, and 3 July 1839, No. 5.
103. Vashishtha, *op. cit.*, p. 162.
104. Proclamation on the part of the British Govt. to the chiefs and the people of Jaipur by Sutherland, dated 18 April 1839, FD, Political Cons., 10 July 1839, No. 37.
105. Batra, *op. cit.*, p. 150.
106. FD, Political Cons., 25 Sept. 1839, No. 169.
107. FD, Political Cons., 20 Nov. 1839, Nos. 60-61.
108. FD, Political Cons., 9 Aug. 1841, Nos. 17-18.
109. FD, Political Cons., 24 Jan. 1842, Nos. 33-34.
110. FD, Political Cons., 31 Aug. 1842, Nos. 50-52.
111. FD, Political Cons., 29 July 1843, No. 106.
112. FD, Political Cons., 3 Feb. 1844, No. 172.
113. FD, Political Cons., 20 Nov. 1847, No. 65.
114. FD, Political Cons., 29 Aug. 1846, Nos. 102-103; and 20 Nov. 1847, No. 65.
115. FD, Political Cons., 8 June 1844, No. 51.
116. FD, Political Cons., 26 Dec. 1846, Nos. 125-126.
117. FD, Political Cons., 17 Oct. 1846, No. 268. Also see V.K.Vashishtha, 'Abolition of Sati in the States of Rajputana' in *Rajasthan History Congress, Proceedings*, Third Session, Udaipur, 1969, pp. 133-35.
118. FD, Political Cons., 17 April 1847, No. 48.
119. FD, Political Cons., 1 May 1847, Nos. 48-50.

120. Banerjee, *The Rajput States and the East India Company, op. cit.*, p. 392.
121. FD, Political Cons., 3 March 1848, No. 49.
122. FD, Political Cons., 4 July 1851, Nos. 167-168.
123. FD, Political Cons., 8 Aug. 1851, Nos. 56-57.
124. *Ibid.*
125. FD, Political Cons., 21 Nov. 1851, No. 17.
126. FD, Political Cons., 7 March 1856, No. 154; and 26 Sept. 1856, No. 156.
127. Batra, *op. cit.*, pp. 173-75.
128. FD, Political Cons., 23 May 1856, Nos. 62-66.
129. FD, Political Cons., 30 Oct. 1856, Nos. 127-128, and 27 Feb. 1857, Nos. 167-168.
130. For example, when Thakur Sumer Singh died in October 1844, the vacancy in the Council was not filled and Thakurs Bhopal Singh and Sur Singh had virtually retired to their homes as they were non-portfolio members of the Council. Later on Thakur Laxman Singh was dismissed and Raja Har Das of Lawan and Thakur Bhim Singh of Diggi were appointed as members.

CHAPTER 3

Revolt of 1857-58 and Inauguration of New Era under the Crown

In 1857 took place a stupendous uprising against the British which has been described as a 'sepoy mutiny'[1] by most of the British writers and a 'national rising'[2] or 'Indian War of independence'[3] by Indian writers. The immediate cause of this revolt was the so-called greased cartridges affair but its real causes lay much deeper and may be found in the last hundred years of the East India Company's rule. In the words of R.C. Majumdar :

> In short, the first century of British rule in India set the stage for and witnessed many rehearsals, though in parts, of the great tragic drama which was to celebrate the centenary of its foundation in blood and tears.[4]

There were several political, administrative, economic, socio-religious and military factors which caused a wide-spread discontentment among the princes, nobles, common people and native sepoys with the Company's rule. The foremost among the causes of the revolt was the aggressive and unscrupulous policy adopted by the British Governors-General towards the Princely States of India. The most prominent feature of this policy was to annex, by fair means or foul, the territories of the States to the British Empire in India. This policy had reached its culmination during the Governor-Generalship of Lord Dalhousie (1848-1856). "The Indian Princes trembled on their thrones as they saw one Princely State after another annexed on the ground of mis-government or failure to produce a natural heir."[5] By his ruthless application of the 'doctrine of lapse' Dalhousie had annexed the States of Satara, Nagpur, Jhansi, Jaitpur, Sambalpur, Udaipur and Baghat. He had contrived war against the Sikh kingdom of Lahore and annexed the Punjab.[6] Despite the unquestionable loyalty of the Nawab of Awadh, he had annexed his State on the plea of gross misrule. Dalhousie's annexations had, undoubtedly, "caused a thrill of uneasiness and suspicion throughout India."[7] He had unjustly deprived Nana Sahib, the adopted son of the late Peshwa Baji Rao II, of the huge annual pension which had been granted to him. Regarding the titular Mughal Emperor of Delhi, it had been decided that on the death of Bahadur Shah II, his successor would leave the ancestral palace. "All these high-handed and unjust measures provoked, as indeed they were bound to provoke, resentment and revolt."[8] Those persons who were the victims of these measures became the prominent leaders of the revolt. But fortunately for the British, a great majority of the Princes and Chiefs did not join the revolt and a large number of them positively supported their Paramount with men and money. Among such notable supporters of the British were the Princes of Rajputana States and the Sikh Chiefs of the Punjab.

None of the nineteen States of Rajputana wavered in their loyalty to the British Government at this critical juncture. As soon as the mutiny of the Bengal army began in May 1857 General George Lawrence, the then Agent to Governor-General, Rajputana States called upon the Chiefs of Rajputana to preserve peace within their borders and muster their troops for co-operating with the British authorities in maintaining order and dispersing the mutineers.[9] The Chiefs readily responded and among those who rendered some sort of useful services may be mentioned the rulers of Bikaner, Marwar, Mewar, Jaipur,

Jaisalmer, Alwar, Bharatpur, Kota, Jhalawar, Banswara, Dungarpur, Sirohi, Dholpur, Karauli, Kishangarh and Tonk. Colonel C.H. Trevor aptly observed :

> What saved Rajputana was the example of leading princes, particularly of Maharana Swaroop Singh of Udaipur, Maharaja Takhat Singh of Jodhpur and Maharaja Ram Singh of Jaipur from whom the other Chiefs and those outside their province took their cue. By standing fast they carried with them the majority of their subjects and thus enabled a handful of British officers to maintain order, and recover the military cantonments from which they had been expelled by the mutiny of the native garrisons.[10]

Maharaja Ram Singh of Jaipur did not belie the expectations of British authorities in the manifestation of his loyalty. As soon as the revolt broke out he placed his contingent of 6000-7000 men at the disposal of the British Political Agent, Captain W.F. Eden. This contingent under the command of Faiz Ali Khan, the State *Bakhshi,* marched along with Major Eden towards Delhi. As Eden reached Rewari he came to know that the district of Gurgaon was in a terrible state of turmoil due to the revolt of the unruly Meos. Instead of advancing further towards Delhi he turned towards the east from Rewari accompanied by the Jaipur troops to take stern action against the rebellious Meos. Near Sohna the Jaipur troops led by Bakshi Faiz Ali Khan attacked and killed the rebel *thanadar* and ravaged a number of Meo villages. Two English ladies and two gentlemen were rescued from their clutches. Thereafter Jaipur force was posted between Palwal and Hodel on the road from Agra to Delhi. Mr. Harvey, the Commissioner and thirty-seven other gentlemen who on account of disturbances were in danger at Hodel, were escorted by the Jaipur troopers and sent back safely to Agra and Mathura. On their return to Jaipur the troops were busily engaged in escorting treasures and British personnel between, Ajmer, Nasirabad and Agra.[11]

In the absence of Captain Eden, the Maharaja took appropriate measures to provide safety and comfort to his family for which he had deputed two of his high officials, Laxman Singh and Pandit Sheodeen. The Political Agent expressed his 'deepest obligations' to the Maharaja for the protection so readily afforded to his family.[12]

When a major part of the Jaipur forces was away on duty in Gurgaon and Mathura districts, the Kota contingent under the command of Captain J.B. Dennys passed through Jaipur on its way to Agra in May 1857. According to Captain Dennys, the Maharaja of Jaipur gave every possible aid; carriage and supplies were plentifully given and the Maharaja lent his own bullocks and gear to assist the guns over the heavy sands of Jaipur. He remarked that but for the assistance rendered to him by the Maharaja, his ministers and Pandit Sheodeen, he could not have moved on with the contingent under his command. He was highly appreciative of the 'civility and assistance' he personally experienced and met with from the Jaipur Darbar.[13] When Captain Dennys and his men returned from Agra, the Jaipur Darbar not only provided an escort of officers but also did all it could to make their journey through Jaipur as comfortable as possible. The Supreme Government expressed thanks for the 'timely cooperation' of the Jaipur Darbar, adding, "such acts of friendship are no less gratifying to the British Government to receive than as they are creditable to the State which renders them."[14]

Towards the end of May 1857 when the sepoys of Nasirabad had mutinied and passed through Jaipur on their way to Delhi, they asked Maharaja Ram Singh to hand over his European proteges to them but the Maharaja not only refused to accept their demand but also offered resistance with whatever small forces he had till they were compelled to march hastily towards Delhi. The British officers whose soldiers had deserted them at Nasirabad and Neemuch were sent with all possible assistance to Agra fort escorted by Thakur Puran Singh of Jaipur.[15] At the request of the Lieutenant-Governor of the Agra province, the Maharaja played an important role in the uninterrupted transmission of mails between Agra and Ajmer.[16]

There were, however, some nobles and officials of Jaipur who harboured feelings of disloyalty towards the British Government and tried to play a dubious role but the Maharaja dissuaded them and even punished them for their anti-British designs. One such high official was Rawal Sheo Singh of Samod. He was the first member of the Council of Regency but actually the Regent and Chief Minister of Jaipur for many years. As minister he exercised much of power and influence and had spent money of the State lavishly. He had bestowed many valuable *jagirs* on his friends and followers, thereby involving the State in debt. He was removed from the office of Chief Minister in 1854 and replaced by his brother Laxman Singh. Rawal Sheo Singh was 'shrewd, intelligent, vain and ostentatious'.[17] He was capable of intriguing against the Maharaja as well as the British. He sought to play the dubious role of a leader of those forces which stood for the extermination of the British influence in India. It was believed that he was present at Delhi at the time of the outbreak of mutiny and stayed there for several days. It was suspected that he had received a secret communication from Emperor Bahadur Shah to reach Delhi along with the troops of Jaipur. He even tried to seduce the young Maharaja from his attachment to the British Government, though in vain. On the other hand, the Maharaja decided to get rid of him. He instructed the Rawal to leave Jaipur immediately which he did, and retired to his ancestral *jagir* of Samod.[18] Thakur Laxman Singh, the brother of Rawal Sheo Singh, continued to be Chief Minister of Jaipur State and he remained fully loyal to the British, extending all possible help to the British Political Agent.

Nawab Wilayat Ali Khan, Faujdar or Chief Magistrate of the city of Jaipur was another State official suspected of indulging in anti-British designs and supporting the cause of Emperor Bahadur Shah. A man was caught with several letters from Delhi addressed to Wilayat Ali Khan. One of these letters was believed to be from Empress Zeenat Mahal in which he was told confidentially that on completing successfully the necessary managements entrusted to him he would be appointed governor of Ajmer. On the basis of these letters he was arrested for trial in a Jaipur court by the orders of the Maharaja. Sadulla Khan who was previously Jaipur's *Vakil* with the Agent to Governor-General and an adopted brother of the

Minister Laxman Singh, was suspected of having given asylum to a wounded rebel, named Zarif Khan. Mian Usman Khan, a fugitive from Bhopal settled in Jaipur for the last three years, was another suspect who was believed to be in secret alignment with the Delhi rebels. In October 1857, W.F. Eden, Political Agent at Jaipur, had got in his possession considerable correspondence which indicated that all of these three Muslim residents of Jaipur were involved in intrigues with the Delhi rebels against the British. Maharaja Ram Singh constituted a special court for the trial of the three suspected conspirators and their accomplices. As a result of the decision of the court Wilayat Ali Khan and Usman Khan were expelled from the city of Jaipur and sentenced to reside as State prisoners in two different forts. Sadulla Khan was merely banished from Jaipur due to the consideration shown by Thakur Laxman Singh for his 'adopted brother'. However, Laxman Singh was made responsible for better conduct of Sadulla Khan in the coming six months; on the expiry of this period the Darbar would review these proceedings and award such other punishment as might seem proper.[19] The Governor-General in Council, on receiving this communication, observed that the sentences passed on these persons were 'too lenient', but added that nothing would now be gained by demanding a heavier punishment.[20]

Tantia Tope, a prominent associate of Rani Lakshmi Bai of Jhansi, after his defeat and discomfiture at Gwalior by the British forces, marched in the direction of Jaipur with his remnant forces. As he passed through the Jaipur territory he failed to secure refuge or assistance, though he was provided with plentiful supplies by some villagers by payment of twice the normal price. He was accompanied by two rebel leaders, named Rao Sahib and Firoz Shah. The British forces sent against these men under the command of Brigadier General Showers and Colonel Holmes received material assistance from the Maharaja of Jaipur and they were routed at Dausa and Sikar.[21]

The Maharaja in a *Kharita* to Governor-General Canning expressed his delight at "gratifying intelligence of the recapture of Delhi, the flight of the rebels and the relief of the Lucknow garrisons with all other particulars." He appreciated the victories of 'brave, powerful and enduring' British troops. Alluding to the services rendered by him to the British Government during the critical period, he expressed his earnest desire to strengthen friendship with the latter and get greater favour in future.[22]

Some scholars opine that the Jaipur State did not have had an untainted record of loyalty to the British Government during the revolt of 1857-58 and that there are demonstrable instances to show that a section of the State sepoys, officials, *jagirdars*, people and even the Maharaja of the State gave evidence of dubious loyalty to the British Paramount.

The Muslim and *Poorbia* sepoys proved 'sinews of the rebellion' in 1857 as they evinced sympathy with the Emperor of Delhi as well as with the rebellious sepoys of Meerut, Delhi, Agra, Neemuch, Nasirabad and Tonk. It was obvious from their revolt in the city of Jaipur, their unwillingness in intercepting the mutineers of Nasirabad and Neemuch through the Jaipur territory, their desertion at Kotputli and later on at Palwal, and defiance of the British Government at Hindaun.[23]

There was anti-British ferment among the people and officials of the Jaipur State. When the Nasirabad mutineers passed through Dudu, Bagru and other territories of the State during 1-4 June 1857 the village officials sympathised with them by extending help in terms of supplying food and not taking any action against them. At the behest of *Kamdar* and village headman the *Banias* supplied large quantities of food and fodder for their cattle by going to their camp near the Dak-bungalow at Bagru. They received food supplies at Manoharpur and some other villages also. The mutineers attacked the Dak-bungalows of British officials at Dudu and Bagru with the tacit support of the *Kamdars* and headmen. Lieutenant C.K.M. Walter (Assistant Commissioner, Ajmer) who was pursuing the mutineers, noticed, to his dismay, feelings of hatred among the mutineers, officials and general masses against the British Government. Likewise he observed, "The Bagru authorities throughout have behaved in a manner far from friendly to the British Government." The *Thanadar* of the *Thikana* of Bagru refused to surrender to the *Sowars* of Lieutenant Walter the four Neemuch mutineers who were under his protection, three of whom subsequently escaped with his connivance.[24] In the absence of Captain W.F. Eden (who had proceeded with Jaipur State forces towards Gurgaon, Rewari, Palwal, etc. to take action against the mutineers) Captain E.I. Hardcastle, Assistant to Agent to Governor-General, Rajputana was sent to intercept the Neemuch mutineers with the support of Jodhpur and Jaipur troops towards the end of June 1857. He marched with the Jodhpur troops towards Hindaun but the Jaipur force lagged behind; the *Sardars* of Jaipur force moved very slowly and halted frequently and consequently this force never reached Hindaun to join Hardcastle. The mutineers won over the greater part of the Jaipur Raj Force at Hindaun. Hardcastle was disgusted to observe the anti-British feelings of the inhabitants of Jaipur State everywhere and the persistent rebellious role of the *Poorbia* sepoys all over the Jaipur State.[25]

Many *Jagirdars* of Jaipur State adopted hostile attitude towards the British Government during the revolt of 1857. Of these, particular mention may be made of Rawal Sheo Singh of Samod, Maji Ranawatji of Khetri and Rao Raja Fateh Singh of Uniara. Rawal Sheo Singh was the most prominent *Thakur* or *Jagirdar* of the State who had occupied the exalted office of Chief Minister of the State. Since his dismissal from this post in 1854 he had turned against Maharaja Ram Singh as well as the British Government. After the outbreak of 'mutiny' in May 1857 he presented *nazarana* to the Mughal Emperor Bahadur Shah II at Delhi and thereafter he made earnest endeavours to win over supporters for the Mughal Emperor in the Jaipur State. He "infused rebellious spirit in the Jaipur State troops at Kotputli as a result of which several of them deserted the camp of Captain Eden and marched to Delhi." He also made efforts, though unsuccessful, for winning over the Maharaja to the side of the Mughal Emperor. He instigated the Mohammedan party at the Jaipur Darbar some of whom adopted hostile designs against the British. He incited the sepoys and people of the State against the British and Europeans. Maji Ranawatji, who was Regent for the minor ruler, Rao Raja Fateh Singh of Khetri, adopted hostile attitude towards the British Government as well as Maharaja Ram Singh. She refused to provide detachment of Khetri troops to W.F. Eden (Political Agent at Jaipur) in June 1857 for intercepting the rebels on the borders of Jaipur State and also gave asylum to the fugitive sepoys of the British Indian army in her territory. Rao Raja Fateh Singh of Uniara was opposed to the dominating influence of the British in the Jaipur State and he adopted anti-British posture during the revolt of 1857. "The Uniara *thikana* stood united in expressing its hostility towards the British Government right from the Rao Raja down to the ryot." The Rao Raja and his people sympathised with the cause of rebels, although he did not involve himself in open armed conflict with the British for which he did not have the requisite military resources.[26]

It has been alleged, and affirmed, that the Maharaja did not extend full and unreserved support to the British against the mutineers in the early stage of the revolt. Rawal Sheo Singh, former Chief Minister of the State, had prevailed upon the Maharaja to play a dual role by giving appearance of a friend of both the British Government and the Mughal Emperor in order to safeguard his own interests as well as that of the State. The Maharaja, therefore, adopted vacillating attitude between the Mughal Emperor and the British Government.[27] The two high officials of the Rajputana Agency at Ajmer, Lieutenant Walter and Captain Hardcastle, were unhappy to note the non-cooperative attitude of the Maharaja, his *Sardars* and officials and also the defection of Jaipur troops. In a letter dated 3 August 1857 addressed to Brigadier-General George Lawrence, Agent to Governor-General, Hardcastle wrote :[28]

> ... from the time we left Jeypoor we were unaccompanied by any *hurkara*, or officer of the Jeypoor Government, which will partly account for the incivility we received and the inconvenience we experienced. The mutineers had Jeypoor officials attached to them during their transit through the territory.
>
> But not only was the defeat or destruction of the rebel army thwarted by the defection of the Jeypoor troops, but other means also which I adopted, were in the same way nullified.

> ...the conduct of the Jeypoor Durbar has been far from satisfactory... It accordingly permitted these several bands of rebels to pass through its territories unmolested and even accommodated them with all kinds of supplies, carriages, etc.

As a result of the capture of Delhi by the British in September 1857, however, there was a complete change in the attitude of the Jaipur Darbar towards the British Government. The Maharaja, as also his Chief Minister, Laxman Singh and Chief Adviser, Pandit Sheodeen, expressed their unflinching loyalty towards the British Government. They took all possible measures to thwart the anti-British designs of the rebels. The Maharaja also punished the rebellious elements of the Mohammedan party and compelled Rawal Sheo Singh to leave the capital Jaipur and retire to his *jagir* of Samod.

A close, candid and dispassionate study of the facts reveals that there was no anti-British ferment on a large scale in the Jaipur State among the *jagirdars,* officials, much less among the people, of the State, nor had Maharaja Ram Singh given unmistakable evidence of dubious loyalty towards the British Government. Only a very few *jagirdars* (not more than three), who harboured some sort of grudge against the Maharaja and the British authorities, showed their sympathies to the mutineers by not taking any action against them, or secretly supplied them food and fodder. Similar was the case with the State officials some of whom, here and there, did not perform their duties scrupulously of giving necessary help to the British commanders like Walter and Hardcastle. There was also a small number of Jaipur sepoys who, probably instigated by Sheo Singh, had defected; others had remained steadfastly loyal to Eden and even saved his life when some rebel-mutineers conspired to kill him. It is significant to observe that there had been no armed revolt anywhere in the territories of the Jaipur State during 1857-58, not even in those of the *jagirdars.* The anti-British ferment, if at all it was there, had not led to any violent revolt against the British in any part of the State. It was all due to the fact that the Maharaja of Jaipur had been whole-heartedly and consistently loyal to the British Paramount and he had taken proper and prompt measures for the maintenance of peace and tranquillity in the State.

In a lengthy letter, dated 14 August 1857, addressed to Brigadier General Lawrence (Agent to Governor-General Rajputana), Captain W.F. Eden, Political Agent at Jaipur, ably refuted the charges levelled by Hardcastle against the Jaipur Darbar in his letter of 3 August 1857, and fully appreciated the pro-British attitude of the Maharaja. Among other things, he wrote :[29]

> ...he (Maharaja) is honestly conscious of having done his best, with the means and materials at his disposal, to aid and co-operate with our Government.
>
> I conceive Captain Hardcastle's urgent demand on the Durbar to supply troops, literally beyond its means, to have been inopportune and indiscreet.
>
> There was a display rather of foresight and prudence on His Highness part, which should for obvious reasons have been better understood and appreciated by Captain Hardcastle.
>
> Captain Hardcastle assumes a knowledge of the resources, the means and appliances of the Jeypore Government, which he does not possess. I contend, that the Jeypore Government had most promptly met our demand for troops and co-operation by sending with me a force of some 6 or 7000 men, the best they had, and I can not but view Captain Hardcastle's proceedings and the threat of the vengeance of our Government held out to the Maharaja as very impolitic and ill-timed.
>
> It is emphatically denied by the Durbar authorities that the mutineers had Jeypore officials attached to them during their transit through the Territory, and I myself believe there were none...
>
> There would seem to have been no virtual defection of the Jeypore Force with Captain Hardcastle, it seems to me that he did not understand them...
>
> I deem it simply an act of public duty I owe to my Government, to myself and to this Court to record at this time, opinions based on a fair knowledge of the young king, of his nobles, his ministers and subjects; of the Army and of its strength, its capabilities, its

> temper and its disposition to act under any and various circumstances.
>
> My own personal experience leads me to record without hesitation that the young Prince has really done his utmost, with a due regard to his own interests, to co-operate with us at this present crisis...

Maharaja Ram Singh evinced 'unflinching loyalty' to the British Government during the crisis of 1857-58, and gave all possible support to the British whenever and wherever demanded, keeping in view his limitations. Immediately after the outbreak of the 'mutiny' he sent 6000 or 7000 Jaipur State forces under the command of Faiz Ali Khan alongwith the Political Agent, Captain Eden, to proceed around Delhi to check the mutineers, but he kept a force of 7000 sepoys and 1800 Nagas (irregular force) for maintaining peace and order in Jaipur and checking the anti-British designs of those who sympathised with the mutineers and the Mughal Emperor, Bahadur Shah. He made proper arrangements for the safety and comfort of Eden's family in Jaipur. A detachment of the Jaipur force escorted safely to Agra twenty Europeans who had taken refuge in a Jaipur camp. He took action against those of his Muslim nobles who were involved in intrigue with the Delhi rebels. Wilayat Ali Khan and Usman Khan, when found guilty by the court, were sent as prisoners in two different forts, and Sadulla Khan was banished from Jaipur city. When Tantia Tope along with his forces passed through the territories of Jaipur with the intention of attacking Ajmer, the Maharaja took prompt measures in consultation with Captain Eden, and foiled his plans. He also gave material assistance to British forces under General Showers and Colonel Holmes who routed the rebels at Dausa and Sikar.

There is no doubt that several rulers of Jaipur State had rendered conspicous services to the Mughals during the times of the great Mughal emperors, but after the disintegration of the Mughal empire when the Jaipur State had to face a dangerous situation due to the incessant invasions of the Marathas and Pindaris, the State was compelled by circumstances to come under British protection in 1818. Since then the British Political Officers had been exercising a dominating influence in the affairs of the State. By the year 1857 when the 'mutiny' broke out, the Mughal empire was a mere 'phantom' and the Mughal emperor Bahadur Shah II only retained nominal authority, having no substantial military resources. He had been compelled by the mutineers of Meerut, Delhi, Agra, etc. to assume leadership of the revolt. Maharaja Ram Singh of Jaipur was a very intelligent and enlightened young Prince. He had Pandit Sheodeen as his able Chief Adviser who had been tutor of the young Maharaja and had inculcated in the latter 'knowledge' and 'wisdom'. Being a very shrewd ruler, the Maharaja had realised that the interests of his State would be more secure by supporting the British against the Mughal emperor. Between the weak wolf and brave lion, he very wisely chose the latter. The future developments in the Jaipur State fully justified his choice and furnished ample proof of his prudence, practical wisdom and foresight. Under the supervision of the representatives of the Paramount Power, as it will be seen in the subsequent chapters, the State witnessed extraordinary progress on modern lines and began to be regarded as the most well-administered State of the region, and its Maharaja earned the reputation of being one of the most brilliant and enlightened Princes of India.

For his unswerving loyalty and meritorious services Maharaja Ram Singh and his principal officers were duly rewarded. The Governor-General in Council, in the beginning of 1858 judged it proper to address a *Kharita* to the Maharaja at once, "acknowledging his good and faithful conduct."[30] The Maharaja was granted the *pargana* of Kot Kasim, lately an appanage of the King of Delhi, in perpetuity. He was highly honoured in many other ways at the Darbar held by the Viceroy and Governor-General at Agra on 30 November 1859. The following rewards were conferred at the same time on officers of Jaipur who were present with the Maharaja in the Darbar :[31]

Bakhshi Faiz Ali Khan, Commander-in-Chief of the Jaipur forces was granted a *khillat* of the value of rupees 2500. Captain Jiwan Ali, Commandant of Jaipur artillery was given *khillat* of rupees 1200. Bhopal Singh, Sobhay Singh and Chaman Lal Dass, the officers of Jaipur State received *khillat* of rupees 1500, rupees 1000 and rupees 500 respectively. Thakur Pratap Singh of Ludana was given *khillat* of rupees 1250. Pandit Sheodeen, Private Secretary to the Maharaja and Mohammad Mohiuddin Khan, Deputy Magistrate of the city of Jaipur, received *khillat* of rupees 250 and rupees 200 respectively.

II

The revolt of 1857-58 is an epoch-making event in the history of British India in general and that of the British relations with the Princely States in particular. As a result of this revolt, the East India Company was abolished and by the Act for the Better Government of India, August 1858, the government of the territories of India together with the paramountcy rights in and over the Indian States were vested in the British Crown. Canning, who was previously the Governor-General of India under the Company, became the first Viceroy and Governor-General of India under the Crown. He was given the authority to conduct relations with the numerous Princely States as the Crown's Representative under the directions of the Secretary of State for India. Highly significant changes took place in the British policy towards the Princely States during the Crown's regime. The Queen's Proclamation, which was read by Canning to the assembled Princes and prominent people at a *Darbar* held in Allahabad on 1 November 1858, declared in clear and unequivocal terms the adoption of a new policy towards the States. The new policy was expounded at length in the Despatch of 30 April 1860 addressed by Canning to the Secretary of State for India.[32]

The main principles of the new policy may be analysed as under :

In the first place, the annexation of the Princely States, which had been the governing principle of the British policy under East India Company, was repudiated once for all. It was remarked in the Queen's Proclamation :

> We desire no extension of our present territorial Possessions; and while we will permit no aggression upon our Dominions or our Rights to be attempted with impunity, we shall sanction no encroachment on those of others.[33]

Canning made a cogent and convincing case against extension of British Empire in India. He emphatically held that instead of extending the British rule, the British Government should give their first care to strengthen their rule within the present limits of the Empire; for they had neither sufficient European force nor the requisite staff of British civil officers nor adequate financial means to launch schemes of further extension of their territory, and any such undertaking would also make it difficult for them to discharge satisfactorily their already existing duties in the administration of justice, the prosecution of public works and in many other ways.[34] He observed, "The safety of our rule is increased, not diminished, by the maintenance of Native Chiefs well affected to us."[35] Sir John Malcolm had said long ago that "if we made all India into *Zillahs,* it was not in the nature of things that our Empire should last fifty years; but if we could keep up a number of Native States without political power, but as loyal instruments, we should exist in India as long as our naval superiority in Europe is maintained."[36] Canning fully agreed with the 'substantial truth' of this opinion and added that the recent events had made it 'more deserving of our attention than ever.'[37] The Secretary of State for India entirely concurred in this viewpoint, adding :

> It is not by the extension of our Empire that its permanence is to be secured, but by the character of British Rule in the territories already committed to our care, and by practically demonstrating that we are as willing to respect the rights of others as we are capable of maintaining our own.[38]

Thus the States were to be perpetuated as an integral part of the Indian system. They were no longer mere transitory governments awaiting the political chances which would permit and justify their gradual extinction.[39]

Secondly, as a concomitant of the principle of non-annexation, the British authorities considered the proposition of granting the right of adoption to the Princes and Chiefs. Before the revolt of 1857, Dalhousie had applied the 'doctrine of lapse' as a result of which he had annexed the States of Satara, Jhansi, Nagpur, Udaipur, Jaitpur, Sambhalpur and Baghat whose rulers had died without natural heirs. In the absence of clear and coherent policy of the British authorities regarding adoption of heirs by the Indian Chiefs there existed 'a haze of doubt or mistrust in the minds of Native Chiefs.' Canning was of the opinion that fears existing in the minds of the Princes and Chiefs should be set at rest and they should be granted the right of adopting heirs in the cases where they had no natural sons to succeed. He suggested to the Secretary of State for India that it would be an act of grace as well as 'sound policy' to give assurance to every Chief above the rank of *jagirdar* (who governed his own territory no matter how small it might be) that the Paramount Power desired to see his government perpetuated, and that on failure of natural heir, his adoption of a successor according to Hindu law and customs of his race (if he be a Hindu) or selection of a successor which might be legitimate according to Mohammadan Law (if he be a Muslim), would be recognised and that nothing would disturb the engagement thus made to him so long as his house remained loyal to the Crown and faithful to the conditions of the treaties or *sanads*.[40] He recommended that such an assurance should be conveyed to each Chief individually and not by a general notification addressed to all.[41] He opined that that was the most opportune time for the proposed step to be taken, for the last vestiges of the Royal House of Delhi had been swept away, the last pretender to the *gaddi* of the Peshwa had disappeared and the Crown of England stood forth the unquestioned ruler in all India.[42] It would have the effect of showing "atonce, and for ever, that we are not lying in wait for opportunities of absorbing territories and that we do deliberately desire to keep alive a feudal aristocracy where one still exists."[43] Her Majesty's Government approved of the principle and recommendation of the Viceroy and Governor-General.[44] The Government of India, thereupon, issued a circular to all the Local Governments and Political Agencies to the effect that Nominal Rolls of the

Princes and Chiefs under their respective charge together with a brief sketch of the history of family of the Chiefs might be submitted confidentially and 'as speedily as possible'[45] so that 'Adoption *Sanads*' might be issued to them individually.

Thirdly, all the treaties and engagements which the East India Company had concluded with the Princes of India were accepted by the Crown and it was declared that they would be 'scrupulously maintained'.[46] It implied that the British authorities in India would abstain from encroaching upon the rights and privileges of the Princes and Chiefs by violating the terms of the existing treaties and engagements.

Fourthly, the British authorities categorically promised that they would "respect the Rights, Dignity and Honour of the Native Princes."[47] Canning addressed another important Despatch to the Secretary of State for India in December 1859 in which he made significant recommendations regarding the grant of titles and honours to the Native Royalties. He observed that the Crown of England should be understood to have assumed to itself the authority, as a Paramount Power, to grant titles and honours to the Native Chiefs and gentlemen, which had hitherto been claimed by the Emperors of Hindustan. He remarked :

> It will be a sounder course and more consonant, I believe, with the feelings of the people at large, if the Crown of England, as a Paramount Power, accepts, and shows respect for the titles and designations which have for many centuries, and under various dynasties, prevailed throughout India.[48]

It would be the best policy, he argued, to adhere closely to the precise titles already in use throughout India and to make no attempt to regulate them by any general rule for all India; for the same titles had a different value, absolutely and relatively in different parts of the country, and some which were used in one part were not known in another.[49] He proposed that this authority should be exercised by the Crown's Representative in India and that an official Roll of all the rightful holders of titles should be kept by the Government of India.[50] The Governor-General opined that he was opposed to attaching, as a rule, any land or grant of money or allowance to the grant of a title. He, however, added that where a substantial reward was due it should be given, but not as a necessary accompaniment of a title. "The tendency in India to consider honours as identical with profit is already too strong, and needs no encouragement'.[51] He also recommended that an order of Knighthood with its badges and insignia of the English style should also be established by the Queen which would be 'an act of wise policy, as well as of Royal Grace', and that such an order should be limited in number and be conferred upon the distinguished Indian Chiefs as well as British born subjects of Her Majesty.[52] Sir Charles Wood, the Secretary of State for India, concurred in the views expressed by the Viceroy and Governor-General.[53]

Fifthly, it was decided by the British authorities that the loyalty and fidelity of the Princes and Chiefs should be ensured so as to create a class of loyal 'feudal aristocracy' which might serve as 'pillars' of the British Empire in India. Canning averred that during the crisis of 1857-58, many Princely States had "served as breakwaters to the storm which would otherwise have swept over us in one great wave", and added that in the event of any danger from an external enemy or any other emergency, "one of our best mainstays will be found in these Native States." But for ensuring this, he held, it was essential to treat the Native Chiefs with consideration and generosity, teaching them that in spite of all suspicions to the contrary their independence was safe.[54]

Sixthly, the authority of the Crown as a Suzerain Power over the Princely States was asserted in clear and unambiguous words. It was stated by Canning :

> The Crown of England stands forth the unquestioned ruler and Paramount Power in all India and is for the first time brought face to face with its feudatories.[55] There is a reality in the Suzerainty of the Sovereign of England which has never existed before, and which is not only felt but eagerly acknowledged by the Chiefs.[56]

Seventhly, while guaranteeing the perpetuation of the rule of the Princes and Chiefs in their States and promising to uphold their dignity and honour, the British authorities reserved to themselves the right, as a Paramount Power, to intervene authoritatively in the affairs of any State to prevent misrule or anarchy, and even to confiscate it in case of disloyalty or deviation from engagements on the part of a Chief. The remarks of Canning in this respect deserve to be quoted verbatum :

> The proposed measure will not debar the Government of India from stepping in to set right such abuses in a Native government as may threaten any part of the country with anarchy or disturbance, nor from assuming temporary charge of a Native State where there shall be sufficient reason to do so. Neither will the assurance, if worded as proposed, diminish our right to visit a state with the heaviest penalties, even to confiscation, in the event of disloyalty or flagrant breach of engagement.[57]

The aforesaid principles of the new policy adopted by the British authorities under the Crown during 1858-60[58], were applied in the British relations with the Jaipur State as also in those of other Rajputana States. In pursuance of the policy of winning over the loyal Princes and Chiefs the British authorities in India, as already mentioned, granted the *pargana* of Kot Kasim to Maharaja Ram Singh and honoured him in many other ways at the Viceroy's Darbar held at Agra in November 1859. The 'most highly-valued' of the privileges conferred upon Maharaja Ram Singh was, however, the right of adoption granted to him by the Viceroy Canning in 1862 by the following *Sanad* :

> Her Majesty being desirous that the Governments of the several Princes and Chiefs of India who now govern their own territories should be perpetuated, and that the representation and dignity of their Houses should be continued, I hereby, in fulfilment of this desire, convey to you the assurance that, on failure of natural heirs, the adoption by yourself and future Rulers of your State of a successor, according to Hindoo Law and to the customs of your race, will be recognised and confirmed.
>
> Be assured that nothing shall disturb the Engagement thus made to you, so long as your House is loyal to the Crown and faithful to the conditions of the Treaties, Grants, or Engagements which record its obligations to the British Government.[59]

The announcement of the new British policy was generally

hailed by the Princes including the Maharaja of Jaipur. They were delighted that their States would be secure, their treaties with the British would be 'scrupulously maintained' and their Princely rights, dignity and honour would be duly respected. But the wide dimensions which the British policy assumed in the course of the following decades in response to the growing requirements of the Paramount Power, belied all their hopes and expectations. Even in violation of the existing treaties and *sanads*, the British authorities began to intervene more and more in the internal affairs of the States, and the Jaipur State was no exception. Such an intervention was exercised chiefly in the matters of succession, arrangements during the minority of the Chiefs, fiscal and economic matters especially pertaining to the issues of tribute, salt, coinage and opium, railways, roads, post and telegraph, armed forces in the State, judicial matters including extradition, boundary disputes among Chiefs, and increasing British control over internal administration of the States, etc. All these matters in respect of the Jaipur State would be examined and analysed at length in the following chapters.

References and Notes

1. Minute of John Lawrence, 9 April 1858, cited in R.C. Majumdar, *The Sepoy Mutiny and the Revolt of 1857* (2nd edition, Calcutta, 1963), p. 441; Charles Raikes, *Notes on the Revolt in the North-Western Provinces of India* (London, 1858), pp. 156-63.
2. Asoka Mehta, *The Great Rebellion* (Bombay 1946), pp. 39-47.
3. V.D. Savarkar, *The Indian War of Independence, 1857* (8th edition, New Delhi, 1970), pp. ix, 1-12.
4. Majumdar, *op. cit.*, p. 242.
5. S.R. Mehrotra, *The Emergence of the Indian National Congress* (New Delhi, 1971), p. 83.
6. It was an act of 'violent breach of trust' on the part of Dalhousie. Major Evans Bell, *The Annexation of the Punjab and the Maharaja Duleep Singh* (London, 1882), p. 13.
7. P.E. Roberts, *History of British India* (3rd edition, London, 1958), p. 361.

8. A.C. Arora, *British Policy towards the Punjab States 1858-1905* (Jalandhar, 1982), p. 21.
9. *Imperial Gazetteer of India, Vol. XXI* (Oxford, 1908), p. 102.
10. Colonel C.H. Trevor, cited in M.L. Sharma, *History of the Jaipur State* (Jaipur, 1969), p. 259.
11. FD, Political Cons., 29 Jan. 1858, No. 142 and Encl.
12. FD, Secret Cons., 29 Jan. 1858, Nos. 293-294.
13. Captain J.B. Dennys to W.F. Eden, Political Agent Jaipur, 28 Sept. 1857, FD, Secret Cons., 18 Dec. 1857, No. 194 and Encl.
14. *Kharita* from Governor-General to Maharaja of Jaipur, 30 Nov. 1857, FD, Secret Cons., 18 Dec. 1857, No. 195.
15. Jadunath Sarkar, *A History of Jaipur* c. *1503-1938*, revised by Raghubir Sinh (Reprint, New Delhi, 1994), p. 343.
16. *Ibid.*
17. Political Agent Jaipur to AGG, 3 Dec. 1857, FD, Secret Cons., 26 Feb. 1858, No. 100, paras 9,10 and 11.
18. K.W., FD, Political Cons., 31 Dec. 1858, No. 4032; also see H.C. Batra, *The Relations of Jaipur State with East India Company* 1803-1858 (Delhi, 1958), p. 182.
19. FD, Secret Cons., 26 Feb. 1858, Nos. 99-100.
20. Governor-General in Council to AGG, No. 498, 3 Feb. 1858, FD, Secret Cons., 26 Feb. 1858, No. 101.
21. Captain W.F. Eden to Brig. General G. Lawrence, 24 July 1858, FD, Political Cons., 17 Sept. 1858, No. 166; Sarkar, *op. cit.*, p. 343.
22. *Kharita* from the Maharaja of Jaipur to the Governor-General in Council, 6 Dec. 1857, FD, Political Cons., 29 Jan. 1858, Nos. 141-142.
23. V.K. Vashishtha, *1857 Revolt in the Princely State of Jaipur* (Jodhpur, 2008), pp. 35-38.
24. *Ibid.*, pp. 39-42.
25. *Ibid.*, pp. 42-44.
26. For details, see *ibid.*, pp. 48-59.
27. *Ibid.*, pp. 22-23.
28. FD, Political Supplementary, 30 Dec. 1859, No. 175.
29. FD, Political Supplementary, 30 Dec. 1859, No. 177. For details, see Appendix IV.
30. FD, Secret Cons., 29 Jan. 1858, Nos. 297-298.
31. GOI to AGG, No. 1574, dated 30 April 1860, FD, Political A, April 1860, No. 607, paras 17 to 28; also Nos. 626-627.
32. Governor-General's (Canning's) Despatch to Sir Charles Wood, Secretary of State for India, No. 43A of 30 April 1860 (hereinafter given as Canning's Despatch of 1860).

33. Queen's Proclamation, 1858, see A.C. Banerjee (ed.), *Indian Constitutional Documents, Vol. II* (Calcutta, 1961), Document No. 3, p. 28; also A.B. Keith, *Speeches and Documents on Indian Policy 1750-1921* (London, 1922), pp. 382-83.
34. Canning's Despatch of 1860, para 33.
35. *Ibid.*, para 34.
36. Malcolm observed elsewhere that extension of territory was "not only undesirable, but hurtful." See K.N. Panikkar (ed.), *John Malcolm : The Political History of India, 1784-1823, Vol.* 2 (New Delhi, 1970), p. 34.
37. Canning's Despatch of 1860, para 35.
38. Political Despatch from the Secretary of State for India to Governor-General of India, No. 59-P of 2 July 1860, para 8.
39. H.H. Dodwell, *The Cambridge History of India, Vol. VI* (Cambridge, 1932), pp. 493-94.
40. Canning's Despatch of 1860, paras 23 and 28.
41. *Ibid.*, para 29.
42. *Ibid.*, para 22.
43. *Ibid.*, para 26.
44. Political Despatch from the Secretary of State for India to Governor-General of India, No. 59-P of 26 July 1860, paras 3-6.
45. Confidential Circular No. 4160, dated 14 Sept. 1860 from the Government of India to all the Local Governments and Administrations.
46. Queen's Proclamation, A.C. Banerjee, *op. cit.*, p. 27.
47. *Ibid.*, p. 28.
48. Governor-General's Political Despatch to the Secretary of State, No. 27 of 24 Dec. 1859, para 7.
49. *Ibid.*, para 3.
50. *Ibid.*, para 4.
51. *Ibid.*, para 6.
52. *Ibid.*, paras 9-13.
53. Political Despatch from Secretary of State to Governor-General of India, No. 81 of 31 Oct. 1860.
54. Canning's Despatch of 1860, para 34.
55. The use of the term 'feudatories' for the Native Princes and Chiefs, in the context of their historical treaty-relationship with the British Government was obviously inapt; but the *de facto* position to which the Native Chiefs had been reduced by the Paramount Power under the British Crown could hardly be said to have been better than that of the feudatories. See Arora, *op. cit.*, p. 95, f.n. 72.

56. Canning's Despatch of 1860, para 22.
57. *Ibid.*, paras 30 and 31.
58. These principles have been reproduced from the author's book, *The Princely States : British Paramountcy and Internal Administration 1858-1948 : A Case Study of the Kapurthala State* (New Delhi, 2001), pp. 43-47.
59. C.U. Aitchison, Comp., *A Collection of Treaties, Engagements and Sanads, Vol. III* (Calcutta, 1932), p. 56.

CHAPTER 4

Succession

The issues of succession in the Native States had furnished circumstances of great importance in the rise and growth of the British paramountcy in India. These circumstances had been caused either by the restless ambition of rival claimants to the *gaddi* or had been created cleverly by manoeuvring on the part of the British diplomats to push forward their Imperial interests. It is a well-known fact that in Bengal the Governors of the East India Company had vary adroitly and insidiously displaced, placed and replaced native Nawabs during 1757-1764 in such a manner as would help in the assertion of British supremacy in that region.[1] In the following decades the Governors-General of the Company, notably Wellesley, Hastings and Dalhousie, continued to follow the policy of taking every possible advantage of succession issues to expand the British dominions and dominance in various parts of the country. In the treaties concluded with Jaipur and other Rajputana States in 1818, there was no provision regarding intervention of the British authorities in the succession matters of these States. Nevertheless, the British Government interfered arbitrarily and authoritatively in all such matters. It was stated by the Viceroy Lansdowne later on in clear words :

> It is the right and duty of the British Government to settle successions in the subordinate Native States. Every succession

> must be recognised by the British Government, and no succession is valid until recognition has been given. This principle is fully understood and invariably observed.[2]

I

Not long after the treaty of 1818 concluded with Jaipur State, the British authorities had to intervene in the affairs of the State due to succession of two minor Chiefs. After the death of Jagat Singh in December 1818, his posthumous son was installed on the *gaddi* who was named as Jai Singh III. He was recognised as the legitimate ruler of Jaipur by the British Government and his mother (the Bhattiani queen) at the same time was recognised as Regent. The British Resident at Delhi, Ochterlony continued to meddle in the internal affairs of the State by taking the side of Mohan Nazir, the Prime Minister as against the Rani Mother. Since Jaipur presented a scene of 'corruption and misgovernment' a special British Political Agent was appointed at Jaipur in 1821 to keep a constant control and supervision over the affairs of the State. The Political Agent interfered continuously and ceaselessly in the administrative affairs of the State throughout the period of Regency of the Rani Mother (1819-1833) to the much annoyance of the latter.[3]

After the death of Maharaja Jai Singh III in February 1835, Ram Singh was installed on the *gaddi* whose succession was recognised by the British authorities. As he was a minor of about two years at that time, his mother Maharani Chandrawat became his Regent. The British Resident at Delhi and Political Agent at Jaipur made the Prime Ministers of their choice and undermined the authority and influence of the Maharani. In 1839 the Maharani was excluded from administrative affairs and a Council of Regency of five Sardars or *Thakurs* was appointed with the British Political Agent as the President. During the next twelve years (1839-1851) it was virtually the rule of the Political Agent. The successive Political Agents notably Thoresby and Ludlow, brought about appreciable improvements in administration and some commendable social reforms, though at least one Political Agent, Rickards, had been found guilty of corruption and misuse of State finances. In September 1851, on attaining the age of 18 years, Maharaja Ram Singh was invested with full ruling powers, and the Governor-General Dalhousie himself participated in the investiture ceremony, presenting a *khillat* of rupees 10,250 to the Maharaja on the occasion.[4]

During 1848-1854 Dalhousie had annexed the States of Satara (1848), Sambhalpur and Jaitpur (1849), Baghat (1850), Udaipur in the Central Provinces (1852), Jhansi (1853) and Nagpur (1854) by the rigorous application of the 'doctrine of lapse'. There were a number of high British officials, such as John Littler, Stephard, Tucker, George Clark and Henry Lawrence who considered the annexation of Native States under the doctrine of lapse as atonce unjust and inexpedient. For instance, Henry Lawrence, the then Agent to Governor-General, Rajputana observed in connection with the proposed annexation of small Rajput State of Karauli :

> The confirmation of the Suzerain is necessary in all cases; he is the arbitrator of all contested adoptions; he can set aside one or other for informality, irregularity or for misconduct; but it does not appear by the rules or practices of any of the sovereignties, or by our own practice with the *Istumrardars* of Ajmere, that the paramount State can refuse confirmation to one or other claimant, and confiscate the State, however, small.[5]

The Home Government, however, refused to approve of Dalhousie's proposal to annex Karauli on the ground that it was 'a protected ally' and not 'dependent'. Even in the cases of the States annexed by Dalhousie there had been prolonged discussions and acute differences among the members of the Supreme Council. Sir Lewis Tupper observes in this connection:

> We were disagreed about our duty, our policy, our rights and about the law and past practice by which we professed to be guided. No wonder, the minds of the princes and people were disquieted and by all this inconsistency and uncertainty and conflict of opinions amongst those whose authority was practically absolute in dealing with their dearest interests and rights.[6]

In the absence of clear and consistent policy of the British authorities regarding adoption of heirs by the Indian Chiefs there existed 'a haze of doubt or mistrust in the minds of Native Chiefs'. During the revolt of 1857-58 a large number of Princes and Chiefs, including those of Jaipur and other Rajputana States, had given ample proof of their loyalty and rendered meritorious services to the British Government. The British authorities had been deeply impressed by their loyalty and services, and decided to adopt a new and more considerate policy towards them. It was announced by the Queen's Proclamation that their territories would no longer be annexed and the British authorities would respect the 'rights, dignity and honour of the Princes'. Canning, the first Viceroy and Governor-General under the Crown, was of the strong opinion that the fears existing in the minds of the Princes and Chiefs should be set at rest and they should be granted the right of adopting heirs in cases where they had no natural sons to succeed. He suggested to the Secretary of State for India that it would be an act of grace as well as 'sound policy' to give assurance to every Chief above the rank of *jagirdar* that the Paramount Power desired to see his government perpetuated, and that on failure of natural heir, his adoption of a successor according to Hindu law and customs of his race (if he be a Hindu) or selection of a successor which might be legitimate according to Mohammadan Law (if he be a Muslim) would be recognised. He recommended that such an assurance should be conveyed to each Chief individually and not by a general notification addressed to all.[7] The Secretary of State accepted the recommendation of the Viceroy and Governor-General.[8] Accordingly Adoption Sanads were issued individually to a large number of Princes and Chiefs in 1862, including Maharaja Ram Singh of Jaipur[9] and other rulers of Rajputana States.

Maharaja Ram Singh was a highly capable and competent ruler, for he was "extremely well-educated, naturally intelligent, and fully alive to the duties which devolved upon him as ruler and anxious to perform them."[10] He ruled successfully for about three decades. During this period he remained steadfastly loyal to the British Paramount and brought about appreciable improvements in various departments of administration under the guidance and supervision of the British Political Agent at Jaipur. He reorganised the administration of the State and constituted a 'Royal Council' of six members to assist him in administrative matters. He took commendable measures for the development of education. The College at the capital flourished under his personal supervision and he got it affiliated to the Calcutta University in 1873. He also established 'Rajput School' for the instruction of the sons of the *Thakurs* and high officials and also a school with several local branches for the education of girls. During his time, there were thirty-three elementary schools and 379 indigenous schools in various districts which were wholly supported by the State. The Maharaja took due care of the health of the people by opening Mayo Hospital and dispensaries in most of the towns of the State. He took a leading part in the establishment of the Mayo College for Princes for which he made a contribution of rupees 1,25,000.[11] He also opened a School of Industrial Arts for which he procured the services of a European, named De Fabeck.[12] He gave a further proof of his administrative acumen by taking necessary measures for forest conservation.[13] Important and valuable irrigation works were undertaken by the Maharaja in fulfilment of his promise made when he was exempted from the payment of progressive tribute. The large sums spent by him on education, public works and irrigation are noteworthy. Probably no other State in India could point to such a large proportion of its revenues spent on works of public utility.[14] The Maharaja did not ignore social reforms in his State. During his minority the Council of Regency under the direction of Major John Ludlow, the Political Agent at Jaipur, had already abolished the evil practices of *sati*, slavery and female infanticide. Being an enlightened ruler, the Maharaja could not tolerate that such practices should raise their ugly heads and he took some practical measures to check these practices and also took action against the culprits. The Secretary of State expressed satisfaction at promptitude displayed by the Maharaja in bringing to justice the offenders.[15] In the course of a severe famine which occurred in Jaipur and some other Rajputana States and neighbouring

British territories in 1868-69, the Maharaja took appreciable measures for the benefit of the famine-stricken people. In recognition of his commendable efforts to mitigate the sufferings of the afflicted fellow beings, the British authorities increased the salute of Maharaja Ram Singh from 17 to 19 guns.[16] He had been honoured with the insignia of G.C.S.I. and C.I.E.

Impressed by the extra-ordinary ability and unswerving loyalty of the Maharaja the British Government nominated him as a member of the first Indian Legislative Council constituted under the Indian Councils Act, 1861; he acted as the Member from 1869 to 1873. It is no less a compliment to the ability and enlightened outlook of the Maharaja that the British authorities nominated him as one of the six members of the Commission constituted to investigate the conduct of Malhar Rao Gaekwad of Baroda.[17] The Maharaja gave his impartial judgement along with the other two Indian members of the Commission by holding the Gaekwad 'not guilty'.

II

Maharaja Ram Singh died on 18 September 1880 when he was about 47 years old. The premature death of this able and popular ruler was an irreparable loss for the State and was deeply lamented by the people of Jaipur and those of Rajputana in general. Colonel Bradford, the then Agent to Governor-General, Rajputana observed that throughout Rajputana there was "but one feeling of sorrow at the premature death of a Chief, whom all classes alike looked upto and respected." Genuine regret was felt by the British authorities also at the death of the Chief whose loyalty to the British Government was 'ever steadfast and true', and to the Agent to Governor-General, as also to many other high British officers who had come into contact with him, the loss was felt as a personal one.[18] The late Maharaja had no natural son nor had he adopted anyone as his heir. After his demise, therefore, the question of succession came to the fore. The issue of succession and successor was discussed in detail by the highest British officers in the Foreign Department of the Government of India.

The questions considered were : Whether, when a Chief dies without either a direct or adopted heir, the State should be regranted to a collateral without conditions ? Whether the new Chief should be asked to pay *nazarana* to the British Government ? Should the nomination of a successor by the late Chief in the presence of British representative be regarded as an informal adoption ? The conclusions arrived at after discussion of these questions were : (i) The British Government had the right to regrant the Jaipur State on such conditions as it might determine but it was not desirable to do so because such a measure was not opportune; it would be inexpedient to inaugurate a distasteful policy with respect to the succession to a Chief of such conspicuous loyalty as the late Maharaja of Jaipur. (ii) No *nazarana* should be taken from the new Chief. (iii) The nomination of a successor by the late Chief in the presence of British representative should be regarded as an informal adoption.[19]

Dr. T.H. Hendley, in charge of the Eastern Rajputana States Agency, had visited Maharaja Ram Singh when he was seriously ill and almost on death-bed. He reported that the Maharaja in the full possession of his mental power and of his own free will, had nominated Kaim Singh, the younger brother of Pratab Singh, the *Thakur* of Isarda. This dying statement of the Chief was written by the Mir Munshi of the Darbar and it was signed by all important nobles, including the members of the Council who were present there. After this, Hendley received a letter from Thakur Fateh Singh to the effect that the two queen mothers and the Maharanis had all approved the adoption by giving their signatures on the letter.[20] After receiving Hendley's report, Agent to Governor-General Rajputana wrote to the Supreme Government of India, informing about the death of Maharaja Ram Singh and forwarding copy of the detailed report of Hendley. He opined that in this difficult and trying position, Dr. Hendley had acted with 'consummate tact and judgement' and that by his prudence in obtaining a clear and unmistakable declaration from the dying Chief, and by the manner in which he elicited the views of the Ranis and those entitled to a voice in the succession, the Jaipur State had been spared the troubles which had always been predicted as inevitable on the death of the late Chief. He pointed out that he had himself known Kaim Singh some years ago when he was being educated at the Jaipur Thakur School. He was then a pleasing boy and was now a tall, well-built youngman, in no way intellectually unfitted for the duties of so high a position, though of course perfectly untrained in matters of administration.[21]

After receiving this communication the Supreme Government directed the Agent to Governor-General to announce that the Government of India recognised succession of Kaim Singh, subject to such conditions regarding present administration and other matters as might hereafter be deemed necessary to impose. Orders were also given for presenting a *khillat* to the new Chief on the occasion of his investiture. Accordingly Kaim Singh was recognised under the title of Sawai Madho Singh as Chief of Jaipur in the ceremony held on 29 September 1880 and a *khillat* of rupees 20,000 was presented to him by the Agent to Governor-General on this occasion.[22] He was about 19 years of age at that time. He was a "young man of nice disposition and pleasing manners, and by no means wanting in intelligence." When quite young he was taught a little English, Hindi and Urdu at the Thakur's School, Jaipur but he had no opportunities whatever of acquiring any knowledge of the duties of a ruler. The Agent to Governor-General, therefore, recommended that though the Maharaja was not a minor, he should not be placed at once in uncontrolled charge of the State. He should continue to be guided by the Council of six nobles with Thakur Fateh Singh as Vice-President and the British Political Agent should, for the present, be given a potential voice in the affairs of the State. He recommended that three of the leading and influential *Thakurs* (Thakur Govind Singh of Chamu, Thakur Sawant Singh of Bugru and Thakur Partap Singh of Diggi) be added to the Council. Besides, Rawal Bijai Singh of Samod, an influential and trustworthy noble, should be appointed in constant personal attendance on the young Chief, subject to the advice of the Political Agent, in the matter of selection of Maharaja's companions. Since the Political Agent had to perform heavy duties in the Eastern Rajputana

States, having the political charge of Bharatpur and Karauli in addition to that of Jaipur, it was recommended that an Assistant to Political Agent, Eastern Rajputana States be appointed who would perform the duty particularly for the supervision of Bharatpur and Karauli.[23]

The Government of India accepted and approved of the recommendation of Col. E.R.C. Bradford, Agent to Governor-General, Rajputana for the conduct of the administration of Jaipur by the Maharaja with the active assistance of the Council of influential nobles till he would have adequate training to take charge of administration in his own hands. The Governor-General in Council considered the suggestion regarding attendance of meetings of the Council by the Political Agent accompanied by the Maharaja and settlement of all important administrative matters with the advice of the Political Agent as suitable, and expressed confidence that Colonel Beynon, an able and experienced Political Agent, would bring the arrangements sanctioned to a successful issue.[24] The Secretary of State for India approved of the proceedings regarding the succession of Kaim Singh as Ruler of Jaipur under the title of Sawai Madho Singh and the administrative arrangements made to assist and guide him.[25]

It was decided by the Supreme Government to confer full powers of administration on Maharaja Sawai Madho Singh on his attaining the age of twenty-one years. Two questions were to be decided in this regard — first, whether a *khillat* should be given to the Maharaja on the occasion of his investiture with full powers; second, whether some conditions should be imposed on the Maharaja while entrusting to him the control of administration of the State.

As regards the first, no uniform practice had been adopted. In the cases of the succession of Chiefs of Mysore and Baroda *khillats* were given both on intimation of succession and on investiture with full powers, with this difference that on succession the British Agent took a *peshcush* also in return. In the case of Udaipur Maharana Surjan Singh received a *khillat* on his accession in November 1874 but no *peshcush* was taken (vide Foreign Dept., Political A, Jan. 1875, Nos. 395-396). No *khillat* was conferred upon him when he was invested with full powers of administration in November 1876 (vide Foreign Dept., Political A, Dec. 1876, Nos. 15-16). In the case of Alwar Maharao Raja Mangal Singh was installed as Ruler in December 1874 and he received no succession *khillat* (vide Foreign Dept., Political A, Feb. 1875, Nos. 120-122). But a *khillat* of the value of rupees 10,000 was conferred upon him on the occasion of his investiture with full powers of administration in December 1877 and a return *khillat* of the same value was received from him (vide Foreign Dept., Political A, March 1878, Nos. 239-243). When Maharaja Sawai Madho Singh was recognised as Ruler of Jaipur State in September 1880, a *khillat* of rupees 20,000 had been conferred upon him but no *peshcush* was taken from him (vide Foreign Dept., Political A, Nov. 1880, Nos. 74-77). After a lot of discussion it was decided by the British authorities that no second *khillat* should be given to the Maharaja of Jaipur on his investiture with full powers of administration and that the Udaipur precedent would satisfy any Rajput Chief.[26]

The Government of India sought information telegraphically whether a second *khillat* to the Jaipur Maharaja on the occasion of assuming full powers of administration was necessary in reply to which the Agent to Governor-General, Rajputana stated that it had not been the custom in Rajputana to give two *khillats* and that the second *khillat* on his investiture with full powers was not necessary.[27]

Regarding the second question, both the Officiating Resident, Eastern Rajputana States and Agent to Governor-General for Rajputana, recommended that it was desirable to impose certain conditions on the authority of the Maharaja while investing him with ruling powers on 6 September 1882. Major W.F. Prideaux, Officiating Resident, Eastern Rajputana States, opined that the inexperience of the young Maharaja and the personal defects of his character necessitated the imposition of certain checks on his authority. Commenting on his character, he remarked, "In temper he is obstinate, and impatient of anything approaching dictation, and yet he is easily led by those who have the tact to humour his whims. Being susceptible of flattery he prefers the society of persons of inferior ranks to that of those whose birth would better fit them as companions. He does not easily forgive, and is apt to gratify his resentment." He suggested the retention of the Council on an improved footing. Four members of the Council, named Purohit Ram Parshad, Babu Jadunath Sen, Thakur Samander Karan and Mir Kurban Ali, should be retired on liberal pension. Each of the three departments — (i) Revenue and Financial; (ii) Judicial; (iii) Foreign and Military — would then consist of one official or working member and one noble of the State as a consulting member. The following conditions should be laid down for observance by the Maharaja and his Council :[28]

(1) No acts or orders which have emanated from the Council during the period that the Resident had filled the office of Joint President should be revised without special reference to the Resident.
(2) The approval of the Resident should be required before sanction can be given to : the annual budget; the appointment or dismissal of a member of the Council; the introduction of any code of rules, judicial or revenue; permanent resumption of hereditary grants in jagir, etc.; the confirmation of capital sentences in criminal cases.
(3) A summary of the proceedings of the Council should be submitted weekly for the information of the Resident, and an annual report on the progress of the administration should be furnished to him for the information of the Government of India.

Lieutenant-Colonel Walter, Officiating Agent to Governor-General agreed with the proposals of Major Prideaux regarding the reduction of the members of the Council by compulsorily retiring four of its members and appointment of two members in each of the three departments. While considering it desirable to impose certain checks on the authority of the Maharaja, he did not endorse the conditions enumerated by the Officiating Resident for observance by the Maharaja and his Council. He expressed the opinion that it would be better to follow the precedents observed at the termination of the minority in

Udaipur and Alwar. He quoted a paragraph from Alfred Lyall's letter No. 2206-253P., dated 10 June 1876 about Udaipur :

> I would lay down no precise rules in any way limiting the Chief's power; but on the other hand I recommend a distinct stipulation that the Maharana shall hold himself bound for the present to consult the Political Agent upon all important matters, and to follow his advice. It might be specified that the concurrence of the Political Agent must be obtained before any important measures or acts of the Council, taken during the minority, can be reversed or disturbed, before any change is made in the present system of administration, etc.

This proposal was sanctioned by the Government of India vide letter from the Foreign Office No. 1674P., dated 18 July 1876. A similar course was followed when the investiture of Maharao Raja Mangal Singh of Alwar with full powers was sanctioned in November 1877.[29]

The Governor-General in Council approved and sanctioned the proposal of the Agent to Governor-General to the effect that the Maharaja of Jaipur should be invested with full powers of administration on his attaining the age of twenty-one years, but that, in accordance with the plan adopted on the accession to power of the Maharana of Udaipur and Maharao Raja of Alwar, the Maharaja of Jaipur should "hold himself bound for the present to consult the Political Agent upon all important matters and to follow his advice"; and that "the concurrence of the Political Agent must be obtained before any important measures or acts of the Council, taken during the minority, can be reversed or disturbed, and before any change is made in the present form of administration." The Supreme Government also gave approval to the retention of the Council on the improved basis which had been determined upon in concurrence with the Maharaja.[30]

Lieutenant-Colonel Walter (Agent to the Governor-General, Rajputana) went to Jaipur accompanied by the Resident and Additional Political Agent Eastern States on 5 September 1882. He read out to the Maharaja and to the members of the Council the draft of a *Kharita* addressed to the Maharaja. It was said in the *Kharita* :

> His Excellency considers it desirable, in bestowing on you full powers, that you should be guided by the following conditions, *viz*, that until such time as Your Highness gains more experience, and is more capable of carrying on the administration unaided, you should consult the Resident upon all important matters and be guided by his advice, that no measures or acts taken or performed by the Council during Your Highness' minority should be altered or revised without the concurrence of the Resident, and further that no change in the administration should be introduced without the advice of the Resident being sought thereon. In all other matters connected with the current work of the administration, Your Highness will be guided by your own discretion and by the advice of the members of your Council.[31]

The Maharaja accepted, without demur and apparently with cordiality, the conditions which it contained. On the following day (6 September) Colonel Walter performed the ceremony of investing the Maharaja with full ruling powers. In a *Kharita* addressed to the Viceroy and Governor-General of India, the Maharaja expressed his thanks to the latter for the great honour conferred upon him, adding :

> The confidence Your Excellency has been pleased to repose in me is very encouraging, and I shall, at all times, earnestly endeavour to make my subjects prosperous and happy, while I rest assured of the kind support of Your Excellency's Government in all matters connected with the administration of my State.[32]

In the following years the Maharaja administered the affairs of the State efficiently under the guidance and advice of the British Resident in all important matters and with the assistance of the Council in other matters. Being impressed with the performance of the Maharaja and his loyalty and ability, the Supreme Government decided in 1886 to remove restrictions on his administrative powers which had been imposed in 1882. The Viceroy Dufferin, in the course of his visit to Jaipur in November 1885, intimated to the Maharaja the decision of the Government to remove restrictions on his administrative powers. Early in May 1886 a *Kharita* was addressed by the Agent to Governor-General, Rajputana to Maharaja Sawai Madho Singh in which he conveyed to the latter, in the name and instance of the

Government of India, a formal announcement of the removal of restriction on his administrative powers — a gratifying proof of confidence reposed in the loyalty and ability of the Maharaja. He expressed confidence on behalf of the Governor-General that the Maharaja would rely in future, as he had done in the past, on the good-will of the Resident and would never fail to attach due weight to the advice of that trusted representative of the British Government. Offering his warm congratulations to the Maharaja, the Agent to Governor-General expressed his earnest hope for the 'long and prosperous reign' of the Maharaja.[33]

III

Early in 1883 some serious differences had arisen between the Dowagar Maharani of Jaipur and Maharaja Sawai Madho Singh. An Agent of the Maharani, named Ganesh Parshad was believed to be responsible for stirring up the strife. A comprehensive memorial was addressed to the Viceroy, Lord Ripon by Maji Sahib Rahtorji, the Senior Dowager Maharani of Jaipur and her two sisters who were also the junior Maharanis of Jaipur. The memorial contained various allegations against the Maharaja, accusing him of improperly slighting the widow of the late Maharaja who held the position of adoptive mother to him. The memorial stated that according to the custom, usage, and traditions of the ruling house of Jaipur, and indeed of all ruling houses in Rajputana, the Senior Dowager Maharani or Queen-Mother performed certain functions and enjoyed certain rights, privileges, and dignities which were being denied to her by the Maharaja and she was being subjected to indignities and insults. Among her numerous grievances listed the following may be mentioned :

That the Maharaja had nominated a Jaipur *Kamdar* for the Queen-Mother's work which was an infringement of her right and opposed to the practice of appointing a Jodhpur man to the post; that at the intervention of Maharaja Jaswant Singh of Jodhpur, who was her own brother, a paper of twelve demands regarding her privileges as Queen-Mother had been prepared of which eight had been accepted by Maharaja Jaswant Singh and assented to by the Maharaja of Jaipur but these conditions were subsequently violated by the latter; that annoyance and insults to which she was subjected became more frequent with the re-admission into Jaipur of Jodiji, the real mother of the Maharaja and his natural maternal uncle, Kalian Singh; that at the Darbar held to celebrate the birthday anniversary of the Maharaja in the *zenana* apartments of the palace, Jodiji took the highest seat which was the Queen-Mother's privilege, and when asked to vacate the seat she abused and insulted the Queen-Mother; that thereafter the Maharaja never came to the Darbar on the Queen-Mother's birth anniversary, or to the celebration of the *Dusehra* and other festivals, and stopped the usual money payments and also the *nazars* payable by himself and the Sardars and officials to the Queen-Mother on such occasions in contravention of the terms agreed upon at the intervention of Maharaja Jaswant Singh of Jodhpur; that the Maharaja enjoined and encouraged the presentation of *nazars* and offerings, instead, to his natural mother, Jodiji; that the Maharaja had set at defiance the authority of the Queen-Mother by taking from the house known as Burra Raj fourteen of the attendants of the Queens and keeping them in a separate place to utilise their services against all rule and custom; that a State official had been placed at the *deori* of the Dowager-Queens to prevent all communications from outside; that to humiliate the Dowager-Queens the Maharaja had prevented their *Gurani* (female spiritual guide) from entering the palace for the due performance of the daily rites of worship; that certain packages containing coloured clothes sent to them in usual course from Jodhpur were stopped in the city and prevented their being taken at once in the *zenana* apartments of the palace; that an order was passed to the effect that the vessels containing water and also supplies of food to be brought into the palace apartments be opened and examined, and a servant named Zorawal Mal of the junior Dowager-Queen had been imprisoned for asking permission to take the water brought for the use of the *zenana* (ladies) into the palace apartments;

that the Maharaja had put into prison three *Naib-Vakils* of the Dowager-Queen because they rightly refused to subscribe on their behalf a document in which the Maharaja had set down some new and humilitaing terms to be observed by them. In the end, the memorialists requested the Viceroy to send a telegram to the Agent to Governor-General, Rajputana directing that the personal humiliating privations to which they had recently been subjected be removed.[34]

Colonel E.R.C. Bradford, Agent to Governor-General, Rajputana while forwarding the above memorial and detailed remarks of J.P. Stratton, Resident, Eastern Rajputana States to the Government of India, opined that there was no substance in the allegations made by the memorialists against the Maharaja of Jaipur. The Maharaja had been most sincerely anxious to do all in his power to bring about an amicable settlement of the misunderstanding which existed between himself and his adoptive mother. The Maharaja had invariably adopted a conciliatory attitude and he had conceded all the terms suggested by Maharaja Jaswant Singh of Jodhpur — terms "far more than she had any right to expect". About the conduct of Maharani Maji Rahtorji, he remarked, "Suffering as she does from a violent and over-bearing temper, she is full of arrogance and self-importance. Such a character cut off from the outside world is easily worked on by evilly disposed persons." He alluded to the notorious discord which existed between her and the late Maharaja Ram Singh. He recommended that the Maji Rahtorji's *Vakil* might be told that the Government of India declined to interfere in her and her sisters' behalf. He added that it was absolutely necessary for the preservation of the dignity of the Maharaja's position that he should be supported in resisting the unwarranted demands that were being made upon him.[35] The Supreme Government accepted the recommendation of the Agent to Governor-General, Rajputana, and declined to interfere in favour of Maji Rahtorji and her sisters. The Agent to Governor-General was directed to extend full support to the Maharaja in resisting unwarranted demands of the memorialists.[36]

IV

To sum up, during the minority of the two successive Chiefs — Jai Singh III (1819-1835) and Ram Singh (1835-1851) — the British Political Agent at Jaipur backed by the British Resident at Delhi intervened continuously and ceaselessly in the administrative affairs of the State. They made and unmade the Prime Ministers who acted as their stooges and eroded the legitimate authority of the Regent (Rani Mother and Maharani) to the much annoyance of the latter. After 1839 when Maharani was ousted from the administrative affairs and a Council of Regency was constituted, the real authority of administration was vested in the British Political Agent who was also to be the President of the Council. There is no doubt that remarkable improvements were effected in every department of administration and some significant reforms, including social reforms, were brought about at the behest and under the guidance of the successive Politial Agents. Even after the termination of the minority of Maharaja Ram Singh and assumption of ruling powers by him, the Political Agent continued to dominate in the affairs of the State from 1851 to 1880.

As a result of the death of Maharaja Ram Singh in September 1880, the question of succession came to the fore. The late Maharaja had no natural son nor had he cared to adopt one. The British authorities proceeded very cautiously but promptly in selecting a successor. Dr. Hendley, in charge of the Eastern Rajputana State Agency, who was present at the death-bed of the Maharaja, tactfully procured a statement from the Maharaja in the presence of leading nobles and officials of the State, nominating Kaim Singh as his successor. He was, therefore, installed on the *gaddi* in September 1880 in the name of Maharaja Sawai Madho Singh when he was about 19 years of age. He was, however, required to conduct administration of the State with the active assistance of the Council of influential nobles, and the British Political Agent was to have a potential voice in the administrative affairs. Upon attaining the age of 21 years in September 1882, he was invested with full ruling powers on the condition that he would be bound for the present to consult the Political Agent on all important matters and to follow his advice, and that his concurrence must be obtained before any important measures or acts of the Council taken during his minority could be reversed or changed. Impressed by the ability and conduct of the Maharaja, the British authorities decided in 1886 to remove restrictions on his administrative powers. But at the same time they expressed the hope that he would rely in future, as he had done in the past, on the goodwill of the Resident and would invariably attach due weight to his advice.

The upshot of the above discussion is that the British Agent or Resident had a decisive voice in all important matters of administration of the State. In fact, it was a main principle of the British policy during the period of the growth of British paramountcy that Political Agent or Resident should play a dominant role in the affairs of the State under his charge. To quote the words of K.M. Panikkar, "The whisper of the Residency is the thunder of the State."[37] Some of the British Political Agents were arrogant and overbearing in their behaviour so as to flout the authority and dignity of the Princes. The Prince of Wales, who visited India during the viceroyalty of Northbrook (1872-1876), was most forcibly struck by the 'rude and rough manner' with which the British Political Officers treated the Princes and the Chiefs.[38] Many vernacular newspapers[39] also condemned in strong terms the general attitude of the Political Agents who interfered unduly in the affairs of the States and frequently insulted and ill-treated the Chiefs. These remarks were true in many cases but they were not applicable to the conduct of all the Political Agents. It was aptly observed by Hamilton, "The worst of the system seems to me that the condition of our relations with the individual States seems to depend entirely upon the character and personal qualities of our Political Agents. If they are Phayres, all goes wrong, and if men like Outram and Clerk, all goes well."[40] This remark is also applicable to the Political Agents at Jaipur. The Political Agents like Rickards and Burton were not only imperious and haughty but they were also covetous and corrupt who tried to fleece the State whose hospitality they enjoyed. On the other hand, the Political Agents like Thoresby and Ludlow were very reasonable in their dealings with the State and made earnest endeavours to reform the administration, taking appreciable measures for the welfare of the people. It is significant to observe in this connection that it was at the initiative of Thoresby that the annual tribute of the State payable to the British Government was reduced from 8 lakhs to 4 lakhs by the Supreme Government. Be that as it may, the dominating position of the Political Agent or Resident in the affairs of the State cannot be denied.

The Government of India generally accepted the recommendations of the Resident — man on the spot — and also those of the Agent to Governor-General Rajputana who forwarded his recommendations with his comments. But sometimes these recommendations were over-ruled by the Supreme Government if they were felt to be unfair to the Chief or not in keeping with the principles of British policy. For example, Major Prideaux, Resident, Eastern Rajputana States, had proposed certain specific conditions to be observed by Maharaja Sawai Madho Singh after assumption of administrative powers to the effect : the approval of the Resident should be required before the sanction of the annual budget, the appointment or dismissal of a member of the Council, the introduction of any code of rules (judicial or revenue), permanent resumption of hereditary grants in *jagir*, the confirmation of capital sentences in criminal cases, etc. etc. But these conditions were not approved by the Agent to Governor-General nor by the Supreme Government. Again it was the Viceroy Dufferin who, in the course of his visit to Jaipur in November 1885, announced his decision to remove all restrictions on the administrative powers of the Maharaja, though the orders of the Supreme Government in this regard were given a few months after. Earlier, in 1883, the Viceroy Ripon had declined to interfere in favour of the Senior Dowager Maharani and two junior Maharanis of Jaipur who had addressed a Memorial to the Viceroy containing various allegations against the Maharaja. Full support was extended to the Maharaja in resisting 'unwarranted demands' of the memorialists.

References and Notes

1. A.C. Arora, *British Policy towards the Punjab States 1858-1905* (Jalandhar, 1982), p. 77.
2. Cited in William Lee-Warner, *The Protected Princes of India* (London, 1894), p. 5.
3. *Supra*, pp. 68-77.
4. *Supra*, pp. 78-86.
5. Parliamentary Paper 442 of 1849 and 50 of 1850 on Adoption by Native Princes ; also Arora, *op. cit.*, p. 79.
6. Sir Lewis Tupper, *Our Indian Protectorate* (London, 1893), p. 106.
7. Governor General's Despatch to the Secretary of State, No. 43A of 30 April 1860.
8. Political Despatch from the Secretary of State to Governor-General, No. 59-P of 26 July 1860.
9. For the Adoption Sanads issued to the Maharaja of Jaipur, see C.U. Aitchison, Comp., *A Collection of Treaties, Engagements and Sanads, Vol. III* (Calcutta, 1932), p. 56.
10. G.B. Malleson, cited in Jadunath Sarkar, *A History of Jaipur*, c.1503-1938, revised and edited by Raghubir Sinh (New Delhi, 1984), p. 339.
11. FD, Political A, June 1871, Nos. 269-271.
12. FD, General A, June 1869, Nos. 54-55.
13. FD, General A, Aug. 1878, Nos. 27-30.
14. RPARS for 1871-72, para 3.
15. FD, General A, May 1870, No. 22 ; FD, Political B, May 1871, Nos. 66-67.
16. FD, General A, April 1869, Nos. 67-70.
17. FD, Political A, March 1875, Nos. 147-154 ; also Aug. 1875, Nos. 111-122.
18. AGG to GOI, 23 Sept. 1880, FD, Political A, Nov. 1880, No. 72, para 2.
19. K.W., FD, Political A, Nov. 1880, Nos. 68-80, pp. 1 – 6.
20. Surgeon T.H. Hendley, in charge Eastern Rajputana States Agency to AGG, No. 1A.P., dated 20 Sept. 1880, FD, Political A, Nov. 1880, No. 73.
21. AGG to GOI, No. 215P., dated 23 Sept. 1880, FD, Political A, Nov. 1880, No. 72.

22. FD, Political A, Nov. 1880, Nos. 74-76.
23. AGG to GOI, No. 231P, dated 2 Oct. 1880, FD, Political A, Nov. 1880, No. 77.
24. GOI to AGG, No. 894 IP., dated 29 Oct. 1880, FD, Political A, Nov.1880, No. 78.
25. Vide FD, Political A, Nov. 1880, Nos. 79-80.
26. See K.W., FD, A–Political-I, Sept. 1882, Nos. 51-52, pp. 1-4.
27. Telegram to AGG, No. 513 I. of 21 Aug. 1882 and Telegram from AGG of 22 Aug. 1882, FD, A-Political-I, Sept. 1882, Nos. 51-52.
28. FD, General A, August 1878, Nos. 27-30.
29. Lieut.-Col. C.K.M. Walter, Offg. AGG to GOI, No. 1775 G., dated 28 June 1882 (Confidential), FD, A-Political-I, Jan.1883, No. 105.
30. GOI to AGG, No. 1541, dated 15 July 1882 (Confidential), FD, A-Political-I, Jan. 1883, No. 106.
31. Translation of a *Kharita* from Colonel Walter, Offg. AGG to Maharaja Sawai Madho Singh of Jaipur, dated 5 Sept. 1882, FD, A-Political-I, Jan. 1883, No. 106B.
32. *Kharita* dated 31 October 1882 from Maharaja of Jaipur to the Viceroy and Governor-General of India, FD, A-Political-I, Jan. 1883, No. 108.
33. *Kharita* addressed by AGG to Maharaja of Jaipur, dated 5 May 1886, FD, Internal A, May 1886, No. 251.
34. Memorial to Marquis of Ripon, Viceroy and Governor-General from Maji Sahib Rahtorji, the Senior Dowager Maharani and two junior Maharanis, dated 12 March 1883, through Pandit Ganesh Parshad (Authorised Vakil), FD, A-General-I, May 1883, No. 180.
35. AGG to GOI, No. 33P., dated 16 April 1883, FD, A-General-I, May 1883, No. 181; Resident, Eastern Rajputana States to AGG, No. 4P., dated 10 April 1883, *ibid.*, No. 182.
36. GOI to AGG, No. 1400 I, dated 29 May, 1883, FD, A-General-I, May 1883, No. 184.
37. K.M. Panikkar, *Indian States and the Government of India* (London, 1932), p. 104.
38. Salisbury to Northbrook, 17 Dec. 1875, Salisbury Papers, Reel 7.
39. See, for instance, *Sahas*, 21 Jan. 1882 and *Akhbar-i-Chunar*, 24 April, 1882 in *Reports on Native Newspapers Punjab and North-Western Provinces* for 1882, pages 44, 285. (NAI).
40. Hamilton to Northbrook, 1 October 1875, Northbrook Papers, Reel 10, p. 259.

CHAPTER 5

Border Disputes

In the post-1858 period several border disputes, major or minor, arose between Jaipur State and the neighbouring States of Karauli, Alwar, Tonk and Patiala. By Article 5 of the treaty of 1818 the Maharaja of Jaipur was bound to refer all such disputes to the arbitration of the British Government. So the British authorities intervened resolutely to settle all these disputes through Agent to Governor-General, Rajputana who received detailed information about all such disputes from the Political Agent, Jaipur and communicated with the Chiefs concerned to settle the disputes amicably. A brief account of these disputes together with the action taken by the Paramount Power may be given as under.

I

The dispute between Jaipur and Karauli commenced in 1859 when a piece of land belonging to Raipur village of Jaipur State was cultivated by the villagers of Bariroond in Karauli State. This dispute continued for about twelve years. The main facts of the case were communicated by the Political Agent, Jaipur to Colonel Keatinge, Agent to Governor-General, Rajputana in 1869, a summary of which is as under[1] :

On 30 September 1859 the Jaipur Darbar represented to the Political Agent that land worth about rupees 1100 to 1200 per annum belonging to Raipur village of Jaipur was cultivated forcibly by villagers of Bariroond of Karauli and that they should pay rent of rupees 75 per annum. The Political Agent sent a copy of the representation to the Karauli *Vakil* adding that the rent of rupees 75 be paid annually to the Jaipur Darbar. On 26 November 1859 the Karauli *Vakil* forwarded a *hundie* for rupees 150 to Agent to the Governor-General (arrears of rent for two years) which was forwarded through Political Agent to the Darbar. On 20 February 1861 the Jaipur Darbar communicated to the Political Agent that the arrears of rupees 187-8 were due plus rupees 75 for the past year and that the amount of rupees 262-8 might be paid and that the Bariroond villagers might be forbidden to cultivate land without permission of the Raj. In November 1862 the Karauli *Vakil* forwarded the amount of arrears and on 24 December he intimated the Political Agent that land in question had been cultivated by Bariroond villagers since Maharaja Gopal Singh's time, or upwards of a 100 years ago; and that he could not understand how Jaipur Darbar wished to dispossess them. On 18 November 1863 the Jaipur Darbar repeated the request to the effect that the Bariroond villagers might be prevented from tilling the land. A copy of this letter was sent to the Karauli *Vakil* with a request that if Bariroond villagers held any *sunnuds* respecting land in question, they should be produced. In 1864-65 all arrears of the rent were paid and intimation to this effect was sent by the Karauli *Vakil* to the Political Agent. On 28 February 1869 the Jaipur Darbar complained to the Political Agent that the *Zamindars* of Bariroond, who were permitted under certain terms to cultivate the land in question, were resisting the Darbar's survey operations of the said land; copy of this letter was sent to Karauli *Vakil* for report. On 13 May 1869 the Karauli *Vakil* stated in reply that the land referred to belonged to Karauli, the Jaipur right in it being confined exclusively to the Karauli annual payment of rupees 75, which it had paid for upwards of 100 years and continued to pay till the present date, and further that the Karauli Darbar could not understand how the Jaipur

Darbar exercised its right to survey it.

Early in November 1869 Colonel Keatinge gave his decision that the best settlement would be for the Political Agent to determine the value of the proprietary right possessed by the Karauli villagers in the Jaipur limit and to invite the Jaipur Darbar to purchase it by a payment of ten years' purchase money. If the Darbar paid the sum assessed, it should be offered to the Karauli *Zamindars*, whose rights would then be considered to have ceased. If the Karauli party refused to accept the compensation, the amount might be held a reasonable time in deposit for them, and in the meantime their claim to assistance from the Agency might be considered as no longer existing.[2]

In January 1871 the Officiating Political Agent, Eastern States, addressed the Officiating Political Agent, Jaipur, in the matter on behalf of the Karauli Darbar. He stated that in his opinion the case had not been fully elucidated. For generations the land had been a bone of contention between the two villages and many lives had been lost in the struggle for it. At length, between 50 and 60 years ago Maharaja Hur Buksh Pal of Karauli encamped for the day near Raipur and he made a settlement on the spot by which the land was to remain in the hands of Bariroond villagers who were actually in possession but the Karauli Darbar was to pay annually rupees 100 to the Khemwallee *Thakur* (to whom Raipur belonged), rupees 75 going to the *Thakur* and rupees 25 to his *Kamdar*. When Raipur became *Khalsa* land, rupees 75 began to be paid into the *Tahsil* of Hindaun, in Jaipur. The Political Agent further remarked that he thought it would be hard now to oust the Bariroond villagers, as proposed by Colonel Keatinge in 1869, and that it would be better to uphold the beneficial arrangement made by Maharaja Hur Baksh Pal.[3]

The Political Agent, Jaipur replied that after carefully looking into the case and discussing it with the Darbar, he was unable to concur with the advisability of the orders already passed in the matter being changed in any way. Soon after, he forwarded to Political Agent, Eastern States, a vernacular note from the Jaipur Darbar, in which complaint was made that, although the purchase money compensating the Karauli villagers for their proprietary right in the land, assessed under the arrangement proposed by Colonel Keatinge was lodged in January 1870, the Darbar had neither been put in possession of the land, nor been paid the rent, which, under the old arrangement, would be due to it by the Karauli Darbar.[4]

In response to the above communication, Political Agent, Eastern States, stated that in his opinion, as Colonel Keatinge's decree involved a transfer of territorial rights, it would not be valid without either the assent of both the Darbars or the confirmation of Government. With regard to the inexpediency of renewing the old arrangement of annual payment, he proposed, to avoid trouble, that Karauli be required to authorise the Agency Treasurer to pay the money regularly to Jaipur. It would then be recovered periodically, with the other sums advanced on account of Karauli, in satisfaction of decrees of the Court of Vakils.[5]

In July 1871 Political Agent, Jaipur forwarded all the correspondence relating to the disputed piece of land to Colonel J.C. Brooke, Officiating Agent to Governor-General, Rajputana States.[6] The latter examined the case thoroughly by going through all the above-mentioned correspondence. Taking all the points into consideration he came to the conclusion that the settlement proposed by his predecessor, Colonel Keatinge was not practicable. He recommended to the Supreme Government that the enquiry be held *de novo* whenever an officer could be spared for the purpose, and that in the meantime the arrangement already existing should hold good, and, to prevent dispute and reference, that the Karauli State be required to arrange payment by the Jaipur Agency Treasurer through the Political Agent to the Jaipur State of the yearly quit-rent in had hitherto been liable to.[7]

The alleged outrage by Karauli subjects on the Jaipur village of Khereyra provided another cause of dispute between Jaipur and Karauli. This could have taken an ugly shape, had Jaipur International Court of Appeals not dismissed the case in consequence of non-attendance of both the plaintiffs and defendants notwithstanding the amplitude of time allowed by the Court to the respective Darbar to produce them. The non-appearance of the plaintiffs before the Court probably suggests that the statement of Karauli subjects in their defence was a correct one. Hence no action was considered necessary by the British Government.[8]

After 1872 disputes between the two States continued to occur from time to time and efforts were also made to settle these disputes through the Agents of the two States under the directions of Agent to Governor-General, Rajputana States. It was in 1883 that the rules were framed for the extradition of criminals between the two States in order to minimise the cause of disputes.[9] Despite these rules, border disputes occurred from time to time between the two States. It was in 1896 that four pending border disputes were disposed of by Lieutenant E. Barnes, the officer specially appointed for the settlement of these cases; the proceedings were confirmed by Agent to Governor-General, Rajputana States.[10]

II

The boundary dispute between Jaipur and Alwar called for settlement. The total boundary of 266 miles in length between Jaipur and Alwar, of which 64 miles had been previously settled, was demarcated by Captain Abbott, Assistant to the Agent to Governor-General, Rajputana in 1871-72. There were 65 disputes to be settled all of which were disposed of by Abbott to the satisfaction of the Agent to Governor-General with the exception of the cases given below.

The Jaipur Darbar appealed to Colonel Brooke against the decision of these cases in August 1872. Brooke instead of disposing of the cases in the presence of the representatives of both the parties, sent the papers to the Maharaja of Jaipur and afterwards in December 1872 personally discussed the matter with the Maharaja again without any intimation to, or the knowledge of the Alwar Darbar. The result of this discussion was that Captain Abbott was ordered to revisit the border from the river Sabee to certain hills lying about five miles south of it. After rehearing the evidence, Abbott adhered to his former decision except as regards the temple which in default of conclusive evidence on either side he assigned to Jaipur.

Colonel Brooke while speaking highly of the skill and judgement displayed by Abbott in the settlement of this difficult boundary, differed from him in the following instances :

(1) Colonel Brooke was willing to uphold Abbott's decision assigning certain piece of land to Alwar, provided the right of occupancy of those who had dug wells in the tract should be respected by the Alwar Darbar.

(2) With regard to certain alluvion cultivated by the Jaipur ryots which Abbott in the absence of conclusive proof on either side had divided equally between Jaipur and Alwar, Colonel Brooke held that the whole of this should be given to Jaipur.

(3) Alluding to a large piece of land cut away by the Sabee river which Abbott had given to Alwar, Colonel Brooke opined that according to the established usage the land cut away by the river taking a new channel became property of the State to whichever side of the main channel it might have been transferred by the river.

The Agent to Governor-General was, of course, the best judge in such matters but his proceedings should be openly and impartially conducted. In this case the decision was given by Colonel Brooke without hearing what Alwar had to say.[11]

The Agent to Governor-General, Rajputana (Colonel Brooke) forwarded copies of correspondence to the Government of India relating to boundary disputes between Jaipur and Alwar, with his opinion and comments thereon. He also requested that sanction be given for payment to Captain Abbott of usual deputation allowance at the rate of rupees 10 per diem during the period he was employed on duty.[12]

Colonel Pelly, the successor of Colonel Brooke, was instructed to enquire into the case as regards the points on which his predecessor reversed Captain Abbott's decision. He was asked to give his verdict after hearing both the parties. In

November 1873 Colonel Pelly informed the Supreme Government that both Jaipur and Alwar Darbars had expressed their willingness to abide by his decision which was arrived at after consulting the Political Agents of both the States. Both of them were of the opinion that Captain Abbott's settlement should be upheld in its entirety, and Colonel Pelly had given his decision accordingly. He had directed Captain Cadell to arrange that the Jaipur cultivators in the land made over to Alwar should be justly treated and had also told Colonel Beynon to move the Jaipur Darbar to explain to them their position in the matter. The Maharaja of Jaipur agreed to abide by Colonel Pelly's decision and his liberal behaviour in the matter deserved appreciation for the concession he made was no light one in his (Pelly's) estimation. Since Pelly's decision amounted to an entire reversal of Brooke's views as conveyed in his letter No. 841G, dated 14 June, Pelly requested that the said letter might be held in abeyance.[13] He also forwarded copies of letters addressed to the Political Agents of Jaipur and Alwar regarding boundary disputes between the two States requesting that Brooke's letter relating to them might be considered as withdrawn.[14]

On the request of Colonel Pelly, the Government of India instructed the Surveyor-General that five copies of each of Jaipur-Alwar boundary maps might be prepared and furnished as early as possible, and promised to remit the cost of the same when recovered from the two States concerned.[15]

Acknowledging the receipt of letter from the Agent to Governor-General for Rajputana, the Supreme Government approved of his proceedings in connection with settlement of boundary disputes between Jaipur and Alwar. The Governor-General expressed satisfaction with the role of Colonel Pelly "whose judicious influence with the Maharaja appears to have saved the Government a delicate and unpleasant task." He also directed that the Maharaja of Jaipur's liberal behaviour in the matter might also be acknowledged in suitable words.[16]

The Government of India was also appreciative of the work of Captain Abbott who had taken great pains in settling the boundary disputes and instructed the Agent to Governor-General to acknowledge his labours in suitable terms. The deputation allowance of rupees 10 per day, amounting in all to rupees 1720, should be paid to him and recovered from the Jaipur and Alwar Darbars in equal shares.[17]

Colonel Pelly informed the Government of India about the continual border disturbances and other quarrels and robberies. He submitted a memorandum on the subject of erection of boundary marks on Jaipur-Alwar border. In response to his letter the Agriculture, Revenue and Commerce Department was requested to arrange for the deputation of a good survey officer to demarcate the boundary pillars; his pay and deputation allowance at the rate of rupees 10 a day being borne by the two States.[18] In reply to this letter Colonel Pelly was informed that arrangements were being made to depute a good survey officer to demarcate Jaipur-Alwar boundary by pillars. It was intimated that the pay and deputation allowance of rupees 10 per day of this officer would be borne by the States concerned.[19]

Colonel Pelly requested telegraphically that the officer who might be deputed to demarcate the Alwar-Jaipur boundary might be directed to proceed to his camp for full instruction prior to going on border.[20] In reply to this telegram the Supreme Government stated that it had been found impossible to provide services of a skilled survey officer at present but that the Surveyor-General would communicate with Captain Strahan, at present employed to the south of Ajmer and see what could be done at close of the working season on his return via Agra. Colonel Pelly was, however, advised to consult Captain Strahan in this regard.[21]

Captain Strahan intimated to the Surveyor-General that he would either undertake the survey of the boundary himself or depute some well-qualified Assistant. Captain Strahan, however, pointed out that the building of pillars or determining sites for them was not the work of his department. He accordingly suggested that information might be sent to him when the pillars were built and thereafter he would send an officer for mapping them. It was also necessary, he added, that this work should be taken in hand in time to complete it before the return of the party to Simla, otherwise some of the valuable spring months would be lost for the prosecution of the survey there.[22]

The Agriculture, Revenue and Commerce Department requested the Surveyor-General to point out to Captain Strahan "that the demarcation of this boundary is of more importance than the survey of Simla, and that the requirement of the latter must entirely give place to those of the former." The Surveyor-General directed Captain Strahan to communicate with the Political Officers concerned, so that the work might be carried out to the best advantage before the close of the present field season.[23]

It may be mentioned that Captain Abbott when settling the boundary in question had erected 'cutcha' pillars which were destroyed soon afterwards. Hence the necessity arose for redemarcation of pillars. The boundary determined on was shown in the maps submitted by Agent to Governor-General for Rajputana, which were with the Surveyor-General. These maps showed the sites fixed for boundary pillars.

Accordingly Lieutenant Yate was asked to proceed to Jaipur and Alwar boundary in order to erect pillars on the demarcating lines laid down by Captain Abbott. The representatives of both Jaipur and Alwar were present on the arrival of Yate at the frontier. The pillars were erected in their presence. It was hoped that the vexed question of Jaipur-Alwar boundary would then be laid at rest.[24]

Certain disputes arose regarding the erection of pillars on the borders of Alwar and Jaipur which called for settlement. Three such disputes were reported by the Political Agent, Alwar to Agent to Governor-General, Rajputana :[25]

(1) The first dispute pertained to *pargana* Thanaghazi in Alwar which had been pending since 20 November 1882. It was about the construction of a pillar on the Hisla Hill. The Alwar Darbar stated that where Jaipur wanted a pillar to build, one did not exist there before; while the Jaipur Darbar asserted that one had been erected according to the boundary laid by Captain Abbott but had been destroyed shortly after. In August 1883 officials of both sides met, but without

result. In 1885 it was decided to let the matter stand over till the slabs which were being substituted for the masonry pillars on the border were erected. Since then the Jaipur Darbar had intimated their wish that the case should be made over for sttlement to a boundary officer when appointed.

(2) The second dispute was regarding pillars on the border between Lotiàwas (Alwar) and Gudha and Maingi (Jaipur) which had been pending since May 1882. There were four broken pillars the erection of which was desired by the Alwar Darbar in accordance with the boundary map and also the removal of a pillar which, it was stated, the Jaipur people had built on a spot where one did not exist before. To fix the site of the broken pillars officials of both sides met repeatedly but failed to come to settlement. The Jaipur Darbar demanded that as there was no prospect of the case being settled mutually, it should be made over to a boundary officer.

(3) The third dispute was about the pillars on the border between Kaler (Alwar) and Barkheri (Jaipur) which had been pending since March 1887. There were eight pillars on this border which were said to have been destroyed. In May 1888 the officials of both the States met and lines were drawn which showed Alwar at 13° 15′ and Jaipur at 13° 0′. After some negotiations it was agreed to fix the boundary at 13° 7½′ and the pillars were built accordingly. In July 1890 the Jaipur Darbar complained that it had been found that the pillars had been built at 18° 45′ instead of 13° 7½′, thereby causing a loss to Jaipur of 22 bighas 10 biswas, besides about 6750 feet in dispute. As the Alwar Darbar objected to reopen the case, the Jaipur Darbar represented that it should be made over to a boundary officer.

Lieutenant-Colonel (previously Captain) H.B. Abbott, Political Agent in response to communication from the Agent to Governor-General, Rajputana suggested that the aforesaid disputes should be settled either by the Resident, Jaipur or by himself (Abbott). He pointed out that he was the officer who originally demarcated this portion of the Alwar border and that the disputes were chiefly concerned with the interpretation of the maps.[26] His letter was forwarded to the Government of India in response to which the latter ordered that the Political Agent at Alwar (Lieutenant-Colonel Abbott) be instructed to settle these disputes as soon as possible.[27]

III

The border disputes between the States of Jaipur and Patiala were not infrequent. To be sure, the Maharaja of Patiala, for his meritorious services to the British Government during the revolt of 1857-58, had been granted as a reward, *inter alia*, the Narnaul division of the confiscated Jhajjar territory in the south-east of the Punjab in perpetuity.[28] The Maharaja did not realise at that time that this additional territory granted to him would cause additional trouble and burden for him, because he would have to take necessary measures for maintaining peace and order in the area inhabited largely by turbulent Muhammadan population. Not only that, the Narnaul territory being contiguous to the Rajputana States of Jaipur and Alwar, the border offences occurred very frequently. It may be observed in this connection that there were criminal tribes like the Meenas in the Jaipur State who would cross the border and freely indulge in loot and plunder. Likewise the inhabitants of Narnaul would also cause disturbances in the Jaipur territory. In the absence of any agreement regarding extradition of criminals between the two States differences and disputes were likely to arise between the governments of these States and the border crimes were likely to increase with the passage of time.

In 1862 a code of criminal rules was drawn by the Maharaja of Patiala which provided for absolute reciprocity in the matter of surrender and trial of the offenders. A list of 30 specified crimes was attached to the rules, on account of which the persons accused were liable to be surrendered. The Maharaja of Jaipur agreed to accept the rules with some modifications. He, however, insisted that whatever code might be adopted, the representation of a Patiala *Vakil* in the Court of Vakils at Jaipur was necessary.[29] The Maharaja of Patiala showed willingness to accept the proposed modifications in the rules, but he said that he would send his *Vakil* to the Political Agent at Jaipur only on the condition that the Maharaja of Jaipur should send his *Vakil* to the Agent to Lieutenant-Governor, Cis-Sutlej States at Ambala. At the same time he opined that the Political Agent, Jaipur could well settle certain cases without the intervention of any *Vakil* and he could refer some cases to the Agent to Cis-Sutlej States, Ambala. The Patiala Chief also forwarded to Political Agent, Jaipur 138 cases connected with Narnaul-Jaipur which called for settlement.[30] The Maharaja of Jaipur was reluctant to send his *Vakil* to Ambala. He pointed out that in 19 cases out of 20, Patiala subjects were plaintiffs and Jaipur subjects defendants, and that the people of Narnaul for generations had been accustomed to come to Jaipur but the Jaipur people had never gone so far north as Ambala. The Political Agent, Jaipur offered certain propositions which were acceptable to the Jaipur Maharaja and they were assented to by the Maharaja. Consequently an agreement was concluded between the two Darbars which provided :[31]

(1) That all petty cases involving tracks of cattle, petty burglaries, etc. were to be settled by the Political Agent, Jaipur in communication with the Nazim of Narnaul.

(2) That in case of difficulty in the appearance of Patiala defendants at Jaipur, the decision was to be deferred till the Political Agent, Jaipur or Agent, Cis-Sutlej States could visit the border.

(3) That all cases involving claims of above rupees 500 but below rupees 2000 in which the Patiala subjects were defendants, would be prepared at Jaipur but would also be referred to Agent, Cis-Sutlej States for concurrent decision and all cases above rupees 2000 were to be tried and decided at Ambala.

(4) That the Maharaja of Patiala had full power to require

any case, in which his subjects were defendants, to be decided at Ambala.

(5) That all the decisions were to be given in conformity with the provisions of the agreement entered into between the two Darbars.

The Rajas of Jind and Nabha also accepted the rules as were agreed upon between the Patiala and Jaipur Darbars.[32]

The difference of race, habits and customs, and the jealousy existing between the Sikh and the Rajput States was so great that the rules agreed upon could not be properly enforced. The Maharaja of Jaipur particularly showed little willingness to enforce the rules. The result was that the borders of Patiala were exposed to the ravages of robbers from Jaipur State and as the subjects of Patiala were generally unarmed they were unable to defend themselves. In 1871, no less than 363 border cases were pending. In September 1872, therefore, the Maharaja of Patiala represented to the Punjab Government that for the last four years the Patiala officials of the Mohindergarh and Narnaul Nizamats experienced great difficulties in the settlement of disputes which arose between those subjects of the Patiala and Jaipur States whose village boundaries adjoined. The Government more than once invited the attention of the Jaipur Darbar to the terms of the agreement of 1862 entered into between Jaipur and Patiala. Although Agent to the Governor-General, Rajputana promised on the part of that Darbar in his letter No. 212 P., dated 5 May 1871 to the Secretary to the Government of India in the Foreign Department, that the provisions of the agreement would be observed, but no action had been taken in this regard. He pointed out with regret that no effect had been produced from the long correspondence held in this matter between the Government of the Punjab, the Political Agent of Jaipur, the Governor-General's Agent for Rajputana and the Supreme Government. References had been made several times to the Government on this subject through the Patiala *Motamid*, Syed Muhammad Ali but the state of border cases was getting worse day by day. He requested that the Jaipur authorities might be induced to fully observe the terms of the agreement referred to.[33]

The Jaipur Darbar desired to amend the rules of 1862. In a communication to the Officiating Agent to Governor-General, Rajputana, Captain E.R.C. Bradford, Officiating Political Agent, Jaipur forwarded a *Kyfeeut* from the Jaipur Darbar with his remarks. The *Kyfeeut* from the Jaipur Darbar dated 24 June 1871, suggested modification of the agreement of 1862 on two principal points : first, that for the mutual surrender of fugitive criminals on the requisition of either of the contracting parties, *prima facie* proof of the refugees' criminality be furnished by the Darbar making the requisition; and second, that the State, in which the *khoj* was ultimately abandoned should be held liable in all cases in which the stolen property or any portion of it might be discovered in that State or in which the criminals might be proved to reside but under all other circumstances the State in which the offence was committed should be held responsible.[34] The Agent to Governor-General, Rajputana forwarded Jaipur Agent's letter along with a copy of the *Kyfeeut* from the Jaipur Darbar to the Punjab Government with the hope that the modifications suggested in the rules of 1862 would be concurred in by the Maharaja of Patiala.[35]

In the last week of September 1872, Major W.H. Beynon, Political Agent, Jaipur wrote a letter to the Officiating Secretary to Government Punjab intimating that he had been furnished by the Jaipur Darbar a statement which showed that as many as 363 cases including both Jaipur and Narnaul, had been unsettled as on 31 December 1871. He informed that he proposed to visit the border during his coming cold weather tour and would dispose of as many of the unsettled cases as possible for which he had sought cordial co-operation of both the parties. He requested that if his proposal met with the approval of the Lieutenant-Governor of Punjab, the Nazim of Narnaul might be directed to exert himself for the fulfilment of the desired object.[36]

Early in November 1872, Lepel Griffin, Officiating Secretary to Government of Punjab, forwarded the letter of the Maharaja of Patiala as well as that of the Political Agent, Jaipur with the comments of the Lieutenant-Governor of Punjab. The Maharaja of Patiala had pointed out that although the enforcement of the rules of 1862 had been approved by the Lieutenant-Governor as well as the Political Agent, little action had yet been taken in the matter by the Jaipur authorities, that the state of the border had become worse and that it was now more imperative than ever to take action for the enforcement of the rules. The Lieutenant-Governor opined that the representation of the Maharaja deserved every consideration. For his border was entirely exposed to the ravages of robbers from Rajputana States and as his subjects were unarmed, they were unable to defend themselves. The Political Agent at Jaipur had expressed his intention of visiting the border during the ensuing cold weather and endeavouring to settle the cases which had long been pending there and which were numerous. The Lieutenant-Governor expressed his conviction of the benefit which would result from this action on the part of the Political Agent and the Maharaja of Patiala had been asked to give the Political Agent of Jaipur every assistance in the disposal of the cases in question.[37]

On receiving the aforesaid letters the Governor-General in Council opined that the state of the Jaipur-Patiala border was 'most unsatisfactory' and that it was absolutely essential that some means should be devised for putting a stop to so serious an evil. The Agent to Governor-General, Rajputana was authorised to enter into direct communication with the Punjab Government and if necessary, Major Beynon (Political Agent, Jaipur) might be sent to Lahore to confer with the Punjab Government on the subject and submit some definite scheme for the consideration of the Governor-General in Council. The most satisfactory arrangement would be the adoption of the rules of 1862 as proposed by the Maharaja of Patiala, and in the main agreed to by the Maharaja of Jaipur. The Supreme Government directed that both the parties might be urged to select specially good men as frontier Nazims, and each might appoint an agent to the Nazim's Court of the other, the joint order of the Nazim and agent for the surrender of offenders or the execution of orders for compensation being considered absolutely binding on the other State concerned.[38]

In January 1873, Agent to the Governor-General

forwarded a letter addressed by the Political Agent, Jaipur to the Punjab Government on 13 January 1873 relating to settlement of border criminal cases between Jaipur and Narnaul. It was stated that the work had by mutual consent been entrusted to a Panchayat of officers equally represented from both sides... one of the conditions being that all such cases as it might not be found either competent or practicable to dispose of were to be submitted for the Agent's orders and decisions which were to be final. From the daily reports which Lieutenant-Colonel Beynon (Political Agent, Jaipur) continued to receive, the Panchayats appeared to be making satisfactory progress. The Political Agent promised to submit a full report in this regard later on.[39] The Secretary, Punjab Government forwarded a copy of letter addressed by him to the Agent to Governor-General Rajputana on 25 January 1873. It was pointed out in this letter that the Patiala Darbar had great disinclination to accept the proposals of the Jaipur Darbar which related to partial modification of Track Rules of 1862. The Lieutenant-Governor of Punjab proposed to depute Lepel Griffin with agents of the Patiala State possessing full powers to decide the question, to meet the Political Agent, Jaipur with agents accredited in like manner by the Maharaja of Jaipur.[40] The Government of India approved of the course of action suggested by the Punjab Government which was in accordance with the instructions already issued by the Governor-General in Council. A copy of the letter was sent to Colonel Brooke, Agent to Governor-General, Rajputana for information with a request that the necessary instructions might be communicated to the Political Agent, Jaipur.[41]

In June 1873, Secretary to Lieutenant-Governor Punjab forwarded a letter dated 3 June 1873 of the *Motamid* of the Maharaja of Patiala to the Government of India. The *Motamid* stated in his letter that regular settlement was in progress in Narnaul district of the Patiala territory. There were, however, several villages bordering on Jaipur territory, including Khetri, in which the boundary was disputed. There was no hope that the Jaipur Darbar would take steps for the settlement of these disputes, and unless they were settled, settlement could not be finalised. He requested that under the existing circumstances a European officer might kindly be deputed to settle the border dispute. He sought the orders of the Government of India regarding the deputation of an officer by the Lieutenant-Governor to settle the border disputes referred to between the States of Patiala and Jaipur.[42]

The Agent to Governor-General was asked to report the wishes of the Jaipur Darbar regarding the deputation of a European officer to settle the border disputes. The Jaipur Darbar entirely acquiesced and wished an officer of the Rajputana Agency to be deputed for the purpose. Accordingly Agent to Governor-General, Rajputana was requested to depute an officer to settle the said border dispute in communication with the Punjab Government.[43] In reply the Agent to Governor-General stated that no officer was available for the settlement of these disputes and accordingly requested the early orders of the Government as to the course to be pursued to prevent the present season being lost.[44] The Government of India, thereupon addressed the Government of Punjab to the effect that since the Agent to Governor-General, Rajputana had no officer available for the settlement of these disputes, the Lieutenant-Governor of Punjab be requested to depute an officer for this duty as originally proposed by him.[45]

The Lieutenant-Governor of Punjab deputed Lieutenant C.F. Massy, an Assistant Commissioner, to settle the border disputes between the Jaipur and Patiala States. Massy commenced his work in 1874 on his return to Narnaul. Subeg Singh was deputed to represent interests of the Jaipur State. Massy had initially a little trouble with semi-independent *Thakurs* of the border areas but he carried on the work almost smoothly. Later on he was joined by Captain Burton, Assistant Political Agent deputed by Sir Lewis Pelly, to represent Jaipur during demarcation of border. Bulk of the work had already been completed before his arrival, save two large disputes which were settled in his presence. The interests of Patiala were carefully guarded by the Nazim of Narnaul Syed Aoolad Ali, the Naib-Nazim Bishambar Das, the Settlement Officer Maulvi Ali Ahmad and his assistant Kishan Dass. From its tri-junction with the Loharu State, the Jaipur-Patiala border was of total 124 miles in length. The Shekhawati Nizamat bordered on northern half while Torawati ran along southern line. There were few Jaipur villages which comprised of *Khalsa* lands (paying revenue to the State) but most of them had been merged in the large *jagir* holdings. The subjects of Jaipur were permitted to carry arms which gave them a considerable advantage over their Patiala neighbours who were unarmed.

It was considered essential first to build boundary pillars which were at length all erected and line reported ready for surveyor, except at 24 points where border was in dispute. Massy claimed that he worked throughout with the object of promoting friendly feelings among villagers on border, thus removing as far as possible the ill-blood invariably engendered by land-quarrels. He encouraged the parties concerned to settle matters amicably, and only when they failed he officially intervened. In many such matters fines were imposed on offenders which were recovered and handed over to the aggrieved party as soon as possible. Massy believed that the infliction of fines would have a good effect, as the news would spread rapidly over the border, and villagers would thus practically learn that a pillar was not to be thrown down with impunity. According to Massy, Jaipur State deserved to be congratulated on having very turbulent portion of border of 124 miles in length settled once for all.[46] Massy also settled the disputed cases between the borders of Patiala and Alwar (29 miles in length). It was decided that the States concerned should share proportionately the cost of the demarcation.

On 16 June 1874 a complaint was received from the Narnaul authorities that seven out of the twelve pillars erected on the border by Lieutenant Massy had been destroyed by the Jaipur people. The Jaipur Darbar was informed about this and requested to take measures for punishing the offenders and securing the future presentation of the boundary marks. The Jaipur Darbar, in reply, asserted the innocence of its subjects and blamed the Patiala party, observing that it had been ascertained from the *Thanadar* of Pucheyree, the official appointed by the Darbar to see that its instructions for the due care of the pillars were carried out, that on it being brought to his notice that two of the marks had been destroyed he went to the spot and succeeded in clearly tracing the offenders to the Narnaul village of Muhammadpur. One or two subsequent communications passed between the Jaipur Darbar and Narnaul authorities, but without eliciting any further definite particulars. In August 1874 a *Chaprasi* was deputed from the Jaipur Agency to see to the immediate repair and re-construction of such pillars as might have been either injured or thrown down on the border line demarcated by Lieutenant Massy. The *Chaprasi* sent a report to the effect that those pillars said to have been destroyed on the border in question had all been replaced under arrangements made in communication with the representatives of both the Darbars. While forwarding a copy of this letter from the Political Agent, Jaipur to the Secretary to Government Punjab, the Agent to Governor-General, Rajputana suggested the necessity of making some rule by which all the villages interested in a boundary mark set up between Native States by the Boundary Settlement Officer should be liable to a penalty in the event of its destruction.[47]

Accepting the suggestion of the Agent to Governor-General, Rajputana, the Lieutenant-Governor of Punjab proposed that Lieutenant Massy might be invested with power to draw up rules for the preservation of boundary pillars as well as with power to discuss and arrange with the representatives of the States concerned the proposed amendments of the extradition and tract rules.[48] In reply to this communication, the Government of India forwarded an extract from the new boundary rules which had been considered suitable for Rajputana and enquired whether the Punjab Government agreed to these rules.[49] The latter replied in affirmative.

There remains to be considered the extradition rules between the two States established at the initiative of the British authorities so as to mitigate the possibility of such disputes.

IV

In March 1873, a meeting took place at Lahore between Lieutenant-Colonel W.H. Beynon, Political Agent at Jaipur and Lepel Griffin, representing the Punjab Government. The two officers, in communication with the representatives from the States concerned, drew up some rules for the pursuit, arrest and extradition of offenders, which were accepted by the two Darbars and sanctioned by the Government of India in the Foreign Department letter No. 1432 P., dated July 1, 1873. A schedule of 23 crimes was appended to the rules, on account of which extradition might be demanded. The main provision were to the effect that whenever any inhabitant of one State committed any crime in the territory of another State and was arrested in that territory, he would be amenable to the courts of that State in the territory of which he was arrested; that whenever any resident of one State after committing crime in the territory of the other State escaped to his own State, he would, without objection or proof demanded of his guilt, be surrendered to the court of that State where he committed crime on the requisition of the authorities of that State. These rules evidently did not require any *prima facie* case to be established against the accused before his surrender, as had been proposed by the Maharaja of Jaipur. In all the cases connected with the crimes specified in the schedule, the Judicial Officer of either State passing the order was to send a copy of his decision to the Darbar of the other State. It was further provided that if at any time the police officers of one State happened to go into the other State in pursuit of a track, the police and other functionaries of the latter State would be bound to assist the tracking party in following up the track and in the recovery of the stolen property and arrest of the offenders.[50]

While giving their sanction to the rules, the Government of India directed the Punjab Government that steps should be taken to procure the acceptance of these rules by the States of Jind, Nabha, Loharu and Alwar. The Agent to Governor-General, Rajputana was also asked to procure the agreement of the Alwar State, and to request the Jaipur Darbar to give its recognition to the rules in respect of Jind, Nabha and Loharu. The Chief of Alwar proposed certain amendments and the Jaipur Darbar had apparently not yet agreed to the extension of rules to Jind, Nabha and Loharu. The Lieutenant-Governor of Punjab suggested that in order to avoid delay, Lieutenant Massy, who was to settle the border disputes between Patiala and Alwar, should be entrusted with the duty of obtaining a definite settlement of the rules between the Rajputana and Punjab States. In his letter dated 15 January 1875, the Officiating Agent to Governor-General, Rajputana reported that the Chief of Alwar had now withdrawn the proposed amendment in the 'Code of International Procedure' between Jaipur and Patiala and agreed to adopt it in respect of Patiala and other Punjab States.[51]

The Jaipur Darbar, however, refused to accept as between that State and Jind, Nabha and Loharu the extradition rules already in force between the Jaipur and the Patiala States.[52] The main ground of its objection was the unsatisfactory working of the rules and the consequent reluctance of the Darbar to enlarge their scope. In 1882, the Punjab Government proposed that it was 'most desirable' that the rules should now be declared to be in force between Jaipur, Jind, Nabha and Loharu. The Jaipur Darbar expressed willingness to accept the proposal of the Punjab Government but suggested two amendments regarding (a) the establishment of *prima facie* evidence of criminality before the surrender of an offender, and (b) liability of the police of the concerned State to punishment for culpable negligence in the matter of the tracking rules.[53] These amendments were considered but they were not adopted. It, however, appears from a Punjab report of 1884 that the Jaipur-Patiala extradition rules had been accepted as between Jaipur and the States of Jind, Nabha and Loharu.[54]

Meanwhile in 1883 rules for facilitating the extradition of criminals between Jaipur on the one side and Bharatpur and Karauli on the other, were framed and sanctioned for one year in the first instance. These rules provided :[55]

1. When any resident of Jaipur committed a crime specified in the schedule attached to these rules and

was arrested in Bharatpur/ Karauli territory, he would be tried by Bharatpur/Karauli courts.

2. When a resident of Bharatpur/Karauli or a Jaipur subject committed in Jaipur territory any of the scheduled offences and escaped into Bharatpur/ Karauli, the *Tahsildar* of the district in which the offence was committed should send a requisition for his surrender to the *Tahsildar* of the Bharatpur/ Karauli district in which he was supposed to be connected. If the man could not be found, the *Tahsildar* might send a person to point him out.

   On the other hand, the *Tahsildar* should at once comply, without excuse or waiting for any proof of guilt, with any such requisition received from a Bharatpur/Karauli *Tahsildar* for the surrender of a resident of Jaipur or a Bharatpur/Karauli subject supposed to be concealed in his district, and he should give every assistance to any person sent by the Bharatpur/Karauli officials to point out the offender.
3. When the hiding place in Jaipur territory of a resident of Jaipur or Bharatpur/Karauli, either of whom was charged with the commission in Bharatpur/Karauli of any of the scheduled offences, had been ascertained, an application by the Bharatpur/Karauli authorities for his arrest should at once be complied with, or if the Bharatpur/Karauli *Tahsildar* or *Thanadar*, accompanied by not more than four followers, desired to make the arrest himself, it would be the duty of the *Tahsildar* or *Thanadar* to go with and assist him, but he would retain custody of the offender pending the receipt of a formal requisition to the Darbar for his surrender. This procedure would be followed in cases of stolen property, but the property would not be made over without a formal requisition.
4. Copies of decisions passed by the Jaipur officials on cases coming under the rules must be sent to the Bharatpur/ Karauli officials of corresponding status. If the decision was passed by the Adalt or Superior

Court, it would be communicated to the Bharatpur/ Karauli Darbar, in accordance with the present custom, through the Agency. No person surrendered would be detained for more than two months : if for any reason a case affecting a Bharatpur/ Karauli subject could not be disposed of in two months, he would be released on security, or if he could not give security, he would be sent back to the Bharatpur/ Karauli authorities to be dealt with as they thought proper.

5. Orders of a Bharatpur/Karauli Court regarding attendance of witnesses etc., received by any *Tahsildar* through a Bharatpur/ Karauli *Tahsildar*, should be complied with within one month from the date of the receipt of the order. Witnesses sent by a Bharatpur/ Karauli *Tahsildar* were to be permitted to depart as soon as their evidence had been taken, and care was to be taken that they were not unnecessarily detained.
6. When Bharatpur/Karauli officials brought a track into Jaipur territory and desired that the place where it terminated should be searched, the Jaipur officials must comply with their request and search the place. In the event of stolen property being found, compensation for the whole or a part of it would be given from the place where the track ended : any disputes regarding the finding of property would be settled by the Court within whose jurisdiction the offence was committed.
7. *Tahsildars* must arrange that no Minas entered Bharatpur/ Karauli territory without a pass. If a Bharatpur/Karauli Mina was arrested in Jaipur without a ticket, the *Tahsildar* would forward him with a written paper to the Bharatpur/Karauli *Tahsildar* of the place where he lived. If a Jaipur Mina arrested without a ticket was forwarded by the Bharatpur/ Karauli authorities and the *Tahsildar* considered him a bad character, he would have him punished, but if he was a Mina of the cultivating class and had merely

gone to Bharatpur/Karauli without a pass through ignorance of the rules, a warning would be sufficient for the first offence.

8. If any *Tahsildar* or *Thanadar* was negligent, or evaded his duty in sending criminals applied for by the Bharatpur/Karauli authorities, serious notice would be taken of his conduct.
9. If by chance any criminal escaped or was in hiding, the *Tahsildar* of the district must make every effort to effect his capture.
10. The *Tahsildar* must take recognizances in a sum of rupees 200 from the villages on the border, to the effect that if they entered into any dispute or fight with the Bharatpur/Karauli villages across the border, they would forfeit to the State the amounts of their recognizances, in addition to any punishment awarded in the case.

Twenty-four crimes were specified on account of which extradition might be demanded. These crimes were the following :

(1) Murder of all kinds. (2) *Dakoiti.* (3) Highway robbery. (4) Burglary. (5) Buying or receiving stolen property. (6) Cattle-theft. (7) Thefts above Rs. 25 in value. (8) *Thagi.* (9) Serious affray, with wounded or other aggravated circumstances. (10) Serious assault, with wounded or other aggravated circumstances. (11) Arson. (12) Forgery. (13) Making counterfeit coin. (14) Rape. (15) Kine-killing. (16) Kidnapping. (17) Administering intoxicating drugs. (18) Cutting or maiming. (19) Aiding or abetting *sati.* (20) Aiding and abetting in suicide. (21) Sedition. (22) Escape from jail or lawful custody. (23) Traffic in slaves. (24) Criminal misappropriation by a servant, except as regards offences by *Lambardars* or *Zamindars* connected with their position as payees of revenue, or village revenue collectors.[56]

From what has been discussed above, it is evident that the extradition rules framed between Jaipur and other Rajputana States and between the Rajputana States and the neighbouring Punjab States (Patiala, Jind, Nabha and Loharu), were based upon the principle of absolute reciprocity. The British authorities did not enforce these rules in accordance with the provisions of the Extradition Act nor by unilateral circulars or orders issued by them, as was done in the case of extradition rules between British India and Native India. On the other hand, these rules were framed in consultation with, and with the consent of, the Darbars concerned. The British Government, no doubt, played an important role in the finalisation of these rules, and subsequently in their enforcement. It is significant to observe that the Imperial Government asserted the principle that all these extradition rules between the various States were sanctioned as arrangements concluded by the British Government with the States, not as agreements mutually concluded between the States[57], and the Supreme Government also took upon itself the responsibility of enforcing these rules.

The British authorities took another significant step to decide the border criminal cases among the Rajputana States. As early as 1840s they instituted five 'International Courts of Vakils' — (i) The Ajmer Court (1842) which dealt with the cases between the States of Kishangarh and Dholpur and the British province of Ajmer. (ii) The Neemuch Court (1842) which decided the cases between the States of Udaipur, Banswara, Dungarpur and Partabgarh. (iii) The Harauti Court (1847) at Kota which exercised jurisdiction over the States of Kota, Bundi and Jhalawar. (iv) The Jaipur Court (1847) which decided the cases between the States of Jaipur, Bharatpur, Tonk and Alwar. (v) The Jodhpur Court which had jurisdiction over the States of Jodhpur, Bikaner, Jaisalmer and Sirohi. The *Vakils* constituting the Courts represented their respective States which were presided over by the Political Agents concerned. These Courts decided 'international' criminal cases arising on the borders of the States concerned. Appeals as well as the decisions of the Court went to the Ajmer Court which was presided over by the Agent to Governor-General, Rajputana or his Assistant. All the cases decided by these courts were recorded and reported regularly year after year.[58]

The British authorities apparently had no direct interest in the matter of border disputes which was the mutual concern of the said States. Their action may, therefore, be explained in terms of their obligation, as well as their right, as a Paramount Power, to maintain peace and order on the borders of the States and to remove the cause of border crimes and border disputes as far as possible.

References and Notes

1. Capt. J. Blair, Offg. Political Agent, Jaipur to Lieut.-Col. R.H. Keatinge, AGG, No. 138, dated 8 Oct. 1869.
2. Lieut.-Col. R.H. Keatinge, AGG, to Capt. E.R.C. Bradford, Offg. Political Agent, Jaipur, No. 1027 G., dated 3 Nov. 1869.
3. Capt. P.W. Powlett, Offg. Political Agent, Eastern States, Rajputana, to Capt. E.R.C. Bradford, Offg. Political Agent, Jaipur, No. 25-12 A, dated 25 Jan. 1871.
4. Capt. Bradford, Political Agent, Jaipur, to Capt. Powlett, Political Agent, Eastern States, Rajputana, No. 250, dated 11 April 1871 and No. 530, dated 19 June 1871.
5. Capt. Powlett, Political Agent, Eastern States, Rajputana, to Capt. Bradford, Political Agent, Jaipur, No. 274, dated 24 June 1871.
6. Capt. E.R.C. Bradford, Political Agent, Jaipur, to Col. J.C. Brooke, Offg. AGG, No. 7-5 G.A., dated 17 July 1871.
7. Col. J.C. Brooke, Offg. AGG, to C.U. Aitchison, Secretary, GOI, Foreign Dept., No. 1384 G., dated 21 Aug. 1871, FD, Political B, Nov. 1871, No. 8.
8. AGG to GOI, No. 371, dated 29 May 1872, FD, Political B, June 1872, No. 323 ; Political Agent, Jaipur to AGG, No. 80/58, dated 20 May 1872, *ibid.*, No. 324.
9. *Infra*, pp. 161-64.
10. RPARS for 1896-97, para 15, p. 40.
11. K.W., FD, Political A, Feb. 1874, Nos. 321-331, pp. 1-2.
12. Col. Brooke, AGG to GOI, No. 841G., dated 14 June 1873, FD, Political A, Feb. 1874, No. 321 and Encls., Nos. 322-323.
13. Col. Pelly, AGG to GOI, No. 2063G., dated 21 Nov. 1873, FD, Political A, Feb. 1874, No. 324.
14. AGG to GOI, No. 772P., dated 22 Nov. 1873, FD, Political A, Feb. 1874, No. 325.
15. Secretary, Govt. of India, Foreign Dept. to Surveyor-General, No. 202P., dated 20 Jan. 1874, FD, Political A, Feb. 1874, No. 326.
16. GOI to AGG, No. 203P., dated 20 Jan. 1874, FD, Political A, Feb. 1874, No. 327.

17. *Ibid.*
18. AGG to GOI, No. 773P., dated 23 Nov. 1873, FD, Political A, Feb. 1874, No. 328.
19. GOI to AGG, No. 205, dated 20 Jan. 1874, FD, Political A, Feb. 1874, No. 329.
20. Telegram from Col. Pelly of 25 Jan. 1874 to Secretary to Govt. of India, FD, Political A, Feb. 1874, No. 330.
21. GOI to AGG, No. 541P., dated 27 Feb. 1874, FD, Political A, Feb. 1874, No. 331.
22. Officer in Charge Rajputana Survey (Strahan) to Surveyor-General of India, No. 7, dated 19 Feb. 1874, FD, Political A, April 1874, No. 161.
23. Surveyor-General of India to Secretary to Govt. of India, R.A.C. Dept., No. 401, dated 27 Feb. 1874 and from Under-Secretary, Govt. of India, R.A.C. Dept. to Surveyor-General of India, No. 143, dated 9 March 1874. See FD, Political A, April 1874, No. 161, also K.W. of this Proceedings.
24. FD, Political B, October 1874, No. 138.
25. Col. Muir, Political Agent, Alwar to AGG, No. 1048-G, dated 16 Dec. 1890 and Encl., FD, Internal A, March 1891, Nos. 315-316.
26. Lieut.-Col. H. B. Abbott, Political Agent, Alwar to AGG, No. 144, dated 16 Feb. 1891, FD, Internal A, March 1891, No. 319.
27. Col. G.H. Trevor, AGG to GOI, No. 369-C., dated 22 Feb. 1891 and GOI to AGG, No. 1143-I, dated 12 March 1891, FD, Internal A, March 1891, Nos. 318, 320.
28. FD, Political Progs..,2 July 1858, Nos. 187-188 ; Lepel H. Griffin, *The Rajas of the Punjab* (Reprint Patiala, 1970), p. 218.
29. FD, Part A, Sept. 1861, Nos. 365-366.
30. FD, Political A, Aug. 1862, Nos. 16-18.
31. FD, Political A, Oct. 1862, Nos. 58-60 ; also see A.C. Arora, *British Policy towards the Punjab States* 1858-1905 (Jalandhar, 1982), pp. 240-41.
32. In 1863, the States of Patiala, Jaipur, Alwar and Bharatpur adopted with respect to each other the code of international rules already operating between Jaipur and the Sikh States of Patiala, Jind and Nabha, with the approval of the Government of India. Vide FD, Political A, Oct. 1863, Nos. 71-74.
33. Maharaja of Patiala to Offg. Secretary to Government, Punjab, dated 16 Sept. 1872, FD, Political A, Dec. 1872, No. 514.
34. Political Agent, Jaipur to AGG, No. 19-7 J A, dated 29 July 1871 ; *Kyfeeut* from the Jaipur Darbar to Political Agent, Jaipur, dated 24 June 1871, FD, Political A, Dec. 1872, No. 516.

35. AGG to Punjab Government, No. 2681, dated 24 Aug. 1871, FD, Political A, Dec. 1872, No. 515.
36. Political Agent, Jaipur to Punjab Government, No. 584, dated 27 Sept. 1872, FD, Political A, Dec. 1872, No. 517.
37. Punjab Government to GOI, No. 1428, dated 8 Nov. 1872, FD, Political A, Dec. 1872, No. 513.
38. GOI to AGG, No. 2438 P., dated 30 Dec. 1872, FD, Political A, Dec. 1872, No. 518.
39. FD, Political A, Feb. 1873, Nos. 260-262.
40. FD, Political A, Feb. 1873, Nos. 263-264.
41. GOI to Punjab Government, No. 336 P., dated 17 Feb. 1873 and to AGG, No. 337 P., FD, Political A, Feb. 1873, No. 265.
42. Punjab Government to GOI, No. 789, dated 19 June, 1873, FD, Political A, July 1873, No. 463 and enclosure, No. 464.
43. FD, Political A, Oct. 1873, Nos. 426-428.
44. AGG to GOI, No. 1098, dated 23 Jan. 1874, FD, Political B, Feb. 1874, No. 34.
45. GOI to Punjab Government, No. 328 P/329 P, dated 4 Feb. 1874, FD, Political B, Feb. 1874, No. 35.
46. K.W. FD, Political B, May 1875, Nos. 136-139.
47. Lieut.-Col. W.H. Beynon, Political Agent, Jaipur to AGG, No. 222-188 G., dated 22 Oct. 1874 and AGG to Punjab Government, No. 4332-3204 G., dated 20 Nov. 1874, FD, Political A, Feb. 1875, No. 90 and its Encl.
48. Punjab Government to GOI, No. 2062, dated 10 Dec. 1874, FD, Political A, Feb. 1875, No. 89.
49. GOI to Punjab Government, No. 355P., dated 3 Feb. 1875, FD, Political A, Feb. 1875, No. 91.
50. FD, Political A, July 1873, Nos. 59-64; also C.L. Tupper, Comp., *Indian Political Practice, Vol. III* (Calcutta, 1895), para 576, p. 95.
51. K.W., FD, Political A, Feb. 1875, Nos. 208-217.
52. FD, Judicial B, Oct. 1875, Nos. 1-5.
53. K.W., FD, A - Political-I, Sept. 1882, Nos. 258-266.
54. Punjab Government to GOI, No. 189, dated 26 May 1884, cit. in Tupper, *op. cit.*, p. 95.
55. FD, A - Judicial-I, July 1883, Nos. 3-8.
56. FD, A - Judicial-I, July 1883, No. 6.
57. Tupper, *op. cit., Vol. I,* para 18, p. 21.
58. V.K. Vashishtha, *Rajputana Agency, 1832-1858* (Jaipur, 1978), pp. 228-29.

CHAPTER 6

Fiscal Matters

As a consequence of the revolt of 1857-58, the Government of India under the Crown was confronted with a financial crisis of great magnitude. It had inherited a huge debt caused due to enormous military operations conducted in suppressing the uprising. It has been estimated that the debt amounted to the sum of £ 71,200,000 in India and £ 26,600,000 in London.[1] Both short-term and long-term measures of varied kinds were envisaged by the Imperial Government for improving the financial condition as well as economic development of the country as a whole. All possible sources for the increase of revenues had to be tapped and all the obstacles that stood in the way had to be removed prudently. As numerous Princely States enjoyed the protection of the Paramount Power, their subordinate co-operation in the fiscal and economic matters was considered necessary. Some of the States were already bound by treaty obligations to pay annual tribute to the British Government or to render military assistance in one form or the other on the requisition of the latter. The British authorities had to impose additional obligations on the Princes and Chiefs in response to their fiscal requirements. For this purpose they concluded new agreements with several States but very often the Supreme Government passed resolutions or issued circulars unilaterally which were enforced in the States through the

British Political Agents or Residents. The fiscal obligations of the States pertained to matters like tribute, salt, opium, coinage, transit duties, etc.

I

Tributes from the Princely States to the Government of India were certainly of great significance as the best acknowledgement of the British paramountcy, but their importance as a source of revenue to British exchequer was also obvious. Being a recurring financial asset, tributes were to the Imperial Government an economic benefit in its most palpable form.[2] The tributes as a source of revenue could not be regarded as insignificant, for quite a large number of Princely States paid annual sums as tributes which together subscribed a considerable amount to the British Government's coffers.

It was laid down in Article 6 of the treaty of 1818 concluded between the British Government and the Jaipur State that the latter would pay annual tribute as follows in return for British protection : tribute was exempted for the first year (owing to devastation of the country); for second year after the date of treaty, 4 lakhs of Delhi rupees; for third year, 5 lakhs; for fourth year, 6 lakhs; for fifth year, seven lakhs; for every succeeding year, 8 lakhs but when the revenues of the principality exceeded 40 lakhs a year, it was required to pay into the British treasury five-sixteenth of the excess in addition to the above-mentioned 8 lakhs.[3] This term of the treaty was plainly unfair, and the considerable amount of tribute appears to have been fixed upon a wrong estimate of the State's income. The yearly instalment of tribute, even when regularly remitted, was not raised without difficulty. As the State became impoverished owing to mismanagement, arrears accumulated and it became evident that the State would neither be able to free itself from the debt which it had incurred nor fulfil for future the promise by which it had bound itself. The Jaipur government struggled on having recourse occasionally to bankers to meet its obligations, but the high rates of interest charged by the latter made the matters worse. In view of financial constraints and heavy tributary obligations of the State, the Maharani (Regent for her minor son Jai Singh III) envisaged a scheme of seizing money from all the subjects who possessed it whether they owed any debt to the State or not, but the British Political Agent, Captain Low refused to sanction this scheme. At this time the British authorities adopted a harsh attitude and the Political Agent gave a warning in August 1827 that if satisfactory arrangements for the payment of arrears of tribute were not made, some *parganas* of the *Khalsa* yielding the amount required would be brought under British management. Thereupon the Jaipur Darbar hastily raised loans and on 7 October 1827 fourteen *Hundies* amounting to eight lakhs of rupees were handed over to the Political Agent. In February 1828 the Maharani made a request to reduce the exorbitant amount of tribute to four lakhs of rupees which was rejected by the Political Agent.[4]

Major Thoresby who became Political Agent at Jaipur in August 1839 and was also the President of the Council of Regency (during the minority of Maharaja Ram Singh) took upon himself the task of improving the financial condition of the State. He felt concerned about "the colossal financial burden under which Jaipur was groaning". He realised that it was mainly due to the heavy tribute which the Jaipur Darbar had to pay to the British Government. During the first twenty years after signing the treaty of 1818 the State had deposited in the British treasury a 'staggering sum' of rupees 1,35,71,000. The taking over of the Sambhar Lake by the British Government in January 1835 had deprived the State of an annual income of about one and a half lakhs of rupees. The State had to incur annual recurring expenditure of about two and a half lakhs of rupees on the maintenance of Shekhawati Brigade. Besides all this, the State also owed heavy debt to bankers amounting to rupees one million or so for which interest amounting to rupees one lakh had to be paid annually. Thoresby took necessary measures to improve finances of the State. On his recommendation the Government of India reduced the amount of tribute of the Jaipur State from rupees eight lakhs to a fixed annual tribute of rupees four lakhs with retrospective effect from November 1, 1840 and also remitted the arrears of tribute amounting to rupees 46 lakhs of rupees. The management and revenues of Sambhar Lake were restored to the Jaipur Darbar.[5] At about this time Major Thoresby addressed a *Kharita* to the young Maharaja, dated 28 August 1842, informing him that the subject of tribute as provided in Article 6 of the treaty of 1818 was under consideration of the Government. But no action was taken in this regard till the end of the year 1870.

On attaining the age of eighteen years, Maharaja Ram Singh was invested with ruling powers in September 1851 and the Council of Regency was abolished. He proved himself an able administrator under the guidance of the British Political Agent. During the revolt of 1857-58 the Maharaja gave an ample proof of his loyalty by rendering meritorious services to the British Paramount which were highly appreciated and duly rewarded with the grant of a *pargana* of Kot Kasim. He continued to take measures for the improvement of administration with unabated zeal and fully cooperated with the British authorities in accepting the principles of their railway policy and readily entered into salt agreement in 1869 as desired by them. But the dread of enhanced tribute deterred the Maharaja from undertaking schemes of irrigation and other works of improvement. Though the annual tribute of the State had been reduced from 8 lakhs to 4 lakhs of rupees in 1842, yet the clause in Article 6 of the treaty of 1818 providing for enhancement of the tribute of 8 lakhs if the revenues exceeded 40 lakhs of rupees by 5/16 of the excess amount, still existed. The Maharaja desired that this obnoxious clause of the treaty should be abrogated.

In 1870, when Mayo was the Viceroy of India, the British Government which had been impressed with the steadfast loyalty and administrative ability of the Maharaja felt that the maintenance of this clause was leading to 'undesirable results'. It held out a direct inducement to the Jaipur Darbar to avoid measures for improving revenues of the State, to conceal from the Political Agent the true condition of its resources, to view with suspicion any enquiries that the British authorities might desire him to make, and to withhold from him the information which, for the interest of the State itself and of the Empire at large, it was desirable that he should possess. During the half a century that had elapsed since the conclusion of the treaty of 1818, the clause had remained a dead letter. After this long interval the Government of India assuredly would never be disposed to exercise the power it possessed under that clause, except in the event of some great political emergency, or as a punishment to the Jaipur State for some serious offence.[6]

Colonel Brooke, Officiating Agent to Governor-General, Rajputana in his communication to the Supreme Government stated that the demand of rupees 8 lakhs as annual tribute and its further enhancement in case of revenues of the State exceeding 40 lakhs by 5/16 of the excess amount, was too high a demand. The Government had been wrongly informed by Jhota Ram (who was a rival of the Rawal) that the annual revenues of the State varied from 60 to 80 lakhs of rupees as he wished to purchase British Government's support for himself. Captain Stewart, the first Political Agent at Jaipur, had also given wrong information to the effect that the State revenue in three years would reach rupees 60 lakhs but actually the State revenue never touched the figure of 40 lakhs and remained at the maximum amount of rupees 34 lakhs. He added that the State had "formerly suffered from evils of our interference on account of this very clause" and recommended that the question of abrogation of this clause should be favourably considered.[7] He forwarded the letter of Captain E.R.C. Bradford, Officiating Political Agent, Jaipur who remarked that though Article 6 of the treaty of 1818 had initially been cancelled, yet it might cause difficulty in future as there was no formal abrogation of the said Article. He opined that the cancellation of this clause of the treaty by the Government and an official intimation to this effect would give immense satisfaction to the Maharaja and the Jaipur Darbar.[8]

The Government of India accepted the recommendation of the Agent to Governor-General, Rajputana and sought the approval of Her Majesty's Government to annul the provision (Article 6 of the treaty of 1818) and to conclude a Supplementary Treaty with the Jaipur Darbar, limiting the payment of tribute to a fixed sum of four lakhs of rupees per annum. While communicating this decision to the Maharaja of Jaipur the Supreme Government informed him of the expectation of the British Government that he should undertake to spend a considerable sum annually upon works of irrigation and improvement with a view to enhance the prosperity of his State. Hope was expressed that the Maharaja would readily promise to adopt this course and being an 'enlightened Ruler' the promise made in this respect would be more than fulfilled by him.[9]

Accordingly Supplementary Treaty was concluded with the Jaipur State on 31 August 1871. It provided[10] :

Article 1. Article 6 of the Treaty of 1818 is hereby cancelled.

Article 2. The Maharaja of Jaipur agrees, on behalf of himself, his heirs and successors to pay to the British Government in perpetuity an annual tribute of four lakhs of Government rupees.

Article 3. This Agreement shall be taken as part of, and supplementary to, the aforesaid Treaty of 1818.

The Maharaja felt himself under 'deepest obligation' to the Government of India for this act of kindness. On his behalf he promised that a reasonable sum would be expended by him annually from revenue of the State upon works of irrigation and public improvement for utmost benefit of his subjects.[11]

II

For a long time there were widely different prices of salt in various provinces of British India and in the Princely States. In the post-1858 period the British authorities desired to abolish this 'fiscal anachronism', to equalise the salt duties throughout India and to acquire monopoly in salt as would enable them to regulate the administration of salt revenues to their advantage. Apart from this, they wanted to give to the people throughout India the means of obtaining an unlimited supply of salt at the cheapest possible cost; the interests of the people and of the public revenue were held to be identical.[12] The attainment of these objects necessitated the acquisition of complete control over the principal salt sources in Rajputana States, the suppression of manufacture of salt elsewhere which might compete with that produced at the principal salt sources and the abolition of transit duties on salt in the Native States. In 1869, therefore, the British authorities opened negotiations with the concerned States of Rajputana, Central India and the Punjab. Maharaja Ram Singh of Jaipur was the first to enter into salt treaty with the British.[13]

By the terms of the treaty of 1869 (signed on 7 August), the Jaipur Darbar agreed to lease to the British Government its right of manufacturing and of selling salt within the limits of the territory bordering on the Sambhar Lake. The lease would continue to remain in force until such time as the British Government desired to relinquish it but in that case an advance notice of two full years would have to be given to the Jaipur Darbar.[14] The Jaipur Darbar would empower the British Government and all officers appointed by the British Government to enter and search, in case of suspicion, houses and all other places, enclosed or otherwise, within the limits hereinafter defined, and to arrest and punish with fine, imprisonment, confiscation of goods, or otherwise, any and all persons detected within such limits in violation of any of the rules or regulations which might be laid down by the British Government in regard to the manufacture, sale, or removal of salt, or the prevention of unlicensed manufacture or smuggling. The limits within which the British Government and its officers were to exercise their jurisdiction were defined : The strip of territory bordering on the shores of the lake, including the town of Sambhar and twelve other hamlets, and comprehending the whole of the territory now subject to the joint jurisdiction of the States of Jaipur and Jodhpur to be demarcated and the whole space enclosed by such line of demarcation would constitute the limits of their jurisdiction.[15]

Within the said limits the British Government or its officers would be authorised to occupy land for building or other purposes, to construct roads, erect barriers, hedges, or buildings, and to remove buildings or other property. If any land paying land revenue to the government of Jaipur be occupied for any of the aforesaid purposes, the British Government would pay to the Jaipur government an annual rent equal to the amount of such revenue.[16] The British Government would constitute a Court who would usually hold his sittings within the above-mentioned limits for the trial and punishment of all persons charged with violation of rules and regulations.[17]

The British Government would from time to time fix the price at which salt manufactured within the said limits would be offered for sale. The Jaipur government would be entitled to receive annually at the place of manufacture from the British Government, for the consumption of the Jaipur State, any quantity of salt which the Jaipur government might demand, not exceeding 1,72,000 British Indian maunds, paying for the same at the rate of nine annas (British Currency) per maund. The Jaipur government would be at liberty to sell such salt at any price that it might fix.[18] Of the stocks held jointly by the governments of Jaipur and Jodhpur at the commencement of the lease, the Jaipur government would transfer its half share to the British Government on these terms — The Jaipur government would transfer its share in 5,10,000 British Indian maunds of salt free of cost. The price to be paid for the share of the Jaipur government in the remainder of the said stocks would be reckoned at 6½ annas per British maund but such a payment to the Jaipur government would only commence when salt in excess of 8,25,000 British Indian maunds was sold or exported by the British Government in any year, and then only on the share of such excess which belonged to the government of Jaipur.[19] No tax, toll, transit duty or due of any kind whatsoever, would be levied by the Jaipur government or would by it permitted to be levied by any other person, on any salt manufactured or sold by the British Government within the said limits.[20] It was specifically provided that nothing in this Agreement would be held to bar the sovereign jurisdiction of the Jaipur government, within the aforesaid limits in all matters, civil and criminals, not connected with the manufacture, sale or removal of salt, or the prevention of unlicensed manufacture or smuggling.[21]

The British Government agreed to pay to the Jaipur government in two half-yearly instalments, an annual rent of rupees 1,25,000 (British Currency) on account of the share of the Jaipur government in the salt sold within the said limits, and rupees 1,50,000 (British Currency) in compensation for duties on salt now levied by the Jaipur government and surrendered under the present Agreement. If the amount of the salt sold in, or exported from, the said limits by the British Government in any year would exceed 8,25,000 British Indian maunds, the British Government would pay to the government of Jaipur on all such excess a royalty at the rate of 20 per cent on the price per maund. The British Government also agreed to deliver annually 7,000 British Indian maunds of good salt, free of all charges, for the use of the Jaipur Darbar; such salt to be delivered at the place of manufacture to any officer empowered by the Jaipur government to receive it.[22] It was clearly stated that the British Government would have no claim on the land or other revenue, unconnected with salt, payable from the town of Sambhar, or other villages or lands included within the aforesaid limits. The British Government also bound itself not to sell any salt outside the limits aforesaid within the Jaipur territory.[23]

If any person employed by the British Government within the said limits would have absconded after committing an offence, or if any person would have absconded after committing a breach of the rules laid down under Article 3, the Jaipur government would, on sufficient evidence of his criminality, make every effort to cause his arrest and surrender to the British authorities within the said limits, in case of his passing through or taking refuge in, any part of the Jaipur territories.[24] It was mentioned in the last Article that none of the conditions contained in this Agreement would be in any way set aside or modified without the previous consent of both Governments; and further, should either party fail or neglect to adhere to these conditions the other party would cease to be bound by this Agreement.[25]

After the conclusion of this Agreement a Proclamation was issued by the Council of Jaipur Darbar on 29 January 1870 to all the *Gumashatas* of *Jagirdars, Mamlaguzars, Bhumias, Nazims, Ziladars, Amils, Taluqadars, Daroghas* of Customs Department, Deputy Superintendents and Officers of Police and Thuggi Department, *Patels, Patwaris, Zamindars, Chaukidars,* etc. within the Jaipur territory. It was said in this Proclamation that from and after the first day of February, the Jaipur Darbar had made over in lease to the British Government the Sambhar Salt Works. From this date, any person who might convey salt from Sambhar through Jaipur State, such salt being carried by a British pass, or in charge of a *Chaprasi* on the part of the British Government would pass through, without being interfered with in any way, nor would any tax, toll or transit due be levied on such salt. If any person would act contrary to the Proclamation, he would be liable to punishment.[26] An English translation of this Proclamation was forwarded by Agent to Governor-General, Rajputana to Secretary to Government of India, Foreign Department.[27]

Similar treaty was signed with the State of Jodhpur on 22 November 1869.

In pursuance of Article 6 of the Salt Agreement, Sambhar Lake Court was constituted in 1870 for the trial of offenders under Article 3 of the Agreement. This Court was to be subordinate to the Court of the District Magistrate, Ajmer. By Notification No. 2112-P issued on 25 September 1875 the composition and jurisdiction of this Court was defined. The Assistant Commissioner, in charge of the British Inland Customs Department at the Sambhar Lake would be the Judge of this Court. He would have powers of a Magistrate of the first class under the Code of Criminal Procedure (Act X of 1872), and he would have according to such powers jurisdiction (a) in respect of all offences committed by subjects of Her Majesty within the aforesaid limits and punishable under the Indian Penal Code, and (b) in respect of breaches of the rules described in Article 3 of the said Treaty, or offences connected with, when committed by any person whatsoever within the aforesaid limits. In the investigation and trial of such offences and breaches of rules and in levy of fines thereof, he would be guided by the provisions of the Code of Criminal Procedure (Act X of 1872 as amended by Act XI of 1874). In all cases in which the salt would be manufactured, carried or stored within the said limits in contravention of the rules, the Court was empowered to declare the said salt confiscated and dispose of it according to the rules in force in the Department of Inland Customs. Any person convicted on a trial held by the Sambhar Lake Court of a breach of the rules or offences connected therewith might petition to the Agent to the Governor-General for the States of Rajputana who, if he deemed fit, might send for the record of the case, and might confirm, reverse, or modify the sentence, or pass any other orders not inconsistent with the aforesaid rules.[28]

A few years after the operation of the aforesaid Salt Agreement with the Jaipur State, the British authorities decided to abolish the Inland Customs Line[29], for they desired to remove restrictions on, and impediments to, internal trade. With that object they had remitted the duty levied on sugar and other sachharine products exported from British territories into Jaipur and other Native States. They sought the co-operation of the Maharaja of Jaipur both by making such arrangements in his own State as would facilitate the abolition of the said Line without risk to the Imperial salt revenue and by abolishing for the relief of his subjects all duties on salt, sugar and other sachharine products, entering, leaving or passing through his State. For attaining this two-fold objective they entered into negotiations with the Maharaja and on 31 January 1879, they concluded another Salt Agreement with him.[30]

By the terms of this Agreement, the Maharaja of Jaipur agreed to suppress, and absolutely prohibit and prevent, the manufacture of salt within any part of the Jaipur State, whether overtly or under the guise of manufacturing salt petre or other saline products except at the Sambhar Lake and the Kuchor-Rewasa Surr, and to destroy and erase all other existing salt works. The *bona fide* manufacture of salt petre at any work then existing within the Jaipur State was, however, permitted.[31] In consideration of the uniform annual payment by the British Government of a net sum of 4 lakhs of rupees (British Currency) the Maharaja of Jaipur agreed to transfer to the British Government 1,72,000 maunds of Sambhar salt which the Maharaja under the Treaty of 1869 was entitled to receive on payment of 9 annas per maund. The said amount of 4 lakhs would be paid in half-yearly instalments.[32] No tax, toll, transit duty, or due of any kind whatsoever would be levied by or with the permission or knowledge of, the Maharaja of Jaipur on salt, sugar or other saccharine products whether exported from, imported into, carried through, or consumed within, the Jaipur State. However, the Maharaja was permitted to levy, according to the existing practice, octroi, *choongi* or other cess or duty on sugar and other saccharine products when imported into towns the population of which exceeded 5000 inhabitants.[33] The Maharaja agreed to forbid the importation into, or the exportation from, the Jaipur State of any salt whatever, other than salt upon which duty had been levied by the British Government, and the Maharaja would duly investigate and punish all contraventions of his orders on this behalf which would come to his knowledge. If any stocks of salt be found to exist within the Jaipur State at the time of conclusion of this Agreement, the Maharaja would, if so required by the British Government, take possession of such stocks of salt, and would give the owners thereof the option either of transferring the salt to the British Government at such equitable valuation as Maharaja might fix, in concurrence with the Political Agent, or of paying the said Agent such duty, not exceeding two rupees eight annas per maund, on such salt as the Governor-General might fix. In the event of the owners as aforesaid accepting the latter alternative they would be allowed to retain the salt on which the said duty might have been paid, but not otherwise.[34]

The Maharaja agreed to permit and authorise the British Government to assume the management of the Kuchor-Rewas Surr, or salt source, and of the works therein situated pertaining to the villages of Rewasa, Kuchor, Nimbora, and Mundpoora. The Maharaja would cause a line of demarcation to be laid down, in consultation with the Political Agent, enclosing the whole of the said salt source. The British Government would be at liberty at any time to close the said salt works, and would further be bound to close them whenever the Maharaja of Jaipur would so require. The Maharaja would have to give notice of twelve months before terminating the arrangement and he would pay to the British Government fair compensation for all standing works and buildings within the line of demarcation.[35] The landholders of certain villages enumerated in Schedule A annexed to this Agreement having hitherto enjoyed certain profits from salt works therein situated, the British Government undertook to pay yearly to the Maharaja, as compensation to the said landholders, the sums entered opposite each village in the said Schedule, and the Maharaja agreed to distribute the said sum accordingly. The Maharaja also agreed to adopt equitable measures to relieve the right-holders in salt works, all feudatories, *jagirdars*, and other landholders or salt workers, from any material losses which might be caused to them by this Agreement.[36]

It was clearly laid down that none of the stipulations set forth in this Agreement would be modified or annulled without the previous consent of both the parties.[37]

Under the Salt Treaties of 1869 and 1870 concluded with the two States (Jaipur and Jodhpur) it was arranged that the Jaipur and Jodhpur Darbars should each receive a royalty of 20 per cent on sales of salt exceeding 8,25,000 British Indian maunds, manufactured and sold by the British Government from that portion of the lake held conjointly by the two States; and that Jodhpur should receive besides a royalty of 40 per cent on sales exceeding 9,00,000 maunds from the Nawagudha portion of the lake, over which it had exclusive rights. When the railway was brought to Sambhar difficulties arose owing to the shifting by the Salt Department of the parts of the lake where they manufactured their salt. In order to settle the differences, Colonel Bradford, Agent to the Governor-General for Rajputana, convened a meeting at Abu of the representatives of both parties so that the exact proportion of the total royalty which each should receive might be fixed. This resulted in mutual agreement between the two Darbars that Jodhpur should receive five-eighths and Jaipur three-eighths of the total royalty payable on excess sales of salt irrespective of the place of manufacture. The Governor-General in Council accorded sanction to this arrangement adding that it was entirely satisfactory in the interests of both the Darbars and of the Salt Department of the Government of India. The Supreme Government also sanctioned the proposal of the Agent to Governor-General for the demarcation of the respective jurisdiction of the Darbars in the bed of the lake.[38]

Whereas the Imperial Government had gained considerably by securing its fiscal interests by the Salt Agreements of 1869 and 1879 concluded with the Jaipur State, the latter had been a loser as a result of these transactions. Maharaja Ram Singh of Jaipur, it has been said in his criticism, did not have any compunction in signing these agreements which were detrimental to the interests of the State. He looked upon the treaty of 1869 as giving him Rs. 2.75 lacs annually but he did not care for its consequences to the common man and still less cared to find out the economic losses to the businessmen of his State or the process of impoverishment which would follow the British monopoly. He surrendered the Jaipur share in the Sambhar Lake for a mere Rs. 2.75 lacs and 7000 maunds of free salt. Ten years later in 1879 he did not hesitate to surrender 1,72,000 maunds of salt, obtained at the rate of Rs. 0.56 paise for the use of the people of the State in exchange for a payment of rupees four lacs.[39] It may also be observed that the petty tradesmen, mostly *banjaras,* were adversely affected; most of them lost their occupation as the trade concentrated in the hands of wealthy merchants.[40]

Besides Jaipur and Jodhpur States, the British Government had also concluded agreements with Alwar, Dholpur, Lawa, Kishangarh, Bharatpur, Sirohi, Jhalawar and Karauli by the terms of which the manufacture of salt was suppressed in each of these States. In the case of Bikaner, Udaipur and Kota the manufacture of salt was prohibited except at certain specified works, a maximum outturn being at the same time provided. To the Bundi, Tonk and Shahpura States which agreed to suppress manufacture of salt the *bona fide* salt petre was expressly permitted.[41]

From what has been discussed above, it will have been obvious that the sole objective of the salt policy of the British Government was to acquire monopoly of the salt of the entire country so that they could make it a substantial source of revenue. With that objective they had concluded salt agreements with Jaipur and other Rajputana States which manufactured salt in greater or smaller quantities. No wonder, they either successfully took over the control of principal salt works or suppressed the manufacture of salt or limited the outturn of salt in various Princely States. For the States which possessed little or no salt it was decided that they would consume salt that had paid British duty, and would thus fall into the same category with several first-class States or groups of minor States which, being situated inland, and having no salt sources of their own or very inferior ones, had always drawn their supplies of salt from sources where British duty was levied.[42] The Imperial Government had, of course, given compensation to the States concerned but it may be observed that compensation paid was often too inadequate. All said and done, the salt policy of the Paramount Power had augmented the fiscal resources of the Imperial Government but it proved detrimental to the economic interests of the Princely States.

It may, however, be argued in defence of the British salt policy that they had got rid of the obnoxious Customs Line which they had initially set up, abolished all taxes, toll and transit duties on salt within the territories of the States. The salt duty was equalised throughout the country and was fixed at two rupees per maund in 1882 and salt began to be supplied at cheap rates to all the people of British India and Native India. Moreover, the salt arrangements made with the rulers of the Princely States were the result of friendly negotiations and agreements, and the States were also compensated for the loss incurred by them, though not as adequate as they had wished.

III

As a result of disintegration of the Mughal Empire, the right of coinage began to be exercised by most of the Chiefs of Native

States who established their own mints, but there were many Native Princes who continued to coin money in the name of the Mughal Emperor. Till 1857 the British Government had authoritatively suppressed the mints in many of the smaller States. It had spared those which were recognised by the treaty and those belonging to the more important States. But it had declared that, "in all future negotiations with Native States possessing Mints" the abolition of those mints was to be held an object of paramount political importance.[43] After the fall of Delhi, and the trial of Bahadur Shah in 1858, Major Nixon, the Political Agent in Bharatpur reported that he had directed the disuse of the Delhi King's name on the coins of the Bharatpur State, which was then under his guardianship, and the substitution of the name of the British Sovereign. He solicited sanction to this measure. At about the same time Captain Eden, Political Agent at Jaipur, intimated that Maharaja Ram Singh of Jaipur (1835-1880) had expressed a desire to discontinue his current coin which bore the name of Bahadur Shah, and to issue a new currency bearing some reference to Her Majesty the Queen. In forwarding these representations to the Government of India, the Agent to Governor-General for Rajputana suggested that it seemed a fitting time to change the coinage of all the Rajputana States, which had hitherto borne the name of the Delhi Emperor. The Government of India in reply authorised the acceptance of the proposal made by the Maharaja of Jaipur, and desired that he might be assured of the Governor-General's appreciation of his 'graceful offer'.[44] The choice of a device for the new coin was left to the Maharaja. And the coins which were issued by him bore the following inscriptions[45] :

Obverse — Zarab-i-Sawai Jaipur 186 — Bahad Malika — Mahajwa — Saltanat — Inglistan — Victoria

Reverse — San Jalus Manus — Maimanat 31 — *Maharajadhiraj Sawai Ram Singhji* — In the 31st year of the fortunate reign of Maharajadhiraj — Sawai Ram Singhji.

At about the same time the Governor-General's Agents in

Rajputana and Central India and the Residents at Hyderabad and Baroda were asked whether the coin current in the States with which they were connected bore the superscription of the King of Delhi. If so, they were to ascertain and report how a proposition to efface that superscription would be viewed by the several Chiefs. The Rao of Kutch had proposed as early as 1846 to C. Napier that the British Government as a Paramount Power in Hindustan should have its name superscribed on native coins and after the revolt of 1857, he resolved to strike his coin in the name of Her Majesty. It has already been mentioned that the Maharaja of Jaipur had volunteered a similar proposal. In response to the information sought the Political Agents reported that all the States had expressed their willingness to efface the obnoxious superscription (of Delhi Emperor). Many of them proposed to issue a new coinage and this coinage, which, however, bore no mark of the dependence of the States on the British Suzerain, was approved by the Government of India.[46] After receiving this communication, the Secretary of State for India remarked :

> The conduct pursued by the Maharaja of Jaipur and the Rao of Kutch seems to show that probably there would have been no difficulty on the part of the other Princes in adopting a similar course if it had been suggested to them, and Her Majesty's Government regret that an opportunity has been lost of denoting by such a proceeding the recognition of the great fact that the supremacy of India is vested in Her Majesty.
>
> It may probably not be too late to repair this omission. In this case you will not fail to take an early opportunity of bringing the subject under the consideration of the various Princes and Chiefs.
>
> Her Majesty's Government would be glad if simultaneously with a change of device an attempt could be made to obtain, as far as that object is attainable, a currency of uniform value throughout India and the withdrawl from circulation of the many spurious and debased coinage which now exist....
>
> Though there is reason to fear that a peculiarly suitable opportunity for a change of this nature has been allowed to pass by, Her Majesty's Government are anxious that the matter should not be lost sight of.[47]

> It appears that no action was taken upon these instructions of the Secretary of State for India as the Government of India did not consider it prudent to follow the course of action at that time.

For about a decade after this, there was no correspondence on the coinage question till 1868 when the issue of short weight counterfeit copper coins in Khetri, a dependency of Jaipur State, came to the fore. It came to the notice of the British Government in this year that there were thirteen mints in Chirawa and nineteen in Surajgarh, both in Khetri, where copper pice was manufactured by the *Sahukars* who had their agents at Agra, Mathura, Ajmer, Gwalior, etc. It was reported that the pice manufactured at these mints were transported to the markets of the said places where these coins were in wide circulation. Both the *Thakur* of Surajgarh and the Raja of Khetri derived profits from this manufacture. The Government of North-Western Provinces reported the facts about the counterfeiting of copper coins at Khetri, enclosing details received from the Inspector-General Police of N.W.P. to the Government of India.[48] Thereupon the latter addressed the following communication to the Agent to Governor-General for Rajputana:

> His Excellency in Council cannot understand how the privilege of coining came to be enjoyed by a subordinate Noble of the Jaipur State. The inexpediency of permitting this to be separated from the other functions of sovereignty, with their attendant responsibilities, is strongly evinced in the present instance, where a Noble, otherwise distinguished for his enlightened method of managing his estates, has been found to add to his sources of revenue by the coinage of light and counterfeit money of other States.
>
> The Jaipur Darbar should be at once called upon to take such measures for keeping the control of the power of coinage in its own hands as shall satisfy the British Government that an abuse of this kind will not again be possible.[49]

Colonel Keatinge, Agent to Governor-General, Rajputana reported that the Political Agent at Jaipur had already taken action in the matter. But he said that the illicit manufacture of counterfeit pice in Khetri was carried on without the knowledge of the Raja and resulted from a want of supervision. The orders of Government had not yet been communicated to the Political Agent, because Keatinge thought they required some modification. He pointed out that in the European sense of the term Jaipur possessed no sovereign rights in Khetri, the Raja exercising complete civil and criminal jurisdiction within his own territory. An arbitrary order to suppress the Khetri mint would be looked upon by the Jaipur Darbar as an admirable opportunity of asserting additional authority, and would be eagerly acted upon, while throughout the minor principalities and in the estates of all the *Thakurs*, the measure would be very unpopular. It was quite possible that resistance might be offered, in which case very troublesome complications might arise. Keatinge remarked that other Nobles in Rajputana had mints and considering the antagonistic position of the great Rulers towards the minor Chiefs and Nobles, he suggested that Government should not in this instance, without great publicity and a clear statement of its intentions, give the weight of its authority to Jaipur.[50]

After receiving this communication the former orders were withdrawn and the Government of India informed the Agent to Governor-General, Rajputana that no further action need be taken regarding the Raja of Khetri except such as might appear called for in connection with the general measures to be adopted in accordance with the new instructions. These instructions were:

> His Excellency in Council is convinced that the right of coining, which has hitherto been unrestrictedly exercised by several of the feudatory Chiefs and Nobles of Rajputana, is calculated to lead to great abuses, and that steps must now be taken to limit this privilege and keep it within due bounds.
>
> Mints must be established and worked only at the capitals of those rulers who have a right to exercise this attribute of sovereign power; that they must be worked under their control and supervision; that mints in the territories of subordinate and feudatory Chiefs and Nobles should be henceforth abolished; and that compensation should be given by their suzerain to

> those *Thakurs* and others who have long usurped or exercised the power of coining and whose revenues would else be impaired.[51]

After these orders of the Supreme Government the Khetri mints were closed for ever.

The Government of India also drew attention of the Agent to Governor-General, Rajputana to the debasement of the coinage which was always going on in Native States and directed him to call the attention of the Rulers who worked mints to this point also.[52]

In the following year (1869) the Finance Department represented that the British Government experienced considerable inconvenience in carrying on its monetary transaction within the jurisdiction of the Native Chiefs, because of the existence of Native coinage differing in value from its own. The Foreign Department was accordingly asked to prepare a complete statement of the mints then existing in the territories of Native Chiefs, and of the titles, character, amount, and value of coinage of each, and to consider "whether any measure could be adopted to induce the several Native Chiefs, or any of them, to forgo the privilege of issuing coins and to close the Mint, or if that appears impossible, to assimilate the coin of the Mints in every respect, except the device, to that of the Government of India, and to admit the coin of the Government of India to legal currency in their territories on the condition that the coin of their Mints be in like manner allowed currency as legal tender in British territories." It was added that it would be a needful condition of such an arrangement that the management of these foreign Mints should be subject to such conditions as might be imposed by the Government of India with the view of ensuring the standard, purity and weight of the coin.[53] Accordingly a circular was sent to various Local Governments, Residents and Governor-General's Agents requesting the preparation and submission of statements of the mints in the Native States under their respective charge with their specific opinion on the matter.[54] After receiving and examining these reports the Government of India issued a confidential Resolution in October 1870.[55] It was said in this Resolution that however desirable and beneficial a uniform coinage for all India might be, it was not possible to introduce a scheme for this purpose, unless the Mints in Native States were closed or their management be taken under the control of the Government of India; but the Supreme Government considered it inexpedient on political and general grounds to adopt this course of action. At the same time the Political Agents be instructed to point out to the Native Chiefs, as opportunity arose, how advantageous it would be for them to co-operate in making the Indian coinage more uniform, and in assimilating it, as far as possible, to that of the British Government. Authoritative interference in the matter should be avoided because the Native Chiefs would not be willing to surrender the prerogative of coining. But if a Native Chief should show a disposition to close his Mint and to ask the British Government for assistance in changing his coinage, he should be encouraged to do so. At the same time those Chiefs who might express a determination not to close their Mints, should be informed that the British Government was willing to help them, as far as it could, to procure good machinery and to improve their assay and process of coining. Where Mints had either been suppressed altogether, or had not been in active use within the last five years, their revival could not be permitted. The British Government also could not permit the establishment of a Mint by any State which had not up to the present time continuously exercised the right of coining without question by the British Government. The Government of India concurred with the Agent to Governor-General, Rajputana as to the propriety of closing the Mint at Shahpura and directed that this should be done.

The Secretary of State for India after perusing the Resolution opined that the object of the Government must be twofold : first, to relieve the inhabitants of Native States from the inconveniences consequent on the number and nature of the coinage in use; secondly, "to secure where this is found feasible, the acknowledgement, on the currency of such Native States as continue to coin money of the supremacy of Her Majesty". He, however, expressed concurrence in the view of the Government of India that no general measure was desirable in the direction of securing an acknowledgement of the supremacy of Her Majesty the Queen in the superscription of the coins of the Native States, and said that the object could be obtained gradually.[56]

The Native Coinage Act, IX of 1876, empowered the Governor-General-in-Council to declare coins of Native States of the same fineness and weight as British coins to be, subject to certain conditions, a legal tender in British India, and authorised Native States to send their metal to the Mints of the Government of India for coinage. The two important States of Rajputana which availed themselves of the opportunity afforded by this Act were Alwar in 1877 and Bikaner in 1893. They called in their silver coins, and dispatched them to Government Mints, whence they were reissued as rupees which bore on the reverse the name of the State and the name and title of the Chief, and which were legal tender in British India. An intimation was given to the two Darbars that as the smaller pieces, the half, quarter, and one-eighth rupee, could not be coined for the States, the British coins of these denominations should be allowed to circulate in the States and they would have full value as legal tender. In 1893, due to silver crisis, the Government Mints were closed to the unrestricted coinage of silver, and the exchange value of all other Native States' rupees depreciated. It was decided that the provisions of the Native Coinage Act were not applicable to the new condition of affairs; but the Government of India agreed to purchase the existing rupees of Native States at their average market value, and to supply British rupees in their place. Eight States of Rajputana took advantage of this offer which involved cessation of the privilege of minting.[57]

Jaipur and six other States[58] continued to have their own coinage. The Jaipur coins were called *Jhar Shàhi* because these coins bore a *Jhar* or spray of six sprigs or branches. Besides the gold *mohurs,* the Maharajas of Jaipur issued a large number of silver and copper coins. The silver coins issued were of one rupee, eight annas, four annas and two annas. The weight of the silver rupee was generally 174 or 175 grains and that of the copper coin 94-96 grains. The rate of exchange between the

Jaipur and British currency varied from time to time. In April, 1899 the Jaipur rupee was worth about 12 annas of British rupee, but towards the end of 1904, 102 *Jhar Shahi* rupees exchanged for 100 British rupees.[59]

IV

The opium policy of the British Government was intended to protect the Imperial revenue and to prevent the Native States from adopting measures which might be detrimental to the interests of the Paramount Power.[60] There were three groups of Native States in regard to the opium arrangements made with them by the British authorities. In the first group were included the States of Rajputana and Central India. The British Government introduced pass system in respect of these States since 1830. The British authorities did not interfere in any way with the cultivation of poppy or the manufacture of opium within these States but they prohibited the import of opium into, and its transport through, British territories except under passes granted by the British officers. These passes, it may be observed, were issued on payment of heavy duty. In the second category fell the States of Western India where the cultivation of poppy was either prohibited or limited, and sales and prices were regulated in the same way as in British territories. In the third group came the Punjab States where there were neither State monopolies nor pass system, but executive measures were taken to prevent smuggling.[61]

The Jaipur State obviously fell in the first category of the States. It had been stated in Memorandum No. 5 appended to the Salt Agreement of 1879 : In the Memorandum from the Jaipur Darbar to Mr. Hume, dated 21 March 1877, the Darbar asked for information regarding the object of the clause of draft Agreement about the prohibition of the export from its territories into British India of *bhang, ganja,* opium, spirits and other intoxicating drugs. It was explained that the import of such articles into British India had always been strictly forbidden and that hitherto it had been mainly prevented by the Indian

Customs Line, which would now be removed. Therefore it had become necessary to request the Jaipur Darbar and all other States bordering upon British India to assist the British Government by prohibiting the export of these articles from their States by the issue of notifications, and by orders to their officials for the arrest and punishment of offenders. The Maharaja was asked to favour the British Government with a *Kharita* engaging to take these and other necessary administrative measures.[62]

In response to this, the Maharaja of Jaipur issued Memorandum No. 6 in which he expressed his willingness, as required by the British Government, to prohibit the export from his State into British territory of opium, *bhang, ganja,* spirits, and other intoxicating drugs. The Maharaja, however, clarified that he had not bound himself that no such articles would ever be smuggled out of Jaipur into British territories; all he had agreed to do was to prohibit publicly such exportation, to direct his subordinate officials of all departments to prevent it, so far as it might be practicable, and to punish all contraventions of his prohibition which might come to his notice. The Maharaja added that he could not undertake to maintain any special establishment to watch illicit traffic of this nature, but so far as might be practicable, with existing establishments he would endeavour to suppress it.[63]

The export, import and transit rates levied on opium in the Jaipur State were very low in comparison with those levied in British territories and in some of the other Princely States, and hence there was a great temptation to smuggle opium from Jaipur into British territory in contravention of the Salt Agreement concluded between the British Government and the Jaipur Darbar in 1869. The Darbar, therefore, thought proper to enhance the duties on opium in order to prevent smuggling. In December 1882 the export, import and transit rates were increased with the consent of the British authorities as indicated by the following table[64] :

STATEMENT SHOWING THE PAST AND PROPOSED RATES OF DUTIES ON OPIUM

				Past Per maund			Present Per maund		
				Rs.	a.	p.	Rs.	a.	p.
	Import rates								
Opium in cakes	...	...	...	40	0	0	50	0	0
" in juice	...	...	...	15	0	0	25	0	0
	Export rates								
Opium in cakes	...	...	...	25	0	0	35	0	0
" in juice	...	...	...	15	0	0	25	0	0
	Transit rates								
Opium in cakes	...	...	...	20	0	0	35	0	0
" in juice	...	...	...	15	0	0	25	0	0
Mapa rates on Jeypore produce consumed within the Jeypore territory									
				Rs.	a.	p.	Rs.	a.	p.
Opium in cakes	...	...	...	6	4	0	35	0	0
" in juice	...	...	...	3	12	0	25	0	0
Mapa rates on Jeypore produce coming into the city of Jeypore									
				Rs.	a.	p.	Rs.	a.	p.
Opium in cakes	...	...	...	25	0	0	35	0	0
" in juice	...	...	...	15	0	0	25	0	0

In 1885, at the request of the Punjab Government, the Maharaja of Jaipur as well as the Chiefs of Bikaner and Alwar were asked to enforce strictly as regards the Punjab the prohibition against the export of opium from their States into British territories as laid down in their Salt Agreements with the British Government. The Maharaja of Jaipur and the other two Chiefs accordingly prohibited the export of opium from their territories into the Punjab, or into the Native States under the control of Punjab Government which were conterminous with the boundaries of the Rajputana States.[65]

In 1890 the Lieutenant-Governor and Chief Commissioner of North-West Provinces and Oudh in a communication to the Government of India suggested the establishment of opium scales in the Jaipur State which would be beneficial in the prevention of smuggling to British territories.[66] The matter was referred to Agent to Governor-General, Rajputana who after getting requisite information from Political Agent, Eastern States, reported to the Government of India that the past statistics of opium cultivation was quite unreliable. The figures furnished by the Jaipur Darbar through the Political Agent regarding cultivation and consumption of opium in its territories as well as its import and export on the frontier were inadequate. Lately consumption per head had been shown during 1887, 1888 and 1889 at 3 *mashas*–3½ *ratis*, 4 *mashas*–7? *ratis* and 8 *mashas*–5? *ratis* respectively but the proper data for the compilation of exact figures was not forthcoming. Until the State could give reliable comparative statistical data regarding its produce and consumption and import and export it was not possible to set up opium scales at Hindaun road. He opined that until he got some further information of reliable nature from the Darbar, the question of opium scales at Hindaun road or elsewhere should be held in abeyance.[67]

The main object of the Paramount Power was that the opium of Native States should not compete with the opium of British India and they endeavoured to prevent the export of illicit opium from the Rajputana States including Jaipur into the British territories. This object appears to have been achieved to a great extent. Thus the Imperial Government secured its revenues from opium which was a considerable source of their income.

References and Notes

1. Michael Maclagan, *Clemency Canning* (London, 1962), p. 258.
2. Sri Nandan Prasad, *Paramountcy under Dalhousie* (Delhi, 1964), p. 167.
3. C.U. Aitchison, Comp., *A Collection of Treaties, Engagements and Sanads*, Vol. III (Calcutta, 1932), p. 68.
4. *Supra*, pp. 91-92.
5. FD, Political Progs., 31 Aug. 1842, Nos. 50-52; also see *Supra*, pp. 101-02.
6. K.W., FD, Political A, March 1871, Nos. 198-201.
7. Offg. AGG to GOI, Foreign Department, No. 505 P., dated 6 Dec. 1870, FD, Political A, March 1871, No. 198.
8. Offg. Political Agent, Jaipur to AGG, No. 147-111G., dated 22 Nov. 1870, FD, Political A, March 1871, No. 199.
9. GOI to the Duke of Argyll, Secretary of State for India, No. 44, dated 15 March 1871, FD, Political A, March 1871, No. 201.
10. FD, Political A, Oct. 1871, No. 120; Aitchison, *op. cit.*, pp. 81-82.
11. *Kharita* from Maharaja Ram Singh of Jaipur to Viceroy and Governor-General of India, dated 29 Aug. 1871, FD, Political A, Oct. 1871, No. 121.
12. Sir John Strachey, *India : Its Administration and Progress* (third edition, Reprint New Delhi, 1977), p. 165.
13. For the terms of the Treaty, see Jaipur Agency Record, Part I, Treaties, File No. 3/1869-70, pp. 1-4; also Aitchison, *op. cit.*, pp. 74-78.
14. Articles 1 and 2 of the Treaty of 1869, Aitchison, *op. cit.*, p. 74.
15. Articles 3 and 4, *ibid.*, pp. 74-75.
16. Article 5, *ibid.*, p. 75.
17. Article 6, *ibid.*, p. 75.
18. Article 7, *ibid.*, pp. 75-76.
19. Article 8, *ibid.*, p. 76.
20. Article 9, *ibid.*, p. 76.
21. Article 10, *ibid.*, p. 76.
22. Articles 11,12 and 13, *ibid.*, p. 77.
23. Articles 14 and 15, *ibid.*, pp. 77-78.
24. Article 16, *ibid.*, p. 78.
25. Article 18, *ibid.*, p. 78.
26. Proclamation issued by Council of Jaipur, dated 29 Jan. 1870, FD, Political A, May 1870, No. 326 A.
27. AGG to GOI, Foreign Department, No. 130 G dated 5 Feb. 1870, FD, Political A, May 1870, No. 326 B.

28. Notification No. 2112-P., dated 25 Sept. 1875, Aitchison, *op. cit.*, pp. 79-81.
29. The Inland Customs Line stretching from a point north of Attock on Indus down to Mahanadi in the South, and covering a distance of 2500 miles had been set up; it had to be patrolled day and night by an army of 12,000 officers and men. See Strachey, *op. cit.*, p. 177.
30. For terms of this Agreement, see FD, Political A, April 1880, No. 179, pp. 1-6; also Aitchison, *op. cit.*, pp. 82-89.
31. Article 1, Aitchison, *op. cit.*, pp. 82-83.
32. Article 2, *ibid.*, p. 83.
33. Articles 3 and 4, *ibid.*, p. 83.
34. Articles 5 and 6, *ibid.*, pp. 83-84.
35. Article 7, *ibid.*, p. 84.
36. Articles 8 and 9, *ibid.*, pp. 84-85; also see Schedule A, p. 86.
37. Article 10, *ibid.*, p. 85.
38. FD, Internal A, Oct. 1884, Nos. 44-58.
39. M.S. Jain, *Rajasthan Through the Ages, Vol. III, from 1761 to 1949 A.D.* (Bikaner, 1996), p. 191.
40. RPARS for 1878-79, p. 3; also see Malti Saxena, *Impact of the British Sovereignty on the Economic Condition of Rajasthan* (Delhi, n.d.), p. 153.
41. C.L. Tupper, Comp., *Indian Political Practice, Vol. I* (Calcutta, 1895), para 186, p. 202.
42. *Ibid.*, pp. 202-03.
43. *Ibid.*, pp. 125-26.
44. GOI to AGG, No. 170, dated 26 Feb. 1858, cited in *ibid.*, p. 126.
45. *Catalogue of the Coins in the Indian Museum*, Calcutta, *Vol. IV*, pp. 238-39; Ashim Kumar Roy, *History of the Jaipur City* (New Delhi, 1978), p. 204.
46. GOI to Governor-General's Agents in Rajputana, Central India and Residents at Hyderabad and Baroda, Nos. 124, 125, 126 and 127, dated 18 Feb. 1858, *Tupper, op. cit.*, p. 126.
47. Despatch from Secretary of State for India to Governor-General, No. 39 of 15 Sept. 1859.
48. Secretary to Govt. N.W.P. to Offg. Secretary to GOI, Foreign Department, No. 633, dated 23 June 1868, and from Political Asstt. to I.G. Police, N.W.P. to Secretary to Govt. of N.W.P., No. 2732, dated 25 May 1868, FD, Finance A, July 1868, Nos. 11-12.
49. GOI to AGG, No. 270, dated 8 July 1868, FD, Finance A, July 1868, No. 13.
50. AGG to GOI, Foreign Department, No. 338 P., dated 15 Aug.

1868, and Political Agent, Jaipur to AGG, No. 127-91 G, dated 5 Aug. 1868, FD, Finance A, Oct. 1868, Nos. 16-17.

51. GOI to AGG, No. 348, dated 3 Oct. 1868, FD, Finance A, Oct. 1868, No. 20.
52. *Ibid.*
53. Tupper, *op. cit., Vol. I,* para 108, pp. 128-29.
54. Col. Keatinge, then Agent to Governor-General for Rajputana, expressed no opinion on the matter but recommended the abolition of the Shahpura Mint; Shahpura alone among the Rajputana States retained the Delhi King's name on its coins.
55. Resolution No. 402 of 6 Oct. 1870, FD, Finance A, Nov. 1870, No. 25; also see Tupper, *op. cit.,* para 109, pp. 129-31.
56. Despatch from the Secretary of State for India to GOI, No. 71 of 31 Aug. 1872.
57. *IGI, Vol. XXI* (Oxford, 1908), pp. 146-47; Tupper, *op. cit., Vol. I,* paras 113, 115, 116, pp. 132-34.
58. These six States were — Bundi, Jaisalmer, Kishangarh, Tonk, Udaipur and Shahpura.
59. *IGI, Vol. XIII* (Oxford, 1908), p. 395.
60. A.C. Arora, *British Policy towards the Punjab States, 1858-1905,* (Jalandhar, 1982), p. 184.
61. Tupper, *op. cit.,* Vol. I, para 185, p. 198.
62. Aitchison, *op. cit.,* p. 88.
63. *Ibid.,* pp. 88-89.
64. FD, A – General-I, March 1883, No. 15.
65. FD, Internal A, July 1885, Nos. 134-151.
66. Secretary to Govt. N.W.P. and Oudh to Secretary to GOI, Dept. of Finance and Commerce, dated 4 July 1890, FD, Internal B, Nov. 1890, No. 111.
67. AGG to GOI, dated 18 Sept. 1890 and its Encl., FD, Internal B, Nov. 1890, Nos. 107-108.

CHAPTER 7

Transport and Communications

The Imperial Government of India desired to have full and exclusive control over the means of transport and communications in the British provinces as well as the Princely States. This was considered essential not only for economic development but also for strengthening the defences of the country as a whole. For achieving this purpose, necessary arrangements had to be made with the States in the matters of construction of railways and roads as well as extension of postal and telegraphic communication.

I

Railways were introduced in India during the Governor-Generalship of Dalhousie (1848-1856). But it was after the assumption of the territories and government of India by British Crown in 1858 that railway lines began to be constructed with greater speed. The principal motive of the British authorities for railway construction in India was, of course, commercial. The railways could help in a big way in the collection and export of raw materials for the British industry and could at the same time open up the vast and hitherto untapped markets in the country for the English manufactured goods. Apart from this, the railways would be highly useful in strengthening the defences of the British Empire in India, improving the efficiency of its administration and catering for the moral and material progress of the country.[1]

As the territories of British India were interconnected with those of the Princely States, it was realised that without the active co-operation of the latter, it would not be practically possible to carry out successfully the country-wide railway projects. The British authorities, therefore, evolved certain principles to ensure the necessary co-operation of Native Royalties in the matters of railway construction and administration. All the railway projects in the Native States, as a rule, were to be reported to the Government of India. Generally the sanction of the Supreme Government, also advice and assistance, if required, was sought before any project was undertaken, and such lines when constructed, were to be inspected and passed as safe before they were opened for traffic. The rulers of the States were also required to co-operate with the Imperial Government in the execution of their railway schemes by providing free of charge in their respective territories all lands needed for the construction and working of the railway lines. They were also expected to cede full jurisdiction in such lands. This rule was to apply to all the railway schemes approved by the Government, whether undertaken by the state agency or by private companies.[2]

In the beginning of 1864 the Government of India laid down three principles of the British policy regarding railways traversing the territories of the States : first the acquisition of land in full sovereignty from the States concerned; second, the acquisition of it free of all charges; third, the acquisition of the right of exclusive administrative jurisdiction in cases in which the Native Chief might object to cede the sovereignty. It was clarified that the Chiefs were generally expected both to bear the loss of revenue on the lands taken up and to compensate the proprietors.[3]

In 1865 the British Government decided to undertake a railway project which aimed at obtaining direct communication with the North-Western Provinces and the Punjab. The proposed railway line was to run from Baroda *via* Partabgarh to Neemuch, thence *via* Deoli, Jaipur and Alwar to Delhi. The line would intersect the States of Bharatpur, Partabgarh, Mewar, Jaipur, Tonk and Alwar. The Chiefs of the Rajputana States concerned were asked to concede three things in the event of the railway line passing through their respective territories : (i) They should give land, averaging 200 feet in breadth for the construction of the railway line, stations, etc., free of all costs. (ii) They should surrender to the British Government full jurisdiction short of sovereignty rights in such land. (iii) They should surrender the right of levying all transit and other duties on goods passing through the railway land.[4]

The Darbars of Mewar, Bharatpur, Alwar, Partabgarh and Tonk readily assented to the three aforesaid conditions regarding the construction of railway line through their territories. The Maharaja of Jaipur, in like manner, consented to the 2nd and 3rd conditions, but only partially to the first, for while prepared to grant the land free of cost he considered compensation for houses, buildings and gardens should be defrayed by the Company.[5]

In a letter addressed to Captain W.H. Beynon, Political Agent, Jaipur, Maharaja Ram Singh of Jaipur expressed his consent to grant 'fair and reasonable' concessions so as to encourage a Railway Company to commence operations within his territory. But he laid down the following conditions keeping in view the interests of his State : (i) whereas he expressed willingness to give up the necessary extent of land, averaging 200 feet in breadth for the construction of the Railway line, stations and bona fide railway purposes, he said that necessary compensation for losses accruing to owners of houses, gardens, wells, etc. in the land ceded must by defrayed by the Railway Company after these had been duly assessed. (ii) He expressed his readiness to concede full jurisdiction in such land short of sovereignty rights to the British Government but on the condition that the Jaipur offenders acting against the State would not be permitted to take refuge within the lands made over to the Railway and would be handed over to the Darbar and that all subjects offending in cases of an international character would be tried by the British Representative of the Jaipur Court. (iii) Whereas the Maharaja was ready to surrender all transit and other duties on goods passing through the railway land, he desired to reserve to himself the right of levying the usual fares on goods breaking bulk, or which might pass to the Railway line from within his territory. (iv) He strongly urged the British Government to make proper provision for the comfort of passengers and see that native passengers should not be ill-treated on the Railway passing through his State. (v) The Maharaja emphatically stated that the fuel required for consumption on the Railway should not be drawn from within his territory as there was already its scarcity owing to the absence of forests or trees in the sandy soil of the State.[6]

The Political Agent, Jaipur while forwarding this letter of the Maharaja to Agent to the Governor-General for Rajputana States, stated that he had endeavoured to explain to the Maharaja the incalculable benefits the proposed Railway would bestow on himself and his subjects generally, that the concessions he was called upon to make, though involved large present sacrifices, were small when compared with the gain that would ultimately be derived by the introduction of a railway through his territory. He said that he had also assured the Maharaja that the interests of the property-holders would be carefully protected and that every possible care would be taken to avoid the needless destruction of property. The Maharaja had, however, promised that he would render all possible assistance as soon as operations were commenced in his territory.[7]

The Government of India directed the Agent to Governor-General for Rajputana States to convey their thanks to the Chiefs of Mewar, Bharatpur, Alwar, Partabgarh and Tonk for having given their ready and cordial assent to the conditions proposed to them. To the Maharaja of Jaipur and other Chiefs who had not given their positive assent he should address letters, explaining to them that they and their people would benefit largely by the construction of Railways in their territory, and that it was, therefore, unreasonable for them to look for compensation on account of the houses, gardens, etc. which might be absorbed within Railway limits. They should be advised to do just as the British Government had done in respect of the Railways passing through British territory, that is, they should themselves make good the losses of private persons within their respective States, for any revenue which they might in this way consent to sacrifice would be soon more than made up to them by the general improvement of their country, which invariably follows upon the introduction of a Railway. As regards the transit duties, if the Chiefs still objected to relinquish this source of revenue, they should be offered to consent to take a specific sum per annum in lieu of duties now leviable on all goods which passed through their territories. With reference to the surrender and trial of offenders the Supreme Government desired that intimation be given to the Chiefs that refugees guilty of heinous crimes, if arrested on the land ceded for Railway purpose, should be given up and that subjects of Native States arrested for crimes in the Railway lands should be tried and punished by the British authorities appointed for such duty.[8]

The Maharaja of Jaipur, on further consideration of the implications of the proposed scheme of railway extension through the Jaipur State, submitted a 'memorandum of conditions' to the Political Agent, Jaipur on 13 July 1867 to be forwarded to the Agent to Governor-General for Rajputana States and thence to the Government of India for their approval and sanction. Many of these conditions were regarded by the Agent as "peculiarly unreasonable and of such a character as could not possibly be taken into consideration". As these conditions were conceived by the Maharaja to protect the interests of his State, they may be mentioned in detail with the reaction and remarks of the Agent to Governor-General for Rajputana States on each of them :[9]

(1) The line of railway, when fixed in detail by survey, to be subject to the approval of the Darbar, prior to the Surveyor's Report being submitted for the sanction of the Government of India.

A.G.G. commented that the Government of India was not prepared to concede to the Maharaja the measure of authority implied in the condition. However, when the survey was submitted for the approval of Government the Maharaja could at that time offer any suggestions or propose any alteration which would be considered fully and impartially by the Supreme Government.

(2) The Darbar to depute some confidential person on its behalf to be present at the survey throughout the whole line.

This was concurred in by A.G.G.

(3) Private property to be carefully avoided as far as it might be practicable.

This was concurred in by A.G.G.

(4) The city of Jaipur and the Ghat to be avoided altogether.

Concurred in absolutely by the A.G.G. so far as the city of Jaipur was concerned. In regard to the Ghat opinion was deferred till the conduct of the survey.

(5) All religious edifices, especially temples dedicated to Mahadeva, to be scrupulously avoided under any circumstances.

A.G.G. remarked that this could not be admitted, for it was absurd to suppose that the line was to be diverted for one and every temple that might fall in the way.

(6) If the Railway Company should require for temporary use any lands beyond the limits agreed upon, the Darbar to have the power to refuse them, or to allow them to be occupied on such terms as it might think proper to fix.

This was concurred in by A.G.G.

(7) If the route of the line should lay at a distance from the city of Jaipur, and the construction of a branch line to connect it with the city became necessary, the Darbar would have a voice in the fixing of the line and of a site for its station house.

This was concurred in by A.G.G.

(8) A *Harkara*, or some other servant of the Raj, to be

posted at each railway station to watch its interests and to convey information.

A.G.G. conceded that no objection would be offered to a Darbar *Harkara* remaining at each station.

(9) No change in the arrangements or system or innovation of any kind relating to the working of the railway to be introduced without the previous knowledge or consent of the Darbar.

A.G.G. opined that it was impossible to admit of a guarantee of this kind, for one set of rules must obtain throughout the length of one line of railway, and could not be determined by the fancy of the Chief of each State through which the railway passed.

(10) All rules and orders which the railway authorities might from time to time issue in connection with this line to be always officially communicated to the Darbar.

This was concurred in by A.G.G.

(11) The Raj to have the power to fix a special tariff on all goods breaking bulk *en route* through the Jaipur State, or passing to the railway line from any part of the country.

This was already concurred in by the Government of India.

(12) Stringent measures to be adopted for the prevention of all ill-treatment of native passengers by the railway servants, and all rules and orders which might be issued for that purpose to be subject to the approval of the Darbar.

A.G.G. assured the Maharaja that all necessary measures for the prevention of ill-treatment of native passengers would be duly borne in mind, and any representations on such subject from the Darbar would be always gladly accepted. But the Government of India could not concede to the Darbar the right of rejecting such rules as might be framed after full and due consideration.

(13) All complaints from the subjects of the Raj to be heard

and decided by the Political Agent of Jaipur in every instance in the presence of the *Vakil* of, and in communication with, this Darbar, and prompt steps be taken by the Railway Company for the removal of the immediate cause or causes of such complaints.

A.G.G. remarked that a special Railway Act was in contemplation for the trial of all railway officials and that he was not prepared in the meanwhile to make any specific assurance without orders from the Government of India.

(14) The Raj to have the power to disallow the purchase or procurement of any particular materials or goods which might be required for railway purchase within the Jaipur territories.

A.G.G. sought clarification whether the condition now under consideration had reference to any other articles besides wood for fuel for the purchase of which the Maharaja had already raised objection.

(15) The Railway Company always to comply readily and promptly with any request which the Darbar might make to any Station Master direct, and the object of which might be the prevention of a criminal escape, or of any unlawful attempt of any of its subjects or servants to leave the territories of Jaipur.

This was concurred in by A.G.G.

(16) The Jaipur Darbar would not be liable to pay any damage for any of its subjects for offences committed within the limits of the railway should they be unable to pay the same : this was applicable specially to thefts committed within the said limits.

This was concurred in by A.G.G.

(17) No railway official or servants to be permitted to live within any city or village, or anywhere beyond the limits of the railway, without the knowledge or permission of the Darbar.

This was concurred in by A.G.G.

(18) A saloon carriage, built at the suggestion and with

the approbation of the Maharaja, to be provided by the Railway Company for his special use, at a fixed rate of fare, to be settled previous to the opening of the line.

This was acceptable to A.G.G. but he added that the opening of the line could not be reasonably postponed simply because the Maharaja and the Company could not arrive at an understanding as to the precise amount of the rate.

(19) Special trains to be also provided for the use of the Raj at a rate of fare to be fixed in like manner.

A.G.G. remarked that rates for special trains could also be fixed upon by mutual agreement.

(20) None of the officials or servants of the Company would be permitted to purchase any landed property within the limits of the Jaipur territories.

This was concurred in by the A.G.G.

The Agent to Governor-General for Rajputana States forwarded the 'memorandum of conditions' on which the Maharaja agreed to the passage of a railway through his territory, together with his remarks as well as those of the Political Agent, Jaipur, to the Government of India.[10] Though the Governor-General in Council concurred generally in the remarks of the Agent to Governor-General on the conditions proposed by the Maharaja, the Supreme Government felt that in respect of conditions Nos. 1, 5 and 9 the Agent to Governor-General had been over-cautious in guarding the interests of the railways and directed that the wishes of the Darbar on these points should be attended to. As regards condition 13 the Government of India instructed that all complaints from Jaipur subjects on matters connected with the railway might be heard and adjudicated by the Political Agent in the presence of a *Vakil* or other representative of the Maharaja, subject to such review and control as was exercised over the Political Agent's decision by the Agent to the Governor-General and the Government of India generally. The Governor-General in Council did not agree to accept condition 14, and ruled that the railway authorities must be allowed to purchase, at reasonable prices agreed upon by both parties, whatever materials might be required by them; otherwise their arrangements would be completely paralyzed. It was suggested by the Supreme Government that an addition should be made to the 16th condition to the effect that the Darbar must do its best to enforce against its subjects any penalties which they might have incurred for offences committed within the limits of the railway.[11] A copy of the communication received from the Agent to Governor-General, Rajputana enclosing 'memorandum of conditions' from the Maharaja of Jaipur as well as that of the orders of Government of India in reply, was sent to the Secretary of State for India for information.[12]

Maharaja Ram Singh of Jaipur was the only Chief in Rajputana who prepared and presented to the British Government a 'memorandum of conditions' containing no less than 20 conditions in connection with the extension of railway line in the territory of his State. It is a compliment to his ability as a ruler to have conceived these comprehensive conditions to safeguard the interests of his State, as well as to his boldness as a subordinate Chief to have submitted this memorandum for the consideration of the Paramount Power. It goes to the credit of the Supreme Government that they accepted most of these conditions which appeared reasonable and fair, but they declined to accept those conditions which were incompatible with the general principles of the British policy laid down in respect of construction and extension of railway lines in all the Native States.

The Maharaja agreed to withdraw the conditions submitted by him earlier. He communicated his decision to do so in a letter addressed to the Political Agent at Jaipur on 5 February 1868. He wrote :

> On reconsideration of the whole subject connected with the Railway question, which has come before me since I last had the pleasure of conversing with you about it, I have made up by mind to withdraw the conditions submitted by me, simply repeating my consent to those originally proposed by the Government of India in letter No. 721, dated 24th March 1865.
>
> In communicating the decision I have thus come to, I have simply

> to state that I rely fully on Government protecting my interests in every possible way when I may have occasion to need its interference, and seeing that all points in dispute are settled strictly in accordance not only with the principles of law and justice, but the circumstances of the country, and the manner, customs and feelings of its people.[13]

Accordingly the Maharaja formally agreed to cede free of cost land required for railway purposes; to defray all necessary compensation for loss accruing to owners of land, houses, etc., in the land ceded; to make over full jurisdiction in the land ceded, short of sovereign rights, absolutely to the British Government; and to surrender all transit and other duties on goods passing through, goods breaking bulk or conveyed to or from the railway being charged either at the prevailing rates or at a tariff to be fixed thereafter.[14]

In October 1869 it was decided to construct Rajputana State Railway from Sambhar to Delhi and Agra, a total distance of 320 miles. The general directions of the line from Agra indicated by the preliminary survey made by the Engineers of the Bombay and Baroda Railway line pointed the route as through Bharatpur, Goodha and Jaipur to Sambhar, and from Delhi through Rewari and Alwar to Goodha, the length of the former being about 190 miles and that of the latter 130 miles. The project was to be carried out under the immediate control of the Government of North-Western Provinces. The Supreme Government decided to divide the Rajputana State Railway as sanctioned into two districts, each to be placed under the charge of a Superintending Engineer. Major F.W. Peile was given the charge of the Agra district where the Railway was to extend from Agra to Sambhar and possibly to Ajmer. Mr. Furnivall was entrusted with the charge of Delhi district where the Railway was to extend from Delhi to the point of junction of the two districts. The executive control was given by the Government of India to the Lieutenant-Governor of North-Western Provinces.[15]

In March 1870 the Public Works Department submitted a Report by Mr. Furnivall, the Superintending Engineer, Delhi Division, Rajputana State Railway, on the question of constructing alternative lines of Railway between Rewari and Jaipur either direct or *via* Alwar. After a careful consideration of the advantages as well as the disadvantages of taking the Railway from Jaipur to Delhi via Alwar, Furnivall arrived at the conclusion that the Alwar route was better. The Foreign Department was requested to issue instructions to the local Political Officers to communicate with the Chiefs concerned and to report their opinions on the proposal.[16] While forwarding the proposal of the Public Works Department to the Agent to Governor-General, Rajputana, the Supreme Government directed that the wishes of the Chiefs of Jaipur, Alwar and Bharatpur on the subject should be ascertained as soon as possible and their answer should be forwarded along with the opinions of local Political Officers and his own views to the Government of India.[17] Furnivall's proposal was accepted.

As required by the office of the Agent to Governor-General, Rajputana, the land plan and schedule of land acquired for the Rajputana State Railway in the Jaipur and Kishangarh territories was supplied by the Political Agent, Jaipur in accordance with the instructions communicated by the Agent to Governor-General.[18]

In regard to the jurisdiction in the lands ceded for Rajputana State Railway, the Government of India, Foreign Department ordered :

Whereas the Maharajas of Jaipur, Kishangarh and Bharatpur have granted to the British Government full jurisdiction within those portions of land forming the Rajputana State Railway, including the lands occupied as stations, out building and for other purposes connected with the Railway, which lie within their respective territories; for the better exercise of such jurisdiction, His Excellency the Governor-General in Council is pleased to issue the following Notification under Sections 4 and 5 of Act XI of 1872 :

The Political Agent for the time being in Jaipur shall exercise the powers described in Section 36 of Act X of 1872 (the Code of Criminal Procedure), and the powers of a Magistrate of the First Class as described in the same Act within such portion of the aforesaid lands as are situated within the limits of the Jaipur Political Agency.

The Political Agent in the Eastern State Agency in Rajputana and the Commissioner of Ajmer as the Agent to Governor-General in Council shall respectively exercise the powers of a Court of Sessions and a High Court as described in Act X of 1872 within the whole of the aforesaid lands.

The administration of the Police within the aforesaid lands shall be delegated to an officer to be designated Superintendent of Rajputana State Railway Police, who shall exercise the same police powers as may be exercised by a District Superintendent of Police under any law for the time being in force in British territory, in subordination to the Political Agent in Jaipur and the Political Agent in the Eastern States of Rajputana within the portions of the aforesaid lands situated within the Agencies respectively.

The Agent to the Governor-General, Rajputana communicated to the Government of India, Foreign Department, a set of Draft Rules for the Rajputana Railway Police prepared by the Superintendent Rajputana State Railway Police in consultation with the Political Agent, Jaipur vide No. 348 G, dated 20 March 1873. According to these rules the Agent to Governor-General was to be the Inspector-General of the State Railway Police. The Superintendent Railway Police was to have a *Vakil* from each State through which the Railway passed as a means of communication between himself and the authorities of the Native State concerned. The Superintendent himself or his Court Inspector would prosecute cases occurring on the Railway line. The total Police Force was to consist of 4 Inspectors, 10 Sub-Inspectors, 39 Head Constables, 222 Constables and 6 European Serjeants which was to be allocated to various Railway Stations according to their importance. The said police staff should be gradually enlisted within the next six months. The total cost of Police Force was estimated at rupees 65,218 per annum and the equipment of the Force would require a further amount of rupees 10,424. Arms and ammunition were to be supplied by the Government and the charges would be debited against the Railway Police.[19]

The Agent to the Governor-General, Rajputana suggested

that the headquarters of the officer appointed to the Police of the Rajputana State Railway might be at Jaipur where he would become acquainted with the Court, and officials with whom his principal work would be. The Public Works Department concurred generally in the views expressed by the Agent to the Governor-General and the Government of India, Foreign Department ruled that the headquarters of the Police be fixed at Jaipur.[20] In 1883 the Agent to the Governor-General, Rajputana wrote to the Supreme Government on the subject of the headquarters of the Superintendent of the Rajputana-Malwa Railway Police, and enquired whether the removal of the office from Jaipur to Ajmer had the approval of the Government of India. He stated that the question had arisen on a letter from the then Superintendent of the Police, who urged that the transfer would be in every way beneficial, seeing that Ajmer was now the centre of the Rajputana-Malwa Railway system, and that if the Police Superintendent were stationed there he would be in personal communications with the Railway authorities, an advantage which he did not enjoy in Jaipur. The Agent to the Governor-General added that this change would involve no un-necessary expense, since the accommodation now supplied at Jaipur was of the most temporary description, while at Ajmer a house already existed for the Superintendent; and further the Railway authorities were ready, on the change being sanctioned, to provide the necessary office accommodation. Taking everything into consideration, the Agent to the Governor-General recommended that the proposed change should be effected, and he requested that early orders be passed in this regard.[21] His recommendation was accepted by the Foreign and Public Works Departments of the Government of India, and necessary orders were issued by the Governor-General in Council, sanctioning the proposal.[22]

The Rajputana-Malwa Railway was under the management of the Government of India. The management of this railway was leased out by the Government to Bombay, Baroda and Central India Railway on January 1, 1885 for 20 years in the first instance.[23] Even under the management of the Government of India the Rajputana-Malwa Railway was not able to meet the operational expenses plus interest on capital invested. It may be observed that the railway construction and management was a source of employment for a large number of high salaried non-technical Englishmen and thus formed part of the process of drain of a large amount of money which could have been utilised in paying off the guaranteed interest. The management either under the private companies or the British Government thus was not likely to leave any money for addition to the State exchequer by the way of revenue.[24]

In 1892 four plots of land in the Jaipur State were acquired for the crossing station on the Rajputana-Malwa Railway. For this purpose plans and schedules were sent by the Agent, Bombay, Baroda and Central India Railway to the Agent to Governor-General Rajputana who communicated the same to the Resident Jaipur. The Resident negotiated with the Jaipur Darbar and acquired the required plots of land for the Rajputana-Malwa Railway.[25] Likewise a strip of additional land measuring 0.136 acre was acquired from the Jaipur Darbar which was required by the Rajputana-Malwa Railway for improving the water arrangements at Dhankia Railway Station.[26]

In 1896 the Jaipur and the Kishangarh Darbar preferred their claims for the trees, fruits, lac, grass, etc. grown in the Railway limits within their territory under the misunderstanding that they had surrendered that land only for the railway purposes and that the rights to land revenue had not been given up. These cases were referred to the Agent to Governor-General for opinion but he refused to admit their claims for such products saying that they had ceded every jurisdiction over the land except the sovereign rights.[27]

In 1904 land was acquired from the Jaipur Darbar for the Rewari-Phulera Chord Railway in response to letter No. 1122 dated 14 March 1904 from Acting Agent, Bombay, Baroda and Central India Railway to the Agent to Governor-General Rajputana sent along with the plan and schedule of land required. Thereafter the Jaipur Darbar was asked to cede jurisdiction over the section of the Rewari-Phulera Chord Railway which traversed the Jaipur State. The Agent to

Governor-General, Rajputana in his letter to the Resident, Jaipur, dated 23 July 1904, communicated the instructions of the Government of India in this regard. In their letter No. 1191-I.B., dated Ist May 1899 with which the Government of India forwarded the revised Form regarding the cession of jurisdiction by all the Darbars of India, they expressly explained that they had not asked for the cession of sovereignty. The Supreme Government at the same time had made it clear in their letter that the various forms of words in which jurisdiction had previously from time to time been ceded by Darbars had proved inadequate in actual practice and it had become necessary to revise the Form in such a way as to cover all the points short of the cession of sovereign rights, that might in future be raised with the line in question. Therefore they had devised the 'short, single and comprehensive' Form of five lines which accompanied their letter. In that letter the Government desired that "the form should be used whenever fresh cessions of jurisdiction are required." The Agent to the Governor-General informed that this Form had actually been used by all Darbars which had ceded jurisdiction since its issue. He quoted the instances of Bikaner, Kota, Tonk, Gwalior, Indore, Jodhpur, Patiala, etc., and added that the Alwar Darbar had very recently adopted this Form in ceding jurisdiction over the section of the Rewari-Phulera Chord Railway within its limits. To insert in the Form a clause limiting the breadth of land required for the Railway would prove inconvenient in the event of its being found essential in future to take up additional land. But the Maharaja of Jaipur might be assured that only so much land as was actually needed for the efficient working of the line would be used, and that, if possible, any surplus land which might not be so needed would be restored to the Darbar. The arrangements for the surrender of extraditable offenders would not be affected by the cession of jurisdiction which the Government had now desired to be obtained from the Darbar. A copy of the Form submitted by the Political Agent, Alwar regarding the cession of jurisdiction by the Alwar Darbar was appended for the guidance of the Jaipur Resident.[28]

Accordingly, the Maharaja of Jaipur submitted the

following Form duly signed by him on 19 August 1904 :

> I, Sawai Madho Singh, Maharaja of Jaipur, hereby cede to the British Government full and exclusive power and jurisdiction of every kind over the lands in the said State which are, or may hereafter be, occupied by the Rewari-Phulera Chord Railway (including all lands occupied for stations, for out buildings and for other railway purposes), and over all persons and things whatsoever within the said lands.[29]

After the cession of jurisdiction over the lands occupied by the Rewari-Phulera Chord Railway by the rulers of Jaipur and Alwar, the Governor-General in Council issued a Draft Notification regarding the administration of criminal justice within the aforesaid portions of land. According to this Notification, the provision of the following acts were to be applied to these lands :

> Act XLV of 1860 (The Indian Penal Code), Act V of 1861 (The Police Act, 1861), Act VI of 1864 (The Whipping Act, 1864), Act I of 1871 (The Cattle Trespass Act, 1871), Act III of 1888 (The Police Act, 1888) and Act V of 1898 (The Code of Criminal Procedure, 1898). Provided that the Code of Criminal Procedure, 1898, would be subject to these modifications, namely (a) that trials before the Court of Session, may in the discretion of the Judge, be without the aid of jury or assessors; (b) that notwithstanding anything in the Code of Criminal Procedure 1898, or the Police Act (V of 1861), the Governor-General may confer on any Police Officer all or any of the powers conferred or conferrable by or under the Code on any Magistrate in regard to particular cases, or to a particular class and to particular classes of cases or to cases generally. The provisions of this Notification would apply to all proceedings except (a) proceedings against European British subjects or persons jointly charged with European British subjects, and (b) proceedings pending at the date of this Notification which shall be carried on as if this Notification had not been issued.[30]

In 1906 an Agreement was concluded between the Jaipur Darbar and the Bombay, Baroda and Central India Railway Company for working the Jaipur State Railway between Sanganer and Sawai Madhopur. Respective obligations of the Company and the Darbar were specified in various articles of the Agreement.

Since the Railway line was confined in the territories of the Jaipur State, the Jaipur Darbar was to have exclusive control in the matters of jurisdiction. The Indian Railway Act, 1890 and Acts for the time being in force in British India relating to railways and the Rules, Conditions and Forms thereunder for the time being applicable to the Rajputana Railway would apply to the Jaipur State Railway. The Railway lines, stations, buildings, dwellings for staff, level crossings, signals, repairing sheds with their machinery and all other necessary appliances for working the line were to be provided by the Darbar and alterations and additions which might be required from time to time would be carried out by or at the cost of the Darbar. As regards the working expenses of the Railway, the Company would charge the Darbar the same percentage of the gross earnings of the State railway as would be the case with the entire B. B. and C. I. Railway. The Darbar agreed to provide and maintain a force of Police for the protection of the line and of property in the trains and at each station thereof. The staff for the Railway was to be recruited from the natives of Jaipur as far as possible. Maharaja of Jaipur's private saloon would be allowed to run free of charge on any train running on the Jaipur State Railway. This Agreement was valid for two years and would be deemed to continue in force until the same would be terminated by notice of not less than 12 months from either party. Any question or dispute which might arise in carrying out the arrangements as laid down in the Agreement would be settled by arbitration, and arbitrators approved by both the parties would be appointed when necessary.[31] A comparison of the working of Jodhpur-Bikaner Railway operated by the State government with the Sanganer-Sawai Madhopur Railway operated by a British Company would make it obvious that the terms of the latter were less favourable for the Jaipur State.[32]

It is pertinent to point out that the Government of India had enunciated its policy very clearly in respect of cession of jurisdiction over railway lands by the Native States in the general circular issued in June 1891. It was laid down in this circular that as long as a railway line was isolated in one Native State and formed no part of a line of communication passing through territory not belonging to the State, the British Government on such a railway would not ordinarily exercise wider authority than considered essential by it as a Paramount Power to assert generally throughout the State. But in cases where the railway lines passed through the territories of two or more Native States, or through British territory as well as that of a Native State, the British Government should assume full and exclusive jurisdiction on such lines, for the inconvenience arising from a multiplicity of jurisdiction could be most serious and intolerable.[33] The copies of this circular were sent for the guidance of all the Local Governments and Political Agencies. As some of the Darbars (notably Patiala and Jind Darbars) had not complied with the contents of this circular in respect of certain Railway lines, the Government of Curzon decided that full and exclusive jurisdiction on such railway lines should be ceded by the rulers of all the Native States on a uniform basis. For this purpose a Form was prescribed in 1899 and the rulers of the States concerned were required to surrender 'full and exclusive' jurisdiction by filling up the Form under their signature. The Maharaja of Jaipur, as already mentioned, had surrendered 'full and exclusive' jurisdiction on this prescribed Form over the lands occupied by the Rewari-Phulera Chord Railway in August 1904.

The British authorities had, of course, no legal right to assume full police, civil and criminal jurisdiction on the railway lines traversing the territories of the States. The assumption of 'full and exclusive' jurisdiction on the lines by the Paramount Power "manifestly marked an inroad on the judicial independence of Indian States."[34] It was observed by the Standing Committee of the Chamber of Princes :

> But no one on the side of either the Government or the States seems to have foreseen that the extension of railways in the states might, and indeed, must lead to the extension of the political predominance of the Government of India over the States' own internal authority. Given the cession of jurisdiction such predominance is an inevitable sequence of the construction of railways.[35]

It may be argued in justification of the policy of the British

Government that as a Paramount Power they considered it to be incumbent upon them to extend railways throughout the country for the benefits of British India as well as for those of the Princely States. Whatever be the original ulterior motive of the British authorities in building railways in India, there is no denying the fact that they were considered essential for the military defence as well as for economic development and prosperity of the sub-continent as a whole. Since the States were to share the benefit, there appeared to be nothing wrong in acquiring lands from them free of charge for the railway lines. The assumption of full and exclusive jurisdiction on the railway lines was also considered essential by the British Government in order to assure safety and justice to the travellers, whether they happened to be subjects of British India or Native India. "For the purpose of uniformly efficient working of the railway lines in the country, as it were, the sovereign rights of the Chiefs were subordinated to the requirements of the Paramount Power."[36]

Despite these justifications, the fact remains that the construction of railways in British India as well as Native India eminently served the economic interests of the Imperial Government and may be viewed as a part of the colonial economy. The British capitalists acquired substantial gains not only in terms of getting adequate and prompt supply of raw material and also country-wide markets for their manufactured goods but many British Companies were also the principal beneficiaries by getting contracts for construction of many railway lines. From the Indian point of view, it proved to be a major factor of the drain of wealth from India to Great Britain. It should also not be forgotten that quite a large number of Englishmen and Europeans were employed on fat salaries on the railways constructed all over the sub-continent including the Princely States. The Europeans were also given special privileges while travelling in the trains and also special provisions were made for their trial by European Judges if they committed crime on the railway lines. The vernacular newspapers were critical of the preferential treatment given to the white passengers who not unoften looked down upon the

Indian passengers. For example, the *Rajputana Gazette* in an issue of December 1895 stated that European passengers were allowed to break railway rules which natives would be punished for breaking. The paper quoted an instance that the other day a European woman travelled in Second Class with an intermediate ticket. At a station an Indian with a Second Class ticket tried to enter her carriage but the woman would not allow him to come in. The European Station Master decided in favour of the woman. The paper also complained that the Railway Companies largely employed Europeans and Eurasians in preference to Natives.[37] *The Rajputana Gazette* pointed out in an issue of February 1896 that natives were not treated properly when travelling by rail. Europeans objected to travelling in the same compartment with them. The other day, the Editor of the said paper and the Editor of *Rajasthan Samachar* got into a Second Class compartment at Nimbhera station on the Neemuch line. There were two Europeans in the carriage, one of whom was 'most rude' to them and 'behaved like a madman'.[38]

Side by side with the railways, roads were also constructed connecting Jaipur with other cities of the State as well as with the cities of British territory and those of the neighbouring States. In the post-1860 period the Jaipur Darbar, as also the other Darbars of Rajputana States, under pressure from the British, had to construct such roads as were considered to be of imperial importance. The British authorities encouraged Maharaja Ram Singh to undertake the construction of roads which could be useful for the economic progress of British India as well as the State. All the roads were under the charge of the Public Works Department and were maintained by the State; and all except the one from Agra to Ajmer were constructed entirely at the cost of the State. The most important of these roads was the metalled trunk road from Agra to Ajmer constructed between 1865 and 1869; its length in Jaipur territory was about 127 miles and its cost was rupees 6.5 lakhs, of which the British Government contributed one-fifth.[39] The Jaipur Darbar took advantage of the 20% subsidy offered by the Government of India to the Indian Princes who constructed roads at their own expense through their territories.[40] The road to Sambhar via

Bagru was also begun by the Jaipur Darbar in 1868 and completed in 1870.[41] In 1873 the principle was laid down by the British authorities that, while the Supreme Government would take upon itself the responsibility for the provision of trunk systems of railway throughout India, the provision of feeder roads was left to Local Governments and Administrations. The Governor-General in Council trusted that the rulers of the Native States would follow the same course as the Local Governments, and the Political Officers were desired to draw the attention of the Native Princes to the subject. The Government of India pointed out that throughout India, except on certain great highways, the means of communication were of the rudest and most primitive kind, suited in a certain degree to the wants of an agricultural and pastoral community, but very inadequate to assist materially in giving a full impulse to traffic and the exchange of commodities, which it was a main object of railways to foster. The Local Governments as well as the Princely States were urged to make "the utmost possible efforts in respect to feeder roads.[42]

Early in 1874 it was decided to open the Agra District of the Rajputana State Railway to Bandikui. Bandikui, it was said, would be an important junction with the Railway to Delhi, which was situated at a distance from any road or line of traffic. It would be a great convenience to passengers to or from Jaipur, and others, if a rough fair weather road on which carts could travel were made between it and the high road from Agra to Jaipur.[43] The Maharaja of Jaipur readily agreed to construct this road for which the Governor-General in Council expressed thanks to the Maharaja.[44]

With the efforts of the Maharaja two other important roads were also constructed — the Jaipur–Tonk Road with 48 miles in Jaipur territory and the Karauli-Mandawar Road, 49 miles long passing through two large towns in the Jaipur State. The latter became a significant artery of trade because of its connecting the Mandawar station on the Rajputana Railway and the town of Hindaun which was the principal mart for cotton, grain, oilseeds, raw sugar, tobacco, etc., grown in the south and east of the Jaipur State.[45]

Among the other roads constructed and repaired by the Jaipur Darbar, mention may be made of Agra Road, Naila Road, Dausa-Sawai Madhopur Road, Gungapur-Hindaun Road, Gungapur-Lalsot Road, Deoli-Rajmahal Road, Niraina-Malpura Road and Bandikui-Madhogunj Road.[46] Besides these roads, many City and Camp roads were also constructed such as Road from Chandpole to Railway Station, New Church Road, Bund-Ka-Durwaza Road, Pumping Station Road, Widening Road at Railway Station Jaipur, Link Road (Huthroi Kothi), Road at Amani Shah, Road at Mission House, etc.[47] It has been estimated that towards the closing year of the period of our study the total length of metalled roads was about 283 miles and that of unmetalled roads about 236 miles.[48]

In December 1882, the Jaipur Darbar abolished all the transit duties on the roads leading to the Rajputana-Malwa Railway within Jaipur territory with the exception of duty on opium. This measure was highly appreciated by the British authorities, and the Viceroy and Governor-General of India conveyed to the Maharaja of Jaipur his "cordial acknowledgements of the enlightened spirit" which had been evinced by the Maharaja in the matter. Thereafter a Notification was issued by the Government of India asking all the Princes and Chiefs to abolish transit duties within their territories through which the railway lines ran.[49]

Thus the roads constructed by the Jaipur Darbar as well as by the rulers of other States together with the abolition of all transit duties on the 'feeder roads', cleared the way for the development of trade and commence without any let or hindrance throughout the length and breadth of the country, and provided another facet of the growth of British paramountcy in the States during the period of our study.

II

The British authorities considered it essential to make certain arrangements with the Princely States of India in order to ensure smooth and efficient working of the Imperial postal system.

For this purpose they had to seek the co-operation of the rulers of States. To begin with, they had to take measures for the safety of Imperial mails in the territories of the States. In July 1866 the Government of India issued a Resolution, which asserted in unqualified terms the absolute responsibility of the States for mail robberies occurring within their territories. In this Resolution[50] the following rules were laid down :

(1) Every State is responsible for secure passage through its territory of Government mail and parcel post.
(2) Where mails or parcel posts are plundered with impunity in consequence of inefficient arrangements for their security on high roads traversing a State, that State will be required to increase the Guards which accompany the mails and strengthen its police stations along the high roads, or same be done by the British Government at the expense of the State concerned.
(3) Where mails or parcel posts are plundered, the Native State into which plunderers are traced and out of which they cannot be traced will be expected to levy compensation from the district for the value of plundered mails or parcel posts.
(4) In estimating such compensation no exemption whatever is to be made on account of bullion, jewellery and other articles of great intrinsic value.
(5) Where men are disabled for life or killed in defence or in carriage of Government mails or parcel posts, claims to pensionary grants will be held to lie against the State held responsible for the outrage.

In pursuance of this Resolution, the British authorities took suitable action against the rulers of Jaipur and other States in whose territories mail robberies occurred from time to time. In April 1872 the case of plunder of Deoli mail between Tomra and Sundara in the Jaipur territory came to the notice of the British Government. There were six suspected perpetrators of the outrage who had taken refuge in the Tonk State. The Tonk Darbar reported that they had arrested only one of the suspects. Thereupon they were told that the other five suspects should be "speedily and satisfactorily accounted for." The Maharaja of Jaipur in a meeting with the Agent to Governor-General, Rajputana held earlier at Jaipur, had assured him that he would not rest satisfied until all the suspected robbers implicated in attack on mails had been accounted for. The Political Agent at Jaipur was instructed to report monthly steps taken by the two Darbars to effect the arrest of suspected culprits and the measures adopted to ensure vigorous action in the matter.[51]

In January 1873 another case of mail robbery in village Mohanpura of Jaipur State was reported. A mail cart was attacked by 15 or 20 armed horsemen at whom the coachman fired his pistol but to no effect. This attack was attributed to 'carelessness and neglect' of escort and patrol establishment. About three months after, on 26 April 1873, another mail cart was plundered in broad day light with 'utmost audacity' in Jaipur territory. The Agent to Governor-General directed the Political Agent at Jaipur to meet the Maharaja to express regret with which the Governor-General had heard of these repeated attacks on Government mails. He further asked him to convey to the Maharaja that severe punishments should be given to the officers whose negligence could be proved. The Jaipur Darbar 'acted with promptitude'; the track of robbers was followed up into Marwar territory. Thereafter the culprits arrested by Marwar Darbar were sent to Jaipur for trial. The Marwar villagers held guilty for harbouring and assisting perpetrators of crime were fined. The Jaipur Darbar was held mainly responsible for the robbery and fined a sum equal to the value of the property plundered, namely rupees 2,985, of which an amount of rupees 273 was to be paid to the sufferers. The remaining amount was to be debited to The Agency Mail Robbery Fund. In these two cases of mail robberies, the conduct of Jaipur police was held to be "of most culpable and unpardonable character." The Darbar was directed to take more stringent action in such cases in future. In another letter the Political Agent suggested three measures for better security of transit of mails : (i) sending an armed guard in the mail cart, (ii) the provision of strong locks in the cart for the mail bags, and

(iii) the prohibition of conveyance of passengers except when booked at post offices.[52]

By referring to the two cases of highway robberies of mails in the Jaipur territory, as discussed above, and the three measures to be adopted for the better security of transit of mails as suggested by the Political Agent, the Director-General of Post Offices of India issued orders for giving effect to the three measures. It was also clarified that the armed guard to be seated in the mail cart was not in substitution of but in addition to the armed *Sowar* who had hitherto invariably accompanied the mail cart. The Political Agent, Jaipur informed the higher authorities that this arrangement was being strictly enforced by the Jaipur Darbar and that it was his duty to see that there was no relaxation or disregard of the measures permitted.[53]

In October 1883 a mail robbery occurred in the Shekhawati district of the Jaipur State. While the postal runner, named Ram Rattan, was carrying the postal transit bag from Surajgarh to Chirawa (in Shekhawati district) on the evening of 20 October 1883, he was attacked by two men on foot armed with *lathies.* They knocked him down, inflicting several wounds on his head, shoulders and arms, and taking the transit bag from him, made off. As soon as the alarm could be given, the tracks of the robbers were followed, and five bags with their contents were recovered a quarter of a mile from the scene of the offence. The sixth bag containing registered and insured packets valued at rupees 325 could not be traced, and the question arose as to who should be held responsible for payment of compensation. It was admitted by the Jaipur Darbar that the robbery occurred in their territory, and was primarily due to the negligence of one of their *Sowars,* named Sher Singh, who had lagged behind instead of keeping pace with the postal runner. But it was contended that the tracks of the robbers had been carried across the Punjab border into the Loharu State which was, therefore, to some extent liable. The Loharu authorities, on the other hand, held that the tracks had not been brought into their territory, or had not been properly made over to their people. As the two Darbars could not agree, the Resident, Eastern Rajputana States, named Dr. J. P. Stratton, had to give his decision. He found that the tracks had not been made over to the Loharu villagers in the manner required by the Track Rules and that, therefore, the whole responsibility for the property lost remained with Jaipur. In accordance with this decision, the Jaipur Darbar had to make good the loss under the compensation rules.[54]

Since the promulgation of rules under the Resolution of 18 July 1866, the question of liability of Princely States for mail robberies occurring in their territories had been considered on several occasions. It was felt that full effect could not properly be given to these strict rules and there had been deviations in certain cases. In 1881, the Secretary of State for India directed that in applying these rules due regard should be paid to the efficiency of the State police and to the vigilance displayed by the Darbar's officials in endeavouring to bring offenders to justice.[55] In 1885, therefore, the Government of India issued another Resolution[56] substituting revised rules for those laid down in the Resolution of 18 July 1866. While reiterating the responsibility of the States for secure passage of Imperial mail through their territories and their *prima facie* liability to pay compensation for the losses caused by robbery, the Resolution of 1885 allowed the State concerned to plead in its defence (i) that its police arrangements were efficient especially with regard to the protection of the mail routes passing through its territory; (ii) that the robbery was committed without complicity on the part of any of its own subjects, or contributory negligence on the part of its local authorities. It was also provided in this Resolution that the compensation paid by the States and the balances of existing Mail Robbery Funds would be credited to the miscellaneous revenue of the Post Office of India, and the Director-General of the Post Office might at his discretion award to consignors or consignees the whole or part of compensation payments to make good the loss caused by the robbery of articles which were neither insured nor of great intrinsic value. The rules of 1885 were approved and sanctioned by the Secretary of State[57], and they were declared to be binding on all the Princely States irrespective of their treaty obligations. These revised rules were generally viewed with feelings of satisfaction by the Princes and Chiefs of various States.

In 1886 the Government of India instructed that all reports about mail robberies in Jaipur and other Rajputana States should be communicated through the Agent to Governor-General.[58] Earlier the Political Agents concerned were required in 1871 (vide Foreign Dept., General A, April 1871, Nos. 43-47) and again in 1883 (vide Foreign Dept., A-General-I, Aug. 1883, Nos. 71-75) to submit copies of their initial reports on mail robberies direct to the Supreme Government. In 1890 a case of mail robbery occurred in the Jaipur territory. The Resident at Jaipur reported the case to the Agent to Governor-General who then forwarded the same to the Government of India. The mails in passing from Chirawa to Surajgarh on 24 March 1890 were plundered on the Raghunathpura-Salukhurd border. The bags contained only rupees 100 in cash and some ordinary letters. One *Sowar* accompanied the postal runner. The *Sowar* stated that seven men on foot and one man on a camel attacked them. The Surajgarh people who followed the trail immediately were joined by Raj *Thanadars* at Narhar and Mandella, two intervening villages. In the limits of the village of Bhomean, four miles from the scene of the robbery, the *Sowar's* horse and the letters were recovered. On 25 March at 12 'O clock noon the tracking party reached Budawas in Bikaner, 30 miles from the scene of the occurrence, where the *Thanadar* of Raburi (Bikaner) was summoned. He attended, but declined to take any action with regard to the continuance of the trail.

The two Darbars (Jaipur and Bikaner) having failed to come to an agreement upon the matter in dispute, the final settlement of the question, according to precedent, was referred to the decision of the Resident at Jaipur. After careful consideration the Resident opined that the tracks of robbers were carried as far as the village of Budawas in Bikaner, and that the *Thanadar* of Raburi failed to take efficient steps to verify the trail or to assist in carrying it further. On the other hand, he considered that the Jaipur authorities were open to censure for not having taken sufficient means to protect the mails. The robbers apparently consisted both of Jaipur and Bikaner men. So he held that the liability to pay compensation to Government for the losses incurred through the robbery should be borne equally by both the Darbars, and that the Bikaner Darbar should pay to the Jaipur Darbar the sum of rupees 52 being half the amount which had already been paid by the latter to the Government of India.[59]

In 1897 a Circular[60] was issued by the Deputy Post-Master General, Rajputana to all postal officials in the Rajputana Circle regarding the escort of mails in the territories of the Rajputana States. The Resident at Jaipur was informed that an unusually large traffic in post parcels containing silver and cash was taking place in these mail lines — Kuchman Road to Sikar, Sikar to Fatehpur and Ramgarh, and Ramgarh to Churu; and he was directed to advise the Jaipur Darbar of the increased responsibility for the safe passage of the parcel mails thrown upon the State and to take necessary measures. After receiving communication from the Resident, the Jaipur State Council made arrangements for providing an adequate escort to secure the safe passage of the parcel mails on the said mail lines. In July 1898 when the parcel traffic had become normal the Jaipur Darbar was informed by the Resident that special escort arrangements were no longer required.[61]

Meanwhile, in the seventies it had begun to be felt increasingly by the British authorities that the existence of diverse and defective postal systems in the Princely States hindered the development of trade in the country, stood in the way of smooth and successful working of the British postal system and caused great inconvenience to the people and their relatives living in the territory of British India and the States. It was, therefore, considered essential to make some arrangements in order to place the matter of the Imperial post in the Princely States on a satisfactory footing. The rulers of the States were asked through the Local Governments and Political Agents to introduce British postal system in their respective territories as far as possible. Maharaja Ram Singh of Jaipur responded partially and he set up a number of Imperial post offices in the Jaipur territories, in addition to a large number of Raj post offices scattered throughout his dominions.[62]

After the demise of Maharaja Ram Singh (1880), the Jaipur Darbar continued to co-operate with British authorities in constructing or providing buildings on rent for British post and telegraph offices and permitting the placing of letter-boxes in various towns of the State, but in many cases the Jaipur Council politely declined to accept their demands on the ground that the revenues of the Raj Postal Department were likely to suffer. Some instances may be given from the Jaipur Agency Record. In December 1887, Deputy Post Master General, Rajputana Circle wrote to the Resident that the Jaipur Post Office which was located in a Raj building, nearly two miles from the Railway Station and almost a similar distance from the city, was in an isolated position far from everybody and everything which was evidently a source of much inconvenience to the public. It was, therefore, decided to remove the Post Office to a central locality and for this purpose a departmental building was constructed close to the Railway Station into which the Post Office would be located at the commencement of the next month. He asked the Resident to inform the Jaipur Darbar that with effect from 10 January next the premises then occupied by the Post Office would no longer be required. For the convenience of the people living at a long distance from the Railway Station a small Post Office was opened near the public garden and the hospital. With the permission of the Jaipur Darbar Seth Nathamal and Jawahirmal rented a house belonging to them to the postal authorities.[63]

The Jaipur Darbar had permitted the placing of a letter-box in the bazar near the Police Station at Bissao for the convenience of the public in 1885. But the Jaipur Council had politely declined the proposals of the Deputy Post Master General, Rajputana Circle to place letter-boxes at a number of places later on. The proposal of placing a letter-box at Ramgarh was not accepted on the ground that revenue of the Raj Postal Department was likely to suffer if the placing of a letter-box was allowed there. Similarly the request for placing a letter-box at Baragaon (in the *pargana* of Jhunjhnu), situated between two villages, Islampur and Guda Gorji, each of which had a Raj Post Office, was not complied with as it would be detrimental to the income of the Jaipur Darbar. The placing of a letter-box at Pilani was also disallowed as the public of Pilani was perfectly satisfied with the existing postal arrangements. The Jaipur Council regretted to be unable to comply with the request of Deputy Post Master General for placing a letter-box at Dausa as it would affect the income of the Raj Postal Department.[64]

In 1898 the Superintendent Rajputana Division submitted a proposal to the Jaipur Darbar through the Resident Jaipur for opening combined Post and Telegraph Offices in the towns of Nawalgarh and Bissao in Shekhawati. It was intimated that a branch telegraph line from Sikar to Nawalgarh, a distance of 18 miles and another from Ramgarh to Bissao, a distance of 10 miles would have to be constructed. The Jaipur Council requested to be furnished with a list of intervening villages between Sikar and Nawalgarh and between Ramgarh and Bissao. In response to this request a list of 8 villages from Sikar to Nawalgarh and of 5 villages from Ramgarh to Bissao was supplied. Thereafter with the permission of Jaipur Darbar the combined Post and Telegraph Offices were opened at the two said towns.[65] In 1902 addition and alterations in the Post Office building at Bissao were permitted by the Jaipur Darbar and the Superintendent Post Offices Upper Rajputana was asked to pay the necessary monthly rent from the date of occupying the building.[66]

In 1899 Deputy Post Master General sought permission from the Jaipur Darbar through the Resident at Jaipur for the construction of new building of combined Post and Telegraph Office at Fatehpur (Jaipur) which fell within the jurisdiction of the Rao Raja of Sikar. As the Rao Raja of Sikar expressed his willingness to meet the additional requirement of Post and Telegraph Office at Fatehpur on the increased rent of rupees 33/- per month, the Jaipur Darbar gave the necessary permission and instructed the Rao Raja through his *Vakil* in attendance at Jaipur to accord necessary facilities and help to the Assistant Superintendent of Telegraph on his visit to Sikar and Fatehpur.[67]

By 1906 there were 32 Imperial (British) Post Offices and no less than 112 Raj (State) Post Offices in the Jaipur State.[68] At about this time the British authorities asked the Jaipur Darbar to adopt Postal Unity, but the latter showed reluctance to do so on the grounds that it would entail loss of revenue, that the British India Postal Department would not allow them any share in the profits which might thereafter be derived from the working of the Department, and, finally, that it would involve loss of prestige. The Agent to Governor-General opined that these arguments were not without weight; at any rate, they still carried great weight with the Darbar and there was no likelihood that they would accept the proposal of Postal Unity.[69]

In May 1906, Rao Bahadur Sansar Chander Sen, Senior Member of the Jaipur Council, addressed a communication to the Resident Jaipur pleading for the orders of Government of India to grant a postal convention to the Jaipur State. He remarked that along with the new lines of railway that had lately been constructed or were under construction in the Jaipur State, the Imperial Postal Department had recently opened their offices in several places as a result of which there was a steady and increasing loss to the Raj Postal Revenue. From the year 1904 the Darbar had introduced various reforms in its own Postal Department with a view to keep pace with the increasing public demand for postal communication within its territory and to raise the standard of efficiency and usefulness of the Department on the same lines as the Imperial Postal system. Consequently, the working of the Raj Postal Department was now perfectly satisfactory, and the Darbar was in a position to guarantee the safety and prompt delivery of all postal communications throughout its territory. Under these circumstances a convention between the Imperial and Raj Postal Departments for exchange of correspondence would be most satisfactory and useful solution. Therefore the Darbar's earnest request might be conveyed to the Government of India to conclude a postal convention with the Jaipur State on the same lines as that already concluded with the Gwalior Darbar and several Punjab States.[70] It may be mentioned that the Government of India had concluded Postal Conventions with Gwalior (April 1885), Patiala (15 September 1884), Nabha (23 March 1885), Jind (3 June 1886), Faridkot (30 November 1886) and Chamba (December 1886). The terms of these conventions for the exchange of correspondence, parcels, money-orders and postal orders, etc. were very reasonable for the States, insofar as they were all on a reciprocal basis. The British authorities also secured from these conventions all the conditions which were considered desirable for the efficient working of the Imperial postal system. The British Indian postage stamps, post cards and embossed envelopes (overprinted with the name of the State concerned but supplied by the British Government at cost price), the British Indian rates, fees and commissions, the British Indian money-order rules, etc., were to be adopted in the Post Offices of the States, and all foreign correspondence originating in the States was to be prepaid only by means of Imperial postage stamps.[71] According to C. L. Tupper, these conventions may be viewed as "a step in advance towards the policy of postal unity"[72], though they recognised the existence of separate State posts.

In reply to the 'earnest request' of the Jaipur Darbar to the British authorities for grant of a postal convention, the Deputy Post Master General, Rajputana informed the Resident, Jaipur that it was not the policy of the Government to extend the convention system any further and that the Jaipur Darbar should be intimated accordingly.[73]

Senior Member of the Jaipur Council, Rao Bahadur Sansar Chander Sen, wrote another letter to the Resident, Jaipur to be conveyed to the Government of India, reiterating the request of the Jaipur Darbar for granting postal convention to the State. He pointed out that the State post had made 'marvellous progress' during the last two years and its working could now be favourably compared with the Imperial Postal arrangements in any of the Rajputana States, that the Darbar had to meet a considerable expense for making extra arrangements for the safety of the Imperial mails, although the State post was quite capable to serve all the places within Jaipur territory, and that the opening of new Imperial Post Offices in Jaipur had been steadily telling more and more on the Raj postal revenue. He added that the Deputy Director-General of the Imperial Post Offices had paid a visit to Jaipur in October last and had recorded his opinion in these words : "The State has lately been taking special interest in its own postal services and has, I believe, developed it considerably."[74]

He enclosed with his letter "Notes on Jaipur State Postal Department" for perusal of the Imperial Department. As these Notes give a comprehensive account of the history and reorganisation of the State Postal Department, it will be useful to reproduce the main contents of these Notes with all the minute details as under :[75]

The existence of postal system in the Jaipur State could be traced as far back as the time of the Mughal rule when it was incorporated in the State Department known as *Mahkma Khabar*. Through its medium the Darbar was kept conversant with all the doings and movements of the Imperial Mughal court, as well as with the conduct of its own officers posted in different parts of the territory. Later on as a demand was felt for a greater facility of communication among the people, the Department was thrown open for the benefit of the Darbar's subjects under the name of *Dak-Khana*. Since 1854, the Darbar had granted permission from time to time to the Imperial Postal Department to open their offices in the capital as well as other important centres of the State. With a view to keep pace with the increasing public demand for postal communication within its territory and to raise the standard of efficiency and usefulness of the Department on the same lines as the Imperial Postal system, the Darbar decided in 1904 to take up in hand the work of thoroughly reorganising its Postal Department. The following important measures of reforms were introduced since 1904 :

(1) *Postal Lines*—The following postal lines were rearranged or newly opened : Jaipur-S.Madhopur Line, Rewanjna-Hindaun Line, Jaipur-Hindaun Line, Jaipur-Newai-Uniara Line, Jaipur-Sambhar Line, Jaipur-Malpura Line, Jaipur-Torawatti Line and Jaipur-Shekhawati Line.

(2) *Railway Arrangements*—Arrangements to carry Raj mails by railway were made from Jaipur to Bandikui and Phulera on the Rajputana–Malwa Railway to Newai on the Jaipur–S. Madhopur Railway and from Phulera to Dabla on the Rewari-Phulera Railway.

(3) *New Post Offices*—Formerly there were 89 State Post

Offices, and 23 new Post Offices were opened since 1904, thus bringing the total number of State Post Offices to 112.

(4) *Letter-Boxes*—Boxes for posting letters, etc., intended to be carried by the State Dak were first placed at different centres in the capital as well as in the districts in July 1904. Since then altogether 130 letter-boxes had been issued, of which 11 boxes had been allotted to the city.

(5) *Postage Stamps*—Adhesive Postage Stamps were first issued in 1904. At first these were printed at the Darbar Press and only stamps of the value of half anna, one anna and two annas were introduced. Subsequently contracts were given for printing State postage stamps in England. Gradually as a demand was felt for stamps of higher value, four anna, eight anna and one-rupee stamps and as well as half-anna embossed envelopes, and single and reply post-cards were issued.

(6) *Date Stamps, etc.*—All State Post Offices had been provided with Date Stamps, Money-Order Stamps, Bearing Stamps, Seals (sealing wax), scales, etc., and their proper use had been enforced as compulsory.

(7) *Village Post-Men*—Formerly there was no village post-man in the districts excepting one at Kishangarh, and the mail runners used to distribute letters on their respective routes. The runners had now been relieved of this duty, which was now performed by village post-men. At present (1906) there were 38 delivery post-men in the districts who delivered postal articles daily.

(8) *Money Orders*—From November 1905, the issue of Money Orders was introduced. At first only 39 Post Offices were authorised to issue Money Orders and 28 to distribute them. From May 1906 all the Post Offices had been empowered to issue and distribute Money Orders. For the public the maximum amount for a single Money Order was fixed at rupees 15 which might soon be increased to rupees 50. For the State

Engineering, Medical and Education Departments, however, the maximum was fixed at rupees 100.

(9) *Reduction in Rates*—Rates for registered letters and parcels (weighing 20 *tolas*) had been reduced from 4 annas to 3 annas and 5 annas to 4 annas respectively. Weight for letters with one-anna stamp had been increased from 1 to 1½ *tola*.

(10) *Raj Service Stamps*—Postage stamps surcharged 'On Raj Services' would be supplied to all the State Departments authorised to send letters free through the State post. This would facilitate service letters work in the Post Offices, ensure accuracy in accounts and check undue use of the free service for private purposes. The arrangements made for Money Order system had made it practicable to introduce Insurance and V.P.P. services, for which a good demand from the public was quite evident.

(11) *Regularity in Time*—Mails of all postal lines, except Malpura, were received in and despatched from Jaipur city by railway, and no regularity in time had been secured. Mails from these lines arrived between 5-30 pm and 9-30 pm and those from Malpura at 6 am on the following morning, and all were sent out for delivery at 7 am every morning.

(12) *Safety of Mails*—Considerable expenses were borne by the State in providing armed *Sowars* as escorts for the safety of the Imperial mails, and additional arrangements had now been made wherever necessary for the State post.

(13) *New Forms*—Several new Forms had been introduced in the Department, copies of which were appended herewith.

(14) *Branch Post Masters*—There were Branch Post Masters in 84 Post Offices some of whom performed postal work exclusively, while others were entrusted with combined postal and intelligence duties. Twenty-seven Branch Post Offices were worked by extra departmental agents.

(15) *Inspectors*—Two Inspectors of Post Offices were appointed on the 1st November 1905 for the Eastern and Western Divisional Circles. The Eastern Divisional Inspector made a tour of 1,582 miles during the year and inspected 45 Post Offices. He opened a new Mail line (Rawanjna-Hindaun Line) with 6 new Post Offices in it. The Western Divisional Inspector made a tour of 1,571 miles and inspected 58 Post Offices, besides opening two new Post Offices and the new mail line from Losal to Sikar. There was another Town Inspector, who looked after the Head Office Circle. Besides, there were one Head Overseer and six Overseers who inspected the Mail lines.

(16) *Superintendent*—The Post Master of the Jaipur Head Office had been entrusted with the additional duty of the Superintendent of State Post. He would proceed on tour whenever necessary, and the various reforms recently introduced in the Department, were effected under his direct supervision.

(17) *Head Office*—The Head Office of the Jaipur city, besides being a Central Post Office for the capital and its suburb, also served as an exchange office between the Imperial Post and the State Post. It had a special department for the *Dak* of the Nagda-Muttra Railway employees. The business in the Head Office had expanded much of late and the question of locating it in a more spacious building was under active consideration.

The Resident at Jaipur forwarded the above-mentioned letter of the Senior Member of the Jaipur State Council with enclosures to the Agent to the Governor-General, Rajputana, requesting that the representation of the Jaipur Darbar might be laid before the Government of India for favourable consideration.[76] The Government of India considered the request of the Jaipur Darbar for the conclusion of a postal convention with the Imperial Post Office. They accepted the principle that a convention might be negotiated, and directed the Agent to Governor-General to take further necessary action in direct communication with the Director-General of the Post Office in India and to work out a scheme acceptable to the Jaipur Darbar and the Government of India.[77]

From what has been discussed above regarding the postal arrangements made by the British authorities in the Jaipur State, it may be concluded that they had succeeded to a great extent in securing the interests of the Imperial postal system in the State. In accordance with the Government's Resolutions of 1866 and 1885 the Jaipur Darbar, like other Darbars, was held responsible for the safety of Imperial mails in its territories. The Darbar took measures for providing guards in the carts carrying mails which were accompanied by the *Sowars* as escorts. If despite these measures robberies of mails took place from time to time in the territory of the State, the Darbar had to make good the loss willingly or grudgingly. The British Government had also succeeded in persuading the Jaipur Darbar to open British Post Offices in the capital as well as other important places in various districts (32 in all by 1906) and also getting placed letter-boxes for Imperial mails in selected towns and villages. They desired that Postal Unity should be introduced in the whole of the Jaipur State but they did not succeed in achieving this objective, for the Jaipur Darbar declined to accept this proposal on the ground that it would be detrimental to the revenues of the State and would also adversely affect the prestige of the Maharaja as a sovereign ruler. The Darbar instead requested the Supreme Government to grant a postal convention to the State on reciprocal basis, as had already been conceded to Gwalior and a number of Punjab States. The Government of India was not inclined to accept this request, stating that the policy of concluding postal conventions with the States was no longer being followed.

It must be said in favour of the Jaipur Darbar that while accepting the reasonable orders of the Paramount Power for securing the interests of the Imperial postal system in the State, it had boldly and resolutely safeguarded the interests of the Raj postal system, and politely declined the demands of the Imperial Government which might involve loss of revenue to the State. The Jaipur Darbar, to its credit, had also thoroughly reorganised the Raj postal system during 1904-1906 so that it had nearly attained the standard and efficiency equivalent to that of the Imperial Postal System. Citing this as the main justification, it repeatedly represented to the Government of India to grant postal convention to the State. At last, in July 1908, the Imperial Government accepted the principle that a postal convention might be negotiated with the State and directed the Agent to Governor-General, Rajputana to take necessary action in this regard.

Keeping in view the political, military, economic and social advantages of the introduction of telegraph system, the British Government under the Crown was keen to extend the system throughout the country. But it could not be practically possible to establish telegraphic communication between various parts of British India without the co-operation of the Princely States. The British authorities, therefore, encouraged and aided all schemes for extension of telegraph system to the States. But for imperial purpose they made it a principle of their policy that all such schemes should operate not only with the sanction of the Supreme Government but should also be subject to the control and supervision of the Director-General of Imperial Telegraphs.

In 1881 the Government of India issued a circular to all the Local Governments and Political Officers in which it was laid down that the Governor-General in Council thought it important to maintain the principle that the general system of telegraphic or telephonic communication throughout the country should be under the Imperial control though there was no desire to interfere with the schemes of a local or quasi-private character. The addressees were, therefore, instructed to report for information and orders of the Supreme Government any project of establishing telegraphic or telephonic communication in Native States under their respective charge.[78]

Subsequently the Foreign and Political Department prepared a summary of the principles to be followed in the matter of telegraph and telephone lines in the Native States :[79]

1. The following are the principles observed in the matter of the construction and maintenance of

telegraph and telephone lines in Indian States :—

(1) Private lines, whether telegraph or telephone (i.e., lines not used by the public and not worked for gain), may be constructed in an Indian State without the previous approval of the Government of India, provided that :—

   (a) the lines shall not pass beyond the boundary of the State concerned ;
   (b) the construction and any subsequent addition to the system shall be notified to the Government of India and a sketch map of the line furnished; and
   (c) no private telephone line shall run into an Imperial Telegraph Office. A private telegraph line may, however, do so on the condition that a deposit account is kept by the State at the office for the transmission of telegrams over the Imperial system.

(2) Telephone systems may be set up and maintained, opened to the public and worked for gain in an Indian State without the previous approval of the Government of India, provided that :—

   (i) the line shall be confined to definite 'local areas', *e.g.*, an important town or its environs within a radius of 10 or 15 miles, and shall not go beyond the limits of a State ;
   (ii) no such local systems shall be connected with one another or with an Imperial Office ;
   (iii) the fact of the installation shall be reported to the Government of India ;
   (iv) the Government of India shall retain the right to buy up any such telephone system in whole or in part, if it is required for Imperial purposes ; and
   (v) the price of such purchase will be a matter for negotiation, but will not be based on the

actual capital expenditure unless the system has been constructed under license from, and regularly inspected by, the Indian Telegraph Department.

(3) No line of telegraph open to the public and worked for gain should anywhere be undertaken in an Indian State without previous reference to, and the consent of, the Government of India.

2. These principles are not intended to include wireless telegraphic installations, the construction of which is confined to British India.
3. Whenever it is proposed by the Telegraph Department to establish a new Imperial Telegraph or Telephone Office with the necessary extension of line, in an Indian State, the Superintendent of Telegraphs should address the Political Officer concerned direct in order to ascertain the views of the Darbar on the project ; when the proposal for the establishment of such an office emanates from the Darbar, the Political Officer will address the Superintendent of Telegraphs. The establishment of a new Imperial office in an Indian State will not require a previous reference to Government ; it should, however, be reported to the Local Government or Administration concerned.

In accordance with the above-mentioned principles, many Telegraph Offices, including Post and Telegraph Offices were established in many cities and towns of the Jaipur State with the consent of the Jaipur Darbar conveyed through the British Political Agent/Resident at Jaipur. It was invariably with the sanction of the Supreme Government and often at the initiative of the British authorities that telegraph lines were set up in Jaipur and other States which were intended to promote Imperial interests. In regard to telephone lines the British authorities would not permit any interference of Native lines with the working of the Imperial system of telephonic communication throughout the country. The Government of India, as a rule, did not permit the existence of such telephone lines in the States which were, or possibly could be, an extension of the general telegraphic and telephonic system of the country, unless such lines were constructed and worked by the Imperial Telegraph Department ; and Jaipur State was no exception.

References and Notes

1. *Imperial Gazetteers of India, Vol. III* (London 1909), p. 66.
2. A.C. Arora, *British Policy towards the Punjab States 1858-1905* (Jalandhar, 1982), pp. 188-89.
3. FD, Political A, Jan. 1864, No. 175.
4. GOI to AGG, No. 721, dated 24 March 1865, FD, General A, March 1865, No. 41.
5. AGG to GOI, No. 1883-353 G, dated 30 Dec. 1865, FD, General A, Jan. 1866, No. 29.
6. Maharaja of Jaipur to Political Agent, Jaipur, dated 25 Sept. 1865, FD, General A, Jan. 1866, Encl. to No. 30.
7. Political Agent Jaipur to AGG, No. 139-71G., dated 9 Oct. 1865, FD, General A, Jan. 1866, No. 30.
8. GOI to AGG, No. 140, dated 26 Jan. 1866, FD, General A, Jan. 1866, No. 31.
9. *Kharita* from AGG to the Maharaja of Jaipur, dated 11 Sept. 1867, FD, General A, Oct. 1867, No. 21 and its Encl.
10. AGG to GOI, No. 1117-60 G., dated 11 Sept. 1867 ; Political Agent, Jaipur to Maharaja of Jaipur, 29 July 1867 ; AGG to Political Agent, Jaipur, No. 1116-111, dated 11 Sept. 1867; see FD, General A, Oct. 1867, Nos. 20-21 and Encl.
11. GOI to AGG, No. 1716, dated 9 Oct. 1867, FD, General A, Oct. 1867, No. 22.
12. Despatch from Governor-General to the Secretary of State for India, No. 43 of 7 Dec. 1867.
13. C.U. Aitchison, Comp., *A Collection of Treaties, Engagements and Sanads, Vol. III* (Calcutta, 1932), p. 71.
14. FD, General A, March 1868, Nos. 24-27.
15. Jaipur Agency Record, Part I, Railway, File, No. 1/1864-69, Prog. No. 46; Office Note, FD, General A, May 1870, Nos. 1-3.
16. Deputy Secretary to Govt. of India, Public Works Dept., to Foreign Department, No. 454 R., dated 14 March 1870, FD, General A, May 1870, Nos. 1-2 and Encls.

17. GOI to AGG, No. 734 G, dated 5 May 1870, FD, General A, May 1870, No. 3.
18. Jaipur Agency Record, Part I, Railway, File No. 5/1875.
19. Jaipur Agency Record, Part I, Railway, File No. 9/1875.
20. FD, General A, June 1872, Nos. 21-22 ; General A, July 1872, No. 19 ; and General A, Aug. 1872, No. 141.
21. AGG to GOI, No. 1971G, dated 28 June 1883, FD, A-General-I, Aug. 1883, No. 92.
22. GOI to AGG, No. 220I, dated 9 Aug. 1883, FD, A-General-I, Aug. 1883, No. 93.
23. RPARS for 1884-85, p. 27.
24. M.S. Jain, *Rajasthan through the Ages,* Vol. III (Bikaner, 1996), p. 309.
25. Jaipur Agency Record, Part-I, Railway, File No. 10/1892.
26. *Ibid.*
27. Jaipur Agency Record, Part I, Railway, File No. R/50/1896.
28. Jaipur Residency Record, Part-I, Railway, File No. 39/1903 and File No. 5/1904-21.
29. Aitchison, *op. cit.*, p. 91.
30. Jaipur Residency Record, Part-I, Railway, File No. 5/1904-21.
31. For details about the terms of the Agreement, see Jaipur Agency Record, Part-I, Railway, File No. R/18/1898-1908, pp. 168-72 ; Aitchison, *op. cit.*, pp. 92-95.
32. Jain, *op. cit.*, p. 312.
33. Circular No. 2665-I of 27 June 1891, FD, Dept. Internal A, Aug. 1891, No. 43.
34. K. M. Panikkar, *Indian States and the Government of India* (London, 1932), pp. 75-76.
35. *The British Crown and the Indian States : An Outline Sketch presented to the Indian States Committee on behalf of the Standing Committee of the Chamber of Princes* (London, 1929), pp. 47-48.
36. Arora, *op. cit.*, p. 200.
37. *The Rajputana Gazette* of 1 Dec. 1895, *Selections from the Vernacular Newspapers*, p. 57.
38. The *Rajputana Gazette* of 8 Feb. 1896, *Selections from the Vernacular Newspapers*, p. 37.
39. *IGI, Vol. XIII* (Oxford, 1908), p. 393.
40. RPARS for 1865-67, Part II, p. 190.
41. Jain, *op. cit.*, p. 306.
42. Jaipur Agency Record, Part I, Railway, File No. 19/1873.
43. FD, General B, Feb. 1874, No. 222.
44. FD, General B, April 1874, Nos. 53-55.

45. Jadunath Sarkar, *A History of Jaipur 1503-1938*, ed. by Raghubir Sinh (Reprint New Delhi 1994), p. 359.
46. For details, see P.W.D. Reports for 1894, pp. 15-18 ; for 1895, pp. 25-29 ; for 1896, pp. 19-21 ; for 1897, pp. 31-33 ; for 1900, pp. 32-37 ; for 1902, pp. 6-7. Also see RPARS for 1892-93, p. 23 and for 1893-94, pp. 27-28.
47. P.W.D. Reports for 1877, pp. 5-6; for 1879, pp. 8-9 ; for 1884,pp. 21-22.
48. *IGI, Vol. XIII*, p. 392.
49. FD, A-General-I, March 1883, Nos. 12-19.
50. Resolution No. 1095 of 18 July 1866, FD, General A, July 1866, No. 56.
51. FD, General B, Jan. 1874, Nos. 46-48.
52. FD, General B, March 1874, Nos. 70-73.
53. FD, General B, April 1874, Nos. 96-98.
54. FD, General A, Nov. 1883, Nos. 84-85, and Internal A, Nov. 1884, Nos. 132-137.
55. Despatch from Secretary of State for India to Governor-General in Council, No. 112 of 3 Nov. 1881.
56. Resolution No. 2495-I of 29 July 1885, FD, Internal A, Oct. 1885, No. 162.
57. Despatch from Secretary of State for India to Governor-General in Council, No. 75 of 15 Oct. 1885, FD, Internal A, Dec. 1888, No. 134.
58. FD, Internal A, Dec. 1886, Nos. 1-4.
59. FD, Internal A, Jan. 1891, Nos. 119-121.
60. Circular No. 23/23 dated 1st July, 1897.
61. Jaipur Agency Record, Part-I, Post and Telegraph, File No. 38/1897.
62. According to Jadunath Sarkar, 38 Imperial post offices were established in Jaipur by 1875 (see Sarkar, *op. cit.*, p. 359) but this figure does not seem to be correct, for only a few British post offices were set up by that time.
63. Deputy Post Master General, Rajputana Circle to Resident Eastern Rajputana States, No. 175, dated 2 Dec. 1887 and Secretary Jaipur Council to Offg. Resident Jaipur, No. 592, dated 17 Sept. 1888, Jaipur Agency Record, Part-I, Post and Telegraph, File No. 19/1887.
64. Jaipur Agency Record, Part-I, Post and Telegraph, File No. 15/1885-1904.
65. Jaipur Agency Record, Part-I, Post and Telegraph, File No. 40/1898.

66. Jaipur Agency Record, Part I, Post and Telegraph, File No. 22/1900-1902.
67. Jaipur Agency Record, Part I, Post and Telegraph, File No. 35/1899 and File No. 60/1904.
68. For details about these places, see Appendix V.
69. AGG to GOI, No. 68-1023 IV, dated 20 March 1907, para 2, Jaipur Agency Record, Part I, Post and Telegraph, File No. 74/1906, p. 167.
70. Senior Member of the Jaipur State Council to Resident, Jaipur, No. 99 dated 17/19 May 1906, *ibid.*, pp. 168-69.
71. Arora, *op. cit.*, pp. 206-07.
72. C. L. Tupper, *Indian Political Practice, Vol. I* (Calcutta, 1895), para 162, p. 178.
73. Deputy Postmaster General, Rajputana to the Resident, Jaipur, No. 8699-F.C.-5, dated 7 Sept. 1906, Jaipur Agency Record, Part-I, Post and Telegraph, File No. 74/1906, p. 169.
74. Senior Member of Jaipur Council to Resident at Jaipur, No. A-243, dated 27/29th Dec. 1906, Jaipur Agency Record, Part-I, Post and Telegraph, File No. 74/1906, pp. 169-70.
75. *Ibid.*, pp. 170-74.
76. Resident, Jaipur to AGG, No. 49, dated 3 Jan. 1907, *ibid.*, p. 169.
77. GOI to AGG, No. 2660-I.A., dated 1 July 1908, *ibid.*, p. 178.
78. Foreign Department, Circular No. 782-I-P. of 24 Oct. 1881, FD, Political A, Feb. 1882, No. 282.
79. Jaipur Agency Record, Part-I, Post and Telegraph, File No. 12/1881-1923, p. 38-I.

CHAPTER 8

Military Matters

Imperial Service Transport Corps

Article 7 of the Treaty of 1818 concluded by the British Government with the Jaipur State provided, "The principality of Jyepoor shall furnish troops, according to its means, at the requisition of the British Government."[1] Similar article was included in most of the treaties of the British Government with the Princely States. In accordance with this stipulation, various Princes and Chiefs rendered useful service to the Paramount Power by sending contingents of their troops to assist the British armies during the Gurkha War, the First Anglo-Afghan War, the First and Second Anglo-Sikh Wars, etc. It has already been mentioned that the Jaipur Darbar had sent the Shekhawati Brigade and the Jaipur forces to the aid of the British army during the First Anglo-Afghan War.[2] In the course of the Revolt of 1857-58, a large number of Princes and Chiefs had sent their troops to fight on the side of the British against the rebels and had also provided supplies wherever required ; the Maharaja of Jaipur had also rendered valuable services to the British Paramount during this crisis.

I

After the Revolt of 1857-58, the British Government of India under the Crown took various measures for the reorganisation of military system in order to safeguard and secure the British Empire in India. The strength of native sepoys in the army was considerably reduced and the number of European soldiers was increased[3]; artillery, as a rule, was to be manned exclusively by the Europeans as far as could be possible. The British authorities also considered it essential to exercise some sort of control over the arms and armies of the Princely States and seek their co-operation in the defence of the Empire against external enemies. They had undertaken the responsibility of protecting the Princes from foreign invasions and internal revolts. In return for this, they required from the Native Chiefs that they should not embarrass the military defence of the Empire ; that they should render active co-operation in securing the efficiency of the Imperial army; and that they should take, in times of emergency, the part assigned to them.[4]

Early in the sixties it had come to the notice of the British Government that some Chiefs of the Central India States possessed troops far larger in number than necessary for internal security. Since the territories of the Chiefs were protected by the British Government the former, it was believed by the British authorities, did not need more military establishments than were required for the maintenance of peace and order in their respective States and for the upkeep of their dignity as sovereigns. Therefore, they decided to restrict the military strength of the States. For this purpose it was essential to acquire detailed information about the military strength of the States. Accordingly a letter was addressed to the Agent to Governor-General, Central India on 29 July 1864, which was then circulated to other Political Agents and Local Governments. The Governor-General in Council directed the addressees to obtain detailed information regarding the ordnance, strength of artillerymen, infantry and cavalry of various States under their respective charge. This was to be done 'without giving umbrage or exciting suspicions and apprehension' in the minds of the Chiefs and 'by the exercise of tact and intelligence' on the part of the concerned British Political Officers. The information regarding ordnance and strength of artillerymen was to be tabulated separately from the infantry and cavalry.[5] Another precautionary measure taken by the British authorities was that the Princely States were not permitted to manufacture arms and ammunition, nor import the same without the consent of the British authorities. They were required to look to the British Government for the supply of such arms. The request of each Chief for the supply of arms was viewed on its merit, and it was accepted or rejected by taking into consideration the nature of arms asked for and the real requirement of that particular State.

Regarding the military strength of the Jaipur State, Colonel J.C. Brooke, wrote in 1868 :

> The Army of Jeypore consists of ten Regiments of Foot, each 600 strong ; and 4000 Nagas, men ill armed and without discipline ; besides a small body 700 cavalry, divided into seven Ressalahs, and 4250 Jagheerdar horse. There are besides 1500 men employed in guarding the seven forts within the territory. The Regiments of Infantry are composed of the same classes as filled the late Bengal Army. The men are badly appointed, and neither the old or unfit men are weeded out of them.
>
> The Nagas are a body of religious mendicants, who are trustworthy and true to the State. They receive the small pay of Rs. 2 a man per month, and Re. one for each child, averaging Rs. 3 per fighting man. In the roll, children are counted as well as adults. They are armed with matchlocks, and will not undergo any discipline.[6]

It is obvious from the above description that the Jaipur army in the late sixties consisted of ill-disciplined and untrained infantry and cavalry besides irregular Nagas and Jagirdari horsemen. At any rate, the military strength of the Jaipur State could not provide the cause of alarm or apprehension for the British authorities.

A detailed information about the military strength of the Jaipur State was compiled by the Resident, Eastern Rajputana States, and forwarded by the Agent to Governor-General in

Rajputana, vide No. 2090 G, dated 17 July 1884 to the Quarter-Master-General in India.[7] As this information is of great importance, it may be reproduced here with all the details :

I. The Jaipur force consists of artillery, cavalry and infantry — the two latter being partly irregular, and partly regular.

II. The artillery comprises 216 guns, mounted in forts, and 65 field and moveable guns, about one-half of which last are unserviceable. Among the guns these are of specified calibre — 6... 3-pounders, 8...6-pounders, 8...9-pounders, 5...18-pounders and 5...24-pounders. These are all old smooth-bore guns, few of which are in good condition, and the carriages are defective. There are 716 artillerymen and about 700 bullocks.

III. The cavalry number 3,578 of whom about 700 are so-called regulars and the rest irregulars. The regulars are armed with swords, lances, and a few with carbines. The latter weapons are old smooth-bore, and the other equipments also are antiquated. With the exception of a few horses of a better class most of the animals are small and light. The irregulars are furnished by the *Jagirdars* of the State, are mounted on small inferior animals, are all poorly armed and are entirely without training.

IV. The strength of infantry is 9,599, of whom some 2,500 are so-called regulars forming four regiments, while the rest constitute the garrisons of forts, etc. Besides these, there are about 5,000 Nagas, Minas, and other special bodies, and some 1,500 armed Najibs and peons attached to the *tahsils*. The regulars are armed and dressed in imitation of native army of British India. The old smooth-bore muskets are mostly worn out, and the equipment otherwise poor and inefficient from military point of view. Drill and discipline are poor. To each regiment of regulars there are attached five 3-pounder guns drawn by bullocks. The Nagas, Minas, etc. are variously armed with sword, matchlock or other weapon. They have no uniform or drill. The Najibs have muskets but no uniform.

V. Even the so-called regulars of all the arms may be said to have no proper training, discipline or equipment, and although they do the work of the State in preserving order, it cannot be said that they are fit for real service in the field.

VI. The pay of the regulars per private soldier ranges from the equivalents of Government Rs. 5-8 to Rs. 6 in the infantry, and from Rs. 6-4 to Rs. 15-8 in the cavalry ; the horse in the former case being the property of the State and in the latter that of the *Sowar*. The pay of the irregulars is low and of too varied amounts to admit of any general statement.

The budget head of the Military Department of Jaipur for all branches except ordnance amounts to some ten lakhs, the ordnance head representing about a lakh more.

VII. In the forts, as elsewhere, there are no guns of modern manufacture. The ordnance is old smooth-bore, mostly honeycombed and with the carriages or other mounts now unsafe or unserviceable.

The garrisons are without proper training or equipment. Of 31 forts of any consequence Ranthambhor, a famous old fortress, is the only large one, and though in a naturally strong position, it is now much out of repair.

VIII. There is no establishment we should class as an arsenal, and no factory of small arms. Gunpowder is manufactured at a few places in the native way sufficient for ordinary requirements of the State.

IX. There are no navigable rivers or any, which are available for transport of military stores.

X. There are no large bridges worth notice, or boat-bridges.

XI. Nor are there any fords of consequence, as in the dry season the stream channels can be crossed anywhere, and in the rains they are only impassable in one way or other at the time of floods.

XII. Camels are the chief means of transport, as much of the country is sandy, and unsuited for wheeled–transport, except in the few districts where *pukka* roads have been made.

As to the number of animals available, 521 were supplied on hire during the late Afghan war... but as the compensation promised for losses of animals was not paid for the many casualties on service, the Jaipur camel-owners, who still continue to complain, would be backward in bringing forward animals for hire if again asked to do so for war service.

There are no stud or breeding establishment for horses kept up.

Similar detailed information about the military strength (artillery, cavalry and infantry) of a large number of other Princely States had been supplied to the Supreme Government much earlier — in the early 1870s. A sizeable number of British bureaucrats at the highest level expressed their opinion, both official and unofficial, in favour of limiting the military strength of the Native States. In response to a letter from Sir Erskine Perry, dated 31 December 1874, pleading the necessity of disbanding all forces of Native States except those required for merely State ceremonials[8], the Viceroy Northbrook wrote that he entirely agreed with him, adding that all that could now be done was to take advantage of every favourable opportunity to reduce them.[9]

In January 1878 a 'Strictly Confidential Circular' was issued by the Government of India to all the Local Governments, Residents and Political Agents which laid down clearly the instructions and principles of the Government's policy regarding military establishments in Native States for the guidance of the addressees:[10] Any requisition for the supply of arms of precision by a Native State was to be declined outright. Stricter watch was to be exercised than hitherto over the military strength of each State and regular reports were to be submitted to the Government of India about the same. No State was to be permitted to maintain more troops than required for the maintenance of internal peace and for the upkeep of the dignity of the Chief. Every opportunity was to be availed of for reducing the military strength of the States. All these principles were to be enforced uniformly in regard to the military establishments in all the States.

The contents of this confidential circular were, however, soon leaked out. Consequently many English newspapers, notably *The Times* (London) and the *Bombay Gazette* published articles pleading the necessity of reducing the armies of the Native States and even recommending their total disarmament. This led to a counter-campaign in the vernacular newspapers strongly condemning the idea of disarming the Princely States.[11]

In 1878 the Government of Lytton passed Indian Arms Act. Under the provisions of this Act, the export of cannons, arms and ammunition, of machinery for manufacturing arms and ammunition, and of military stores from British India into Native States was prohibited except under license from British authorities. It was further provided in the Act that no person would bring into British India any arms, ammunition or military stores except under a licence. The Maharajas, Rajas and Nawabs were, however, exempted from the prohibition directed against the unlicensed carrying of arms while in India for their own private use; but they could not import machinery for making arms or ammunition.[12] With a view of acquiring accurate information regarding the number and quantity of arms and ammunition imported each year into Native States for the use of either natives or Europeans the Supreme Government directed that special attention should be given by the Political Officers to the matter of registration and they should furnish a copy of every license of arms and ammunition. Instructions were also issued for furnishing in future half-yearly returns of arms and ammunition exported to the Native States.[13] The Government of India also sent instructions to Agents to Governor-General in Rajputana and Central India, as also to Residents in Hyderabad, Kashmir and Mysore, etc., for proper enforcement of Rule 8(c) of the Arms Act Rules, which required persons desirous of exporting arms to obtain the consent of the Magistrate or Political Officer of the place of consignment. It was stated in the Supreme Government's letter No. 2735-I, dated 8 July 1889 :

> It is a matter of the greatest importance that effectual measures should be taken to prevent arms exported for retail sale in a Native State from getting into the hands of persons unfit to possess such weapons, but after a license for a consignment has been given, it is practically impossible to secure any control over the ultimate disposal of the arms covered by it. It is not, therefore, advisable that the export of rifles, guns and revolvers for sale in the Native States should ordinarily be permitted, except under the restriction in the 3rd paragraph of this letter.[14]

The 3rd paragraph laid down that Political Officers should be instructed not to give in future certificates of their consent to intending importers of arms without first satisfying themselves that the arms were actually required for the personal use of some responsible and respectable person who would be entitled to possess them under the Arms Act Rules if he were in British India.

In June 1880 the Maharana of Udaipur applied for permission to export by rail from Jaipur *via* Ajmer and Nasseerabad 50 maunds of gunpowder for the use of the Kumalgarh Fort. On the recommendation of the Agent to Governor-General, Rajputana the Government of India granted the necessary permission, adding that under the existing rules separate licenses would have to be issued for the import of gunpowder from Jaipur into Ajmer, and for its transport through Ajmer. The import license could be granted by the Commissioner of Ajmer, and the transport license could be granted by the Deputy Commissioner of Ajmer under Rule 2 of the Rules framed under the Indian Arms Act, 1878. The necessary licenses were issued and the request of the Maharana of Udaipur was complied with.[15]

In September 1880 it was proposed by the Foreign Department, at the behest of military authorities, to sell surplus accoutrements of the 33rd Regiment of Native Infantry to the Maharaja of Jaipur on reasonable rates but the Jaipur Darbar expressed unwillingness to purchase the same.[16] The matter was not pressed any further.

In 1884 M/s Manton and Company of Calcutta applied for a license to export a pair of cannons to Jaipur for the Maharaja. Considering that the State already possessed 65 cannons, irrespective of 46 mounted in forts, both the Resident at Jaipur and Agent to Governor-General, Rajputana opined that no more cannons were needed. The Jaipur Darbar was informed accordingly and the license for exporting the cannons was not granted to the said company.[17]

The Government of India issued a Circular No. 2778-I dated 9 August 1893 to all the Local Governments, Agent to Governor-General, Rajputana and others on the subject of disposal of arms in Native States by persons to whom licenses to go armed on a journey had been granted by Form IX of the Arms Act Rules, and enquired if there was any reason to believe that traffic in arms with Native States was carried on in this manner to such an extent as to require any action. In response to this the Resident, Jaipur informed the Agent to Governor-General, Rajputana that there was no reason to believe that any such traffic in arms was carried on in the States under the Jaipur Residency. He, however, pointed out that the manner in which licenses in question were generally prepared advantage might be taken by 'unscruplous persons' for carrying on illicit traffic of this nature, for the licenses generally contained 'most meagre and imperfect' description of the license and the arms. Such persons would have no difficulty in bringing English made guns to a Native State and exchanging them for weapons of local manufacture. Similarly the holders of these imperfectly prepared licenses proceeding from a Native State to British India could take with him arms of local manufacture and exchange them for superior English made weapons. He suggested as a remedy that the fullest information of the license and a detailed description of the weapon should be given in the license.[18]

In 1900 the Jaipur Darbar expressed desire to return certain arms and ammunition[19] which had been acquired on payment from the British Government to be used for preventing famine. The Supreme Government accorded sanction for the return of these arms and directed the Agent to Governor-General Rajputana to send the whole supply into the store at Ferozepur

Arsenal, the amount of cost being refunded to the Jaipur Darbar.[20]

By the Resolution of the Government of India in the Foreign Department, No. 3129 I.-A, dated 19 August 1901 all the Residents posted in various States and Political Officers in Rajputana States were empowered to grant licenses for the export of arms and ammunition to the States under their political charge, irrespective of whether they were required for personal use or for sale. It was subsequently decided by the Resolution No. 3001 I.-A, dated 27 June 1903 to modify the restrictions imposed earlier, firstly, by removing rifles of .577 bore of the Snider pattern and also magazine pistols from the category of military weapons, and, secondly, by authorising Political Officers to grant licenses, in certain cases, for the export of rifles of .303 bore and of .450 bore of the Martini-Henry pattern, and of a limited quality of ammunition for use with those weapons.[21]

In 1905 the following rules were enforced under Arms Act for the better control of the trade of fire-arms and ammunition in the Jaipur State by the Resident, Jaipur in accordance with the instructions from Agent to Governor-General, Rajputana[22]:

(1) All dealers in and manufacturers of fire-arms and ammunition would be required to take an early license from the Judicial Member.

(2) They would maintain a register of their stock and all transactions.

(3) Their business premises, registers and stock would at all times be open to inspection by the City and District Magistrates over the Inspectors of Police.

(4) They would not sell to *Bhils, Banjaras, Sansis* and persons to whom they might be prohibited by the Inspectors of Police in writing from selling fire arms and ammunition.

(5) Each dealer would affix a definite registered trade mark to all fire-arms made or sold by him.

(6) Whosoever dealt in or manufactured fire-arms or ammunition without a license in contravention of rule 1, or sold arms and ammunition to *Bhils* and others in

contravention of rule 4 would be liable to be punished with imprisonment for a period not exceeding 8 months or with fine not exceeding rupees 500 or with both.

(7) If a dealer failed to maintain the register by rule 2 or to affix a trade mark as required by rule 5 he would be liable to fine not exceeding rupees 100 and to have his license, granted under rule 1, cancelled.

(8) No one might have in his possession without a license more than 10 seers of gunpowder, even though it was not for sale; and any one infringing this rule would be liable to a fine which might amount to rupees 100 provided that contractors of the Public Works Department and bona fide cultivators would be granted such licenses gratis for blasting purposes.

Thus under the Arms Act, 1878 and general ratification, circulars and orders issued from time to time thereafter, the British authorities exercised strict control over arms and ammunition in the Native States. The export of cannons, arms and ammunition as well as machinery for manufacturing arms and ammunition from British India into the States was strictly prohibited except under license from British authorities. The Political Officers were required to give yearly and later on half-yearly reports duly registered about the arms and ammunition exported to the States. The persons desirous of exporting arms were required to obtain the consent of the Magistrate or Political Officer of the place of consignment. Effective measures were taken to prevent arms exported for sale in a Native State from falling into the hands of irresponsible and undesirable persons. Precautionary measures were also taken to prevent illicit traffic in arms in Native States by persons to whom licenses to go armed on a journey had been granted by Form IX of the Arms Act Rules. Rules were also enforced for better control of fire-arms and ammunition in Jaipur and other States. All the dealers and manufacturers of fire-arms and ammunition were required to obtain license from the Judicial Member, maintain a register of their stock and of all transactions, affix a definite registered trade-mark on all fire-arms made or sold by them, and they would not sell fire-arms and ammunition to *Bhils, Banjaras, Sansis,* etc. For violation or infringement of any of these rules, they were to be punished with fixed amount of fine or imprisonment for a number of months or both. It may be observed that these rules pertaining to restrictions on the use, sale or manufacture of fire-arms and ammunition were as much applicable on the people of British India as on those of the States. At any rate, a close supervision and control was exercised not only over the arms and ammunition but also over the armies of the Native State through the Political Officers — in the case of Jaipur State by the Political Agent, Jaipur.

II

The Government of Lytton had, at first, viewed with distrust the military establishments of the States and had decided to restrict them and, if possible, to reduce them. But the British involvement in the Afghan War (Second Anglo-Afghan War) brought about a substantial change in the attitude of the British authorities towards the armies of the States. Quite a large number of Princes and Chiefs, including the Maharaja of Jaipur, offered their services to the Paramount Power, and were even prepared to send their armies for the help of the British Government during this War.[23] The British authorities, however, decided to utilise the services offered by these Punjab Chiefs — Maharaja of Patiala, the Rajas of Jind, Nabha, Kapurthala and Faridkot and the Nawabs of Bahawalpur and Malerkotla. The several contingents of these Punjab Chiefs were constituted into a Brigade, comprising 3,000 infantry, 1,000 cavalry and 13 guns. These contingents were employed on the arduous duties pertaining to garrisoning of posts, holding General Roberts' line of communication from Kohat to Kurram and furnishing almost daily escorts to convoys and officers from 22 February to 5 June 1879. Brigadier-General Watson spoke highly of the services rendered by these contingents. Even the Viceroy was impressed with the excellent behaviour of the contingents and was highly appreciative of the services rendered by them.[24] The happy experience of the employment of Punjab Chiefs' contingents on the frontier "furnished an indisputable cause which set the course of thinking of the British policy-makers towards the organisation of Imperial Service Troops."

Meanwhile in response to the telegraphic message from Her Majesty the Queen to the Viceroy of India on the subject of the success of the British in Afghanistan, Maharaja Ram Singh of Jaipur, like other Princes and Chiefs, expressed his feelings of loyalty to the British Crown and his best wishes for the success of British arms in these words :

> Nothing can be more gratifying to Princes and people of India than to hear the success of British arms to which they owe peace and prosperity they enjoy, and under the protection of which they feel themselves perfectly secure from foreign aggression and free from internal discord. May Her Majesty's puissant arms always remain invincible and keep enemies of the Empire in awe and horror.

While forwarding this letter of the Maharaja to the Agent to Governor-General, Rajputana for onward transmission to the Government of India, Political Agent at Jaipur added that the Maharaja of Jaipur had held a Special Darbar at the Palace on Christmas Day, when Her Majesty's message was read out, both in English and Vernacular.[25]

When the Maharaja of Jaipur received the 'most welcome intelligence' that Amir Yakub Khan of Afghanistan had proceeded in person to Gandamak to confer with the British authorities and had there signed a treaty of peace with the British Government, he telegraphically communicated his 'warmest and most loyal and friendly congratulations' to the Viceroy of India which were cordially acknowledged.[26]

During the following decade, numerous Princes and Chiefs expressed their earnest desire to render material and military assistance to the British Government on the Indian frontiers as well as in the far off War in Africa. For instance, in 1882 when the Government of England sent forces to Egypt to quell the rebellion of the national leader Ahmad Arabi, spontaneous offers of military assistance were received by the British

Government of India from many Princes and Chiefs, notably those of the Punjab but these offers were declined with thanks.[27] In 1885 at the time of the Panjdeh crisis which posed impending danger of war between England and Russia, a large number of Native Chiefs came forward with enthusiasm to place their resources in terms of men and money at the disposal of the British Government ; these offers, though cordially acknowledged by the Government of India, were politely declined.[28] According to Stuart Beatson, "The danger which then seemed imminent was happily averted, but the feelings which had been raised by it did not die away, and both in the Native States and elsewhere the idea began to gain ground that some scheme for utilizing the military resources of the Chiefs ought to be worked out."[29] On the occasion of the Silver Jubilee Celebrations of the Queen-Empress in the summer of 1887, the Nizam of Hyderabad and many Chiefs of Rajputana and Punjab States came out with voluntary offers of monetary and military assistance towards the defence of the Empire[30]; others remained silent only because they had freely placed their resources at the disposal of the Government of India two years before. Being impressed by these sincere and generous offers, the British authorities began to consider seriously the proposition of associating the troops of Indian Princes in some organised form for the defence of the Empire.

Mortimer Durand, Foreign Secretary to the Government of India, initiated the proposal. He opined that the Native States were maintaining large undisciplined forces which could never be used by the British Government in the time of war against a potential foreign enemy, and might prove 'a source of material weakness and danger'. He, therefore, suggested that the number of these forces should be reduced and out of them should be formed an efficient and powerful reserve maintained at the cost of the States themselves. He emphatically remarked :

> The safest game now is the bolder game of trusting the Native States and carrying them with us. So long as we are doing well in front, we have nothing to fear behind. The policy of isolating the Native States and keeping their armies inefficient, and therefore at best useless, is as unsuitable to the altered condition

> of affairs as would be the policy of arming our Native troops with smoothbore muskets. My hope is to get a serviceable reserve at small cost and weaken rather than strengthen the Native States as against ourselves, while at the same time opening up for Imperial purposes new recruiting grounds which would otherwise be closed to us and from which we can draw troops wholly unconnected with our army.[31]

He suggested that the scheme should be launched from the Punjab States who possessed good indigenous fighting material and the British authorities could also count upon the loyalty and co-operation of their Chiefs.[32] The scheme was approved in principle by Dufferin, the then Viceroy and Governor-General of India. Major Howard Melliss of the Bombay Staff Corps was consequently selected to visit the Punjab States of note and to submit a report on the actual condition and future capabilities of the armies of these States. Major Melliss travelled through many of the Punjab States and submitted his report on 7 March 1888 which positively recommended utilization of the forces of these States.[33] The consent of the Chiefs of Patiala, Bahawalpur, Jind, Nabha, Kapurthala and Faridkot was obtained for the scheme. Thus a beginning of the scheme was made with the armies of the Punjab States, because from their position near the North-West Frontier and the martial spirit of the population they seemed specially suitable for the experiment.[34] A committee consisting of Frederick Roberts, Commander-in-Chief, James Lyall, Lieutenant-Governor of the Punjab, Lieutenant-General G.T. Chesney, and Mortimer Durand, Foreign Secretary to the Government of India, was then appointed to work the details of the scheme and give specific recommendations. The committee recommended that the States of Patiala, Bahawalpur, Jind, Nabha, Kapurthala, Malerkotla and Faridkot should maintain contingents of infantry (1000, 300, 300, 300, 600, 150 and 150 respectively), cavalry (600, 150, 150, 150, 150, 50 and 50 respectively) and 16 guns in all (4 each by Patiala, Jind, Nabha and Kapurthala), fit to join the Imperial forces in the field. The Governor-General in Council accepted the recommendation of the committee, subject to future modifications, on 24 October 1888, and announced that the

Viceroy would meet the Chiefs concerned next month at Lahore and Patiala to explain to them personally the main principles of the scheme.[35]

Accordingly, Dufferin visited Lahore and Patiala, and in a Darbar held at Patiala on 17 November he explained to the Chiefs present the main principles of the scheme. He said that the Government of India did not think it necessary, or in all respects desirable, to accept from the Native States of India the pecuniary assistance which they had so freely tendered. What the British Government proposed was to ask those Chiefs who had specially good fighting material in their armies to raise a portion of those armies to such a pitch of general efficiency as would make them fit to go into action side by side with the Imperial troops. But the Government would in no case ask a Native State to maintain a larger force of this description than it could well afford to support. To help these Chiefs in maintaining the troops selected for service a few English officers would be appointed as advisers and inspectors. These officers would have their headquarters at some central point in British territory, and would visit the several States in turn. Capable Native Drill Instructors would also be lent to the Native States from the British Indian regiments. The selected troops would be armed with breech-loading weapons presented to the States by the British Government — carbines for the cavalry and Snider rifles for the infantry. Thus while each force would remain a purely State force recruited in the territories of its Chief, and serving within them, the troops composing it would gradually be made so efficient as to enable the Imperial Government to use them as part of its available resources to meet any external danger. In the end, the Viceroy expressed happiness to say that the principal States of the Punjab had fully concurred in this scheme, and arrangements would be made to carry it into effect.[36]

Hardly had the scheme been approved by the Supreme Government when Dufferin had to relinquish the office of Viceroy, and he was replaced by Lansdowne. The new Viceroy was as enthusiastically favourable to the scheme as his predecessor, for he considered it beneficial for the Government as well as the States.[37] In March 1889, the Government of India addressed a comprehensive Despatch to the Secretary of State for India explaining the principles of the scheme. The main principle of the scheme, it was said, was that the Princely States of India ought to be associated with British India in any measure for the defence of the country. There could be no doubt that so long as the Princely States were asked to maintain in a condition of efficiency only such forces as they could keep up without undue strain upon their resources, the Chiefs would undertake the duty with pleasure and regard it as in the highest degree honourable to themselves and to their people. Therefore it was 'right and wise' to invite the co-operation of the Princely States in this matter, to show them that they were trusted and to welcome in the ranks of the Imperial army the contingents of the Princely States. Stress was then laid upon the important point that the troops to be raised should be State troops proper, that they should be composed and officered, as far as possible, by the natives of the States and that they should be completely under the control of the Chiefs. It was pointed out that the scheme of raising such contingents had been initiated from the Punjab States due to the proximity of these States to the North-West Frontier and that the total strength of troops expected to be raised would be about 15,000 troops from Kashmir and States of Punjab and Rajputana, and 10,000 from those of Hyderabad, Mysore and Gwalior.[38] The Secretary of State accorded sanction to the scheme and called for a report on the progress of the scheme after eighteen months or two years.[39] Thus came into being a new organisation of the selected troops of Princely States which, according to Government of India Circular No. 2660-I of 9 August 1890, was officially designated as 'Imperial Service Corps' or 'Imperial Service Troops'.[40]

The five States of Rajputana who were associated with the scheme of Imperial Service Troops were : Alwar, Bharatpur, Bikaner, Jaipur and Jodhpur. The Jaipur State raised the Jaipur Transport Train between 1889 and 1891, "the Maharaja Madho Singh choosing to forego the prestige and *eclat* attaching to the possession of combatant troops in order to contribute what he believed to be more useful and more likely to be called into requisition in Imperial defence."[41] In 1889 the Maharaja offered to maintain a transport train of 1,000 ponies fully equipped for service under the British Government on an emergency arising.[42] Considerable progress was made in the following years to organise the Transport Corps as desired by the British authorities. Workshops had been added and several other changes and improvements were made in the corps. The men had been properly armed and disciplined, and the carts and ponies began doing useful service. On 31 March 1892 the strength of the corps was as under[43] :

Officers	5
Non-commissioned officers	48
Drivers	321
Veterinary establishment	2
Farrier department	5
Ponies	699
Carts	205
Saddlers, Carpenters and others	28

Every effort was being made to raise the corps to its contemplated strength. The corps was inspected by the Maharaja, Colonel Trevor and Colonel Melliss.[44]

III

Not long after the organisation of Imperial Service Troops, they were partially employed in one form or the other for active service in the warfare on the frontiers in which the British were involved. In 1895, a large number of Chiefs, including those of the Punjab and Rajputana, offered their Imperial Service Corps for employment in the contemplated Chitral expedition.[45] The Inspector-General of Imperial Service Troops in his telegraphic communication to the Foreign Secretary to Government of India, pleaded for their employment. He expressed the fear that if these troops were not utilised for service on this occasion the Chiefs might be disappointed, and they would entertain the idea of getting rid of the useless expenses upon the maintenance of transport and war-material for these troops.[46] In reply the

Supreme Government instructed the Inspector-General to make the Chiefs understand that the required forces had already been mobilised for the expedition and that due to difficulty of carriage and need of prompt action it could not be possible for the Government to utilise the Imperial Service Troops other than the Jaipur and Gwalior transport trains.[47]

The Jaipur Transport Corps was employed on service for the first time in the Chitral campaign of 1895. It was composed of 1000 ponies and 500 carts. It was divided into eight troops, each of 150 ponies and 75 carts, and was maintained complete in every particular with hospitals, veterinary establishment, and workshop.[48] The corps left Jaipur within forty-eight hours of receiving orders, in six special trains, each train containing a troop with its ponies, carts, equipment, and workshops. At first it was employed as a cart-train between Jallala and Dargai ; but later on during the campaign it was sent up to Dir, 90 miles distant, with provisions for the Chitral garrison which it put down at Dir in seven days without the loss of a single bag or pony. From Dir it returned to Dargai for more train-work but again moved forward into the Swat Valley in July. Towards the end of September the corps moved to Nowshera and returned by rail to Jaipur.[49]

Throughout its field service the corps maintained 'an excellent spirit'. In all weathers and at all hours all ranks turned out punctually and cheerfully for convoy work, which was always performed in a most exact manner, bringing the men a great reputation for honesty and regularity, whilst for a non-combatant corps the general standard of discipline was distinctly high.[50]

Colonel H. Mellis, Inspector-General, Imperial Service Troops, raised the question of proposed *bhatta* for the Gwalior and Jaipur Transport Trains during their employment with the Chitral Relief Force. He wrote to the Supreme Government that in accordance with the ruling conveyed in the Foreign Department letter No. 1912-I, dated 14 June 1895, all the ranks of Jaipur and Gwalior Imperial Service Transport Corps while on field service were to be treated as fighting men and they had been drawing *bhatta* at the rates shown in paragraph 46-C,

Army Regulations, India, Volume I, Part II[51], the rate for drivers being Rs. 8 per mensem. The mule drivers of the Government Transport Department had been allowed *bhatta* at Rs. 8 per mensem while on service. Melliss proposed that this privilege might be extended to the men of the Jaipur and Gwalior Corps as they would forfeit Rs. 2 per mensem for the privilege of drawing fighting men's rations. He opined that the Government should do as much for these trains as possible because it is for the first time they had been out and they had done 'excellent work'.[52] It was observed by high officials of the Foreign Department that the concession suggested by Colonel Melliss could not be granted without creating heart-burning among the Government transport mule drivers who did not have the advantage allowed to fighting men. Colonel Melliss was, therefore, informed that the Military Department was averse to the question being re-opened, and since the former did not wish to press the matter, it was dropped.[53] The British authorities were highly appreciative of the 'excellent' work done by the Jaipur Transport Corps in the Chitral Relief Expedition and expressed their thanks to the Maharaja of Jaipur. The salute of the Maharaja was increased with the sanction of the Queen Empress. On recognition of his services with the Chitral Relief Force, Rai Bahadur Dhanpat Rai, Superintendent of Jaipur Transport Corps, was honoured by the Government of India with his admission to the Order of British India.[54]

The Maharaja of Jaipur, to show his appreciation of the honour conferred upon him for the Chitral expedition, desired to increase his Transport Corps by 200 ponies and 100 carts. He sounded Colonel Melliss unofficially in this regard and sought his advice through Colonel Tate as to whether his offer was likely to be accepted or not. Thereupon Colonel Melliss addressed a D.O. letter to W.J. Cuningham, Foreign Secretary. The latter consulted the Viceroy and wrote back that if the offer was put forward officially[55], by the Maharaja it would be 'both accepted and appreciated'.

Accordingly, the Maharaja of Jaipur submitted his proposal officially to the Resident at Jaipur. He wrote that he had been much gratified to learn from the official despatches the appreciation in which the services of the Jaipur Transport Corps were held by Their Excellencies the Viceroy and the Commander-in-Chief and since the Corps' return to Jaipur he had been considering the plan for increasing the strength and efficiency of the Corps. At the same time, to mark his gratitude for the honour that had been conferred on him by Her Majesty the Queen-Empress by the increase of his salute, and to keep his contribution to Imperial Defence commensurate with the higher rank thus bestowed upon him, he wished to increase the strength of ponies and carts composing the Jaipur Transport Corps. He proposed for the present to increase the number of ponies by 200.[56]

While forwarding the Maharaja's letter to the Supreme Government, R.J. Crosthwaite, Agent to the Governor-General, Rajputana remarked that the Maharaja's desire to increase his Transport Corps, which had rendered such good service in the Chitral expedition, would no doubt be fully appreciated, and he sought the permission to convey thanks of the Government to the Maharaja for his offer.[57]

The Viceroy read with much interest and satisfaction the Maharaja's letter to Colonel Law (Resident at Jaipur) and was pleased to observe the close personal attention which the Maharaja paid to the Corps. He remarked that the efficiency and usefulness of the Corps had been fully proved, and the Government of India had much gratification in accepting the Maharaja's highly valuable offer which "affords one more proof of the distinguished loyalty and zeal of the Jaipur State".[58] The Government of India informed the Secretary of State for India that the Maharaja of Jaipur had expressed a wish to increase the strength of the Jaipur Imperial Service Transport Corps which, Her Majesty's Government were aware, had rendered excellent service in the Chitral expedition, and that they had no hesitation in accepting the Maharaja's offer.[59]

It may be noted that the Maharaja had initially proposed to add 200 ponies and 100 carts to his Transport Corps but later on in his official communication he only mentioned the increase of 200 ponies. While accepting this offer the British authorities deliberately omitted the reference to the 100 carts.[60] It has been recorded in the Administration Report of Rajputana States for 1896-97 that the increase of 200 ponies sanctioned by the Maharaja had been given a practical shape. The strength of 1200 ponies was divided into eight troops and 520 carts. The corps was inspected by the Viceroy in November 1896. Lieutenant-Colonel Tate, the Inspecting Officer, left in November and was succeeded by Captain Cookson.[61]

As a result of the employment and utilisation of the Jaipur and Gwalior transport corps during the campaign for the relief of Chitral, the British authorities began to realise the increasing value of the organised Imperial service transport corps. While the Imperial Service Cavalry and Infantry (except those of Kashmir) had been hitherto useless, they felt, the transport corps would be always of value in any important expedition as the present one and would be far more valuable than infantry or cavalry in the event of mobilisation of whole force by the British. The example set by Jaipur and Gwalior would perhaps be emulated by some other States, such as Udaipur and Kota. "When they (Udaipur and Kota) see to Jaipur and Gwalior Crops return to their homes with honour (and I trust reward), a hint only would perhaps be necessary to induce them to follow the example set by Jaipur." But it would be unwise to ask any Chief now maintaining Imperial Service Troops to substitute transport for any portion of them. They were likely to receive such a proposition with feelings of disappointment and mortification, and some might even entertain the idea, or rather suspicion, that the British were about to break faith, and that the aim and object of the Imperial Service scheme was to reduce the whole of their armies to a vanishing point altogether, for it should be understood that the rest of their armies had either gone, or were melting away, to meet the cost of the Imperial Service Troops. Undoubtedly one great object in the original scheme was, if possible, to effect reductions in the large standing armies of the Native States — and this object appeared to have been happily achieved. Whereas the British high-ups (both in the Army and the Foreign Department) were convinced of the greater utility of the transport corps in any campaign on the North-West frontier, they did not consider it prudent or wise to ignore the trained infantry and cavalry of the Imperial Service Troops of certain States (notably Punjab States) which had really good fighting material.[62] And in the North-West Frontier campaign in the following year (1897) they judiciously decided to utilise the services of both the transport corps of some States and selected troops of infantry of some other States.

In 1897 when the British Government was involved in warfare on the North-West Frontier, a large number of Native Princes and Chiefs offered their troops of infantry and cavalry as well as transport corps for employment.[63] The British authorities decided very cautiously to employ only one battalion of infantry from the Punjab States of Patiala, Jind, Nabha and Kapurthala and a company of Sappers and Miners from Sirmur and Malerkotla. It was also decided by the Supreme Government to accept the services of the Jaipur and Gwalior Transport Trains which had done excellent work in the Chitral expedition and had again been put at the disposal of the Government 'in the most patriotic manner' by the Maharaja of Jaipur and Maharaja Sindhia of Gwalior.[64] The thanks of the Government of India had been ordered to be conveyed to all the Chiefs from whom offers of troops and transport corps had been received.

In connection with the mobilisation of Imperial Service Troops of the said States for active service, it was decided that they were to make their own arrangements for food and forage until the date of crossing the external frontier of India, or leaving the frontier station, as the case might be. The Chiefs concerned were also to meet the expenditure of their respective troops in respect of ordinary pay of the troops, land transport other than by rail, first supply of clothing and all articles required for full equipment of the troops for mobilisation on active service. But the expenses incurred on ammunition and other explosives, renewal of field service clothing, maintenance of mobilisation equipment during the period of active service, transport by rail both within and without the limits of their States, free rations to all combatants and authorised regimental followers across the frontiers, compensation for dearness of provisions if free rations were not supplied, and on the field *bhatta* as permissible to the soldiers of Indian army, were all to be borne by the British Government.[65]

The Jaipur Transport Corps was detailed for service under the orders of the General Officer Commanding the line of communication, Tirah Expeditionary Force, and mobilized in September 1897, arriving at Kushalgarh by the 13th of that month. On the 2nd October the corps commenced a staging system between Kohat and Shinaori, a distance of 47 miles, and carried about 460 maunds of stores daily. Later on, 560 ponies were used, under pack, for the transport work of two British regiments. These animals were used in the operations in Tirah and retirement of the force by the Bara Valley, the carts being railed to Peshawar. The cart train was thus set working in the Khyber Pass in February and March. The work done by the corps was 'excellent'. During the whole campaign the departments of supply were indented on for nothing but food for men and animals, the entire clothing, equipment, and materials for repair being taken with the corps. The water carts and invalid *tangas* of the corps proved of the greatest use. The health of the men throughout was excellent and but few of the ponies lost condition despite the severe work.[66] Having done its work to the entire satisfaction of the British commander under whom it had been placed, the Jaipur Transport Corps returned from Peshawar in April 1898 after the breaking up of the Tirah Force. While communicating this information to the Maharaja of Jaipur, the Agent to Governor-General, Rajputana conveyed the thanks of the Government of India for the 'admirable service' rendered by the Jaipur Transport Corps. The Maharaja responded by expressing his thanks for the favourable terms in which the Government of India had acknowledged the services rendered by the Jaipur Transport Corps on the field service.[67] Rai Bahadur Dhanpat Rai, C.I.E., the Superintendent of the Jaipur Transport Corps, was given 'the very highest possible praise' for his exceptional energy and ability.

The Commander-in-Chief recorded his appreciation of the good services rendered by the infantry battalion of Patiala, Jind, Nabha and Kapurthala, as also by the Jaipur and Gwalior transport corps, during operations on the North-West Frontier.

George Hamilton, the Secretary of State for India, was 'agreeably surprised' to learn so good reports of the efficiency of Imperial Service Troops despite the obvious disadvantage under which they worked.[68]

During the viceroyalty of Curzon, it was decided for the first time to send Imperial Service Troops for employment outside India in 1899-1900 when the British were involved in Wars in South Africa and China. A large number of Native Chiefs came out with their offers of troops. But the British authorities decided to employ only a limited number of horses from the Imperial Service Troops of some Punjab States in case of war in South Africa, and Imperial Service Infantry and Imperial Service Sappers from the States of Bikaner, Alwar, Jodhpur and others in case of war in China. Curzon remarked that both in South Africa and China the Imperial Service Troops had 'behaved splendidly' and he claimed the credit for having employed them for the first time out of India.[69]

Though the Jaipur Transport Corps had not been on active service during the year 1900-01, it had waged a most successful campaign against the famine, in regard to which its services had been 'invaluable'. The strength of the Transport Corps at that time amounted to 744 men (including officers), 1159 ponies, 556 iron carts, and 16 *tongas*. The corps had the honour, in January 1901, of being inspected by the Commander-in-Chief.[70] The corps continued to maintain its high standard of efficiency under the most capable Commandant, Sardar Bahadur Dhanpat Rai, C.I.E. Dhanpat Rai's self-invented transport and ambulance carts were receiving great attention all over India, and had much impressed all the military visitors, foreign and English, who had visited his lines.[71] In October 1902, over 400 transport carts and *tongas* and 900 ponies of the Jaipur Transport Corps were employed in the Delhi manoeuvres, and afterwards in connection with the Viceregal Camp at Delhi. The manner in which the work was carried out brought great credit on Rai Bahadur Dhanpat Rai, and on the officers and men of the Corps.[72] Rai Bahadur Dhanpat Rai and Daffadar Abdul Rahman Khan received silver medals in Delhi Darbar.[73]

In 1903 when the British were involved in War in

Somaliland, many Chiefs including those of Patiala, Bahawalpur, Jind, Nabha, Bikaner, Bhavnagar and others offered their Imperial Service Troops for employment but the Government of India, while appreciating the offers informed the Chiefs concerned politely that their services were not required by the Government.[74] The employment of Jaipur Transport Corps had been suggested for Somaliland. But no offer had been made by the Maharaja of Jaipur in this regard. Curzon remarked that he was not disposed to ask the Maharaja for it and that he deprecated the suggested employment of the corps ; for if the Native States were ordered or even requested to send their contingents, whenever we desired it, for active service in outlying parts of the Empire, the character of Imperial Service movement would be completely changed.[75] The Secretary of State for India concurred in the views expressed by the Viceroy.[76]

In spite of the fact that the Jaipur Transport Corps was not employed for service in Somaliland, the ruler of Jaipur, like other Chiefs, thought it a privilege to send his Imperial Service corps for assisting the Paramount Power in any war on the frontiers of India or beyond in foreign countries in which the British were involved from time to time. Indeed the Native Chiefs vied with another in offering voluntarily the services of their trained troops and they felt disappointed if their services were not, or could not be, accepted. Despite this, the British authorities were not unanimous in their opinion regarding the usefulness and trustworthiness of the Imperial Service Troops. The three successive Viceroys — Dufferin, Lansdowne and Elgin — were, of course, favourably inclined towards the scheme of associating trained troops of some selected States for Imperial service. But there were others who were averse to the scheme due to one reason or the other. Sir Donald Stewart, a distinguished militarist considered it as 'entirely useless'.[77] Sir A.P. Macdonnell, the Lieutenant-Governor of North-Western Provinces and Oudh, looked askance at the scheme and considered it a 'mistake'.[78] Sir William Lockhart, the Commander-in-Chief, viewed the whole scheme "not merely as nonsensical but even as dangerous and would like to abolish the entire Imperial Service Contingents by a stroke of pen tomorrow."[79] Curzon was also at first inclined to doubt whether the movement had in it any permanent vitality.[80] It is significant to observe in this connection that the total strength of the Imperial Service Troops was a little upwards of 19,000 only.[81] And the scheme remained confined to 23 States[82], although many other States had expressed their keen desire to join it.

Jaipur was one of the five States of Rajputana which were associated prominently with the scheme of Imperial Service Troops. It was due to the keen personal interest of the Maharaja of Jaipur that the Jaipur Imperial Service Transport Corps was employed usefully in the Chitral expedition (1895), and it was as a result of his initiative that 200 ponies were added to the Jaipur Transport Corps after this expedition. In 1897-98 the Jaipur Transport Corps, as already mentioned, did 'excellent' work in the Tirah campaign on the North-West Frontiers of India. The British authorities were appreciative of the 'admirable service' rendered by the Jaipur Transport Corps.

In appreciation of his loyalty and services to the Paramount Power, the Maharaja of Jaipur was appointed as Honorary Colonel of the 13th Rajputs (the Shekhawati Regiment), by His Majesty the King Emperor in 1904. The Maharaja held a special Darbar in the City Palace on 2 September 1904 in honour of this appointment, in which besides Colonel Pears, British Resident at Jaipur, many other high British dignitaries participated. Colonel Pears remarked that the appointment was an 'unusual honour'; the only other Chiefs enjoying a similar distinction were the Raja of Nabha, Honorary Colonel of the 14th Sikhs, and the Maharaja of Kashmir, Honorary Colonel of the 37th Dogras. He then reproduced a brief history of the Shekhawati Regiment which had been supplied to him by Lieutenant-Colonel Fairbrother, commanding the Regiment at that time.[83] He extended his 'hearty congratulations' to the Maharaja for the honour which had been conferred on him by His Majesty, and expressed the hope that under the benign care of the Maharaja the Regiment would continue to uphold its tradition of loyalty and bravery.[84] The Maharaja thanked Colonel Pears and other British Officers for taking the trouble in coming to the Palace Hall and participating in the 'joyous ceremony'. He requested the Resident to convey his sense of loyalty and devotion to His Majesty the King Emperor through the proper channel.[85] The Agent to Governor-General, Rajputana, forwarded the letter of the Resident at Jaipur along with a copy of the speech delivered by the Maharaja on 2nd September to the Government of India, requesting that the expression of the Maharaja's loyalty and devotion to His Majesty the King Emperor might be conveyed to the latter.[86] Accordingly the request of the Maharaja of Jaipur was conveyed by the Governor-General in Council to His Majesty's Secretary of State for India.[87]

The Maharaja of Jaipur continued to remain loyal and faithful to the Paramount Power. During the First World War the Jaipur Transport Corps rendered useful service to the British in Mesopotamia and Palestine. After the World War I, the Jaipur State Forces, like the State Forces of other principal States, were reorganised under the guidance of British Officers. The troops were classified into three categories — Class A, Class B and Class C.[88]

References and Notes

1. C.U. Aitchison, Comp., *A Collection of Treaties, Engagements and Sanads, Vol. III* (Calcutta, 1932), p. 68.
2. *Supra*, p. 83.
3. In 1864, out of a total strength of 2,05,000 men in the army, 65,000 were Europeans; there was an overall decrease of about 40 per cent in the total strength, but an increase of 60 per cent in the number of European troops. Vide *IGI, Vol. IV* (London, 1908), p. 345.
4. *Ibid.*, pp. 85-86; also see A.C. Arora, *British Policy towards the Punjab States 1858-1905* (Jalandhar, 1982), p. 248.
5. FD, Political A, June 1865, Nos. 165-167.
6. J.C. Brooke, *Political History of the State of Jaipur* (Calcutta, 1868), p. 12; Jadunath Sarkar, *A History of Jaipur 1503-1938*, revised and edited by Raghubir Sinh (New Delhi, 1984), p. 383.
7. K.W., FD, A-Military-I, Aug. 1884, Nos. 9-27, see No. 14, pp. 8-10.

8. Sir Erskine Perry to Northbrook, 31 Dec. 1874, Northbrook Papers, Reel 9, pp. 305-06.
9. Northbrook to Sir Erskine Perry, 12 Feb. 1875, Northbrook Papers, Reel 10, p. xvii.
10. Foreign Department Circular No. 119 of 15 Jan. 1878, FD, Secret Supplementary, Dec. 1879, No. 338.
11. For details, see Arora, *op. cit.*, pp. 256-58.
12. C.L. Tupper, Comp., *Indian Political Practice, Vol. I* (Calcutta, 1895), para 125, pp. 145-46.
13. Jaipur Agency Record, Part-I, Arms Act, File No. 1/1878, pp. 29-30.
14. *Ibid.*, p. 89.
15. FD, General A, Dec. 1880, Nos. 10-12.
16. FD, Military B, Feb. 1881, Nos. 6-7.
17. FD, Notes and Orders, B-General-I, June 1884, Nos. 235-242A.
18. Jaipur Agency Record, Part I, Arms Act, File No. 4/1891.
19. 500 Breech Loading Carbines acquired from Madras Arsenal and 1200 Breech Loading Carbines, 1 Muzzle Loading Carbine, 1000 bayonets and 28,000 Ball Cartridges got from Ferozepur Arsenal.
20. FD, Internal B, Oct. 1900, Nos. 433-435.
21. Jaipur Agency Record, Part I, Arms Act, File No. 5/1895-1909, pp. 130-31.
22. Jaipur Agency Record, Part I, Arms Act, File No. 7/1905-1914.
23. FD, Secret Supplementary, Dec. 1878, Nos. 320-416.
24. FD, Secret Supplementary, July 1879, Nos. 153-154.
25. Maharaja of Jaipur to Political Agent at Jaipur, dated 25 Dec. 1878; Political Agent, Jaipur to AGG, No. 1-P, dated 3 Jan. 1879; AGG to GOI, No. 41-P, dated 23 Jan. 1879. See FD, Secret Supplementary, Feb. 1879, No. 324.
26. FD, Secret Supplementary, Sept. 1879, No. 201 of Nos. 179-361, pp. 6-7.
27. FD, A-Political-E, Sept. 1882, Nos. 32-42 and 123-125.
28. FD, Secret E, Feb. 1886, Nos. 260-499.
29. Stuart Beatson, Comp., *A History of the Imperial Service Troops of Native States* (Calcutta, 1903), Preface, p. ii.
30. FD, Secret I, Nov. 1887, Nos. 30-41; also Secret I, March 1888, Nos. 1-47.
31. Note by H.M.D., 7 Aug. 1887, K.W.I, FD, Secret I, March 1889, Nos. 95-103, pp. 1-3.
32. *Ibid.*, p. 4.
33. Melliss to Punjab Govt., 7 March 1888, FD, Secret I, March 1889, No. 98.

34. Beatson, *op. cit.*, p. iii.
35. FD, Secret I, May 1889, Nos. 21-22.
36. Speech by Lord Dufferin delivered at Patiala on 17 Nov. 1888, FD, Secret I, May 1889, No. 29; *Speeches by the Marquess of Dufferin and Ava* (Calcutta, 1889), pp. 365-68; Beatson, *op. cit.*, pp. iv-vii.
37. *Speeches by the Marquess of Lansdowne, Vol. II* (Calcutta, 1895), pp. 434-35.
38. Secret/Internal Despatch from Governor-General in Council to Secretary of State, No. 41 of 13 March 1889, FD, Secret I, May 1889, No. 62; Tupper, *op. cit., Vol. I*, pp. 150-52.
39. Secret Despatch from Secretary of State to Governor-General in Council, No. 18 of 31 May 1889 and No. 29 of 6 June 1889, FD, Secret I, Dec. 1889, Nos. 18-19.
40. FD, Internal A, Aug. 1890, No. 150.
41. Beatson, *op. cit.*, p. 47.
42. RPARS for 1888-89, p. 35.
43. RPARS for 1891-92, pp. 58-59.
44. *Ibid.*, p. 59.
45. FD, Secret I, July 1895, Nos. 5-23.
46. Telegrams from Inspector-General Imperial Service Troops to Foreign Secretary, dated 23 and 25 March 1895, FD, Secret I, July 1895, Nos. 1-2.
47. Foreign Secretary, GOI to Inspector-General, Imperial Service Troops, 27 March 1895, FD, Secret I, July 1895, No. 4.
48. Beatson, *op. cit.*, p. 47.
49. *Ibid.*, pp. 47-48.
50. *Ibid.*, p. 48.
51. Vide FD, Internal A, Aug. 1895, No. 281.
52. Col. H. Melliss, Inspector-General, Imperial Service Troops to Secretary to GOI, Foreign Department, No. 1156, 9 Oct. 1895, FD, Internal A, Nov. 1895, No. 125.
53. D.O. from Lieut.-Col. A.C. Talbot to Col. H. Melliss, 4 Nov. 1895, K.W. No. 2, FD, Internal A, Nov. 1895, No. 125, p. 3.
54. FD, Secret I, February 1896, No. 42 of Nos. 23-48.
55. D.O. letter from Col. H. Melliss to W.J. Cunnihgham, dated 23 March 1896 (Confidential); D.O. letter from W.J. Cuningham to Col. H. Melliss, dated 27 March 1896. See K.W. No. 2, FD, Internal A, June 1896, Nos. 305-308, p. 5.
56. Maharaja of Jaipur to Col. V.E. Law, Resident at Jaipur, dated 17 April 1896, FD, Internal A, June 1896, No. 306.
57. AGG to GOI, No. 1788-G., dated 4 May 1896, FD, Internal A, June 1896, No. 305.

58. H.S. Barnes, Offg. Secretary to the GOI to AGG, No. 1645-I., dated 19 May 1896, FD, Internal A, June 1896, No. 307.
59. Despatch from GOI to Secretary of State for India, No. 115, dated 16 June 1896, FD, Internal A, June 1896, No. 308.
60. K.W. No. 1, FD, Internal A, June 1896, Nos. 305-308, p. 2.
61. RPARS for 1896-97, p. 39.
62. For a detailed discussion among the British high-ups about the comparative utility of the Transport Corps and Infantry and Cavalry of Imperial Service Troops, see K.W. No. 4, FD, Internal A, June 1896, Nos. 305-308, pp. 1-7.
63. FD, Internal A, Oct. 1897, Nos. 372-456.
64. K.W. No. 3, *ibid.*
65. FD, Internal A, Jan. 1898, Nos. 192-196.
66. Beatson, *op. cit.*, pp. 48-49.
67. FD, Internal A, Aug. 1898, Nos. 367 and 370.
68. Hamilton to Elgin, 2 Dec. 1898, Elgin Papers, Reel 3, No. 45.
69. Curzon to Roberts, 19 June 1901, Curzon Papers, Reel 6, No. 39.
70. RPARS for 1900-1901, p. 22.
71. RPARS for 1901-02, p. 17.
72. RPARS for 1902-03, p. 17.
73. RPARS for 1903-04, p. 16.
74. FD, Internal A, March 1903, Nos. 5-45.
75. Telegram from Viceroy to Secretary of State for India, No. 3283-D, dated 28 June 1903, FD, Internal A, Aug. 1903, No. 31.
76. Telegram from Secretary of State for India to the Viceroy, dated 29 June 1903, FD, Internal A, Aug. 1903, No. 32.
77. Hamilton to Curzon, 21 Dec. 1899, Curzon Papers, Reel 1, No. 75.
78. Macdonnell to Curzon, 29 Sept. 1899, Curzon Papers, Reel 8, No. 109.
79. Curzon to Hamilton, 11 Jan. 1900, Curzon Papers, Reel 2, No. 2.
80. *Ibid.*
81. Tupper, *op. cit.,, Vol. I*, para 141, p. 158.
82. These 23 States were : Alwar, Bahawalpur, Bharatpur, Bhavnagar, Bhopal, Bikaner, Faridkot, Gwalior, Hyderabad, Indore, Jaipur, Jind, Jodhpur, Junagarh, Kapurthala, Kashmir, Malerkotla, Mysore, Nabha, Navanagar, Patiala, Rampur and Sirmur.
83. The nucleus of the 13th Rajputs was originally a small force of Jaipur troops handed over to the command of Lieutenant Forster in January 1835 for the suppression of lawless bands in

Shekhawat and other territories adjacent to Jaipur. He gradually formed a Brigade, afterwards known as the Shekhawati Brigade. The Brigade consisted of Artillery, Cavalry and Infantry and had its headquarters at Jhunjnu, about 90 miles north of Jaipur. During the next ten years Lieutenant Forster and his Brigade were constantly engaged in suppressing crime and in attacking and dismantling the forts of the powerful Shekhawat Chieftains whose troops were making raids either into other States or into the territories of their brother Chieftains in Jaipur. In 1845 the Brigade took part in the First Anglo-Sikh War and distinguished itself at the battle of Aliwal. In 1847 the Artillery and Cavalry of the Shekhawati Brigade were disbanded and the Infantry became part of the regular army with the designation of the Shekhawati Battalion. During the Revolt of 1857-58 the Regiment remained loyal and rendered excellent service. In 1858 Forster was promoted to the rank of Colonel and he retired from service in the same year. The Regiment went on foreign service in Malta and Cyprus in 1878, and on its return to India took part in the Afghan campaign in 1879-80, in the Sikkim and Manipur expeditions in 1888 and 1891, and in the relief of Chitral in 1895, the Punjab Frontier and Mahsud Waziri campaigns in 1897, and 1902. By an order passed in 1893, the Regiment was composed wholly of Rajputana Rajputs.

84. Resident, Jaipur to AGG, No. 5246, dated 9 Sept. 1904, FD, Internal A, April 1905, No. 7, Encl. and Sub-Encl. 1.
85. Speech delivered in the Darbar on 2 Sept. 1904 by the Maharaja, *ibid.*, Sub-Encl. 2, Encl. I.
86. AGG to GOI, No. 309, dated 21 Sept. 1904, FD, Internal A, April 1905, No. 7.
87. GOI to AGG, No. 1197-I.A., dated 29 March 1905, FD, Internal A, April 1905, No. 8 ; GOI to His Majesty's Secretary of State for India, No. 61, dated 30 March 1905, *ibid.*, No. 9.
88. For details about the Jaipur State Forces, see H.H. The Maharaja of Jaipur, *A History of the Indian State Forces* (New Delhi, 1967), pp. xvi-xvii, 55-62.

CHAPTER 9

British Impact on Internal Administration

The British Government exercised a significant impact on the internal administration of Jaipur, as also on other States in the post-1858 period. Although the treaty of 1818 concluded by the British Government with the Jaipur State precluded the British authorities from interfering in the internal administration of the State, yet the British policy-makers considered it their duty to improve the administration of the State which should be conducive to the welfare and happiness of the people. During the period of the East India Company the British governors-general from the time of William Bentinck (1828-35) had begun in British India the process of 'civilising mission', for he had been prominently influenced by the utilitarian movement of England, and the process had acquired a great momentum by the time of the governor-generalship of Dalhousie. The British governors-general deemed it a 'White Man's Burden' to take measures for the welfare and happiness of the people. The 'civilising mission' was initiated in the Princely States in the post-1858 period, more specifically during the viceroyalty of John Lawrence (1864-69) and it reached its fruition during the tenure of Curzon's viceroyalty (1899-1905). But it must be underlined that behind this 'civilising mission' lay the predominant imperial interests of the Paramount Power.

In accordance with the so-called 'civilising mission', the British authorities persuaded the rulers of the Jaipur State to bring about reforms in the administration which might lead to the well-being and happiness of the subjects. In 1867 the practice of preparing Annual Reports on the Political Administration of Rajputana States, including Jaipur, was started by the British authorities. In these reports was recorded the progress in various branches of the administration of the State, and even comments were given on the character and conduct of the then Maharaja. These reports were regularly published, and as such compelled the rulers to effect necessary improvements in administration, otherwise they would fall in the esteem of the people and the press. The rulers were not expected to behave like irresponsible despots but act as benevolent rulers who should be assisted and guided by a council of competent officials and nobles. More important still, the British Political Agent/ Resident at Jaipur acted as the most effective check on the authority of the Maharaja, and as his main adviser and guide he persuaded the latter to reform the administration on modern lines. "The creation of an administrative structure, patterned after the British Indian model was a major part of this civilising process."[1]

I

During the time of Maharaja Ram Singh (1835-1880) a State Council known as 'Royal Council of Jaipur' was constituted in 1867.[2] Its purpose was to assist the Maharaja in running the administration efficiently. The Council originally consisted of six members. In its initial working the Council did not come up to the expectation of the British authorities. There was 'a want of independent action among its members' and "the tendency of its operations is less to induce in Executive Officers individual energy than to relieve them of the responsibility involved in their position." Captain Bradford, the British Resident/Agent at Jaipur opined that with the exception of Nawab Faiz Ali Khan who was the head of the Royal Council, the other members of the Council were 'men of no calibre' and majority of them were 'inert, old and unprogressive'. The good government of the country was largely due to Nawab Faiz Ali Khan[3], and not to the other members. Yet the Council was a sort of moral force on which the Maharaja relied in order to claim, if need be, that he was governing in accordance with the wishes of his people, when as a matter of fact it did not represent their interests in any way.[4] Be that as it may, Maharaja Ram Singh had succeeded in carrying out commendable administrative reforms with the assistance of the Council.

After the demise of Maharaja Ram Singh in 1880, Kaim Singh, who was 19 years old at that time, succeeded to the Chiefship in the name of Sawai Madho Singh. The new Maharaja was directed to conduct the administration of the State with the active assistance of the Council (consisting of influential nobles); he was required to be guided by the advice of the Political Agent in all important administrative matters who was also to attend the meetings of the Council accompanied by the young Maharaja.[5] On the suggestion of Colonel Bradford it was decided in 1881 to add three more members to the Council who were the respective heads of three chief clans, namely Chomu, Diggi and Bugru, so far unrepresented, so that the Council was given more national and representative character. The Council now consisted of nine members who were the following :

1. Thakur Gobind Singh (of Chomu)
2. Thakur Partab Singh (of Diggi)
3. Thakur Sawant Singh (of Bugru)
4. Thakur Samunder Singh
5. Thakur Simbhu Singh
6. Purohit Ram Parsad
7. Babu Jadu Nath Sen
8. Babu Kanti Chander Mukerji
9. Mir Kurban Ali

The Maharaja of Jaipur and the Political Agent were to sit in the meetings of the Council as joint heads (Presidents) of the Council. No matters could be decided by the Council without concurrence of the Political Agent. Hakim Salim Khan was to act as Secretary of the Council. Thakur Fateh Singh was the Vice-President of the Council.[6]

For administrative convenience three main departments were established — (i) Revenue and Financial Department; (ii) Military, Foreign and Miscellaneous Department; (iii) Judicial Department. Three members of the Council were associated with each of these three departments. Partab Singh, Simbhu Singh and Jadu Nath Sen were allocated Revenue and Financial Department. Gobind Singh, Ram Parsad, and Kanti Chander Mukerji were to deal with Military, Foreign and Miscellaneous Department. Sawant Singh, Samunder Singh and Kurban Ali were entrusted with the work of Judicial Department.[7] Fateh Singh, who was the Vice-President of the Council, was to look after all these departments and he was to be guided by the Political Agent in all important affairs of administration.

In his Report of 11 May 1881 Beynon, Political Agent, recorded his impressions about Fateh Singh and other members of the Council.[8] Thakur Fateh Singh was a self-made man of strong will and indomitable energy. His extraordinary memory was 'a mine of information' which gave him easy mastery over his colleagues in dealing with State questions. He was capable of doing much and had Raj interest at heart but his strong tendencies to nepotism and monopoly of power needed to be watched carefully. Thakur Gobind Singh, a premier noble of the State was a highly respectable gentleman who was fairly educated and possessed tolerable knowledge of English language and 'good stock of common sense'. He was fast rising in popularity and becoming a special favourite of the young Chief. Thakur Partab Singh was a 'very amiable native gentleman' who was selected for loyalty and capability shown in the management of his large estate. He was painstaking, industrious and a 'straight forward and faithful adherent to the Raj'. Thakur Sawant Singh, belonging to old and loyal stock of Rajputs, was a 'perfect gentleman'. He possessed sound common sense and his strong attachment to the Raj 'makes him safe and reliable counsellor of the State'. Thakur Samunder Singh, elder brother of Thakur Fateh Singh, possessed a considerable force of character. He was shrewd, energetic and well-informed on all matters pertaining to revenue affairs of the State. Purohit Ram Parsad, a spiritual adviser of the late Maharaja, was 'exceedingly popular'. He was a harmless and well-disposed man who adhered firmly to the *gaddi*. Babu Jadu Nath Sen, a Bengali gentlemean, owed his position to his long connection with the late Maharaja. He did not possess enough energy to do more good or harm. He was a non-partisan and as such virtually a 'nonentity'. Babu Kanti Chander Mukerji was a principal working man of the Council. He possessed considerable mental calibre and was a brilliant administrator capable of accomplishing much if his energies were properly applied and directed. Mir Kurban Ali, another working element of the Council possessed fair knowledge of law and procedure, and as such he was well-fitted to perform his functions as Judicial Member of the Council. "His judgements are generally sound and his views clear; while painstaking care and method with which he performs his work are very praiseworthy."

In July 1881 a serious charge of misappropriation of money was levelled against Thakur Fateh Singh, Vice-President of the Council. On 14 July 1881 Colonel Bannerman, the Officiating Resident, Eastern States of Rajputana, submitted an official report on the subject of allegation made against Fateh Singh. It had come to Colonel Bannerman's ear that some time before his death the late Maharaja (Ram Singh) had been much incensed with Fateh Singh, owing to reports having been made to him that Fateh Singh had taken large bribes. He had tried to win over favours from the Maharaja by making a large present to him — of Rs. 50,000 in cash and Rs. 1,75,000 in currency notes; the latter being in a sealed up envelope, which was kept sealed up in the charge of one Kishen Lall, the keeper of the Maharaja's *Kupperdwara* or private property. Some six or eight days after the death of Maharaja Ram Singh, and before the recognition by the British Government of the present Maharaja, Fateh Singh is said to have obtained possession of this envelope from Kishen Lall. Colonel Bannerman was anxious that a careful examination should be made of the contents of the *Kupperdwara*, knowing that if, at some future time, deficiencies were found, the blame of carelessness would be cast upon the administration of the time, when the Political Agent was responsible for it. He spoke to the Maharaja on the subject but the latter raised objections on the ground that the *Kupperdwara* contained all the *zenana* jewels which had never before been seen by an outsider, and no examination of its contents had ever been made before. Colonel Bannerman expressed himself quite willing not to press an examination of the *zenana* jewels.

The whole story had been first brought to the notice of Colonel Bannerman by Babu Kanti Chander Mukerji and Thakur Gobind Singh, two members of the Jaipur Council. The Babu, who had been for years Fateh Singh's rival for power in the State declared that some months before his death the late Maharaja had told him that he had caused Fateh Singh to disgorge some of his ill-gotten gains and that "he had that day received from him Rs. 50,000 in coin and Rs. 1,75,000 in notes in a sealed envelope, which he had not looked at himself, but had told Fateh Singh to make it over to Kishen Lall." Fateh Singh was summoned and told exactly what had been said about him. He entirely denied the story of the currency notes for Rs. 1,75,000 but he confessed that he did, after the late Maharaja's death, obtain from the *Kupperdwara* an envelope which he had before, by the late Maharaja's orders, given to Kishen Lall to keep but he said that the envelope only contained some private accounts belonging to the Maharaja. Fateh Singh demanded a full enquiry. Colonel Walter, Agent to Governor-General, Rajputana was anxious to get the truth of the story and therefore he asked Colonel Bannermen to make such an enquiry.[9]

After investigating the whole matter, Colonel Bannerman expressed his opinion to the effect that Thakur Fateh Singh's conduct was open to such grave suspicion that he ought to be removed from the post of Vice-President of the Council, and required to leave the Jaipur State. For, if he remained in the State after his removal from power, he would, with his extensive connections, become a focus of intrigue and prejudicial influence.[10] Colonel Walter, Officiating Agent to Governor-General for Rajputana, agreed with Colonel Bannerman that very grave suspicion rested on Thakur Fateh Singh who, he observed, had long held a not very enviable notoriety in Jaipur;

and he opined that the present opportunity should be taken advantage of to dispense with his services as a member of the Council, and that, to prevent future complications, he should not be allowed to remain in the State.[11]

The Viceroy and Governor-General in Council, after full consideration of the papers submitted, came to the conclusion that the enquiry had proved nothing against Thakur Fateh Singh and that the case afforded no ground for dispensing with his services or for refusing him permission to remain at Jaipur. The Supreme Government ordered that this decision should be communicated to the Maharaja who should be informed that if he desired Thakur Fateh Singh to be reinstated as Member of the Council the Government of India would have no objection. It, however, directed the Agent to Governor-General that the office of Vice-President of the Council might be discontinued.[12] Fateh Singh continued to be a Member of the Council.

By this time the Council conducted its business 'methodically'. References from various departments were openly discussed and orders recorded. The Political Agent and the Maharaja took part in its proceedings. On attaining the age of twenty-one years, Maharaja Sawai Madho Singh was invested with full ruling powers on 5 September 1882 but he was required to consult the Resident upon all important matters and be guided by his advice. He was also to get advice and assistance from the Members of the Council in the day-to-day administrative affairs of the State.[13]

Later on some changes took place from time to time in the Members of the Council. Two prominent Members of the Council, Thakur Gobind Singh and Babu Kanti Chander Mukerji died in 1900. They were replaced by Thakur Debi Singh of Chomu and Babu Ishan Chander Mukerji respectively. Thakur Umrao Singh of Kotla and Nawab Faiz Ali Khan were appointed as the other two Members of the Council. The former was a well-known and experienced *Jagirdar* of the United Provinces who was connected by marriage with Maharaja Madho Singh. Nawab Faiz Ali Khan was a Member of the Legislative Council of the United Provinces.[14] In 1902 when the Maharaja left for London to attend the coronation of the King-Emperor Edward

VII, the administrative work of the State in his absence was carried on by the Council. Thakur Umrao Singh had been selected by the Maharaja to be specially responsible for the conduct of affairs. He had been instructed to keep the Resident informed and to take his advice in all matters of importance.[15]

It is significant to observe that all administrative affairs of the Jaipur Darbar were conducted in the name of the Jaipur Council and all correspondence with the British Resident was carried on by the Secretary of the Council on behalf of the Council. The creation of a Council of officials to regulate the administration of the State according to clearly laid rules and procedures deriving its power from the ruling Prince and acting on his behalf was the surest way of announcing a new spirit in the administration.[16] This was, of course, done under the British impact.

II

The Jaipur State was divided for administrative purposes into two main divisions — the Eastern and Western divisions. Each of these divisions was under a Revenue Commissioner or *Diwan*. Each division was further divided into districts or *Nizamats*. There were ten *Nizamats* in all : Shekhawati, Torawati, Hindaun, Dausa, Sawai-Jaipur, Sawai-Madhopur, Gangapur, Kot Kasim, Malpura and Sambhar. Each *Nizamat* was under a *Nazim* who was assisted by a *Naib-Nazim*. They were administrative as well as judicial officers like the Deputy Commissioners or Collectors of British districts. The *Nizamats* were sub-divided into thirty-one *Tahsils*.[17] Each *Tahsil* was under the charge of a *Tahsildar* who performed administrative as well as judicial functions. According to the Administration Report of 1905-06, there were eleven *Nizamats*, Bandikui being the eleventh and the number of *Tahsils* was thirty-three.[18]

There were a large number of *Thakurs* or feudatory nobles who owed allegiance to the Maharaja of Jaipur. The principal nobles who paid regular tribute to the Jaipur Darbar were the chiefs of Khetri, Sikar and Uniara.

The land revenue system of the State was gradually reformed and reorganised. Earlier there was 'endless variety of land tenures' and general assessment of the whole territory was called for. By the orders of Maharaja Ram Singh a survey under native agency was begun but it made little progress. Beyond the *Khalsa* land there was very little known of actual revenue receipts of the State.[19] Under the British impact it was decided by the Jaipur Council unanimously that revenue survey on scientific principles be conducted.[20] The State government was persuaded to agree to land survey operations; the advantage of fixity of land revenue and the possibility of future higher revenue returns were brought home to them. Babu Kanti Chander Mukerji, a Member of the Jaipur Council and an expert in the land revenue matters, prepared a comprehensive account of the land revenue system of the Jaipur State. He submitted a Memorandum on the various tenures of land in the State, the different methods of assessing the revenue, and the modes of collection in force. The main features of the Memorandum may be summarised as under :

(i) Tenures : The tenures of the village occupants in the Jaipur territory were *Ryotwari,* each cultivator paying rent for his holding direct to the Raj. The *Zamindari* system was almost unknown. The occupants of every village had the right of cultivating all the land included within the boundaries of their village. Where the villages were few in number and could not bring under cultivation all the cultivable land within their village boundaries, the occupants of adjacent villages were allowed to take up land in the village provided they had no cultivable land of their own. The villagers who thus took up land in another village were called *pae-kashts.* The occupants of every village had the right of grazing their cattle and taking the *punni* (grass) and *pulla* (seeds) as well as wood growing on the uncultivable and fallow portions of their village land.[21]

Some ryots were proprietors of their respective holdings and this proprietary right was hereditary. They enjoyed undisturbed possession of their holdings so long as they continued to pay the rent fixed. They also enjoyed the right of transfer by sale or mortgage. Such proprietors were called

Biswedars and their holdings *biswas*. The rest of the land within the boundary of a village was taken up by cultivators who did not possess any proprietary rights like the *Biswedars*. In some villages the principal occupants were regarded as the cultivating proprietors of the entire village. They were jointly held responsible for the total rent due by the villagers. They distributed the land to cultivators subordinate to them on conditions fixed by them and realized the rent due. These village proprietors enjoyed this right so long as they continued to pay the total amount of rent due on account of the entire village. The cultivators were mere tenants-at-will; they had no hereditary rights in the land, but the right of cultivation descended from father to son and was recognised by the State; it could not, however, be transferred without the sanction of the Darbar.[22]

Diwan Moti Lall tried to introduce what he called '*chakbundi*' system. He decided to measure the *chahi* and *barani* lands belonging to each village, and to redistribute the same among the cultivators fixing a certain rate per bigha in accordance with the nature of the soil as well as the caste of the cultivator. But as the villagers everywhere opposed this measure, the Diwan had to abandon it. He then took an average of the past five years' actual revenue derived from each village and offered to let out for ten years each village to the occupants, jointly or separately as they preferred, on an annual rental based on the above average. The cultivators declined to take on themselves joint responsibilities and applied for separate leases, agreeing to pay for their respective holding proportionate share of the rental fixed for the whole village. Land was accordingly redistributed among them. However, wide discontent prevailed among a large number of cultivators and many of them deserted their villages; with the result, Moti Lall's *chakbundi* system remained in force over less than half of the Jaipur territory, and the old system of distributing land to the cultivators at the beginning of each agricultural season prevailed over the greater portion.[23]

There was another class of proprietors in most of the *Khalsa* villages who were known as *Bhumias*. A *Bhumia* was originally the guardian of the village, and as such he was entitled to a share of the produce of each field within the village boundaries. In some villages the *Bhumias* paid a nominal quit-rent to the Raj and took the entire revenue from the village. There were rent-free holdings also in almost every *Khalsa* village, namely *Ooduk* (a religious grant made under a solemn oath), *Inam* (grant made for meritorious service) and *Tankha* (grant made in lieu of pay).[24]

(ii) Method of Assessment of Revenue : There were three different methods of assessment prevailing in villages which had not been brought under the *chakbundi* system — first *batai* or division of the produce; second *bhej* or money rates per bigha; third *halsera* or money rates per plough. There were four different methods of *batai* : (1) *seedha batai* or actual division by measuring the corn by an earthern pot called *mutka;* (2) *kankut* or division of the produce by conjectural estimate of the crop on the field; (3) *dal batai* or division by conjectural estimates of the ears of corn gathered in heaps; (4) *reh* or *guntabundi,* that is, after reaping, the corn was gathered and bound into sheaves. Any of the four ways of *batai* was adopted as desired by the cultivator or thought convenient by the *Tahsil* officer. The *batai* method of assessment was almost always adopted in regard to all foodgrains of *spring* or *rabi* and autumn or *kharif* produce, such as wheat, barley, gram, *bajra, jawar, til, moong, urd,* etc. When the State share had been settled, the cultivator was sometimes allowed to retain it by paying the money value at the market rate. In case the market rate was not favourable, the Raj share of the produce was taken to and deposited in the State granaries. The share of the produce taken by the State varied everywhere in accordance with the caste and sometimes with the occupation of the cultivator. The agriculturist by caste and profession had to give the State one-half of the produce of his fields, and this was the maximum rate. The Brahmans, Rajputs, Jats and Gujars, etc. had to pay less. The Brahmans and the Rajputs were allowed to cultivate land on the most favourable terms. The State share of the produce varied from one-half yielded by ordinary agriculturist to one-fifth paid by the Brahman and the Rajput.[25]

In villages where the *chakbundi* system had not been introduced, a money cess was also levied on the cultivator called *mulba.* The *Bhumia* of the village was allowed to levy a separate cess on the cultivator's share of the produce which was called *bhum* or *paona,* as one *pao,* i.e. one-fourth of a seer was taken by the *Bhumia.* The village *Patel, Patwari, Chaudhri* and *Kanoongo* were allowed to take jointly one and a half seers per maund from the cultivator's portion in return for the assistance they rendered in the management of the village affairs. The corn thus obtained was equally divided among them. Another cess called *nalbut* was levied by the Raj on fields irrigated from wells belonging to the State. This rate varied from twelve to four annas per bigha.[26]

Bhej or money rates were generally applied to valuable crops other than food-grains and varied with the kind of crop sown, the caste and occupation of the cultivator as well as with the nature of the soil. Cotton, sugarcane and *mukka* were the chief autumn or *kharif* crops, and opium, tobacco and *jeera* the chief spring or *rabi* crops, for which *bhej* or money rates were taken. These rates varied from one rupee to seven rupees per bigha. The *bhej* rates were higher or lower in accordance with circumstances connected with the advantages of irrigation available. The land irrigated from wells paid a higher rate than the land irrigated from *talaos* or tanks. The *bhej* rates were on the crop and for the season, not for the year.[27]

The third method of assessment was *halsera* or cash rates per plough which the cultivators brought to the field. These rates varied from Rs. 3-2-0 to Rs. 1-4-0 in accordance with the nature of the soil affording greater or less facility to the agriculturist. The *halsera* rates were levied irrespective of the caste of the cultivator and of the crops sown. This method of assessment was generally adopted in villages which included within their boundaries a considerable area of cultivable land, while the villagers were very few in number and no *pae-kashts* came forward from the surrounding villages. The *halsera* was allowed for limited periods with the sanction of the Diwan.[28]

In all *chakbundi* villages cash rents were taken from the cultivators on the measured *puttis* or holdings irrespective of the crops sown. Each cultivator had to pay a proportionate share of the revenue fixed for the whole village in accordance with the average of the past five years' collection. The *chakbundi* system had not in any way interfered with the interests of the *Biswedar*. He still paid the rent fixed for his holding at some remote period. Deducting from the total revenue, fixed for the village, the amount payable by the *biswedars* and the favoured castes, as well as by the village officers, the remainder was realised from the non-proprietary cultivators, each being required to pay a share in proportion to the areas of the *putti* assigned to him. Under this system no *mulba* or extra cess was levied.[29]

Land was always granted rent-free to the cultivators for building hamlets. However, a cess called *jhoopra* or cottage rate was taken from artisans and others (goldsmiths, blacksmiths, carpenters, weavers, *kolis, chamars,* etc.) which varied from twelve to six annas per cottage for the year. Another extra cess was levied on the occupants of every village who kept flocks of sheep and goats grazing on the village waste. This cess was called *chelliginti* and its rate was one anna a head per annum. Cows, bullocks and buffaloes were generally exempted from the payment of this cess.[30]

(iii) Mode of Collection and System of Accounts : At the end of each agricultural season, i.e. *kharif* and *rabi* the *Tahsildar* of the *pargana* sent *Shahnas* to the villages included in the *pargana* under his charge to make preliminary arrangements for *batai* and the realization of *bhej* rates. They were required to be present in the villages assigned to them separately twenty days or a month before reaping commenced. The *Shahnas* were selected and employed by the *Tahsildar* each season. Their appointment was temporary lasting for six months (three months for *kharif* and three months for *rabi* crops) and they were paid rupees 5 per month for the period they were employed. As soon as the *Shahnas* reached the respective villages assigned to them they summoned the *Patel, Patwari, Chaudhri* and *Kanoongo* of the village. The village cultivators were also assembled. In the presence of all the *Shahna* took from the village officers a statement of the number of fields under cultivation that season, together with particulars regarding the crops sown, the caste of the individual cultivators, the nature of the tenure and the method of assessment prevailing. The *Shahna* then inspected

each field in company with the village *Patel* and *Patwari* as well as the cultivator. The *Shahna* then sent the statement to the *tahsil* and asked *Tahsildar*'s permission to commence reaping. After reaping, when the produce was ready for division the *Shahna* sent a report to the *Tahsildar* and sought his permission for commencing *batai*. The *Tahsildar* then sent out another temporary employee called *Tupdar* to superintend the *batai* operations. Thus the *batai* operations commenced under *Tupdar* and *Shahna's* directions in the presence of village *Patel, Patwari, Chaudhri* and *Kanoongo*. The *Tupdar's* appointment lasted for about 15 days each season and his allowance was R. 1-8 per diem. When *batai* or division was over, the Raj share was sometimes commuted into money payment in accordance with the market rate.[31]

With regard to *bhej* or cash rates, likewise, when the crop was ready each field was measured in the presence of the *Tupdar, Shahna,* village officers and the cultivator concerned. When the number of bighas had been ascertained by actual measurement, the *bhej* rate per bigha, in accordance with the crop, the nature of the soil, as well as the caste or occupation of the cultivator, was demanded. In case of the cultivator's inability to pay the rent on demand, he was not allowed to remove the produce from the field. The *Bohra* or money-lender, who was often present on such occasions, offered to pay the money for the cultivator, and the latter was bound down by a written agreement to pay the money by instalments, together with interest at exorbitant rates varying from 12 to 24 per cent.[32]

The villages of each *pargana* were divided into a number of small circles called *talukas* each of which was placed under an officer called *Talukadar* who was subordinate to the *Tahsildar*. Each circle, or *taluka* included villages yielding an aggregate annual revenue of about Rs. 12,000. While the *Tupdar* and *Shahna* were employed in assessing and collecting revenue the *Talukadar* went round and inspected each village. The *Talukadar's* monthly salary varied from Rs. 7½ to 15 in accordance with the prepondence of the *bhej* over the *batai* method of assessment in his circle. Sometimes the *Tahsildar* went out and inspected the operations personally. In *chakbundi* villages cash rents were taken, as already stated, for produce of every description whether food-grains or the more valuable crops. In this case also the cultivator was not allowed to take home the produce of his fields until he paid the rent due to him.[33]

The system of accounts was as under :

When *batai* or division of the produce took place, and the *bhej* or cash rates were in the course of realization *Novisindas* or *Mutsudier* from the *tahsil* office were sent out to get the *khusra* and *khuttuni* (rough *jummabundi* accounts) prepared on the spot. It was the duty of the village *Chaudhri* to prepare the *jammabundi* accounts and to make three copies of the same. Each of the three copies was signed by the *Patel*, *Patwari*, *Chaudhri* and *Kanoongo* of the village. The tahsil *Novisinda* took one copy and submitted it to the Tahsildar. Of the other two copies one remained with the *Patel* and the other with the *Chaudhri*. In case of *batai* the *jummabundi* accounts showed the name and caste of the cultivator, the kind and amount of grain in the field, and the share accruing to the State. The accounts also showed the equivalent in money when the Raj share was commuted into its money value. The *bhej jummabundi* accounts showed the name and caste of the cultivator, the area of the field, the nature of the soil, the crops sown, the rates applicable, and the total amounts resulting.[34]

The Government of India was highly appreciative of the Memorandum submitted by Kanti Chander Mukerji on the land revenue system of the Jaipur State which was found to be highly 'instructive and interesting'. So much so that the Supreme Government sent copies of this Memorandum to all the Local Governments and Administrations to be distributed for information among selected revenue officers of the provinces.[35]

In order to provide irrigation facilities to the cultivators, huge reservoirs were constructed year after year since 1868 under the able supervision of Colonel Jacob; these irrigation projects will be discussed in some details in section IV. It is, however, significant to observe that land settlements as operated in British India, were not introduced in the Jaipur State during the period of our study.

The land revenue system of the Jaipur State suffered from

all the defects and deficiencies which could be witnessed in the *Ryotwari* system in operation in various provinces of British India. The agriculturists by caste and profession (peasants or cultivators) had to pay one-half of the produce to the State in addition to many other cesses. The *Shahnas* and *Tupdars* who were temporary employees sent by the *Tahsildar* to do the important business of assessment and collection of revenue, were generally corrupt. They were "more mindful of filling their own pockets than attending the interests of the State or of the cultivators." They often won over the *Patel, Patwari* and other village officers to their side and all of them exploited the cultivators who had also to pay exorbitant rate of interest to the money-lenders. With the result, the condition of the ryots or cultivators became miserable many of whom often remained indebted to the greedy money-lenders. In the lands under the *jagirdars* also the condition of the peasants was no less miserable. Only the condition of the *Biswedars* was good who were the proprietors of the land and enjoyed many privileges.

Land revenue constituted a major source of income of the State. The State also derived considerable income from other sources. An estimate of the annual finance (income and expenditure) of the State can be formed from the following figures of the last decade or so of the 19th century[36] :

Year	*Receipts* Rs.	*Expenditure* Rs.
1887-88	61,96,000	49,34,251
1888-89	61,90,669	48,41,429
1889-90	65,54,850	49,84,201
1890-91	61,91,276	54,11,510
1891-92	61,66,559	54,89,704
1892-93	68,18,651	53,89,911
1893-94	64,18,406	51,77,186
1894-95	65,27,577	52,02,517
1895-96	66,56,536	56,15,092
1899-1900	45,03,123	108,71,398
1901-02	65,88,000	67,14,242

It is obvious from the above figures that the average annual income of the State during the years 1887-1896 was about rupees 65 lakhs. The chief sources of revenue were : land revenue (about 42 lakhs); customs (9 lakhs); receipts under the Salt Agreements of 1869 and 1879 (about 7.5 lakhs); tribute from *jagirdars* (4 lakhs); and irrigation rates (about 3 lakhs).[37] The average annual expenditure was about rupees 52 lakhs, the main items being civil and Judicial staff (figure not available); army, including the Imperial Service transport corps (about 10 lakhs); public works, including irrigation (about 7 lakhs); tribute to British Government (4 lakhs); police (about 2.4 lakhs); privy purse, palace and charities (figure not available); education (rupees 84,000) and medical institutions and vaccination (rupees 70,000).[38] Thus the annual budget during the decade 1887-1896 was consistently surplus budget, the average annual revenue being about 13 lakhs more than the average annual expenditure. Evidently the financial administration of the State was very well managed. It was due to the keen personal interest of the Maharaja and efficient functioning of various departments at the hands of the members of the Council who were guided by the Political Agents and ably assisted by the British officers employed in various departments on high jobs. The fall of revenue and considerable increase of expenditure in 1899-1900 was due to severe famine which had broken out in various parts of the State. It was, indeed, creditable for the Jaipur Darbar that it had remitted or reduced land revenue of the cultivators adversely affected by the famine, and at the same time spent a considerable sum of money in providing relief to the famine-stricken people. It is significant to note that the extraordinary expenditure thus indicated had been met without recourse to borrowing.[39] As a result of rigid economy and other measures for increasing the revenue, the State improved its financial administration within two years, as is indicated by the figures of receipts and expenditure in 1901-02.

III

Under the British impact Maharaja Ram Singh endeavoured to reform the administration of justice. In 1870-71 he appointed a committee of high officials of the State to look into the judicial administration and submit a report regarding the preparation of suitable civil and criminal procedure codes. It was also to compile rules and regulations for the guidance of district judicial officials. But the progress in this regard, however, was far from satisfactory.

In March 1883 Lt.-Col. E.R.C. Bradford reported that in his recent visit to Jaipur he found that there was urgent need of the attention of the Jaipur Administration to the conduct of the Judicial Department. After discussing the matter with the Maharaja, the Council and the Resident, he came to the conclusion that it would be desirable to appoint an experienced judicial Member of the State Council, to have charge of the Judicial Department. He suggested the name of Pandit Maharaj Kishen, Extra Assistant Commissioner, Punjab, after consulting Sir Charles Aitchison, the Lieutenant-Governor of the Punjab who had no objection to the temporary transfer of his services to the Jaipur State.[40] The Maharaja of Jaipur expressed his willingness to accept, for three years, the services of Pandit Maharaj Kishen who would have a seat in the State Council and would be allowed to draw from the Raj Treasury Rs. 500 per mensem, besides the usual pension contribution. He enclosed a *rubakar* of the Jaipur Council, stating in brief the nature of the duties particularly to be entrusted to the new officer together with a memorandum of confidential instructions for him.[41]

It was stated in the Council's *rubakar* that the administration of justice of the Jaipur State was not efficient as might be desired; there were no written rules and regulations, and no fixed procedure for the courts of justice; the working of the subordinate courts, both in the *Sudder* and in the *Mofussil,* was not properly looked after. The defects that had been noticed could not be rectified without the appointment of an experienced judicial officer. It was accordingly proposed that the Government be requested to lend to the Raj the services of an experienced Hindu judicial officer for a period of three years. The officer should first of all go through all the existing civil and criminal procedures, as well as the rules, *rubakars,* and orders that had from time to time been issued since the organisation of the courts. He should also see the rules that had been drawn up by the Legal Committee and submitted to the Maharaja, together with any additions and alteration which the officer might think proper. He should also inspect different courts of justice, both in the *Sudder* and in the *Mofussil,* and submit his report to the Maharaja, suggesting reforms which he might think necessary.[42]

The Governor-General in Council gave approval to the proposal of Agent to Governor-General, Rajputana and accorded sanction to the transfer of Pandit Maharaj Kishen's services to the Jaipur State on the terms proposed.[43]

As a result of the efforts of Pandit Maharaj Kishen necessary reforms were brought about in the judicial administration of the State on the pattern of judicial system operational in various provinces of British India. Suitable civil and criminal procedure codes were prepared. Rules and regulations for the guidance of the courts, both in the Sudder and in the Mofussil, were compiled. The powers and jurisdiction of the judges of various courts were clearly defined.

The powers of all the courts in civil and criminal cases from the lowest, the *Tahsildar*'s court to the highest, the Council were as under[44] :

The lowest courts were those of *Tahsildars* which numbered twenty-two, nine of these officials not being invested with judicial powers. They tried civil suits not exceeding Rs. 50 in value, and in the criminal cases they could give punishment of imprisonment up to one month and fine up to Rs. 11. But the *Tahsildar* of Shekhawati had enhanced powers. He tried civil suits not exceeding Rs. 100 in value, and in the criminal cases he could give punishment of imprisonment up to three months and fine up to Rs. 50.

The ten *Nazims* could try any civil suit arising in their districts, while in the criminal cases nine of them, the *Nazim* of Shekhawati having special powers, could punish with imprisonment up to two years and fine up to Rs. 200. They could pass a sentence of whipping not exceeding twenty-five stripes. They could also hear appeals against the decisions in civil and criminal cases of the respective *Tahsildars* under them, except in the case of the *Tahsildar* of Shekhawati. The *Nazim* of Shekhawati, however, had the same original criminal powers as the *Faujdari Adalat*. The ten *Naib-Nazims* could try civil suits up to the value of Rs. 100 and in criminal cases could punish with imprisonment up to three months and fine up to Rs. 50.

There were three *Munsifs* at the capital who disposed of civil suits not exceeding Rs. 300 in value. Similarly there were *Naib-Faujdars* at the capital who tried less important criminal cases and could give punishment with imprisonment up to six months and fine up to Rs. 100.

The *Adalat Diwani* or civil court consisted of two judges who, sitting separately, decided civil suits beyond the powers of the *Munsifs*, while jointly they heard appeals against the *Tahsildar* of Shekhawati, the *Naib-Nazims*, and the *Munsifs*.

The *Faujdari Adalat* or court of the chief magistrate, could punish with imprisonment up to four years and fine up to Rs. 400. It disposed of criminal cases beyond the powers of the *Nazim* (excluding Shekhawati) and of the *Naib-Faujdars*. It also heard appeals against the decisions of the *Tahsildar* of Shekhawati and the *Naib-Nazims*.

The next higher court was called the Appellate Court. It consisted of four judges, two on the civil and two on the criminal side. The former disposed of all appeals in civil cases against the decisions of the *Nazims* or of the civil court, while the latter, besides hearing appeals in criminal cases against the orders of the *Naib-Faujdars, Nazims*, and the *Faujdari Adalat*, tried original cases beyond the powers of the latter, or of the *Nazim* of Shekhawati, and could punish with imprisonment up to five years and fine up to Rs. 500.

The Council was the highest court in the State and the final appellate authority in all matters, civil, criminal and revenue. It dealt with all the serious criminal cases beyond the powers of the Appellate Court, and, when presided over by the Maharaja, could pass sentence of death on Jaipur subjects.

Pandit Maharaj Kishen had issued a large number of circulars on criminal and civil procedure, police, registration, stamps, etc. He had redistributed judicial powers among the various tribunals as a result of which the work was more evenly divided among the law officers, both civil and criminal. Under his orders the courts were required to submit monthly returns of work done by them. This necessity for reporting progress resulted in clearing off many outstanding cases in the *Nazim's* courts. The submission of returns by various courts also facilitated the collection of statistics.[45]

In the 1840s the British authorities had established five 'International Courts of Vakils' for the trial of offenders on the inter-state borders. Of these, the Jaipur Court (1847) had jurisdiction over the States of Jaipur, Bharatpur, Tonk and Alwar.[46] The *Vakils* from Jaipur constituted the bench of the Court of Vakils over which the Political Agent presided. This court decided the cases of offenders who committed crimes on the borders of the said four States. Appeals against the decisions of this Court of Vakil were taken up by the Ajmer Court which was presided over by the Agent to the Governor-General or his Assistant. The Jaipur Court of Vakils continued to work successfully throughout the period of our study. The work done by this court was recorded in detail and reported year after year. For instance, the Administration Report for 1891-92 recorded : 21 cases were admitted during the year in addition to 9 cases pending from the previous years. Of these, 23 cases were disposed of and 7 were kept pending. Six offenders were arrested of whom 5 were convicted; 2 were awarded life imprisonment, 2 six months' imprisonment and 1 fourteen years' imprisonment. The claims for compensation amounted to Rs. 20,245 and the amount of fines was Rs. 2,680. There were six appeals against the decisions of the court. The sentences in four of the cases were confirmed one sentence was enhanced and one appeal was dismissed.[47]

The International Courts of Vakils in the four Agencies and at the headquarters proved quite successful in settling the disputes involving inter-state relations. These courts in course of time became agencies to spread British message which could not be done in a formal manner. They also served to make the Political Agent much more powerful. By a process of indirect control, a State's *Vakil* could be easily influenced to carry out the wishes of the Paramount Power represented through the Political Agent.[48]

Apart from bringing about necessary reforms in the judicial administration of the State, the main interest of the Paramount Power was to secure the interests of British Indian subjects in Jaipur, as also in other Princely States. With the construction and extension of railway lines in the territory of Jaipur State, establishment of British post and telegraph offices in various cities of the State, appointment of many European officers and British Indian native officers on high jobs in the State, development of external trade of the State, etc., a sizeable number of British Indian subjects resided temporarily for a short or longer time in the State. It became the duty of the British Government to make necessary provisions for safeguarding the interests of all these British Indian subjects.

The British jurisdiction in all the Princely States in regard to the British Indian subjects was exercised in two forms, namely personal jurisdiction and territorial jurisdiction. As regards personal jurisdiction, the Indian Legislature had been given the power to make laws and regulations for the British subjects and servants in the Native States under the Indian Councils Act, 1861, supplemented by the Act of 1865 and the Act of 1869.[49] The British territorial jurisdiction in the Native States was exercised by the orders of the Governor-General in Council which, in fact, wielded extra-territorial powers far wider than those exercised by the Indian Legislature. Such powers and jurisdiction had from time to time been delegated to Political Agents and others acting under the authority of the Governor-General in Council.[50]

European British subjects within the Native States of India were amendable to British Indian Courts and British Indian law. C.L. Tupper aptly remarks in this connection :

> The right of ex-territoriality belongs to every European British subject in the Feudatory Native States of India; and as such subjects are amenable to the courts of British India for offences committed by them in Native States, no question of extradition arises.[51]

The British Government had assumed full civil and criminal

jurisdiction over the lands occupied by the railways in the Jaipur State. In respect of the Rajputana State Railway, the Governor-General in Council authorised the Political Agent at Jaipur to exercise the powers of a Magistrate of the First Class (in regard to Code of Criminal Procedure) in such portions of the aforesaid lands as were situated within the limits of Jaipur Agency. Likewise, the Political Agent in the Eastern State Agency in Rajputana and the Commissioner of Ajmer as the Agent to Governor-General in Council were authorised to exercise respectively the powers of a Court of Sessions and High Court within the whole of aforesaid lands.[52]

In 1868 an Extradition Treaty was concluded between the British Government and the Maharaja of Jaipur apparently on the basis of reciprocity.[53] Various articles of the treaty provided for mutual surrender of persons accused of committing a heinous offence. Article 1 of the treaty laid down that any person, whether a British or Foreign subject, committing a heinous offence in British territory, and seeking shelter within the limits of the Jaipur State, 'shall' be apprehended and delivered up by the latter Government to the former. Article 2 provided that any person, being a subject of Jaipur, committing a heinous offence within the limits of the Jaipur State, and seeking asylum in British territory 'will' be apprehended and delivered up by the latter Government to the former. Article 3 provided that any person, other than a Jaipur subject, committing a heinous offence within the limits of the Jaipur State, and seeking asylum in British territory, will be apprehended and the case investigated by such Court as the British Government may direct. As a general rule such cases will be tried by the Court of the Political Officer in whom the political supervision of the Jaipur State may at the time be vested. Article 4 stated that in no case shall either Government be bound to surrender any person accused of a heinous offence, except on requisition, duly made by, or by the authority of, the Government within whose territories the offence shall be charged to have been committed, and also upon such evidence of criminality as, according to the laws of the country in which the person accused shall be found, would justify his apprehension and sustain the charge if the offence had been committed. Article 5 defined the heinous offences.[54] Article 6 provided that the expenses of any apprehension, detention or surrender made in virtue of the foregoing stipulations, shall be borne and defrayed by the Government making the requisition.[55]

The signing of the extradition treaties (with Jaipur and other Rajput States, "opened another front from which internal autonomy of the states was considerably reduced. Though generally supposed to have been so these treaties were not on grounds of reciprocity or equality."[56] The British Government could requisition the return of a non-British subject also which was not allowed in the case of Jaipur and other Rajput States; the States could requisition the return of their own subjects only. According to Article 3 of the treaty, any foreign subject (other than a Jaipur subject) committing a heinous offence within the limits of the State and seeking asylum in the British territory would be apprehended and tried in such court as the British Government might direct. Generally such cases were to be tried by the Court of the Political Agent in whom the political supervision of the State was vested. Article 4 of the treaty stated that evidence of criminality of the person accused justifying his apprehension had to be furnished to the satisfaction of the Government from whom the surrender was demanded. The British Government's request would be made through the Political Agent whose wishes could not be defied by the Darbar. But there was no agency for making the request for the return of criminals fleeing from the State and the request was rarely accompanied by evidence which might be found satisfactory by the British Government.

In 1870s the British Government made new extradition rules under Act XI of 1872 and Act XVI of 1879 which were to be applicable to all the Native States except those with whom extradition treaties had been concluded. Under these rules the British subjects were exempt from trial in the courts of Native States. Chapter IV of the Act XXI of 1879 gives the Political Agent a discretionary power to refuse extradition and to dispose of the case himself. The general custom in the absence of treaty provision to the contrary had been for Political Agents to retain jurisdiction in all cases in which the accused were servants of the British Government, or servants of the Political Agent, or of any officer of Government officially employed within the State. However in regard to Jaipur and other Rajput States with whom extradition treaties had been concluded, the extradition rules laid down under the Act of 1879 were not applicable. An interesting case came to the fore in this regard in 1886. Seth Srichand, a Jaipur subject, who, being under trial on a charge of criminal breach of trust, absconded from Jaipur into British territory. The Resident, Eastern Rajputana States, issued a warrant, under section 11 of the Act of 1879 for the arrest of the absconder. The Counsel of the accused banker, Messrs Woodroffe and Evans of Calcutta Bar, held that section 11 of the Act did not apply to the cases in which there was a treaty, specifying the offences for which extradition might be demanded and laying down the procedure to be adopted when such extradition was applied for. They argued :

> Between the Government of British India and the Jaipur State there is such a treaty... Its provisions and the procedure therein laid down are therefore to be followed in any cases falling within the scope. Criminal breach of trust and criminal misappropriation of property are amongst those enumerated in article 5 as coming within the category of the heinous offences for which extradition may be demanded, and the procedure therein laid down for procuring the extradition of a person committing these or any other of such heinous offences is a requisition by the Maharaja of Jaipur to the Government of India when the supposed offender seeks asylum in British territory. The action of the Political Agent, therefore, assuming him to have issued a warrant for the arrest of Seth Srichand in supposed pursuance of section 11 of Act XXI of 1879 is illegal, and the banker cannot be arrested thereon in, or removed from, British territory.[57]

In this case the procedure prescribed by the Extradition Treaty (of 1868) should have been followed to the exclusion of the procedure laid down in Act XXI of 1879. As a matter of fact since the passing of this Act, Political Agent in Jaipur and other Rajputana States had been in the habit of issuing extradition warrants against certain offenders on their escape from

Rajputana State territory into British territory; nor before the occurrence of the case of Seth Srichand, had any objection been raised in any quarter to this practice. The Supreme Government did not contest the opinion of the Law Counsels, but thought that there was no reason why the extradition treaties should not be modified in order to allow the more convenient procedure of the Extradition Act to be adopted.[58]

The British authorities claimed and asserted their superiority over the governments of Princely States in extradition matters on two principal grounds : first, they considered it to be their prerogative as a Paramount Power; secondly, they believed that the Princely States lagged behind in the advancement of civilization and their judicial norms were far more backward than those of the British Government.[59]

Connected with the judicial administration was the administration of police and jails which also witnessed some significant changes and reforms under the British impact. The police of the State may be divided into two bodies — City Police and District Police. The City Police maintained law and order in the city of Jaipur. The *Kotwal* was the chief of the city police who worked under the supervision and control of the *Faujdar* or City Magistrate. The *Kotwal* was assisted by two *Naibs*.The entire police force under these officers consisted of 10 *Mohurrirs,* each drawing salary of Rs. 8 or Rs. 10 per mensem, one *Jemadar* on Rs. 6 per mensem and 396 Constables and Lance-Jemadars. Besides this police force, there were 333 *Chaukidars* for watch and ward at night in the city of Jaipur, the pay of each *Chaukidar* being Rs. 4 per mensem.[60] The District Police was under the control of a Superintendent who drew salary of Rs. 300 per mensem. He had his headquarters at Jaipur but he was constantly moving about the districts. Besides the Superintendent, the District Police consisted of 11 Deputy Superintendents, 160 *Thanadars,* 582 Constables and 11,058 *Chaukidars.*[61]

In 1885-86 the district and border police were under Narain Singh, the Superintendent of the Thagi and Dakaiti Department. In accordance with Dr. Stratton's advice the Jaipur Darbar had given Narain Singh an assistant, had confined *Thanadars* and

Dakaiti officials to the exercise of police functions only and had redistributed the *thanas*.[62]

In 1866 the Government of India issued a Resolution which asserted absolute responsibility of Native States for Imperial mail robberies occurring in their territories.[63] In pursuance of this Resolution, the British authorities took suitable action against the rulers of Jaipur and other States in whose territories mail robberies occurred from time to time. At the behest of the British Political Agent, the Jaipur Darbar had to take certain police measures for better security of transit of mails such as sending an armed guard in the mail cart in addition to the armed *Sowar* accompanying the mail cart. In some cases the Jaipur Darbar had also to pay compensation for the loss caused due to mail robberies which occurred in the territories of Jaipur.[64]

As already mentioned, the British Government had assumed full civil and criminal jurisdiction on the lands occupied by railways in Jaipur and neighbouring territories. They had also to make necessary police arrangements for the security of the railway lines and the passengers along with their goods travelling in railway trains. The police administration of the Rajputana State Railway was entrusted to an officer designated as Superintendent of Rajputana State Railway Police, and the Agent to Governor-General Rajputana was to be the Inspector-General of the State Railway Police. The Superintendent was to have a police force consisting of Inspectors, Sub-Inspectors, Head Constables and Constables under his control, and his headquarters was to be at Jaipur.[65]

The administration of jails was also modernised under the British impact. In medieval times the criminals were kept in forts. Since 1840 prisoners began to be lodged in the city jail at Loon Karan Natani's *haveli* in which the city *Kotwali* had already been established. The present Central Jail was constructed in 1854 in the vicinity of Jaipur, in the south of the city walls.[66] It was reported in 1867-68 that the practice of indoor jail labour and a system of management similar to that existing in the jails of British India had been introduced in the Jaipur Jail. In the same year the sanitation of the jail and control of prisoners had been placed under the supervision of a European officer, and the obligation of providing proper accommodation and subsistence for the prisoners had been apparently recognised by the Jaipur Darbar.[67] It was reported in 1869-70 that the discipline of the jail had been good, but there was more than the average amount of sickness owing to overcrowding for a period of six months.[68] Major C.A. Baylay observed in 1878 that the administration of the jail was "very well conducted... and a great credit to the State."[69]

Up-till 1889 the only jail was at the capital which had accommodation of about 370 prisoners and was always overcrowded. The construction of an additional jail was started in 1887, and the building was completed and occupied in 1889. The latest improvements in sanitation were introduced in the new building. Colonel Jacob and Dr. Hendley took pains in their respective departments to ensure that the health of the prisoners should be maintained on a normal footing.[70] Those two institutions, known respectively as the Central and District jails, had accommodation for 1144 prisoners (1034 males and 110 females).[71] The health of the prisoners both in the old and new jails was generally satisfactory. It was recorded in the Administration Report for 1891-92 that there were only 30 deaths during the twelve months (1891) compared with 81 of the preceding year, or 24.86 per thousand against 55.63. This decrease was said to be due to the absence of any epidemic, an improved scale of diet and more equal distribution of the prisoners between the two jails.[72] In November 1896 Mr. J. Fox who was Deputy Superintendent in the Alipore Jail (Bengal) was appointed as the new Superintendent of Jaipur jails. He "brought with him the highest encomiums from Bengal" and he improved the condition of the prisoners considerably.[73] In 1897 a new female jail was constructed at Jaipur having two wards with provisions of a hospital, dispensary, store room and bath room, well ventilated and protected by iron bars.[74] A distinct advance was made in the jail manufactures — carpets, cotton rugs, dusters, etc. It was hoped that under Sardar Hira Singh's skilful management the Jaipur jail carpets would rival those of Bikaner. Money wisely expended in fostering manufactures provided the means of enormously reducing the cost incurred in maintaining the State jails.[75]

IV

A separate Public Works Department was established in the Jaipur State by Maharaja Ram Singh. Since 1860 this department had been under a British officer lent by the Government of India and it "takes rank with any similar institution in British India."[76] In addition to roads and buildings, this department looked after the gas and water-works, public gardens at the capital, conservation of forests, the cotton presses and the numorous irrigation works in the districts.

The British authorities were keenly interested in developing means of transport in the Princely State, having three motives in view, *viz.* defence and security, administrative efficiency and promotion of British trade. With these motives Jaipur and other States were directed to construct roads and introduce railways in their territories. In the post-1860 period, therefore, with the efforts of Maharaja Ram Singh, roads were constructed connecting Jaipur with other towns of the State as well as with the cities of British India and those of the neghbouring States. The most important of these roads was the metalled trunk road from Agra to Ajmer constructed between 1865 and 1869; its length in Jaipur territory was about 127 miles (75 miles east joining the Bharatpur State and 52 miles west joining the Kishangarh State) and its cost was rupees 6.5 lakhs, of which the British Government contributed one-fifth.[77] The two other important roads constructed were : the Jaipur-Tonk Road with 47 miles in the Jaipur territory and the Karauli-Mandawar Road, 49 miles long passing through two large towns in the Jaipur State.[78] Among the other roads constructed and repaired by the Public Works Department, mention may be made of Agra Road, Naila Road, Dausa-Sawai Madhopur Road, Gungapur-Hindaun Road, Gungapur-Lalsot Road, Deoli-Rajmahal Road, Niraina-Malpura Road and Bandikui-Madhogunj Road.[79] Besides these roads, many City and Camp roads were also constructed, such as Road from Chandpole to

Railway Station, New Church Road, Bund-Ka-Durwaza Road, Pumping Station Road, Widening Road at Railway Station Jaipur, Link Road, Road at Amani Shah, Hawa Mahal Road, Road at Mission House, etc.[80] It has been estimated that towards the closing year of the period of our study the total length of metalled roads was about 283 miles and that of unmetalled roads about 236 miles.[81]

The roads proved highly useful for the people to travel from one place to another, and led to the development of trade and commerce (both internal and external) of Jaipur State. The British were the principal beneficiaries from the roads as well as the railways in the Jaipur territories, for they could acquire raw material and sell their manufactured goods without paying transit duties (since 1882).

During 1868-1906 some important railway lines were constructed at the behest of the Supreme Government by certain Railway Companies. The Jaipur Darbar had to cede lands free of charge required for Rajputana State Railway and Rajputana-Malwa Railway together with full jurisdiction on these lands. In 1904 land was acquired from the Jaipur Darbar for the Rewari-Phulera Chord Railway. Thereafter Maharaja Madho Singh of Jaipur ceded full and exclusive power and jurisdiction over the lands occupied by this Railway on the Form prescribed by the British authorities.[82] In 1897 the Jaipur Darbar initiated the project of constructing its own Railway from Jaipur to Sawai Madhopur. Order was issued by the Darbar for survey of the proposed Metre Gauge Railway line. The work was placed by Colonel S.S. Jacob, Superintending Engineer in the hands of C.E. Scotherd.[83] After getting the approval of the Government of India the work of constructing the line was started. Colonel Jacob spoke highly of the excellent work done by Mr. Scotherd for the Darbar in connection with the projected Railway line.[84] In 1902-03 the whole line had been practically completed as regards earth work, ballast, bridge-work and station buildings. In the following year six and a half lakhs of rupees (Imperial Currency) had been placed in deposit in the State Treasury for the purchase of permanent-way materials required for the first section of the line. The Darbar ordered through Government of

India materials for a section of the Jaipur Sawai-Madhopur Railway at a cost of Rs. 36,500 and accepted tenders for the supply of sleepers, etc. It was expected that the first section of 32 miles would be ready for traffic by the autum of 1905.[85] In 1906 Agreement was concluded between the Jaipur Darbar and the Bombay, Baroda and Central India Railway Company for working the Jaipur State Railway between Sanganer and Sawai Madhopur.[86]

The British Government considered it their right as well as duty as a Paramount Power to extend railways throughout the country for the benefits of British India as well as for those of the Princely States ; railways were considered essential for the military defence as well as for economic development of the sub-continent as a whole. Whatever be the original ulterior motive of the Imperial Government in extending railway lines in Jaipur and other States, there is no denying the fact that the railways added considerably to the prosperity of the Jaipur State and proved immensely useful for the people of the State.

Necessary measures were taken by the Jaipur Darbar for providing medical facilities on modern lines to the people of the State. A General Hospital was opened at Jaipur by Maharaja Ram Singh. The foundation stone of this hospital was laid by the Viceroy Mayo on 14 October 1870 at the request of the Maharaja, and it was named as 'Mayo Hospital' after the name of the Viceroy. The design of the hospital was prepared by Dr. De Fabeck, the talented Principal of the School of Arts. The planned double-storeyed building of the hospital consisted of Surgical Ward, Medical Ward, Opthalmic, Women's Ward, a Dispensary, Surgery, *Varandahs* on east and west, consulting-rooms, baths, Doctors' quarters, store rooms and offices. The total cost was estimated at Rs. 95,692 and the building was expected to be completed in 18 months.[87] The front of the hospital was equipped by Mayo Fountain and Well which were designed by Dr. Fabeck.[88] New dispensaries were opened or repaired at places like Bandikui, Sambhar, Mhowa, Hindaun, Lalsot, Dausa, Chatsu, Malpura, Gungapur, and Sawai Madhopur.[89] The Mayo Hospital and all the dispensaries were under the able superintendence of Surgeon-Major T.H. Hendley.[90]

In 1904-05 there were in all 29 hospitals and dispensaries, including the small hospitals attached to the jails and the lunatic asylum, in the Jaipur State. Of these institutions, 22 were maintained by the Darbar and the remaining 7 by the *jagirdars.* In 1904 the number of cases treated was 2,09,041 of whom 3,937 were in-patients, and 10,808 operations were performed.[91]

Vaccination was nominally compulsory everywhere, but was especially backward in some of the *Thikanas* (*jagir* estates). In 1904-05 a staff of 47 vaccinators under a native Superintendent and the Residency Surgeon successfully vaccinated 79,000 persons, or about 30 per 1000 of the population.[92]

Maharaja Ram Singh who had stayed in Calcutta for a long time as a Member of the Imperial Legislative Council, had been deeply impressed by the cultural amenities of the Metropolitan city and he "conceived the plan of making Jaipur a second Calcutta". In imitation of the Eden Gardens of Calcutta, he laid out the Ram Niwas Garden at Jaipur which covered an area of 2200 feet by 1500 feet.[93] On the model of the Calcutta Public Library, the Maharaja founded a Public Library at Jaipur in 1871. He established a small zoo in Jaipur emulating the Calcutta Zoological Garden. Getting inspiration from the Town Hall of Calcutta, he planned to construct Albert Hall in Jaipur of which the foundation stone was laid by the Prince of Wales on 6 February 1876. It was designed by Dr. Fabeck.[94] The total expenditure on the construction of the Hall amounted to Rs. 4,80,602 against the sanctioned estimate of Rs. 5,18,619.[95] The Maharaja also constructed a Museum at Jaipur. Its building was of a novel type which had been designed by Colonel S.S. Jacob, who was Engineer of the State. Mr. Adem, another British officer who was Assistant Commissioner, Inland Customs, Sambhar, rendered valuable services in the establishment of the Museum for which he was presented a gift of gold watch by the Maharaja of Jaipur.[96] It is significant to observe that it was during the period of Maharaja Ram Singh that the Jaipur city was made a pink city. The Maharaja at first tried colouring all the streets in different colours, green, yellow, pink etc.; finally pink was adopted for the whole city.[97]

Major Ludlow, the British Political Agent, had taken initiative in 1840s to provide pure water to the city of Jaipur by constructing a dam over the *Aman-i-Shah nullah*, but due to faulty construction the embankment gave way in 1855. Subsequently the Public Works Department took the city water-work in hand. In 1874 Colonel S.S. Jacob, the State Engineer, constructed a dam and set up an engine which pumped the water about 104 feet high into service reservoir through which water was delivered in iron pipes for transmission to the city. In 1882 the Jaipur Darbar appointed a European officer, named John Dominy as Assistant Engineer in Jaipur water-works after obtaining sanction for his appointment from the Supreme Government.[98] Thereafter water was delivered regularly year after year into the service reservoirs. For example, in 1892-93 the total number of gallons delivered was 32,86,25,728, or a daily average of 8,97,884 gallons. The cost of raising the quantity of water was Rs. 51,879, that is about 2½ annas per 100 gallons.[99] The statistics for the following year were 3,37,410,200 gallons, with an average of 9,24,411 daily and the average cost of raising the quantity of water was a little above 2¼ annas per 1000 gallons.[100] A scheme for supplementing the water-supply to the Jaipur city was started in October 1905 as a result of which an average of 8,00,000 gallons of water per day were supplied during the first half of the year 1906.[101]

Necessary measures were also taken by the Public Works Department of the State for generating gas required for lighting the city and palace. The total quantity of gas generated together with its cost and the gas consumed year after year, was recorded in the annual reports. For example, the total quantity of gas generated and the cost of gas for a thousand cubic feet and its consumption in the years 1891 and 1892 was as under[102] :

	1891	*1892*
Average number of jets	No. 601	No. 670
Gas consumed	3,122,220 cubic feet	2,884,170 cubic feet
Cost of gas per thousand cubic feet	R. a. p. 9 3 6½	R. a. p. 9 0 1½

The revenue derived from gas consumed amounted to Rs. 2,829 in 1892. In the following year the total quantity of gas consumed was 30,04,940 cubic feet. The revenue derived amounted to Rs. 2,190. The cost of gas per 1000 cubic feet was Rs. 9-5-11½, or 5 annas and 10 pies more than in the previous year.[103] The operations of the gas works continued to be satisfactory in the following years. In 1904 the cost of gas production was about Rs. 10 per thousand cubic feet including maintenance charges. The average number of jets lit daily for 5 $^2/_3$ hours was 759 at a cost of about Rs. 43 per jet per annum.[104]

Under the British impact, forest-conservation occupied the attention of Maharaja Ram Singh for the first time in 1867-68.[105] To be sure, the forests in the Jaipur State covered an area of about 283 square miles, and were divided into reserved (71 square miles), demarcated (93 square miles) and undemarcated (119 square miles); the reserved portion was mostly located in the *Nizamats* of Sawai Jaipur and Madhopur.[106] The forests, more especially those near Ranthambor and Kandahar, were very valuable Mr. E.M. Moir, Deputy Conservator of Forests in the North-Western Provinces, submitted a report on them in March 1886 which engaged the attention of the Jaipur Darbar. The chief difficulty anticipated in the preservation of forests was the interference which it would necessarily entail with the prescriptive rights of villages lying on their out-skirts. To overcome this difficulty, the Political Agent recommended strict enclosures of the forest areas. In November 1885 the Jaipur Darbar had procured the services of Bhai Sadhu Singh, an officer of the Punjab Forest Department, and appointed him as Superintendent of forests.[107] He proved to be an excellent officer. Colonel S.S. Jacob spoke highly of his 'tact, energy and ability'.[108] Under his able supervision the task of forest-conservation made a good progress. Effective steps were taken for the preservation and development of forests.

Bhai Sadhu Singh returned to the Imperial Forest Service in the Punjab in October 1892, as the Punjab Government expressed its inability to spare his services any longer. After his departure the Council began to look after the forest matters. The forest produce, such as firewood, bamboo, grass, fruits, honey and *lac,* began to be sold in larger quantities. With the result, the forests became a profitable source of income year after year. It was recorded in the Administration Report for 1896-97 that there was no change of forest area under 'reserved' while the 'undemarcated' forest area was lessened by 430 acres owing to the transfer of a grass preserve for the use of Imperial Service Transport Corps. The revenue from forests for the year was Rs. 29,568 and the expenditure Rs. 12,523, giving a net profit of Rs. 17,045.[109] Although many of the road-side avenue trees had been destroyed during the famine of 1899-1900, yet the revenue from the forest for the year 1901 amounted to Rs. 24,000 as against the expenditure figures of Rs. 8,500, thus leaving a substantial profit.[110] The receipts from the forests for the year 1903 were Rs. 25,957 and the expenditure Rs. 8,5,48.[111]

The first State-owned cotton-press was established at Jaipur in 1885 which was managed by the Public Works Department. In order to secure its success, the Jaipur Darbar raised the export tax on unpressed cotton from Re. 1-4-0 to Re. 1-12-0.[112] In 1888-89 the total income from the cotton-press amounted to Rs. 70,744 as against expenditure of Rs. 35,630, thus showing a profit of Rs. 35,114.[113] In 1892 a new cotton-press was sanctioned at Mandawar, near the Hindaun Road Station which started working in the following year. In 1893-94 the capital outlay on the Jaipur cotton-press was Rs. 2,24,714 while the net revenue was Rs. 49,898, thus giving a return of 22.20% on the total outlay. Owing 'to the unfavourable season and the scanty cotton crop, there was a fall in the number of bales pressed from 21,193 in the previous year to 13,839. The business at the cotton-press of Mandawar was also very slack, only 290 bales having been pressed during the whole year. This was due to the same reason as stated above.[114] In 1904 the gross revenue derived from the two cotton-presses at Jaipur and Mandawar was Rs. 62,162. This gives a percentage of 5.83 on Rs. 2,30,019, the capital cost of the Jaipur Press, and a percentage of 6.04 on Rs. 1,18,869, the capital cost of the Mandawar Press, as against 11.04 per cent and 10.94 per cent respectively last year. Owing to the late rains of October 1903, the cotton crop had not been good during the year. The price of cotton fluctuated from Rs. 17 per maund to Rs. 25. It has been estimated that in 1904 about 3,730 tons of cotton and 4 tons of wool were pressed.[115]

Numerous irrigation works undertaken by the Public Works Department constituted a laudable achievement of the Jaipur Darbar. In 1871 when a Supplementary Treaty had been concluded with Jaipur, limiting the annual tribute of the State to four lakhs of rupees, the British authorities had informed the Maharaja of the expectations of the Supreme Government that he should undertake to spend a considerable sum annually upon works of irrigation and improvement with a view to enhance the prosperity of his State. And the Maharaja did not belie these expectations. Even earlier, in 1868 he had appointed Colonel S.S. Jacob as the State engineer who applied his energy and efforts first in repairing the old irrigation works and then undertaking the new irrigation projects year after year. By the year 1902-03 about 200 irrigation works had been completed. The total expenditure on irrigation works in the State since 1868 was nearly Rs. 63 lakhs and the revenue realized therefrom about Rs. 52 lakhs.[116] These irrigation works reflect great credit on the enlightened liberality of the Jaipur Darbar, and the energy of Colonel Jacob who had directed and superintended their construction. As a reward of his meritorious work Colonel Jacob, the Superintending Engineer of the State, was awarded gold medal of the Kaisar-i-Hind Order, and the title of K.C.I.E. was conferred upon him.[117] It was recorded in the Administration Report for 1904-05 that the total expenditure on irrigation from 1868 to end of August 1904 had been Rs. 66,86,500 and the total estimated returns Rs. 58,89,159. The revenue derived from irrigation during the year was Rs. 1,16,815 as against Rs. 81,946 in the previous year. The total area irrigated had been 38,938 acres. No less than thirty-four surveys were carried out during the year in connection with new or existing irrigation projects.[118] In 1905-06 twenty new irrigation tanks were added to the 202 already in existence. The total expenditure on irrigation works in the State since 1868 to date rose to Rs. 70,91,575.[119] Some of the important irrigation works were the following :

(i) The dam of the Tori-Sagar tank in the south-west, close to the town of Malpura, was about $1^1/_3$ miles long. This tank had 2 canals, with 58 miles of distributaries, and irrigation from it began in October 1885.[120]

(ii) The work on the dam of the Buchara tank across the Sota stream, in the Torawati hills, 60 miles north of the capital, was started in 1886. The canals connected with this tank, which was about 1¾ square miles, were under construction. The work was completed in 1889. The reservoir could hold up water sufficient to irrigate about 17 square miles. The total expenditure to 1903 was about Rs. 3.4 lakhs and the revenue realized about Rs. 2.8 lakhs.[121]

(iii) One of the most remunerative of the larger irrigation works was the Kalakh Sagar, about 30 miles north-west of the capital. It was completed in 1883 at a cost of Rs. 2 lakhs and could, when full, irrigate nearly 8 square miles. It had 55 miles of main canals and 118 miles of distributaries. The total expenditure to 1903 was about Rs. 3 lakhs, and the revenue during the same period no less than Rs. 6.4 lakhs.[122]

(iv) In 1896 sanction was accorded for the construction of Ramgarh Reservoir, only twenty miles from Jaipur. Steps were being taken to carry out the project. By 1901 it had progressed well, 47 feet of the reservoir having filled out of 70 feet high water level. Irrigation thereon had started proceeding. The total amount sanctioned for the Ramgarh irrigation works was Rs. 5,63,970 while the expenditure in 1903-04 was Rs. 5,02,304 and Rs. 16,830 during 1904-05.[123]

(v) Among the smaller irrigation works may be mentioned the Fateh Sagar in the Hindaun district in the east. Its cost, including repairs, was less than Rs. 15,000. During the year 1902-03 the revenue from this tank was Rs. 13,900, that is more than 95 per cent on the capital outlay.[124]

The average amount expended by the Public Works

Department on its various branches was about Rs. 7 lakhs a year.[125] It has been estimated that between 1868 and 1901 the total amount of more than Rs. 234 lakh was spent by the Public Works Department which "testifies to the wise and generous policy" of Maharaja Ram Singh and Maharaja Sawai Madho Singh. It is significant to observe that for more than three decades the Public Works Department in all its branches was very creditably managed under the able and experienced superintendent of Colonel S.S. Jacob who had attained the rank of Superintending Engineer in the State. His "professional qualification and untiring zeal and interest in all the different branches of the Department cannot be too highly praised."[126] As already mentioned, for his meritorious services he was awarded gold medal of the Kaisar-i-Hind Order and honoured with the title of K.C.I.E. In April 1902 Colonel Jacob was succeeded by C.E. Scotherd as in charge of Public Works Department who proved to be equally energetic and efficient.[127]

V

Education on modern lines made a remarkable progress in the State under British impact. It was as a result of the initiative of Major Ludlow, the British Political Agent at Jaipur, that first modern school was established at Jaipur. Pandit Sheodeen, Maharaja Ram Singh's tutor, was appointed as the first Headmaster of the school. After attaining his majority in 1851, Maharaja Ram Singh evinced keen personal interest in the school which made a rapid progress. Two Directors of Public Instruction, North-Western Province, named Stewart Reid and Kempson, who visited the school in 1861 and 1863 respectively, were greatly impressed with the progress of the school and awarded prizes to mark the educational success of the institution and the zeal and industry of the scholars.[128] In 1864 Babu Kanti Chander Mukerji was appointed as Headmaster of the school and under his stewardship the school made great progress. In 1867 four boys of the school passed the Matriculation Examination of the Calcutta University.[129] In 1873 the school was raised to the status of a college of the Intermediate (then called F.A.) standard and was affiliated to the Calcutta University, thanks to the personal efforts of the Maharaja. Next year three students from the college appeared in the F.A. Examination for the first time since its affiliation with the Calcutta University.[130] The college began to be called the Maharaja's College. A Thakurs School (also called Rajput School) was also established by Maharaja Ram Singh, which, however, could not attract the expected number of Thakurs' sons. It was "more frequented by the sons of bankers than by pupils of the class for the benefit of which it was intended".[131]

Female education was not ignored. In 1866 first girls' school was established at Jaipur. To begin with, two lady teachers, named Sada Kunwari and Jiwani, were appointed and 25 girls enrolled themselves as pupils.[132] In 1867 an experienced lady teacher from Calcutta, Mrs. Ockelton was appointed Headmistress and the number of pupils rose to 35, but soon after many of these girls left the school. Due to the personal interest of Maharaja Ram Singh the number of girls in the school rose to 160 by the end of 1868. Several girls qualified themselves as teachers and one of them was appointed to teach female prisoners in the Jaipur Jail. During the tenure of the next Headmistress, Miss Jane E. Joyce the school made a commendable progress and a number of branch and auxiliary girls' schools were opened.[133] Gradually the number of girls' schools in Jaipur and other districts rose considerably.

In 1861, due to the efforts of Dr. Kingsford Burr and munificence of Maharaja Ram Singh a medical school was established at Jaipur which was the first institution of its kind in Rajputana. Dr. Burr was appointed as the Superintendent of the Medical School which progressed well for about three years. But in 1865 there were serious differences between Dr. Burr and Captain Beynon, the then Political Agent, which led to the suspension of the former and also to the closure of the school.[134]

In 1867 Maharaja Ram Singh in the course of his visit to Calcutta was much influenced by the advice of Sir Charles Trevelyan to open a school of industrial arts in his State. On his return to the Capital, the Maharaja established the Jaipur School of Arts in June 1867. Dr. C.S. Valentine, the personal physician of the Maharaja, was appointed as the first Principal of the school. The branches of industry in which instructions were given were : blacksmith's work, carpentry, carving in wood, bone and ivory, jewellery, pottery, coach-building, practical and analytical chemistry, lithography, drawing and book-binding.[135] In October 1869, Dr. De Fabeck, whose services were temporarily lent to the Darbar by the British Government, was appointed as the next Principal.[136] He soon introduced new branches in the school, such as geometrical, mechanical and architectural drawing and mapping; printing, electroplating, photography, ornamental embroidery, etc. During the tenure of the two succeeding Principals, Scorgie (1872-1874) and Upendra Nath Sen (1875-1907), the school made a remarkable progress.[137]

It was recorded in the British Agent's report in 1875, "In Jaipur public instruction has made greater progress than in any other State in Rajputana during the administration of the present Maharaja Ram Singh."[138] Education continued to make progress during the long reign of his successor, Maharaja Sawai Madho Singh (1880-1927). Like his predecessor, the new Maharaja evinced keen personal interest in the development of education. The year 1887 is an important landmark in the development of education in the State. In that year Babu Hari Das Shastri, the newly appointed Principal of Maharaja College and Director of Public Instruction, Jaipur State reorganised the schools and increased the number of inspecting staff. A comprehensive system of scholarship for promising students in the primary and higher schools was sanctioned by the State, and lower schools were connected with the higher schools and higher schools with the Maharaja College. In 1888-89 there were 164 educational institutions in the State with 7,390 scholars. Besides, there were 305 private schools with 7,661 scholars as against 277 schools and 6,614 scholars in the previous year. In 1891-92 there were 167 schools under State support and 432 private institutions. The number of scholars in attendance at the former was 7,896 and at the latter 13,661, showing a total increase of 1,280 pupils and 96 schools. It is significant to note that two students of the Maharaja's College passed with Honours the B.A. Examination of the Calcutta University in 1888; they were the first to take a university degree from the Jaipur State. In 1891, of the seven students who appeared for the B.A. Examination three graduated, and for the Intermediate, Entrance and Middle Class examinations, of the 40 candidates who appeared, all were successful. In 1891-92 there were eight schools for girls, having in all 594 students, under the management of Lady Superintendent, Miss Hemming.[139]

In 1896 the Maharaja's College was raised to M.A. standard, and was affiliated to the Calcutta University for M.A. Examination[140], whereas for the lower B.A. and Intermediate examinations it had been affiliated to the Allahabad University. In 1896-97 there was a marked advance in the education department of the State. The number of public institutions rose to 110 and that of the pupils to 8,750 against 109 and 8,622 respectively of the previous year. The private schools numbered 623 and the scholars 16,100 as compared with 551 and 15,638 respectively for the year 1895-96. The total number of institutions in the State was 733 and that of the pupils under instructions 24,850 (24,325 boys and 525 girls).[141]

In 1901 Babu Sanjivan Ganguli was appointed Director of Public Instruction. At this time there had been a decrease both in the number of schools and of scholars, the latter being now only two-thirds of what they were reported to be two years back. It was mainly due to the severe famine of 1899-1900 which affected greater part of the Jaipur State. As a result of the keen efforts of Babu Ganguli there was an increase of 26 schools and 1,029 scholars compared with the previous year. The good results of the University Examinations were also noticeable; 5 out of 6 candidates passing the B.A., 11 out of 12 the F.A. or Intermediate, and 23 out of 26 the Entrance Examinations. It was felt that the extension of primary education and the systematic inspection and supervision of all schools were urgently needed.[142]

In 1902 the Director of Public Instruction recommended that in order to provide sufficient funds for opening new primary schools in the districts local education cess on land assessment should be imposed. The recommendation was accepted which resulted in the opening of many *halqabandi* or circle schools throughout the State like those in the United Provinces.

The progress in education continued to be satisfactory in the following years. In 1903-04 there was a marked increase in the total number of schools and scholars in the State, *viz.* 661 schools and 21,078 scholars as compared with 482 and 15,388 in the previous year. The private institutions recorded an increase of 151 schools and 3,911 scholars. Of the *Thikanas* who maintained schools, particular mention may be made of Khetri, Sikar, Chomu, Uniara, Malsisar, Nawalgarh and Siwar. In the meanwhile the Maharaja College made further progress. A substantial grant from the Maharaja had enabled the college authorities to procure the necessary apparatus for science subjects, and affiliation for the Bachelor of Science degree had been granted to the college by the Allahabad University. The college showed good results in the University examinations; 4 out of 5 candidates passed the B.A., 13 out of 15 the Intermediate, and 13 out of 22 the Entrance examinations. The college staff had been strengthened and their salaries raised during the year.[143] At that time it was the only first-grade college affiliated to the Allahabad University in the whole of Rajputana. In 1904 two distinguished educationists, named Vrendenburg, Curator of the Geological Survey of India and Professor Frederick J. Smith of the Trinity College, Oxford, visited the college and both of them were appreciative of its working.[144]

In 1904 there were 753 educational institutions in the State, 151 public and 602 private. Of the former 77 were maintained by the Darbar, and 74 were under private management, though more or less under the supervision of the Education Department. Of these 74 private institutions, 18 were maintained by *jagirdars,* 12 by the Jain community, 10 by the United Free Church of Scotland Mission and 34 by bankers or private individuals. Of the total number under instruction at the end of 1904, 78 per cent were Hindus, about 9 per cent Muhammadans, and 12 per cent Jains. There were eleven girls schools in the State, namely, nine at the capital,one at Amber, and one at Sambhar; they were attended in 1904 by 797 girls.[145] Education was provided free throughout the State, no fees being charged anywhere.

There was a further progress in education in 1905-06. For the period ending 31 August 1906 there were in all 882 schools (public and indigenous) in Jaipur, with 25,733 scholars on the rolls. Of these pupils 19,921 were Hindus, 3318 Muslims, 2120 Jains and 374 Christians. The Jaipur College had maintained its high reputation in the University and other examinations, such as M.A., B.A., Intermediate and Entrance examinations of Allahabad University, Jaipur Sanskrit examinations (Acharya, Sastu, Upadhyay and Pravisika) and Panjab University examinations (Munshi Fazil, Munshi Alam and Munshi). The *Pioneer* in its issue of 5 July 1905 commented that the most remarkable feature of the results of Entrance Examination of the Allahabad University was the success attained by the Maharaja's College, Jaipur. The School of Arts had maintained its reputation. There were 14 teachers in the school and 88 pupils had received instructions in Drawing, Engraving, Pottery, Carpentry and other handicrafts.[146]

An educational institution of the deepest significance to Rajputana in the foundation of which Maharaja Ram Singh took a leading part was the Mayo College for Princes at Ajmer, which was "an Eton in India for the sons of aristocracy." In a Darbar held at Ajmer on 22 October 1870, Mayo suggested to the Princes and Chiefs present there that a college should be founded at Ajmer where the future rulers and nobles of Rajputana might receive such an education as would fit them for their high position and important duties. The college was to be maintained at the joint expenses of the British Government and the 'feudatory' Princes. The latter contributed nearly six lakhs of rupees of which Maharaja Ram Singh of Jaipur contributed Rs. 1,25,000.[147] Colonel Loch, the designated Principal of the college viewed the establishment of the college as a 'political experiment'. The college aimed at making the sons of aristocracy admirers and not slavish imitators of British institutions, manners and customs. Besides the sons of Princes, young Political Officers were attached to the college for six months.

This provided them an opportunity to meet the future Princes and Chiefs at a time when they were young and of an impressionable age. The college was expected to play a great role in transforming the outlook of the Princes as it was to be an institution for political indoctrination, for controlling the wayward behaviour of the Princes. The goal was to create a generation of rulers who would look up to the Political Agents for advice and would do their bidding.[148] The college also provided a forum to the Viceroys and Agents to the Governor-General to exercise their influence on the Native Royalties. It is significant to observe that almost every Viceroy visited the Mayo College. The Viceroy Curzon (1899-1905) took special interest in bringing about reforms in this college, as also in the other Chiefs' colleges at Lahore, Rajkot, Nowgong and Indore. In March 1904 Curzon convened a conference at Ajmer in which detailed suggestions for the improvement of Mayo College were worked out. Consequently the college came to have the English Staff of one Principal, one Vice-Principal and two Assistants in addition to Native Staff of eight Assistants. The Viceroy and Agent to Governor-General for Rajputana became respectively the ex-officio President and Vice-President of the Council of this college.[149]

Summing up it may be said that education on modern lines made great strides in the Jaipur State during the second half of nineteenth century and early years of the following century. It was largely due to the keen and consistently zealous interest evinced by the two successive Maharajas, Ram Singh and Madho Singh, who functioned thoroughly under the influence of the Political Agents and Viceroys of the period. Even in the establishment of Mayo College at Ajmer, the then Maharaja of Jaipur (Ram Singh) had made a liberal contribution — the institution which aimed at giving western education and training to the sons of Princes and Chiefs so as to prepare them for becoming competent rulers subsequently fully loyal and faithful to the Paramount Power.

VI

Under the influence of the 'civilising mission' of the British authorities some significant social reforms were brought about in the Jaipur State. During the minority of Maharaja Ram Singh, Major John Ludlow, the British Political Agent at Jaipur (1844-1847) had taken necessary measures, with the co-operation of Rajput nobles of the Council of Regency, for the abolition of inhuman practices of *sati*, female infanticide and slavery in the State.[150] But despite these measures, the said evil practices, which had their roots in the Rajput tradition since medieval times, could not be liquidated entirely. In the post-1858 period the Jaipur Darbar had to take strict action against the culprits whenever and wherever it got reports about the occurrence of incidents pertaining to such criminal practices.

The following incidents of *sati* which occurred from time to time together with the action taken thereupon by the Jaipur Darbar may be mentioned briefly :

(i) On 6 May 1869 a case of *sati* took place in the hamlet of Monata in the Khetri district (about 16 miles from Khetri). Nandram Singh, a Rajput, died at 11 am His widow aged about 40 years (having four children, aged from 12 years to 2½ months) burnt herself with the deceased at about 2 pm on the same day. The Jaipur Darbar acted promptly in punishing those concerned in the commission of crime. Two culprits, named Sarupa Chakur and Away Singh, who carried body of the deceased and also raised funeral pyre on which the widow was immolated, were sentenced to 3 years' imprisonment with hard labour. A fine of Rs. 1000 was imposed on the hamlet in which the *sati* took place, and 11 persons in the vicinity of the hamlet from which the spectators gathered to watch the scene were fined Rs. 100 each. The *Thanadars* of the Singhana *pargana* were fined Rs. 25 each for want of vigilance. The Jaipur Darbar also inflicted a fine of Rs. 1000 on the chief of Khetri. When the whole case was reported by the Agent to Governor-General, Rajputana to the

Viceroy and Governor-General in Council, the latter approved of the action taken by the Jaipur Darbar with the remark that 'sufficient punishment' had been inflicted on those who were concerned in the crime.[151] The Secretary of State for India expressed satisfaction at promptitude displayed by the Jaipur Darbar in bringing to justice the offenders, adding that 'exemplary punishment' was awarded to the culprits.[152]

(ii) On 5 February 1873 a case of *sati* occurred in the village Baori-Khera of Jaipur State. Upon the death of the son of *Patel* of the village, his widow was immolated on the funeral pyre of her husband. Full enquiry was made of this incident by the Jaipur officials and severe punishments were given to the persons implicated in the case. The *Patel* of the village, who was the father-in-law of the immolated widow, was sentneced to 7 years' imprisonment and his Biswedari rights were absolutely forfeited. Four persons who carried the body and prepared funeral pyre were awarded 3 years' imprisonment each. The *Patwari* and *Chaukidar* of the village were given punishment respectively of 4 years' and 3 years' imprisonment. The *Thanadar* of the area was dismissed from service. The Agent to Governor-General for Rajputana considered the punishments awarded for the crime as 'sufficient' and directed the Political Agent to see that the punishments were rigorously carried into effect. The Governor-General in Council in their letter No. 2530 P., dated 27 October 1873, addressed to the Agent to Governor-General, Rajputana, expressed satisfaction as to the adequacy of the punishments which had been awarded by the Jaipur Darbar to those concerned in this crime and desired that the punishments should be effectively carried out by the Political Agent.[153]

(iii) On 7 October 1882 a fatal case of *sati* occurred at the village Utarna situated on the hilly border between

Jaipur and Bundi which fell within the *jagir* of the Rao of Duni, in the Jaipur State. Upon the death of Thakur Sham Singh (who belonged to the Naruka clan of the Kachhwaha tribe of Rajputs), his widow immolated herself on the funeral pyre of her husband. The Jaipur Darbar promptly despatched Munsif Sri Narain to the scene of occurrence to enquire into the case. On the basis of his report the Judicial Department of the Jaipur Council decided that Sadool Singh, Hameer Singh and Onar Singh, the sons, and Deo Singh and Roop Singh, the brothers, of late Sham Singh, were offenders of the first class and should be imprisoned for a term of seven years each; Bukhtawar Singh, Roor Singh, Suja, Zalma, Nanda, Lukhmana, Jeykishna and many others, who were offenders of the second class for being present to witness the scene, should be imprisoned for a term of one year each and fined Rs. 50 each. The Maharaja in his order dated 25 December 1882 approved of the punishment given to the sons and brothers of the deceased but he ruled that the punishment awarded to second class offenders was too light and should be increased to three years' rigorous imprisonment (without any fine). There was no satisfactory proof that the *Thikana* of Duni was in any way to blame; the Rao of Duni at the time of occurrence of the event was lying sick at Jaipur and had no cognizance of it. The Governor-General in Council in their letter No. 185 I., dated 24 January 1883, addressed to the Agent to Governor-General, Rajputana, expressed satisfaction at the promptitude with which the Maharaja of Jaipur acted in bringing to justice the persons who aided and abetted in the crime. A copy of the correspondence about the whole case was forwarded to the Secretary of State for India for information.[154]

Female infanticide was another cruel practice which had been prevalent among the Rajputs since medieval times. The British Government made earnest endeavour to put an end to this practice in British India as well as in the Native States. Certain Draft Rules were envisaged for the suppression of female infanticide in Jaipur and other States. The opinion of Maharaja Ram Singh was invited in the matter. The Maharaja remarked that the operation of the said rules had mainly been based on proportion of girls to the non-adult population. He opined that this criterion could not, for reasons which appear too apparent to require mention in details, be relied on in all cases. He expressed the opinion that to initiate very strict rules in a matter in which the honour of a family was affected, was likely to cause considerable heart-burning and discontent. This 'unnatural crime', he observed, was attributable mainly, if not entirely, to two causes — first, to a want in so many cases of suitable matches for daughters in point of family; and secondly to enormous expenses incurred on marriages. So long as these causes were in existence the entire prevention of crime of female infanticide could hardly be hoped for or expected. He suggested that measures with a view to removal of these causes should be adopted first. This could alone be done through the leading members of each clan whose very position would point them out as the fittest persons to interfere in these domestic and private affairs. With the co-operation of these leading members of clans and the assistance of Panchayats formed from amongst them to overcome the difficulties coming in the way, the disappearance of this inhuman crime would be only the work of time. The Maharaja added that he was already engaged in endeavouring to introduce measures in this regard by degrees.[155]

As a part of the 'civilizing mission' of the British authorities, slavery had been abolished in British India and, under the British impact, in the Princely States also. In 1868 a minor incident came to the fore regarding the confinement of a slave girl in the Jaipur jail. The Kishangarh Darbar solicited the interference of the British Political Agent for the surrender of the girl who actually belonged to the Kishangarh territory. A copy of Kishangarh Darbar's requisition was sent by the Political Agent to the Jaipur Darbar for enquiry and necessary action. It was reported by the Jaipur Darbar that the girl had been duly made over to her claimants.[156]

Colonel Keatinge, Agent to Governor-General for Rajputana, after noticing this case, issued a circular to all the Political Agents of Rajputana States in which he stated that they should in no way recognise or let continuance of the practice of slavery which was repugnant to all British law and custom. In order to curb this practice the Political Agents were instructed to refuse assistance for the capture or extradition of any persons who were described as slaves assigning reason for so doing.[157] The Viceroy and Governor-General in Council accorded their approval to the action taken by the Agent to Governor-General, Rajputana.[158]

VII

During the second half of the nineteenth century famines occurred frequently in various parts of India. The immediate cause of each of these famines was generally the failure of monsoons and deficiency of rainfall, but the underlying factors leading to the recurrence of such frequent famines are considered to be "poverty of the agricultural masses and growing destitution among them, rising prices of foodgrains and stationary wages, and the increasing population obtaining little scope for employment outside agriculture."[159] Jaipur and many other Princely States also experienced fury of famines from time to time, greater or lesser in intensity. The Chiefs had to take necessary measures to help the famine-stricken people by providing them all possible relief and also to prevent recurrence of famines. British authorities desired that adequate measures should be taken by the Native Royalties in this regard. They kept a watchful vigilance over the steps taken by the Darbars and expressed readiness to provide them all possible help and guidance.

In 1868-69 a severe famine occurred in Jaipur and some other Rajputana States because of failure of crops owing to scarcity of rain and attack by locusts. It caused wide-spread misery and distress among the people. Maharaja Ram Singh took the lead in taking measures for the relief of the famine-stricken. The early measures taken by him included the construction of a *'pucca bund'* across kukoas river near Amber, a *dharmsala* in immediate vicinity of the city (intended to serve as a depot for distribution of alms and relief to the aged and infirm), repairing and erecting of new buildings within and without the capital, reparation of forts, temples, *talaos* and laying out of a large garden. All these works were undertaken in order to provide employment to the impoverished people. The number of men employed on the said works was estimated at 17,179. The levying of all sorts of taxation in Jaipur principality was abolished, with a view to enable the *Mahajans* to import grain without any hindrance or inconvenience.[160] A sum of rupees 20,000 was spent for the purchase of grain, and food to the value of rupees 1,31,652 had been distributed among labouring classes, instead of cash payments. The Maharaja suspended the payment of rent and succession duty amounting to rupees two lakhs. He devoted nearly equal sum to relief works, irrespective of ordinary public works.[161] The gracious and 'enlightened' measures taken by the Maharaja for the benefit of the famine-stricken people not only of Jaipur but also of neighbouring States and British territory, were appreciated by the British Government. It was observed by Colonel Keatinge, Agent to Governor-General, Rajputana States, "The benefits which will be derived from the Maharaja's liberality by the British district of Ajmere and the famine-afflicted Native States of Rajputana cannot be stated in rupees, but will be balanced by countless saving of human life and human misery."[162] In recognition of his self-sacrificing efforts to mitigate the sufferings of the afflicted fellow beings, the Government of India recommended that the personal salute of the Maharaja of Jaipur be increased by 2 guns, that is, from 17 to 19 guns; the Secretary of State readily accepted this recommendation.[163]

In 1877 there was a grass famine, and 30 per cent of the cattle perished, while in 1878 the rains were late and prices rose almost to famine rates, but the distress was partial and brief. Relief works were started by the Jaipur Darbar, and 6,000 persons were employed daily for two months till the rains set in.[164]

In 1891-92 there was scarcity in the western and south-western parts of the State. The Jaipur Darbar promptly gave *takkavi* advances, remitted a portion of the land revenue and threw open for grazing the forest Reserves.[165]

The famine of 1899-1900, "the greatest in extent and intensity which India had experienced during the last two hundred years"[166], also seriously affected the Jaipur State. Maharaja Madho Singh took energetic and efficient measures to combat this calamity. The British authorities evinced keen interest in examining the intensity of the famine in the affected areas of the State and the relief measures taken by the Jaipur Darbar to help the famine-stricken. Major J.R. Dunlop Smith, Famine Commissioner, Rajputana personally visited some of the famine-affected areas and scrutinised the relief measures. He submitted a comprehensive report about the famine relief works undertaken by the Jaipur Darbar in January and February 1900.[167] He observed that measures to cope with the distress were taken in time and they were wisely and liberally framed. During the last two months (Jan.-Feb.) the numbers on relief works, excluding those employed on the Rewari-Phulera Railway, had risen by over one hundred per cent to 36,081 and the total in receipt of gratuitous relief had been quardrupled. K.C. Mukerji, Chief Member of Jaipur Council, under the orders of Maharaja Madho Singh, supervised all the branches of the famine administration, and all returns and accounts were submitted direct to him. Three special officers were appointed to superintend the operations on the spot.[168]

The Public Works Department under Colonel Jacob took major relief works scattered all over the State which included construction of new roads and buildings and repair of old ones, development of extensive irrigation works. Up till 3 March 1900, as many as 83 works involving an expenditure of nearly four lakhs of rupees had been sanctioned, and Colonel Jacob had under consideration proposals for nearly as many more. These were mainly irrigation projects, notably the construction of a new reservoir near Malpura, the new road from Dudu to Malpura and the hospital and hutting arrangements. The daily average number of persons employed on the works under the

Public Works Department was 14,265, exclusive of the labour employed in the permanent institutions.[169]

The construction of the Rewari-Phulera Chord Railway Line was started as a relief work on 4 November. The two sections of the Railway in the Jaipur State were in charge of Lieutenant Garrett. Over twenty miles of earthwork had been completed during the said two months and as many as 13,935 persons had been employed.[170]

The services of the Jaipur Imperial Service Transport Corps were utilised to the utmost in the general scheme of relief operations. The energetic Superintendent of the Corps, Rai Bahadur Dhanpat Rai had at his command a well-disciplined force. He opened poor-houses or rather collecting depots at Jaipur, Chagsu, Malpura, Lalsot, Madhorajpura and Dausa. In addition to these chief centres many small institutions called forwarding depots were also established; 42 transport carts specially fitted up as ambulances and 25 hand stretchers had been distributed among these depots. Branch hospitals were attached to all the main depots which were provided with qualified hospital staff and a stock of medicines. The head depot established at Jaipur consisted of one *duffadar*, one *havildar* and four sweepers. The people were fed twice a day on the work which was nearly a mile from the camp. Many people were working in the bed of the Amanishah *nullah* outside the city. One day's reserve of grain was kept up in one of the garden houses. All cases of non-contagious sickness were removed to the Mayo Hospital in the city but a camp segregation hospital had been opened near the transport lines. The orphanage attached to this relief was the most useful institution. There were 21 girls and 31 boys in this orphanage most of whom had been picked up on the roads or fields of different parts of the districts by Sardar Dhanpat Rai himself. "The share taken by Sardar Dhanpat Rai and the men under his command in the famine campaign is a most important one. In addition to the care of nearly ten thousand people collected at different centres they form what may be called the famine police of the State."[171]

The petty works under district officers consisted of the sinking of new and repairing of old wells, small tanks and repairs of buildings. Most of these projects were carried out by the *Tahsildars* of Newai and Toda Rai Singh. The average monthly amount sanctioned for these petty works had been over 17,000 rupees, exclusive of *takkavi* advances. The *Khalsa* forests had been freely opened to needy cultivators for grazing and the collection of fuel.[172]

A humane policy had been adopted by the Darbar towards all the *jagirdars*. Those of the petty *Thakurs* who were themselves in distress were allowed to withdraw their *Sowars* temporarily from service and no *Tafawat* fees was charged from them so long as the famine lasted. The residents of *jagir* villages were freely admitted to all relief works and poor-houses. The bigger *Thakurs* had in some instances started projects of their own.[173]

Gratuitous relief in various forms was issued in the towns and villages. In addition to the works described above, doles of grain were given to the sick, infirm and cripples in various villages. A large poor-house was opened in the city of Jaipur. The people gathered in large enclosure at the back of the Mayo Hospital. The poor-house which was under the supervision of Major Durrell Pank was looked after by Pandit Baij Nath who was assisted by staff of many employees. The poor-house was visited everyday by Major Pank. Food was distributed twice a day.[174]

At an early stage of the famine the Darbar had made arrangements for the purchase and import of grain (barley) in order to sell it to the poorer classes at a privileged rate. Till the middle of February 1900, the daily sales averaged 6000 local rupees and the loss to the Darbar came approximately to 20 per cent.[175]

Thus famine relief in the Jaipur State "is administered on thoroughly sound principles, while no expense is spared in carrying these into action". The administration was fully prepared to meet any emergency. The Darbar had grasped the situation from the outset and had shown both 'skill and commonsense' in combing the various branches of relief.

The following table shows the number of persons on relief in Jaipur State month by month since October 1899 :[176]

Month	*Works*	*Gratuitous*	*Total*	*Percentage of Population*
Oct. 1899	7,000	48,732	55,732	3.0
Nov. "	25,400	Not reported	25,400	-
Dec. "	33,338	7,017	40,355	2.3
Jan. 1900	35,340	24,928	60,268	3.4
Feb. "	41,961	32,212	74,173	4.2
March "	42,700	37,432	80,132	4.6

The famine (1899-1900) was probably as successfully combated in Jaipur as in the adjacent British Indian territory. The Jaipur famine operations were in advance of most of the other States in Rajputana. More significant still, the Jaipur Darbar had no recourse to borrowing from Imperial sources. The famine was fought, and well fought, by the State with its own funds and for the most part with its own personnel.[177]

The Viceroy Curzon in his speech delivered in Calcutta Town Hall on 16 February 1900 mooted the proposal of creating an All India Famine Fund. Thereafter a preliminary draft of scheme for administration of proposed trust for the fund was prepared and sent to the Political Agents with the instructions to invite suggestions of the Princes and the Chiefs. Maharaja Madho Singh of Jaipur gave some suggestions in the draft scheme which were forwarded to the Government of India. Consequently, in June 1900 Indian Peoples' Famine Trust was created. The Princes and Chiefs were asked to make contributions towards this Trust Fund the interest of which would be utilised for helping famine-stricken people in any part of India. The Maharaja of Jaipur made a liberal contribution of rupees fifteen lakhs to be invested in Government Promissory Notes. He also expressed desire to pay interest on 15 lakh rupees for six months from January to June 1900. The Maharaja's munificent gift following so closely upon public appeal made by the Viceroy afforded much gratification to the Government of India. It was in keeping with Maharaja's generous disposition and with his traditional loyalty, and it had set an example which, it was hoped, would stimulate others to similar benevolence.[178]

Soon after, the Maharaja made a further endowment of one lakh rupees to the Famine Trust. In response to this the Supreme Government addressed a letter to Agent to Governor-General, Rajputana, requesting him to convey to Maharaja of Jaipur "an expression of high appreciation of Her Majesty's Government of His Highness's humane and public-spirited action."[179]

In November 1905 when Prince and Princess of Wales visited Jaipur, the Maharaja, on behalf of himself and his senior Maharani, subscribed another amount of four lakhs of rupees to the Indian Peoples' Famine Trust.[180]

It is obvious from the afore-mentioned account that the British authorities took zealous interest in the famine administration of Jaipur, as also in that of other Native States; and their attitude was 'not one of apathy but of sympathy and vigilence'.[181] They desired that similar relief measures should be adopted by Native Chiefs in their territories as were taken by the British Government in its own territory. For the guidance of the Chiefs abstracts of Famine Codes were supplied to them. In accordance with these Codes the Darbars were required to start relief works, open poor-houses and provide gratuitous relief to the people and they were to submit monthly reports, intimating in details the progress of measures taken by them. The Imperial Government's concern about the famine relief measures in the States was actuated by two main considerations. First, in the absence of such measures many people from the States might migrate to the relief works in operation in the adjoining British territory; such a mass migration, if unchecked, was likely to upset the famine-relief schemes of the British Government. Secondly, the Paramount Power during the period under study was genuinely interested in the welfare and happiness of people of the States. At any rate, the Supreme Government could not tolerate that due to negligence of responsibilities on the part of the Darbars, their subjects should starve, suffer and die in the course of famines. But it must be said in all fairness to Maharajas Ram Singh and Madho Singh of Jaipur that both of them had taken prompt and adequate relief measures for the famine-stricken people of the State — measures which were highly appreciated by the Government of India as well as by the Secretary of State for India. The former Maharaja was even rewarded by the Secretary of State with the grant of two additional guns in his personal salute, from 17 to 19 guns.

VIII

The British impact on the internal administration of Jaipur State was exercised largely through the British Political Agent (later on Resident). He interferred in the day-to-day administration of the State and gave his advice, sought for and unsought for, in all important matters to the Darbar. His advice was virtually tantamount to order which generally had to be carried out. It was through him that all the communications of the Jaipur Darbar were sent to the Agent to Governor-General, Rajputana who on his part sent directions of policy matters to the former. The Agent to Governor-General forwarded all the correspondence of the Darbar to the Government of India with his comments. It is significant to observe that during the period of our study (1858-1905) the Viceroy-in-Council began to play a decisive role in framing the British policy towards the Princely States more or less on a uniform basis. It was by resolutions passed or circulars issued by the Supreme Government to all the Political Agencies and Local Governments that various facets of the British policy, notably pertaining to the internal administration of the States, were carried out. Thus the Viceroys of the period began to play the most significant role in moulding the personal conduct and determining the tone of internal administration of Princes and Chiefs.

John Lawrence was the first Viceroy of the period who asserted authority of the Paramount Power irrespective of the existing treaties, engagements and *sanads*. He, inter alia, directed the Princes and Chiefs to establish efficient internal administration leading to the welfare and happiness of the subjects. "Good Government was the condition on which Lawrence maintained the ruling Chiefs in power."[182] In his speeches delivered at various Darbars he admonished the Native Chiefs to apply their energy and efforts for improving their administration. For instance, in the course of his speech delivered at Agra Darbar on 19 November 1866 to the great Chiefs of Rajputana and Central India, he exhorted them to have good laws, well-selected officials, an efficient police, a well-managed revenue, schools for the education of the young and hospitals for the cure of the sick... "The Chief who made his people happiest would be the best friend of the British Government"... "Of all fame that great men can acquire, that alone is worth having which is accorded to a just and beneficient ruler. The names of conquerors and heroes are forgotten. But those of virtuous and wise Chiefs live for ever."[183] Convinced of the fact that British administration was far superior to Native administration, he took advantage of every favourable opportunity to introduce the same in the States. Lawrence was highly appreciative of the efficient internal administration of Maharaja Ram Singh of Jaipur whom he considered 'the best friend of the British Government'. On the other hand, he was highly critical of incapable and inefficient Chiefs and their officials. He did not hesitate even to depose a Chief if he was found guilty of gross misrule or of an atrocious act.

Following in the footsteps of Lawrence, his successor Mayo also exhorted the Princes and Chiefs to establish good administration based on the welfare and happiness of the people. In the course of his speech addressed to the Princes and Chiefs of Rajputana in a Darbar held at Ajmer on 22 October 1870, he said :[184]

> ...If we respect your rights and privileges you should also respect the rights and regard the privileges of those who are placed beneath your care. If we support you in your power, we expect in return good government. We demand that everywhere, throughout the length and breadth of Rajputana, justice and order shall prevail; that every man's property shall be secure; that the traveller shall come and go in safety; that the cultivator shall enjoy the fruits of his labour, and the trader the produce of

> his commerce; that you shall make roads, and undertake construction of those works of irrigation which will improve the condition of the people and swell the revenues of your States; that you shall encourage education, and provide for the relief of the sick.
>
> ...Be just and merciful to your people. We do not ask whether you come with full hands, but whether you come with clean hands. No presents that you may bring can buy the British favour; no display which you may will raise your dignity in our eyes; no crying or flattery will gain my friendship. We estimate you not by the splendour of your offerings to us, nor by the pomp of your retinue here, but by your conduct to your subjects at home. For ourselves, we have nothing to ask of you. But for your people we demand good government, and we shall judge of you by this standard alone.

In the same Darbar Mayo announced the foundation of the prestigious educational institution for the sons of the Princes which was named Mayo College after the name of the Viceroy. In the foundation of this institution Maharaja Ram Singh of Jaipur took a leading part, and of all the Princes of Rajputana he subscribed the maximum amount of rupees 1,25,000. It is significant to observe that after Mayo almost all Viceroys of the period under study (Northbrook, Lytton, Ripon, Dufferin, Landsdowne and Curzon) visited this College, and the speeches delivered by them in the presence of Princes and Chiefs strengthened the bonds of relationship between the Paramount Power and the 'Feudatory' Chiefs.

Of all the successors of Mayo, Curzon exercised the deepest impact on the conduct of the Princes and the administration of their States. This energetic Viceroy evinced keenest interest in the 'Indian India' and he is reported to have personally visited forty Princely States.[185] The imperious Viceroy put forth the theory that the rights and privileges of the States were derived directly or indirectly from the Paramount Power and that "No Native Chief in our opinion is in possession of sovereignty of his state."[186] "The sovereignty of the Crown", he remarked, "is everywhere unchallenged. It has itself laid the limitations of its own prerogatives."[187] It was "a claim not to paramountcy but to complete sovereignty."[188] At the behest of Curzon many ruling Princes of India, including Maharaja Madho Singh of Jaipur, had been sent to London in 1901 to participate in the Coronation ceremony of the King-Emperor, Edward VII as a mark of their allegiance to the British Sovereign. In order to further strengthen the bonds between the Native States and the British Suzerain he chalked out a magnificent programme for holding a Coronation Darbar at Delhi to proclaim the accession of the new Sovereign on 1 January 1903. In this Darbar, too, the Maharaja of Jaipur duly participated.

Curzon regarded the Princes as "no longer detached oppendages to the Empire, but its participators and instruments". In the course of his very first of the speeches about the Native States delivered at Gwalior on 29 November 1899, he had remarked, "The native Chief has become, by our policy, an integral factor in the Imperial organisation of India. He is concerned no less than the Viceroy or the Lieutenant-Governor in the administration of the country. I claim him as my colleague and partner."[189]

There is little doubt that during Curzon's period of Governor-Generalship earnest efforts began to be made by many Princes and Chiefs to improve the administration of their States, for they desired that good annual reports should be sent by their Residents or Political Agents about their administration and conduct to the Supreme Government. The internal administration of Jaipur State under Maharaja Madho Singh was highly efficient as testified by the annual Administration Reports during Curzon's time, and Curzon had nothing to complain against it, as also against the conduct of the Maharaja. During the famine of 1899-1900 also the Maharaja had taken commendable relief measures for helping the famine-stricken people, and these measures, as already mentioned, had evoked high appreciation from the Viceroy as well as Secretary of State for India. Not only that, the Maharaja had also fully cooperated with Curzon's scheme of instituting Indian People's Famine Trust and had contributed liberally towards the Trust fund.

IX

From what has been discussed in the foregoing account, it may be concluded that the internal administration of the Jaipur State during the post-1858 period was, on the whole, highly satisfactory. It was mainly because of the personal qualities of the two successive Maharajas (Ram Singh and Madho Singh) of the State. Both of them were able and enlightened rulers who had developed western outlook and drawn considerable inspiration from the highly modernised administrative machinery of British India. They had very wisely established a Council of able and experienced officials and *Thakurs* of the State, and the Council rendered valuable assistance to the rulers in the day-to-day administration of the State. Not only that, both the Maharajas were guided by the sane advice of the British Political Agent at Jaipur as well as by the Agent to Governor-General, Rajputana. They were also influenced by the periodic speeches of the Viceroys who poured into the ears of all the Native Princes to work for the welfare and happiness of their subjects.

This is, however, not to suggest that the administration of the State was not free from defects and deficiencies. In the first instance, many patriotic elements in and out of the State felt that the administration of the State under the two Maharajas was a slavish imitation of the British Indian administration without taking into consideration the noble traditions, usages and customs of the Rajputs which had been guiding the administration of the Rajput rulers for the past many centuries.

It is further alleged that the annual reports about the administration of Jaipur, howsoever complimentary to the Maharajas, did not represent the true picture about the plight of common people. The land revenue system, as pointed out elsewhere, was oppressive for the peasants who had to pay 50 per cent land revenue besides many other cesses; with the result they were often indebted to the moneylanders. Of the agriculturists, only the *Biswedars* and *Jagirdars* appeared to have been prosperous. The prosperity of the State was confined only to the upper classes. The British officials in the State — and they were many in numbers — drew fat salaries and European British subjects were given preferential treatment in every matter. The annual administration reports prepared by the British authorities, as also the annual reports prepared by the Darbar, generally presented a rosy picture of the administration of the State. The two said Maharajas of the State were fully loyal and faithful to the Paramount Power and were ever ready to accept the orders and circulars of the Supreme Government issued to promote their Imperial interest, even though they compromised with, and even denied, the internal sovereignty of the Chiefs. Little wonder, therefore, that the British authorities generally spoke well of their conduct as well as of the administration of the State.

Quoting an extract from the Rajputana Administration Report for 1895-96 about the administration of Jaipur State, the *Rajputana-Malwa Times* in a leading article considered this Report as misleading. It was said in this Report, "His Highness the Maharaja of Jeypore is to be congratulated on the excellent and progressive administration of his State, and much credit is due to Rao Bahadur Kanti Chander Mukherji, C.I.E., and the Council." The writer of the article characterised these remarks as "being uncommonly misleading to the public at large." Instead of describing the Prime Minister's administration as excellent and progressive, the writer went on to say, "our worthy Agent to the Governor General (Mr. Crosthwaite) would have approached the mark had he termed Kanti Chander's management of affairs as oppressive and regressive to the extreme." If the Agent to the Governor-General believed that any Prime Minister notorious for persecuting his own subjects and capable of acting in concert with an unworthy Political *more rapacious than rapacity itself,* would serve the purpose of good government in a Native State, it would then be very difficult to find out a single dominion in the whole world of which misrule could in any sense be predicated. He commented that Babu Kanti Chander was hated by all classes in the State, that the Council was a mockery and the position of the titular Maharaja was only a tool in his hands. The Prime Minister was practically the ruling despot in the land with the Resident, Colonel Law, and the Maharaja himself as his right and left arms by which he "strikes terror into the heart of all individuals far off or near about or around." The writer concluded by warning the Maharaja to look to the sufferings of his subjects lest a terrible catastrophe should visit his dominions.[190]

There is obviously an exaggeration in the scathing criticism of Jaipur administration by the writer of article in the said newspaper. Nevertheless, the fact remains that despite some irrefutable merits of the administration of Jaipur State, the common people, notably the peasants, were not really happy. In the hay day of Indian nationalism the people of the State gradually became more and more conscious about their rights which resulted in the formation of Jaipur Praja Mandal in 1938 under the presidentship of Seth Jamuna Lal Bajaj. The main objects of the Mandal were to establish responsible government in the State, to abolish undue taxes, to secure elementary rights of citizenship for the people and to bring about all round improvement in the State.[191]

References and Notes

1. M.S. Jain, *Rajasthan through the Ages, Vol. III* (Bikaner, 1996), p. 266.
2. RPARS for 1867-68, p. 3.
3. In October 1869 the Maharaja of Jaipur conferred the title of 'Mumtaz-Ood-Dowla' on Nawab Faiz Ali Khan, the head of the Royal Council, for long and faithful service to the State. Vide FD, Political A, Jan. 1870, Nos. 170-183.
4. RPARS for 1869-70, p. 8.
5. *Supra*, pp. 149-51.
6. FD, Political A, Jan. 1882, No. 176 of Nos. 166-183.
7. *Ibid.*
8. FD, Political A, Jan. 82, Nos. 178-181.
9. K.W. No. 1, FD, Political A, Oct. 1881, Nos. 241-252, pp. 1-2.
10. Lieut.-Col. P.W. Bannerman, Political Agent, Eastern States of Rajputana to AGG, No. 18 P., dated 28 July, 1881, FD, Political A, Oct. 1881, No. 250.
11. Lieut.-Col. C.K.M. Walter, Offg. AGG to GOI, No. 215 P, dated 1 Aug. 1881, FD, Political A, Oct. 1881, No. 246.

12. GOI to Offg. AGG, No. 6431 P., dated 15 Aug. 1881, FD, Political A, Oct. 1881, No. 251.
13. *Supra*, pp. 154-55.
14. RPARS for 1900-01, p. 21 and for 1901-02, p. 16.
15. RPARS for 1902-03, p. 16.
16. Jain, *op. cit.*, p. 271.
17. *IGI, Vol. XIII*, p. 394.
18. Annual Administration Report of the Jaipur State for 1905-1906, p. 3.
19. K.W. No. I, FD, Political A, Jan. 1882, Nos. 166-183.
20. AGG to GOI, No. 156 P, dated 21 June 1881, FD, Political A, Jan. 1882, No. 166, para 5.
21. Memorandum by Kanti Chander Mukerji on the Land Revenue System of the Jaipur State, 1882, FD, A-Rev-I, Sept. 1883, No. 4, paras 1-3.
22. *Ibid.*, paras 4-7.
23. *Ibid.*, para 10.
24. *Ibid.*, paras 8 and 11.
25. *Ibid.*, paras 12-16.
26. *Ibid.*, paras 18-22.
27. *Ibid.*, paras 23-29.
28. *Ibid.*, para 30.
29. *Ibid.*, para 31.
30. *Ibid.*, paras 32-33.
31. *Ibid.*, paras 34-35.
32. *Ibid.*, para 36.
33. *Ibid.*, paras 37-38.
34. *Ibid.*, para 41.
35. Secretary to GOI, Revenue and Agriculture Department to Local Governments and Administrations, dated 22 Sept. 1883, FD, A-Revenue-I, Oct. 1883, No. 5.
36. See RPARS for 1888-89, p. 36; for 1891-92, p. 59; for 1892-93, p. 4; for 1896-97, p. 38; for 1900-1901, p. 23; for 1901-1902, p. 17.
37. *IGI, Vol. XIII*, p. 395.
38. *Ibid.*
39. RPARS for 1900-1901, p. 22, para 12.
40. AGG to GOI, No. 915 G, dated 30 March 1883, FD, A-General-I, April 1883, No. 43.
41. Maharaja Sawai Madho Singh of Jaipur to J.P. Stratton, Resident, Eastern Rajputana States, dated 22 March 1883, FD, A-General-I, April 1883, No. 44.
42. *Ibid.*, Encl.

43. GOI to AGG, No. 976 I., dated 19 April 1883, FD, A-General-I, April 1883, No. 45.
44. *IGI, Vol. XIII,* pp. 394-95.
45. RPARS for 1885-86, pp. 39-40.
46. The other four courts were : The Ajmer Court (1842) having jurisdiction over the States of Kishangarh and Dholpur and the British province of Ajmer, which was also the Court of appeal for other Courts of Vakils; the Neemuch Court (1842); the Harauti Court (1847) at Kota; the Jodhur Court (1847).
47. RPARS for 1891-92, p. 60, para 12.
48. Jain, *op. cit.*, p. 116.
49. Sir Courtenay Ilbert, The *Government of India : Being a Digest of the Statute Law Relating Thereto* (London, 1898), p. 444.
50. *Ibid.*, pp. 452-53.
51. C.L. Tupper, Comp., *Indian Political Practice, Vol. III* (Calcutta, 1895), para 542, p. 67.
52. *Supra,* pp. 244-45.
53. Similar extradition treaties were also concluded between the British Government and the Rajput States of Banswara, Bikaner, Bundi Dholpur, Dungarpur, Jaisalmer, Jhallawar, Jodhpur, Karauli, Kishangarh, Kota, Pratapgarh, Tonk and Udaipur in 1868 or 1869.
54. There were 19 heinous offences in the list : murder, attempt to murder, culpable homicide, thugee, poisoning, rape, causing grievous hurt, child-stealing, selling females, dacoitee, robbery, burglary, cattle-theft, arson, forgery, counterfeiting coin, criminal breach of trust, criminal misappropriation of property and abetting the above offences.
55. FD, Political A, Sept. 1868, No. 255; C.U. Aitchison, Comp. *A Collection of Treaties, Engagements and Sanads, Vol. III* (Calcutta, 1932), pp. 72-73.
56. Jain, *op. cit.*, p. 121.
57. Tupper, *op. cit., Vol. III,* para 549, p. 73.
58. FD, Internal A, July 1886, Nos. 336-338 and Nov. 1886, Nos. 77-81.
59. Arora, *op. cit.*, p. 238.
60. Annual Administration Report of the Jaipur State for the period from Ist April 1905 to 31st August 1906, p. 4.
61. *IGI, Vol. XIII,* p. 397.
62. RPARS for 1885-86, p. 40.
63. FD., General A, July 1866, No. 56.
64. For details, see *supra,* pp. 189-96.

65. Jaipur Agency Record, Part I, Railway, File No. 9/1875.
66. Sarkar, *op. cit.*, p. 355.
67. RPARS for 1867-68, p. 4.
68. RPARS for 1869-70, p. 9.
69. Cited in Sarkar, *op. cit.*, p. 355.
70. RPARS for 1888-89, p. 36.
71. *IGI, Vol. XIII*, p. 398.
72. RPARS for 1891-92, p. 58.
73. RPARS for 1896-97, p. 38.
74. P.W.D. Report for 1897, p. 25.
75. RPARS for 1901-02, p. 17.
76. *IGI, Vol. XIII*, p. 396.
77. *Ibid.*, p. 393; P.W.D. Report for 1868-69, p. 6.
78. P.W.D. Report for 1874-75, p. 5, paras 28-30.
79. For details, see P.W.D. Reports for 1894, pp. 15-18; for 1895, pp. 24-29; for 1896, pp. 19-21; for 1897, pp. 31-33; for 1900, pp. 32-37; for 1902, pp. 6-7.
80. P.W.D. Reports for 1876-77, pp. 5-6; for 1877-78, pp. 5-6; for 1878-79, pp. 8-9; for 1883-84, pp. 21-22.
81. *IGI, Vol. XIII*, p. 392.
82. For details, see supra, pp. 208-15.
83. P.W.D. Report for 1897, p. 17.
84. P.W.D. Report for 1899, p. 15.
85. RPARS for 1901-02, p. 16; for 1902-03, p. 16 ; for 1903-04, p. 15; for 1904-05, p. 72.
86. For terms of the Agreement, see Aitchison, *Vol. III*, op. cit., pp. 92-95.
87. P.W.D. Report for 1871-72, pp. 4-5.
88. P.W.D. Report for 1873-74, p. 5.
89. P.W.D. Reports for 1895, p. 23; for 1896, pp. 15-16.
90. RPARS for 1885-86, p. 42.
91. *IGI, Vol. XIII*, p. 399.
92. *Ibid.*
93. P.W.D. Report for 1873-74, pp. 3-5 and for 1877-78, p. 4.
94. P.W.D. Report for 1875-76, pp. 2-3.
95. RPARS for 1889-90, p. 21.
96. FD, General B, Dec. 1871, Nos. 77-80.
97. Ashim Kumar Roy, *History of the Jaipur City* (New Delhi, 1978), p. 80.
98. FD, General B, Aug. 1882, Nos. 164-168.
99. RPARS for 1892-93, p. 24.
100. RPARS for 1893-94, p. 29.

101. Annual Administration Report of Jaipur State for 1905-06, p. 7.
102. RPARS for 1892-93, p. 24.
103. RPARS for 1893-94, p. 28.
104. RPARS for 1904-05, p. 72.
105. RPARS for 1867-68, p. 4, para 27.
106. *IGI, Vol. XIII*, p. 391.
107. RPARS for 1885-86, p. 42.
108. RPARS for 1892-93, p. 24.
109. RPARS for 1896-97, p. 37.
110. RPARS for 1901-02, p. 17.
111. RPARS for 1903-04, p. 16.
112. RPARS for 1885-86, p. 41.
113. RPARS for 1888-89, p. 36.
114. RPARS for 1893-94, p. 28.
115. RPARS for 1904-05, p. 72; *IGI, Vol. XIII*, p. 392.
116. RPARS for 1902-03, p. 16.
117. *Ibid.*
118. RPARS for 1904-05, p. 72.
119. Administration Report of the Jaipur State for 1905-06, p. 7.
120. RPARS for 1885-86, p. 42.
121. *Ibid.*; also see *IGI, Vol. XIII*, p. 391.
122. *IGI, Vol. XIII*, p. 391.
123. RPARS for 1900-01, p. 22, and for 1904-05, p. 72.
124. *IGI, Vol. XIII*, p. 391.
125. The highest and lowest amounts during 1885-1905 were spent in the following years :

Highest		*Lowest*	
1885-86	= Rs. 11,00,000	1904-05	= Rs. 5,71,954
1892-93	= Rs. 10,90,719	1903-04	= Rs. 6,64,969
1902-03	= Rs. 10,09,741	1896-97	= Rs. 7,18,731
1888-89	= Rs. 8,77,867	1891-92	= Rs. 7,61,923
(RPARS for 1885-86, p. 41; for 1892-93, p. 22; for 1902-03, p. 16; and for 1888-89, p. 36)		(RPARS for 1904-05, p. 72 ; for 1903-04, p. 15; for 1896-97, p. 38; and for 1891-92, p. 58).	

126. RPARS for 1893-94, p. 29.
127. RPARS for 1902-03, p. 16 and for 1903-04, p. 15.
128. FD, General A, Progs. Feb. 1864, Nos. 86-87; also see G.C. Verma, 'Educational Development in Jaipur' in J.N. Asopa (ed.), *Cultural Heritage of Jaipur* (Jodhpur, 1982), pp. 164-65.
129. RPARS for 1866-67, p. 186.
130. RPARS for 1874-75, p. 89.
131. RPARS for 1869-70, p. 9.

132. RPARS for 1866-67, p. 186.
133. RPARS for 1868-69, pp. 86-87; Verma, *op. cit.*, p. 170.
134. FD, General B, Oct. 1866, No. 130.
135. RPARS for 1869-70, p. 9.
136. Both the Jaipur Darbar and the Political Agent considered that special European supervision was necessary to give the institution a fair start. On their request the British Government lent the services of Assistant Surgeon De Fabeck, who was essentially an artist, for a period of one year in the first instance on a salary of Rs. 1000/- a month. Vide FD, General A, June 1869, Nos. 54-55.
137. Verma, *op. cit.*, p. 174.
138. Cited in Sarkar, *op. cit.*, p. 356.
139. RPARS for 1888-89, p. 36, and for 1891-92, p. 58.
140. Report on Public Instruction in Jaipur State (1897), p. 11.
141. RPARS for 1896-97, p. 37.
142. RPARS for 1901-02, p. 17 and for 1902-03, p. 16.
143. RPARS for 1903-04, p. 15 ; also verma, *op. cit.*, p. 168.
144. Report on Public Instruction in Jaipur State (1904), p. 2.
145. *IGI, Vol. XIII*, pp. 398-99.
146. Annual Administration Report of Jaipur State for the period from 1 April 1905 to 31 August 1906, pp. 10-11. For further details, see Appendix VI.
147. FD, Political A, June 1871, Nos. 269-271; also Sarkar, *op. cit.*, p. 357.
148. Sherring, *Mayo College, Vol. I*, pp. 166,179; also Jain, *op. cit.*, pp. 240-41.
149. FD, Internal A, July 1904, Nos. 3-42; Lovat Fraser, *India Under Curzon and After* (London, 1911), pp. 222-23; Anju Suri, 'Curzon and British Paramountcy in the Princely States' in *Indian History Congress Proceedings*, 63rd Session, 2002, pp. 539-40.
150. *Supra*, p. 102.
151. Jaipur Agency Record, Part-I, Suttee, File No. 2/1869.
152. Despatch from Secretary of State for India to Govt. of India, No. 27 of 17 March 1870, FD, General A, May 1870, No. 22.
153. Jaipur Agency Record, Part I, Suttee, File No. 4/1873.
154. FD, A — General-I, Jan. 1883, Nos. 64-69; Jaipur Agency Record, Part I, Suttee, File No. 6/1882.
155. FD, Political B, May 1871, Nos. 66-67.
156. K.W. FD, General B, October 1868, Nos. 174-176.
157. Circular No. 619 G, dated 12 Aug. 1868, issued by Agent to Governor-General, Rajputana to all Political Agents in Rajputana

States, FD, General B, Oct. 1868, No. 175.

158. Governor-General in Council to AGG, No. 1838, dated 22 Oct. 1868, *ibid.*, No. 176.
159. B.M. Bhatia, *Famines in India* (Bombay, 1963), p. 8.
160. FD, General A, Dec. 1868, Nos. 64-66; also Jan. 1869, Nos. 54-56.
161. RPARS for 1869-70, p. 8.
162. FD, General A, April 1869, Nos. 67-70.
163. *Ibid.*
164. *IGI, Vol. XIII*, p. 393.
165. *Ibid.*
166. Sir John Elliot (Government Meteorologist), cited in H.S. Srivastava, *The History of Indian Famines, 1858-1918* (Agra, 1968), p. 242.
167. FD, Internal A, April 1900, No. 95 and Encl., pp. 119-138.
168. *Ibid.*, para 2.
169. *Ibid.*, paras 4-6.
170. *Ibid.*, para 7.
171. *Ibid.*, paras 8-14.
172. *Ibid.*, paras 15-16.
173. *Ibid.*, para 17.
174. *Ibid.*, paras 18-19.
175. *Ibid.*, para 20.
176. FD, Internal A, May 1900, No. 290 of Nos. 267-304.
177. RPARS for 1900-01, pp. 21-22.
178. FD, Internal A, Sept. 1900, Nos. 94-105.
179. FD, Internal A, Nov. 1900, Nos. 186-190.
180. Annual Administration Report of Jaipur State for 1905-06, p. 2.
181. Srivastava, *op. cit.*, p. 250.
182. Charles Aitchison, *Lord Lawrence* (Oxford, 1894), p. 139.
183. Cited in Bosworth Smith, *Life of Lord Lawrence, Vol. II* (London, 1883), pp. 506-08; Charles Aitchison, *op. cit.*, p. 140.
184. W.W. Hunter, *Life of Earl of Mayo, Vol. I* (London, 1875), pp. 208, 213-14.
185. Lovat Fraser, *India Under Curzon and After* (London, 1911), p. 237.
186. Curzon to Northcote, 18 June 1903, Microfilms, Curzon Paper, Reel 9, No. 106 (NAI).
187. Thomas Raleigh, *Lord Curzon in India : Being a Selection from his Speeches as Viceroy and Governor-General of India* (London, 1906), p. 226.
188. *The British Crown and the Indian States : An Outline Sketch Presented to the Indian States Committee on behalf of the Standing Committee of*

the Chamber of Princes (London, 1929), p. 66.

189. Raleigh, *op. cit.*, pp. 217-18.
190. *The Rajputana-Malwa Times*, dated 2 Nov. 1896, cited in *Selections from the Vernacular Newspapers for the fortnight ending 15 Nov. 1896*, pp. 357-58.
191. *The Hindustan Times*, dated 9 May 1938, cited in F.K. Kapil, *Rajputana States, 1817-1950* (Jodhpur, 1999), p. 136.

CHAPTER 10

Findings in Retrospect

The year 1818 marks the beginning of British paramountcy in Jaipur State. In this year a highly significant treaty was concluded with Jaipur and 18 other States of Rajputana as a result of planned and persistent efforts of C.T. Metcalfe, British Resident at Delhi, who had the full support of the Governor-General, Marquess of Hastings. According to the terms of this treaty the British Government agreed to protect the territory of the principality against all enemies; the Maharaja of Jaipur and his successors were bound to act in subordinate co-operation with the British Government, to acknowledge its supremacy, to refer their disputes with other Chiefs to the arbitration and award of the British Government and to furnish troops and supplies at the requisition of the British Government. It was specifically provided in Article 6 of the treaty that annual tribute would be paid in perpetuity by the Jaipur State amounting to rupees four, five, six, seven and eight lakhs of rupees during the second, third, fourth, fifth and sixth year respectively which would be further increased, if the revenues exceeded forty lakhs of rupees at the rate of five-sixteenths of the excess in addition to rupees eight lakhs. It was laid down clearly in Article 8 of the treaty that the Maharaja, his heirs and successors "shall remain absolute rulers of their territory and their dependents."

In the course of the following four decades of the East India

Company's rule the British authorities intervened almost continuously in the internal affairs of the State in gross violation of the aforesaid Article 8 of the treaty. The opportunities for such intervention were provided by the minority of the two successive Maharajas, Jai Singh III and Ram Singh, which together extended over a period of thirty-two years (1819-1835 and 1835-1851). In 1821 the British authorities appointed a Political Agent at Jaipur in order to exercise effective control and supervision over the affairs of the State, and this was done in spite of the opposition of the Regent Rani (the Bhattiani queen) and the Prime Minister, Rawal Bairisal. The Political Agent backed by the British Resident at Delhi and since 1834 by the Agent to Governor-General for Rajputana at Ajmer, placed himself in opposition to the Regent Rani and did not permit her to wield her prerogative of having a Prime Minister (*Mukhtiar*) of her choice. During the minority of Ram Singh (since 1835) the Political Agent and Agent to Governor-General continuously eroded the authority of the new Regent, Rani Chandrawat, and made and unmade the *Mukhtiar* of their choice. In 1839 the Regent Rani was excluded from the administrative affairs of the State and a Council of Regency of five Sardar *(Thakurs)* of the State was appointed with the British Political Agent as its President. It was to all intents and purposes the rule of the Political Agent, and the Council of Regency played a second fiddle to him in all important administrative matters.

The minority administration of the State was made use of by the British authorities, through the Political Agents, to safeguard and promote fiscal and other imperial interests of the British Government. They made sure that the full amount of annual tribute, howsoever unfair, was paid regularly by the Jaipur Darbar to the British Government under all circumstances even of financial stringency. In order to check frequent robberies and lawlessness in the Shekhawati region 'Shekhawati Brigade' was organised under the command of Major Forster which virtually remained under the exclusive control of the Political Agent; the services of the Brigade could be, and were actually, utilised by the Imperial Government for employment even out of the Jaipur State. After 1851 when Maharaja Ram Singh had been invested with ruling powers, the Political Agents, who enjoyed the support of Agents to Governor-General, Rajputana, continued to dominate in the affairs of the State.

Thus the roots of British paramountcy in the Jaipur State, as also in other Princely States in a greater or lesser degree, could be perceived during the period of the East India Company which had virtually become the Paramount Power by the end of Dalhousie's period (1856). Only a definite theory or system remained to be evolved and this was done during the first half a century of the Crown's regime.

During the Revolt of 1857-58 a large number of Princes and Chiefs, including the Maharaja of Jaipur, rendered valuable services to the British Government. For his unswerving loyalty and meritorious services Maharaja Ram Singh and his principal officers were duly rewarded; the Maharaja was also granted the *pargana* of Kot Kasim as a reward for his services. As a result of this Revolt, a new era was inaugurated in the British policy under the Crown towards the Princely States of India. The Queen's Proclamation, which was read by the Viceroy Canning to the assembled Princes and prominent people at a Darbar held in Allahabad on 1 November 1858, declared in clear and unambiguous terms the adoption of a new policy towards the States. The new policy was expounded at length in the Despatch of 30 April 1860 addressed by Canning to the Secretary of State for India. In the first place, the annexation of Princely States, which had been the governing principle of British policy under the East India Company, was abandoned once for all. To use the words of the Queen's Proclamation, "We desire no extension of our present territorial possessions". Secondly, solemn promises were given to respect the 'rights, dignity and honour' of Native Princes and to 'scrupulously maintain' all the treaties and engagements which the Princes had made with the East India Company. In pursuance of the new policy 'Adoption Sanads' were issued by the Viceroy Canning in 1862 to all the Princes and Chiefs individually, including the Maharaja of Jaipur, by which the right of adopting a heir or nominating a successor was granted to them in case of failure of natural son.

In the following decades the British Government began to intervene more and more in the internal affairs of Jaipur State in gross violation of Article 8 of the treaty of 1818; consequently the Maharajas of Jaipur no longer remained "absolute rulers of their territory". The Imperial Government gradually asserted new claims as a Paramount Power and exacted corresponding new obligations from the Maharajas. They "arrogated to themselves arbitrarily in the name of 'paramountcy' whatever rights they pleased—paramountcy which was deliberately left undefined."

The British Government considered it their right and duty as a Paramount Power to settle issues of succession in the subordinate Native States and they made it a principle of their policy that every succession must be recognised by the British Government and that no succession would be valid until recognition had been given. Even during the East India Company's period the British Government had given recognition to the accession of two minor Maharajas, Jai Singh III and Ram Singh, and made administrative arrangements during their minority. It has already been mentioned that the British Political Agent at Jaipur, backed by the Resident at Delhi and later on by Agent to Governor-General at Ajmer, played a dominating and decisive role in all important administrative matters during the minority of the two Chiefs. In 1880 Maharaja Ram Singh died. He had left no natural son nor had he adopted anyone as his heir. It was reported that the late Chief had nominated a collateral named Kaim Singh as his successor in the presence of British representative, Dr. T.H. Hendley. The Supreme Government, therefore, recognised Kaim Singh as the new Chief of the State under the title of Sawai Madho Singh. At that time he was a young man of 19 years, and it was decided by the British authorities that he should conduct administration of the State with the active assistance of the Council of six nobles to which three more influential *Thakurs* were added; the meetings of the Council would be attended by the Political Agent accompanied by the young Maharaja. Upon attaining the age of 21 years in September 1882, the Maharaja was invested with full ruling powers on the condition that he would be bound to consult the Political Agent on all important matters and to follow his advice. In fact, it was a main principle of the British policy during the period of the growth of British paramountcy that Political Agent or Resident should play a decisive role in the affairs of the State under his charge.

In accordance with Article 5 of the treaty of 1818 the British authorities acted as arbitrators in the settlement of border disputes which arose from time to time between Jaipur and the neighbouring States of Karauli, Alwar, Tonk, Bikaner and Patiala. The Agents to Governor-General for Rajputana obtained detailed information about such disputes from the Political Agent, Jaipur, and communicated with the Chiefs concerned to settle the disputes amicably. In the case of Jaipur-Patiala border disputes the representatives of the Lieutenant-Governor of Punjab and *Motamids* of Patiala were also involved in the settlement of disputes. The British authorities instituted five 'International Courts of Vakils to decide the border criminal cases of the Rajputana States. Of these, the Jaipur Court decided the cases of offenders belonging to the States of Jaipur, Bharatpur, Tonk and Alwar. The *Vakils* constituting the bench of this Court represented their respective States and it was presided over by the Poloitical Agent. All the cases decided by the Court were reported regularly year after year and appeals against its decisions could be taken to the Ajmer Court which was presided over by the Agent to Governor-General, Rajputana. With the sanction of the British Government extradition rules for the exchange of offenders were framed between Jaipur and other Rajputana States and between Jaipur and the neigbouring Punjab States (Patiala, Jind, Nabha and Loharu) which were based on the principle of absolute reciprocity. Significantly, the Supreme Government asserted the principle that all these extradition rules between the various States were sanctioned as arrangements concluded by the British Government, not as agreements mutually concluded between the States. The action of the British authorities may be explained in terms of their obligation, as well as their right, as a Paramount Power to maintain peace and order on the borders of the States and to mitigate the cause of border crimes and border disputes as far as possible.

As numerous Princely States enjoyed the protection of British Government, their subordinate co-operation to the Paramount Power in fiscal and economic matters was considered necessary whether it was in accordance with, or in violation of, the existing treaties. According to Article 6 of the treaty of 1818 the Jaipur State was bound to pay an annual tribute of rupees four lakhs which tended to increase year after year amounting to rupees eight lakhs in the fifth year and much more if the revenues of the State increased beyond rupees forty lakhs. As this term was unfair and unreasonable, Maharaja Ram Singh of Jaipur represented to the Supreme Government repeatedly for the reduction of the amount of tribute. At last a supplementary treaty was concluded with the Jaipur State in 1871 by which the annual tribute was fixed at rupees four lakhs in perpetuity. The Maharaja felt obliged to the Government of India for this act of kindness. Be that as it may, tributes from Jaipur and many other States constituted an important source of income for the Imperial Government.

For the purpose of securing the monopoly of salt throughout the country and making it a regular source of revenue, the British authorities concluded treaties with Princely States concerned. They concluded two Salt Agreements in 1869 and 1879 with the Jaipur State. By the former the Jaipur Darbar agreed to lease to the British Government its right of manufacturing and of selling salt within the limits of the territory bordering on the Sambhar Lake in return for an annual amount of rupees 2,75,000 (an inadequate compensation indeed) to be paid in two half-yearly instalments by the British Government; by the latter the Jaipur Darbar agreed to suppress and absolutely prohibit and prevent the manufacture of salt within any part of the Jaipur State.

The opium policy of the British Government was intended to protect the imperial revenues and to prevent the Princely States from adopting measures which might be detrimental to the interests of the Paramount Power. In pursuance of this policy the export of opium, *bhang*, *ganja*, spirits and other intoxicating drugs from the Jaipur territories into British India was strictly forbidden, and necessary orders were issued by the Jaipur Darbar in this regard to the officials of the State.

After the fall of Delhi and trial of the Mughal Emperor Bahadur Shah II, the Maharaja of Jaipur was among the first Princes who expressed willingness to efface the obnoxious superscription of the Delhi Emperor from his coins and to issue a new currency bearing some reference to Her Majesty the Queen. Gradually the British Indian currency had been adopted by a large number of Princely States, including many Rajputana States. But Jaipur and six other Rajputana States, however, continued to have their own coinage; the Jaipur coins were called *Jhar Shahi* which were issued in silver and copper metals in addition to gold *mohurs.*

In accordance with the principles of British policy regarding extension of railway lines in the territories of Princely States, the Jaipur State was asked to cede lands free of charge required for railway construction together with full jurisdiction short of sovereign rights in the relevant lines. Maharaja Ram Singh at first submitted a 'memorandum of conditions' for the proposed scheme of railway extension through the territories of the Jaipur State in order to safeguard the interests of his State. But when the Supreme Government declined to accept those conditions which were incompatible with the general principles of British policy he withdrew the conditions submitted earlier. The Jaipur Darbar, therefore, ceded all the lands which were required for Rajputana State Railway, Rajputana-Malwa Railway and Rewari-Phulera Chord Railway, and also ceded to the British Government "full and exclusive power and jurisdiction of every kind over the lands" occupied by these Railways, and "over all persons and things whatsoever" within the said lands. The judicial powers over the said lands were exercised by the Political Agent and police powers by the Superintendent of Rajputana Railway Police with his headquarters at Jaipur and subsequently at Ajmer. It may be observed that the British authorities had no legal right to assume full police, civil and criminal jurisdiction on the railway lines traversing the territories of the Princely States. The assumption of such jurisdiction by the Paramount Power "manifestly marked an inroad on the judicial independence of Indian States."

Side by side with the railways, roads were also constructed connecting Jaipur with other cities and towns of the State as well as with other cities of British territories and those of the neighbouring States. It was under pressure from the British authorities that Jaipur Darbar had to construct such roads as were considered to be of imperial importance. Of these roads, particular mention may be made of the trunk road from Agra to Ajmer, Jaipur-Tonk road, Jaipur-Sambhar road (via Bagru) and the Karauli-Mandawar road. The Jaipur Darbar was urged to make 'the utmost possible efforts' in respect of constructing feeder roads connecting the important places with the railway stations. In December 1882 the Jaipur Darbar had abolished all the transit duties on the roads leading to the Rajputana-Malwa Railway within the Jaipur territory for which the Supreme Government expressed thanks to the Maharaja of Jaipur for the 'enlightened spirit' evinced by him in the matter. Thus the roads constructed by the Jaipur Darbar as well as by the rulers of other States together with the abolition of all transit duties on the 'feeder roads' paved the way for the development of trade and commerce without any let or hindrance throughout the length and breadth of the country, and provided another facet of the growth of British paramountcy in the States.

The British authorities considered it essential to make certain arrangements with the Princely States of India in order to ensure smooth and efficient working of the Imperial postal system. The Supreme Government unilaterally, by means of issuing resolutions, imposed certain rules upon the Princely States, including the Jaipur State, holding them prima facie responsible for mail robberies committed in their territories; they were held liable to pay compensation not only to the Government for whatever was taken or destroyed but also to the carriers of mails or their families. Several cases of mail robberies occurred in the Jaipur territory from time to time for which the Jaipur Darbar had to pay compensation as decided by the British authorities. As suggested by the British Political

Agent, the Jaipur Darbar had to take measures for better security of transit of mails, such as sending an armed guard in the mail cart and making provision of strong locks in the cart for the mail bags. The rulers of the States were asked through the Political Agents to introduce British postal system in their respective territories as far as possible. The Jaipur Darbar responded partially and set up a number of Imperial post offices in the Jaipur territories, in addition to a large number of Raj post offices scattered throughout the dominions of the State. In 1906 there were 32 Imperial Post Offices and no less than 112 Raj Post Offices in the State. The British authorities desired to introduce Postal Unity in all the Princely States except the six States (Gwalior, Patiala, Jind, Nabha, Faridkot and Chamba) with whom postal conventions had been concluded in the 1880s. The Jaipur Darbar had brought about drastic reforms in its Postal Department during 1904-1906, making the Raj postal system as efficient as the Imperial postal system. Therefore, it represented to the British authorities repeatedly to conclude a postal convention with the State, declining politely the proposal of Postal Unity. At last in 1908 the Supreme Government gave directions to work out a scheme of postal convention acceptable to the Jaipur Darbar and the Government of India.

Actuated by political, military and economic considerations the British authorities were keen to extend the telegraph system in the whole sub-continent, including the Princely States. They, therefore, encouraged and aided all schemes for extension of telegraph system to the States. But for imperial purpose they made it a principle of their policy that all such schemes should operate not only with the sanction of the Supreme Government but should also be subject to the control and supervision of the Director-General of Imperial Telegraphs. Many Telegraph Offices, including Post and Telegraph Offices were established in many cities and towns of the Jaipur State with the consent of the Jaipur Darbar conveyed through the Political Agent. It was very often at the initiative of the British authorities that telegraph lines were set up in Jaipur and other States which were intended to promote imperial interests.

As a matter of fact, in the fiscal and economic matters, as also in the means of transport and communications, it was the deliberate policy of the British Government that all these important matters in respect of British India as well as Native India, should be under 'a single charge'. It was by unilateral resolutions passed and circulars issued by the Government of India in all these matters that the policy of the Imperial Government was sought to be enforced more or less uniformly in the Princely States; some relaxation was, however, made in the case of Jaipur State in the matters of coinage and postal system, as already indicated.

The British Government under the Crown adopted two-fold policy regarding military establishments in the Princely States — first, to keep a strict control over the armies and arms of the States; second, to utilise the services of selected troops of selected States for the imperial cause. In pursuance of the first, the British authorities kept themselves fully and regularly informed about the ordnance, strength of artillerymen, infantry and cavalry maintained by the States, including the Jaipur State. The States had to depend on the British Government for the supply of all arms and their requisition for arms, if considered unnecessary by the military authorities, could be rejected by the Supreme Government. Under the Arms Act, 1878 strict control was exercised over arms and ammunition in Jaipur State, as in all other States. The export of cannons, arms and ammunition from British India into the States was strictly prohibited except under license from British authorities.

As regards the second, Jaipur State was one of the twenty-three selected States which were associated with the scheme of Imperial Service Troops launched in 1889. The Jaipur Darbar organised Imperial Service Transport Corps originally composed of 1000 ponies and 500 carts (complete in every particular with hospitals, veterinary establishment and workshop). The corps was employed for service for the first time in the Chitral campaign of 1895. Throughout its field service the corps maintained an excellent spirit. The British authorities were highly appreciative of the work done by the corps for which they expressed their thanks to the Maharaja of

Jaipur Gratified by the honour done to him, the Maharaja voluntarily offered to increase the strength of the corps by 200 ponies. The Supreme Government accepted the Maharaja's 'highly valuable offer' with thanks. The Jaipur Transport Corps was again employed for service in the Tirah campaign on the North-West Frontier. The Government of India expressed their thanks to the Maharaja of Jaipur conveyed through Agent to Governor-General, Rajputana for the 'admirable service' rendered by the Jaipur corps.

The British Government exercised a profound impact on the internal administration of Jaipur State. Actuated ostensibly by the 'civilising mission' the British authorities earnestly desired that the ruler of the State should reform his administration on modern lines and take necessary measures for the welfare and happiness of the people. He should not behave like a malevolent despot but act as a benevolent ruler who should allow himself to be assisted and guided by a Council of competent officials and nobles. Maharaja Ram Singh, therefore, constituted a State Council in 1867 which initially consisted of six members. After the accession of Kaim Singh (Sawai Madho Singh), three more members, who were prominent *Thakurs*, were added to the Council. In due course of time all the administrative affairs of the State began to be conducted by the Council in the name of the Maharaja. More important still, the British Political Agent at Jaipur acted as the most effective check on the authority of the Maharaja, and as his main adviser and guide he persuaded the latter to effect reforms in every department of administration.

The Jaipur State, for administrative purposes, was divided into ten *Nizamats* or districts. Each *Nizamat* was under a *Nazim* who was an executive as well as judicial officer like the Deputy Commissioner or Collector of a British district. The *Nizamats* were divided into thirty-one (later on thirty-three) *Tahsils*, each under the charge of a *Tahsildar*..

The land revenue system of the State was gradually reformed and reorganised. The State government was persuaded to undertake land survey operations. Kanti Chander Mukerji, a prominent member of the Jaipur Council and an expert in the land revenue matters, prepared a comprehensive account of the land revenue system of the State. He submitted a Memorandum on the various tenures of land in the State, the different methods of assessing the land revenue, the modes of collection and the system of keeping accounts. The *Ryotwari* system was prevalent in the State, each cultivator paying rent for his holding direct to the Raj. The Government of India was highly appreciative of the Memorandum which was found to be highly 'instructive and interesting'. In order to provide irrigation facilities to the cultivators, a large number of reservoirs were constructed year after year since 1868 under the able supervision of Colonel S.S. Jacob, the State Engineer. These irrigation works "reflect great credit on the enlightened liberality of the Jaipur Darbar, and the energy of Colonel Jacob who had directed and superintended their construction." The financial administration of the State was very well-managed year after year due to the personal interest evinced by the Maharaja and efficient functioning of various departments at the hands of the members of the Council who were guided by the Political Agents and ably assisted by the British officers employed in various departments on high jobs.

The judicial administration of the State was re-organised on British pattern under the able supervision of Pandit Maharaj Kishen, Extra Assistant Commissioner, Punjab whose services were borrowed by the Jaipur Darbar for a number of years. Suitable civil and criminal procedure codes were prepared. The jurisdiction and powers of all the courts in civil and criminal cases from the lowest, the *Tahsildar's* court, to the highest, the Council, were clearly defined. Apart from bringing about necessary reforms in the judicial administration, the main interest of the Paramount Power was to safeguard the interests of British Indian subjects, especially the European subjects, in the Jaipur State. For this purpose an Extradition Treaty was concluded between the British Government and the Maharaja of Jaipur in 1868, apparently on the basis of reciprocity but actually according a preferential treatment to the British Indian subjects. Connected with the judicial administration was the administration of police and jails in the State which also witnessed significant changes and reforms under the British impact.

The Public Works Department was established in the State by Maharaja Ram Singh which, since 1860, had been under the charge of a British officer lent by the Government of India, and it "takes rank with any similar institution in British India". Apart from constructing a large number of roads within the city of Jaipur and outside, it raised many buildings of public interest. In order to provide medical facilities to the people of the State on modern lines a General Hospital was opened at Jaipur which was named as Mayo Hospital. Many dispensaries were also opened at various places in the State; the Hospital and the deispensaries functioned under the able superintendence of Surgeon-Major T.H. Hendley. In imitation of the Eden Gardens of Calcutta, Maharaja Ram Singh laid out Ram Niwas Garden at Jaipur. The other notable buildings raised at Jaipur were Albert Hall and Museum. In order to provide pure water and light to the city, water-works and gas-works were undertaken by the Public Works Department in addition to numerous irrigation works under the charge of Colonel Jacob. For the conservation of forests the Jaipur Darbar procured the services of Bhai Sadhu Singh, an officer of the Punjab Forest Department and appointed him as Superintendent of forests.

Education on modern lines made a remarkable progress in the State under British impact. Starting with a modern school at Jaipur which was raised to the status of a college in 1873 called the Maharaja College, the Jaipur Darbar gradually established a large number of primary and higher schools, including many girls' schools. By the end of 1904 there were 753 educational institutions in the State, 151 public and 602 private. Of the former 77 were maintained by the Darbar and 74 were under private management, though more or less under the supervision of the Education Department. There were eleven girls schools in the State which were attended in 1904 by 797 girls. The Jaipur College had maintained its high reputation in the university examinations, such as M.A., B.A., Intermediate and Entrance examinations of Allahabad University, as is evident from the good results shown by it in the examinations held in 1905. The Jaipur School of Art, a notable technical institution of the State, made a great progress under the principalship of Dr. De Fabeck whose services were temporarily lent to the Jaipur Darbar by the British Government in 1869. It maintained its reputation in the next over three decades. A good number of pupils of this school had received instructions and training in drawing, engineering, pottery, carpentry and other handicrafts. An educational institution of great significance, in the foundation of which Maharaja Ram Singh took a leading part, was the Mayo College of Princes at Ajmer. Of the total amount of rupees six lakhs contributed by a number of Chiefs for its maintenance, the Maharaja of Jaipur contributed rupees 1,25,000. Thus in the development of education the Jaipur State was second to none in the whole of Rajputana. And in this development the Britishers had played a highly significant role directly or indirectly.

Under the British impact the Maharajas of Jaipur took commendable famine-relief measures during the famines of 1868-69 and 1899-1900 which occurred in various parts of the State. In order to help the famine-stricken people in the course of the first famine, Maharaja Ram Singh suspended the payment of rent and succession duty, abolished duties on the import of grain, spent a considerable amount to provide food to poor and labouring classes and undertook many works, including a 'pucca bund', a *dharmsala,* repair of forts, temples, *talaos,* laying out of a large garden, etc. in order to provide employment to the impoverished people. The prompt and 'enlightened' measures taken by the Maharaja for the benefit of the famine-stricken people not only of Jaipur but also of neighbouring States and British territory were highly appreciated by the Government of India which decided to increase the personal salute of the Maharaja from 17 to 19 guns, with the approval of the Secretary of State.

During the famine of 1899-1900, which was much more severe in intensity, Maharaja Madho Singh took energetic and prompt measures to combat the calamity. Major J.R. Dunlop Smith, Famine Commissioner, Rajputana personally visited some of the famine-affected areas and scrutinised the relief measures. In his comprehensive report about the relief works undertaken by the Jaipur Darbar, he pointed out that the measures to cope with the distress were taken in time and they were wisely and liberally planned. Major relief works were taken under the directions of Colonel Jacob and Lieutenant Garrett, which included construction of new roads and buildings and repair of old ones, development of extensive irrigation works, commencement of earthwork in connection with Rewari-Phulera Chord Railway line — works on which thousands of persons were employed daily. The services of Jaipur Imperial Service Transport Corps under its energetic Superintendent, Rai Bahadur Dhanpat Rai, were utilised to the utmost in the general scheme of relief operations. Many poor-houses and depots were opened at various places to which branch hospitals were attached. Arrangements were made for providing food to the poor and medicines to the sick. An orphanage was opened for the helpless orphan boys and girls. A large poor house was opened at Jaipur where food was distributed twice a day. Thus the severest famine in Jaipur State was as successfully combated as in the adjacent British Indian territory.

The British impact on the internal administration of Jaipur State was exercised largely through he Political Agent at Jaipur who was the channel of communication between the Jaipur Darbar and the Agent to Governor-General, Rajputana. But during the period 1858-1905, the Viceroys and Governors-General played a highly significant role in moulding the personal conduct and determining the tone of internal administration of the Maharajas of Jaipur, as also of other Princes and Chiefs. In their speeches the Viceroys, notably John Lawrence, Mayo and Curzon, admonished the Native Chiefs to improve their administration and take measures for the welfare of people which alone would be the criteria for them to win over the goodwill of the Supreme Government. The administration of both the Maharajas of the period, Ram Singh and Madho Singh, was highly efficient as testified by the annual Administration Reports, and the British authorities had also nothing to complain against their conduct.

Behind the benevolent consideration for welfare and happiness of the people of Princely States lay the predominant imperial consideration which determined the British policy towards the States. The British authorities asserted and promoted their imperial interests almost uniformly in all the Princely States in the matters of succession; administrative arrangements during the minority of the Chiefs; salt, coinage, opium-trade, railway, post and telegraph; personal and territorial jurisdiction of the British subjects in the States; extradition between British India and Native India and between the States themselves; disputes between the States and their isolation from one another; military establishments in the States; employment of British and European officers in the States; interference with the internal administration of the States; and allegiance of the Princes and Chiefs to the British Sovereign. The claims of the Supreme Government in all these matters were asserted very often in clear violation of the existing treaties and engagements. The British paramountcy thus assumed wide dimensions in response to the growing requirements of the Imperial Government. With the result, the Princes were left with only a limited exercise of authority in internal affairs, and that too subject to overall control and supervision of Political Agents representing the Paramount Power. "The attitude of the Paramount Power was overbearing and dominating, reminding the Princes, at every step, of their absolute dependence and subordination to the Government of India."

The process of the growth of British paramountcy had started during the viceroyalty of John Lawrence (1863-1869) and reached its culmination towards the end of Curzon's viceroyalty (1899-1905). The year 1905 has, therefore, been chosen as marking the close of our study. After 1905, with the growth of militant Indian nationalism, there was some relaxation in the restrictions imposed on the Princes, and they were gradually permitted to meet on a common platform which led to the formation of Chamber of Princes in 1921. Nevertheless, there was no substantial change in the nature of all-pervasive British paramountcy. The Report of the Indian States Committee submitted in February 1929 frankly admitted that the

Paramount Power had to take decisions and exercise the functions of 'paramountcy' beyond the terms of treaties for imperial purposes and further that "Paramountcy must remain Paramount." So the paramountcy remained paramount in respect of Jaipur and numerous other States.

APPENDICES

Appendix-I

Treaty of 1818

TREATY between the HONOURABLE ENGLISH EAST INDIA COMPANY AND MAHARAJAH SEWAEE JUGGUT SING BAHADOOR, RAJAH of JEYPORE, concluded by MR. CHARLES THEOPHILUS METCALFE, on the part of the HONOURABLE COMPANY, in virtue of full powers granted by HIS EXCELLENCY THE MOST NOBLE THE MARQUIS of HASTINGS, K.G., GOVERNOR-GENERAL, &c., &c., and by THAKOOR RAWUL BYREE SAUL NATTAWUT on the part of RAJ RAJINDER SREE MAHARAJ DHEERAJ SEWAEE JUGGUT SING BAHADOOR, according to full powers given by the RAJAH, — 1818.

ARTICLE 1.

There shall be perpetual friendship, alliance, and unity of interest between the Honourable Company and Maharajah Juggut Sing and his heirs and successors, and the friends and enemies of one party shall be the friends and enemies of both parties.

ARTICLE 2.

The British Government engages to protect the territory of Jeypore and to expel the enemies of that principality.

Article 3.

Maharajah Sewaee Juggut Sing and his heirs and successors will act in subordinate co-operation with the British Government and acknowledge its supremacy; and will not have any connection with other Chiefs and States.

Article 4.

The Maharajah and his heirs and successors will not enter into negotiation with any Chief or State without the knowledge and sanction of the British Government; but the usual amicable correspondence with friends and relations shall continue.

Article 5.

The Maharajah and his heirs and successors will not commit aggressions on any one. If it happen that any dispute arise with any one, it shall be submitted to the arbitration and award of the British Government.

Article 6.

Tribute shall be paid in perpetuity by the principality of Jeypore to the British Government through the treasury of Delhi, according to the following detail :—

First year from the date of this Treaty, in consideration of the devastation which has prevailed for years in the Jeypore country, tribute excused. Second year, four lakhs of Delhi Rupees. Third year, five lakhs. Fourth year, six lakhs. Fifth year, seven lakhs. Sixth year, eight lakhs.

Afterwards eight lakhs of Delhi Rupees annually, until the revenues of the Principality exceed forty lakhs.

And when the Rajah's revenues exceed forty lakhs five-sixteenths of the excess shall be paid in addition to the eight lakhs above mentioned.

Article 7.

The principality of Jeypore shall furnish troops according to its means, at the requisition of the British Government.

Article 8.

The Maharajah and his heirs and successors shall remain absolute rulers of their territory and their dependents according to long established usage; and the British civil and criminal jurisdiction shall not be introduced into that principality.

Article 9.

Provided that the Maharajah evince a faithful attachment to the British Government, his prosperity and advantage shall be favourably considered and attended to.

Article 10.

This Treaty of ten Articles having been concluded and signed and sealed by Mr. Charles Theophilus Metcalfe and Thakoor Rawul Byree Saul Nattawut, the ratifications of the same by His Excellency the Most Noble the Governor-General and Raj Rajinder Sree Maharaj Dheeraj Sewaee Juggut Sing Bahadoor shall be mutually exchanged within one month from the present date.

Done at Delhi, this 2nd day of April, A.D. 1818.

C.T. Metcalfe.
Thakoor Rawul Byree
Saul Nattawut.
Hastings.

This Treaty was ratified by His Excellency the Governor-General, in Camp near Toolseypore, on the 15th of April 1818.

J. Adam,
Secretary to the Governor-General.

Source: Aitchison, C.U. (Compiler), *A Collection of Treaties, Engagements and Sanads, Vol. III*, Calcutta, 1932, pp. 68-69.

Appendix-II

Governors-General and Viceroys of India

Governors-General under the East India Company

Earl of Moira, Marquess of Hastings	...	1814-1823
Earl Amherst	...	1823-1828
Lord William Bentinck	...	1828-1835
Earl of Auckland	...	1835-1842
Earl of Ellenborough	...	1842-1844
Viscount Hardinge	...	1844-1848
Marquess of Dalhousie	...	1848-1856
Earl Canning	...	1856-1858

Viceroys and Governors-General under the Crown

Earl Canning	...	1858-1862
Earl of Elgin	...	1862-1863
Lord Lawrence	...	1863-1869
Earl of Mayo	...	1869-1872
Earl of Northbrook	...	1872-1876
Earl of Lytton	...	1876-1880
Marquess of Ripon	...	1880-1884
Marquess of Dufferin	...	1884-1888
Marquess of Lansdowne	...	1888-1894

Earl of Elgin	...	1894-1899
Marquess Curzon	...	1899-1904 and 1904-05

Source : Mersey, Viscount, *The Viceroys and Governors-General of India 1757-1947*, London, 1949.

Appendix-III

Agents to Governor-General, Rajputana States

Name		*Year of Assumption of Office*
Lieutenant-Colonel A. Lockett	...	1832
Major Nathaniel Alves	...	1834
Lieutenant-Colonel John Sutherland	...	1841
Colonel John Low	...	1848
Colonel George St. Pierre Lawrence	...	1852
Lieutenant-Colonel Henry Montgomery Lawrence	...	1853
Colonel George St. Pierre Lawrence	...	1857
Colonel E.K. Elliot	...	1864
Colonel W.F. Eden	...	1865
Colonel R.H. Keatinge	...	1867
Colonel J.C. Brooke (Offg.)	...	1871
Colonel L. Pelly	...	1874
A.C. Lyall	...	1874
Major C.K.M. Walter	...	1876
Colonel E. Bradford	...	1878
Colonel C.K.M. Walter	...	1887
Colonel G.H. Trevor	...	1890
R.J. Crosthwaite	...	1895

A. Martindale	...	1898
E.G. Colvin	...	1905

Source : *Imperial Gazetteer of India, Vol. XXI*, Oxford, 1908, p. 142.

Appendix-IV

Letter from Political Agent, Jaipur to Agent to Governor-General, Rajputana

From
Captain W.F.Eden
Political Agent Jeypoor
To
Brigadier General G.St.P. Lawrence
Officiating Agent Governor General Rajpootana

Dated Jeypore 14 August 1857

Sir,

I have had the honor to receive your letter No. 65A dated 8th instant forwarding copy of a letter from your Assistant Captain Hardcastle of the 3rd instant, upon which you invite me to make such remarks, as I may desire to offer.

2. I had an interview with the Maharajah this morning simply for the purpose of speaking to him on the points embraced in Captain Hardcastle's report.
3. I find His Highness perfectly indifferent to the report itself, as he is honestly conscious of having done his best, with the means and materials at his disposal, to aid and co-operate with our Government. The

capacity and quality of his troops are not matter for discussion.

4. I will take Captain Hardcastle's report as nearly as possible in the course it is written. His application to the Pundit Sheodeen, I conceive to have been received in a most proper spirit and further conceive Captin Hardcastle's urgent demand on the Durbar to supply troops, literally beyond its means, to have been inopportune and indiscreet, the more manifestly, so, as he knew the Maharajah had, sent little short of all his available Troops with me on service towards Delhi.
5. Captain Hardcastle's laudable desire to do good service, or to distinguish himself in exterminating the mutinous Regiment from Neemuch must, I apprehend, have rendered him totally regardless of the efficiency of the means about to be placed at his disposal for that purpose; the disappointment to which he was subjected had doubtless led him to throw unusual, and I think, very unmerited culpability and censure, on the Jeypore Government. If the Jeypore Government had given him 5000 Nagas and 5000 Meenas and 2000 Horse, the result of his untoward and romantic expedition would have been precisely the same; so soon as I heard of his intention, however spirited, and commendable it appeared, I observed to His Honour the Lieutenant Governor of Agra, that it was not a difficult matter to foretell the result.
6. The display of lukewarmness referred to by Captain Hardcastle in his 3rd para; and reported to you demi-officially, the Maharaja cannot acknowledge to have been made, and I am disposed to agree with him. There was a display rather of foresight and prudence on His Highness part, which should for obvious reasons have been better understood and appreciated by Captain Hardcastle. The answer or refutation to this charge you have already before you, vide your

Khureeta to His Highness of the 16th June, written unhappily I think, upon your Assistant's demi-official communication, my letter No. 41 of 21st June to you, and lastly your letter in English of the 28th June of His Highness. It is manifest to me that had Captain Hardcastle reported the extent and nature of the Maharaja's co-operation already afforded, you would not have addressed His Highness in a tone, which not only offended him and his Court, but tended to discourage the entire Durbar in their efforts to aid our Government more than they had already done; nor would you I conclude have written a separate letter to the Minister, Thakoor Luchhman Singh, who is helpless to act without the orders of his Chief; I repeat, it is idle to suppose that the Durbar had the means at his disposal to give effective aid to Captain Hardcastle, while it was simply absurd in that Officer to have threatened the Pundit Sheodeen in the manner and words set forth by him.

7. Captain Hardcastle's expressed and, I believe, recorded sentiments have been ever unfavourable to the Government of Jeypore and disparaging to its troops, and if these were well grounded they should have kept him alive to the character and temper of both as received by him; when I come indeed to consider the whole affair, I am really better disposed to commend, rather than to censure, the reported dilatory proceedings of the Durbar in giving the few extra troops they could command at the moment of Captain Hardcastle's hasty requisition; it would appear as if they foresaw, what Captain Hardcastle in his blind zeal, would not or could not comprehend, a defeat of the levies by the mutineers would assuredly have spread a panic throughout Jeypore and caused irremediable mischief and disorganization, and possibly been productive of most disastrous consequences; and that a defeat would have followed a collision, no one in his senses will

deny. Your own more matured experience must reveal to you the utter inability of taking the Troops of any native State to bear the brunt of a collision with disciplined Forces.

8. In his 4th paragraph Captain Hardcastle assumes a knowledge of the resources, the means and appliances of the Jeypore Government, which he does not possess. I contend, that the Jeypore Government had most promptly met our demand for troops and co-operation by sending with me a force of some 6 or 7000 men, the best they had, and I cannot but view Captain Hardcastle's proceedings and the threat of the vengeance of our Government held out to the Maharajah as very impolitic and ill-timed.

9. I have, of course, called upon the Pundit both in private and in the presence of the Maharajah for some explanation in regard to the "impertinence" complained of by Captain Hardcastle : the Pundit most respectfully denies the charge, tho' he may have expressed himself with some display of earnestness and warmth, and there is little to be surprised at, if he did so; he observes that, Captain Hardcastle at once and distinctly stated (I use the Pundit's own words) "that the British Government was in no way satisfied with the Jeypore Government for their not being forward in giving assistance, & ca. To this, the Pundit explained the nature and extent of the aid his master had already so promptly afforded to the British Government, observing that if in spite of all His Highness' efforts to meet our wishes, the paramount power should be still displeased, it rested with that power to do whatsoever it might think fit with this principality and ascertaining that Maharajah had been really or in any way insincere or slow to co-operate with us.

10. I can perceive nothing foolish, nothing intemperate or impertinent in such a remark; but rather a plain and simple statement with which I apprehend

Captain Hardcastle should have been satisfied; the Pundit's so called excuse was a palpable truth, and as such well worthy of consideration, at a time too, when such intense excitement was prevailing everywhere : in no place more so perhaps than in Jeypore itself.

11. The Maharajah conceived and very properly, that tranquillity within his own Territories, and more especially peace and good order at his own capital should be maintained; to ensure the latter, there were, His Highness informs me, when Captain Hardcastle arrived here, some 1500 Nagas and 700 sepoys, there were also a few Thakoors with their followers; all who had been summoned had not arrived, considerable apprehension existed that the Mahomedan population, (and in the mind of the Maharajah this was considerably increased by some unpleasant facts that had come to his knowledge in regard to the fidelity of one of the highest and influential Sirdars at his Court) many of whom came from Delhi and have their relations there, would take an early and ready occasion to create disturbance and incite other to join them with a view to plunder the city.
12. In no place, for manifest reasons, would such an event have caused less surprise I think, and in my humble opinion it speaks well for this Court, that no such melee has yet occurred, I quite concur in the remark by His Highness and by the Pundit, that it would not have been a wise measure to denude this city so much of Troops brought together for its protection; while against if the inconsiderable force placed at Captain Hardcastle's disposal had been induced by some unforeseen or unexpected miracle to meet the mutineers, their certain defeat would assuredly have led to very serious and bad results, while the event would have been eagerly seized by the disaffected in the city to carry out their own vile plans and intentions, rumours of which were rife and enough.

13. With regard to the reported worthlessness of the force sent with me, the Pundit begs respectfully to observe, that he simply stated, (what I myself knew well) that perfect reliance could not be placed in the men, I will give you his own words "I did say to Captain Hardcastle, that the Troops of the Native States are unable to withstand against the disciplined Troops of the English, and a man of ordinary understanding will testify the truth of this assertion, more so at this critical time when Musselmen, who compose a larger portion of the Army will show sympathy for the King of Delhi."
14. Referring to the 5th, 6th, 9th and 10th paras: of your Assistant's letter, I would simply refer to the Abstract translations marked A and B of papers I have received from the Durbar in explanation.
15. It is monstrous to expect the same rapidity of action from Durbar Troops, as we would expect from our own; the small contingent given to Captain Hardcastle was composed nearly entirely of footmen, of the most Irregular description, with Guns, who could not possibly keep up with Horse men and it is notorious, that however great their numerical superiority, they will not advance without their Guns.
16. The 7th and 8th paras : refer to the Jodhpore Troops. Captain Hardcastle is not surprised, he says, with their indifferent, and questionable conduct, which ended, though he does not mention it, with a large number of them joining the Mutineers. The display of regard for the honour of their King, is very commendable, but the last few lines from the 8th para: "they were naturally etc.", are thus peculiarly applicable to the Jeypore Troops.
17. The impertinence Captain Hardcastle refers to in the first portion of the 9th para: is in no wise brought under proof and from the fact of his allowing that on hearing a man call out, *"Oh Oont Wallah"* he took it for granted that he must be the *"Oont Wallah"* in

question manifestly shews there was a predisposition to construe every word or look into a display of hostility or aversion to himself personally, conclusions not borne out even by his own statement. The conclusions, he comes to at the end of his 10th para cannot with justice be entertained or admitted, I take on myself to point out a palpable error, and a very mischievous one in such a report, "When the Nusseerabad mutineers passed this", Captain Hardcastle says "thousands of Troops and the principal Nobles of the land were assembled" this is simply a myth, they had not all been summoned ever or but very recently and had not arrived.

18. The statement of the Government *Chupprassee* as set forth in the 9th para: must be taken at its value, I have no complaint against Bugroo from Lieutenant Walter; I now learn for the first time from Captain Hardcastle's report that "Jeypore has long been distinguished for her inhospitality – and incivilities to travellers". I have been barely ten months at this Court, and I can bear witness to the contrary, since my incumbency at least, and you I apprehend, only know by report what is so indelicately put forth by Captain Hardcastle as a fact; Regiments have passed through and officers with their families and many other Travellers and I have only one complaint of a trifling nature, such as that about a cup of milk, against Doodoo, and a report from the officer Commanding the 15th Regiment N.I. that no supplies were ready at Moakhunpoore, the stage between Bugroo and Doodoo belonging to the Bichone Thakoor.

19. What Captain Hardcastle states as to his own discomforts at Bugroo, shall be closely inquired into.

20. It is emphatically denied by the Durbar authorities that the mutineers had Jeypore officials attached to them during their transit through the Territory, and I myself believe there were none; Captain Hardcastle

must have dreamt it or he would have stated the matter more clearly.

21. There would seem to have been no virtual defection of the Jeypore Force with Captain Hardcastle, it seems to me that he did not understand them, and very unreasonably expected a great deal more than they were either able, or perhaps under his orders, disposed to do; the ability of Captain Hardcastle to destroy the rebels never existed and, therefore, could not have been thwarted or opposed. Captain Hardcastle has displayed considerable courage and zeal, but I fear without much judgement. I look on the result of his expedition as rather a happy incident to himself personally, and an event happier still to the interest of Jeypore, and Rajpootana generally.

22. In the course of conversation with the Maharaja, I observed, that his mind had been not a little disturbed by the letter you had been pleased to write to his minister, Thakoor Luchhman Singh. You may possibly have written it on some demi-official report of your Assistant Captain Hardcastle, as you wrote a *Khureeta* on the same day to the Maharaja, which I have referred to in the 6th para, of this letter, and you will, I trust pardon my presumption. If I observe, that the seeming intention of that letter was calculated only to produce considerable dissatisfaction, if not positive mischief; indeed I fear it has in no inconsiderable measure done so; the letter was an invitation to the Thakoor, as a *Sirdar* of the State, to do what he could only undertake by the orders of his chief, while at the same time it might be (as it has been by the King and others) construed as implying a determination on your part in the name of the British Government to confer a portion of the Jeypore Territory upon the Thakoor as a reward for services expected of him, further more it has been construed as implying or conveying a suspicion of the integrity or fidelity of the King himself.

23. I conclude I was right in assuring His Highness that the letter could not possibly be intended to convey such imputation. Indeed that I had only to refer him to your letter in English addressed to him on the 28th June last; whatever the impressions were or may still exist on this point, I have thought it right to mention it to you.
24. I would not that, I should be considered as making myself the champion of this Durbar. I deem it simply an act of public duty I owe to my Government, to myself and to this Court to record at this time, opinions based on a fair knowledge of the young king, of his nobles, his ministers and subjects; of the Army and of its strength, its capabilities, its temper and its disposition to act under any and various circumstances. There is much in the condition of this principality to be deplored though the Maharajah displays a strong and eager desire to amend its errors, the faults however are not I apprehend with the present system obtaining, but with the administration of previous years which forced the system on this Government.
25. My own personal experience leads me to record without hesitation that the young Prince has really done his utmost, with a due regard to his own interests, to co-operate with us at this present crisis; his efforts have not met with that success we could hope for, the reason of this is manifest, and may resolve itself into a question (on which our future interest may be allowed in some degree to depend) which should engage the intervention too, not only as regards Jeypore, but many native states in India. In truth there never was a time so favourable in all its conditions for turning over a new leaf, so to speak, in the annals of an old community.

I have & ca:
Sd/- W.F. Eden
Political Agent Jeypore.

Jeypore Political Agency Office
14th August 1857.

True Copy
Asstt. Agent Governor General

Source: Foreign Department, Political (Supplementary) Cons. 30 December 1859, No. 177 (NAI); Vashishtha, V.K., *1857 Revolt in the Princely State of Jaipur*, Jodhpur, 2008, Appendix-III, pp. 91-98.

Appendix-V

List of Jaipur State Post Offices in the year 1906

No.	*Mail Lines*	*Post Offices*	*Remarks*
1.	Jaipur-S. Madhopur	S. Madhopur	
2.		Bhagwatgarh	
3.		Kherni	
4.		Malarna Chorh	
5.		Mandauri	
6.		Lalsoth	
7.		Ramgarh	
8.		Lawan	
9.		Khandar	
10.		Bonli	
11.		Malarna Dungar	
12.		Lemali	
13.		Moran	
14.		Bamanwas	
15.		Gangapur	
16.		Wazirpur	
17.		Tunga	
18.		Jathwara	1 Government Post Office
19.		Bassai	Ditto...
20.	Rewajena-Hindaun	Rewanjena	
21.		S. Madhopur Railway Station	

22.		Banas	
23.		Jatwara	
24.		Gangapur	
25.		UJai	
26.	Jaipur-Hindaun	Hindaun	1 Government Post Office
27.		Walghat	
28.		Toda-Bhino	
29.		Manpur	
30.		Secundra	
31.	Jaipur-Hindaun	Bandikui	1 Government Post Office
32.		Ratanzila	
33.		Ghosla	
34.		Mohwa	1 Government Post Office
35.		Sikrai	
36.		Gijgarh	
37.		Baswa	1 Government Post Office
38.		Guda Katta	
39.		Kala Khoh	
40.		Babai (Barhyal)	
41.		Dausa	1 Government Post Office
42.		Sainthal	
43.	Jaipur-Newai-Uniara	Sheodaspur	
44.		Do. Railway Station	
45.		Chaksu	
46.		Do. Railway Station	
47.		Newai	
48.		Do. Railway Station	
49.		Simar	
50.		Isarda	
51.		Baneta	
52.		Jhilaya	
53.		Uniara	
54.	Jaipur-Sambhar	Asalpura	1 Government Post Office
55.		Kalak	
56.		Thalera	1 Government Post Office
57.		Naraina	Ditto
58.		Dadoo	
59.		Sambhar	1 Government Post Office
60.		Kishengarh	Ditto
61.		Lasol	Ditto

No.	*Mail Lines*	*Post Offices*	*Remarks*
62.	Jaipur-Sambhar	Jobner	
63.	Jaipur-Malpura	Sangener	1 Government Post Office
64.		Renwal	
65.		Madhorajpura	
66.		Phagu	
67.		Malpura	
68.		Toda-Raisingh	
69.		Churu	
70.		Mozamabad	
71.		Nasrida	
72.		Dooni	
73.		Punwar	
74.		Lawa	
75.	Jaipur-Torawati	Amber	
76.		Jamuna-Ramgarh	
77.		Manoharpur	
78.		Shahpura	
79.		Amarsar	
80.		Ajitgarh	
81.		Thoi	1 Government Post Offie
82.		Kanwat	Ditto
83.		Nim-ka-thana	Ditto
84.		Dabla	(Dabla) 1 Government
85.		Patan	
86.		Jelo	
87.		Khetri	1 Government Post Office
88.	Jaipur-Torwati	Peragpura	
89.		Bairath	
90.		Kotputli	1 Government Post Office
91.	Jaipur-Shekhawati	Babai	
92.		Chomoo	
93.		Khajroli	
94.		Gobindgarh	
95.	Jaipur-Shekhawati	Hasterah	
96.		Badhal	1 Government Post Office
97.		Sri Madhopur	Ditto
98.		Khandela	
99.		Udeypurwati	
100.		Nawalgar	1 Government Post Office
101.		Jhonjhunu	Ditto
102.		Gudagari	Ditto, newly opened

103.		Sikar	Ditto
104.		Ringus	Ditto
105.		Malsisar	
106.		Islampur	
107.		Chirawa	1 Government Post Office
108.		Mandawa	Ditto
109.		Singhana	Ditto
110.		Dehmi	
111.	Jaipur-Sambhar	Jobner (experimental	
112.	Head Office	Jaipur City	2 Government Post Offices

Source: Jaipur Agency (Residency), Part I, Post and Telegraph, File No. 74/1906, pp. 174-76.

Appendix-VI

Education in Jaipur State 1905-06

Babu Sangiban Ganguli continued to be Director of Public Instruction for the period under review.

It was apprehended that the distress of 1905 would have effected educational statistics, but this has not been the case.

For the period ending 31st August 1906 there were 882 schools (public and indigenous) in Jaipur, with 25,733 scholars on the rolls. The class of institutions are as follows :

(1)	Public Schools	3
(2)	Secondary " (State and private)	30
	Anglo Vernacular and Vernacular —	
(3)	Primary Schools (State and private) —	
	For boys	126
	For girls	10
	Technical Schools —	
	Advanced	93
	Elementary	615
	Total ...	882

Of the pupils, the Hindu Scholars number	...	19,921
Mussalman "	...	3,318
Jains "	...	2,120
Christians "	...	374
Total	...	25,733

The Jaipur College has maintained its high reputation in the University and other examinations as will be seen from the list below :—

Allahabad University Examination —

	No. of Candidates who went up	*Passed*
M.A.	2	1
B.A.	9	8
Intermediate	17	11
Entrance	30	25
Jaipur Sanscrit Examinations —		
Acharya	3	3
Sastu	6	5
Upadhyay	17	5
Pravisika	12	4
Panjab University Examinations —		
Munshi Fazil	5	4
Munshi Alam	10	7
Munshi	10	8
Other Examinations —		
Vernacular Fusil	33	20
Upper Primary	138	86
Lower Primary	397	221

On the results of the Entrance examination of the Allahabad University, the Pioneer in its issue of the 5th July of 1905 made the following appreciative comment. "The last issue of the United Provinces Gazette contains the results of the Entrance examination of the Allahabad University held in April last. The most remarkable feature of the results is the success attained by the Maharaja's College at Jaipur."

The State expenditure on education for the past year was Rs. 91,995

Local cess	1,584
Thikanas	13,745
Other sources	43,386
	Total... Rs. 1,50,710

The Schools in the districts have been regularly inspected during the period under report.

Only one boy, Bishen Singh of Bissau, was sent by the Darbar to the Mayo College at Ajmer during the period under report.

SCHOOL OF ARTS

The School of Arts has maintained its reputation. There were 88 pupils under training during the period under report who have received instructions in Drawing, Engraving, Pottery, Carpentry and other different handicrafts.

There are 14 teachers, and a sum of Rs. 3,812-6-6 was awarded in Scholarships to the pupils.

Source: Administration Report of Jaipur State for the period from 1 April 1905 to 31 August 1906, pp. 10-11.

Glossary

Amil	:	Collector of land revenue in a *pargana.*
Amir-ul-Umra	:	Premier noble; title of a noble of high order.
Ashvamedha yajna	:	A horse-sacrifice ceremony generally performed by great ancient Hindu kings.
Bajra	:	Spiked millet.
Bakhshi	:	A paymaster of troops; a military commander.
Bania	:	A Hindu trader or shopkeeper.
Bara kotri	:	Twelve chambers of the Kachha-waha house.
Barani	:	An arid tract dependent on rain; unirrigated.
Batai	:	Division of produce.
Bhang	:	Hemp.
Bhatta	:	An allowance.
Bhej	:	Cash rates per bigha.
Bhet	:	Religious offering to Raj temples.
Bhum	:	Cess taken by *Bhumia* on cultivator's

		share of produce, generally ¼th of seer.
Bhumia	:	Originally the guardian of a village.
Biswa	:	Sub-division of a bigha; unit of land.
Biswedar	:	Holder of a *biswedari* tenure.
Biswedari	:	A type of land tenure.
Bohra	:	A money-lender.
Chahi (land)	:	Land irrigated from well.
Chakbundi	:	Consolidation of land-holdings.
Chaprasi	:	A peon.
Chaudhri	:	A chief person of village usually rich and influential.
Chaukidar	:	A watchman.
Chauth	:	Maratha cess taken in lieu of providing protection generally amounting to ¼th of the revenue.
Chelliginti	:	A cess levied on occupant of grazing animals.
Choongi	:	Toll (tax).
Dak/Dak-khana	:	Post/Post-office
Dakoiti	:	Robbery by a gang.
Dal batai	:	Division by conjectural estimates of the ears of corn gathered in heaps.
Darbar	:	Royal court; state government; audience hall.
Darogha	:	A superintendent; police officer above the rank of *thanadar*.
Deori	:	An entrance to a house or building.
Dharmsala	:	Rest-house.
Dusehra	:	An Indian festival celebrated in commemoration of the victory of Lord Rama over the forces of Ravana by burning effigy of the latter.
Du-aspa-sih-aspa	:	Rank of a *mansabdar* with additional obligations.

Farman	:	Royal order.
Farzand	:	Son; a title.
Faujdar	:	A commander of troops; administrator of a *sarkar* under the Mughals.
Faujdari	:	Military and civil governorship of an area.
Gaddi	:	Royal seat or throne.
Ganja	:	Hemp
Gola	:	A slave boy.
Goli	:	A slave girl.
Gumashata	:	A collector of land revenue; agent of a *jagirdar*.
Guntabundi	:	Gathering of the corn and binding into sheaves after reaping.
Gurani	:	A female spiritual guide.
Halsera	:	Cash rates per plough.
Halqabandi (schools)	:	Circle or area schools.
Harkara	:	Messenger or representative of government.
Hundie	:	Payment draft; promissory note.
Inam	:	Gift or grant awarded for meritorious service.
Istumrardar	:	Holder of permanent tenure of land.
Jagir	:	An estate granted by the ruler to a noble in lieu of military service; assignment of land revenue for services rendered or to be rendered.
Jagirdar	:	Holder of a *jagir;* holder of any assignment of revenue.
Jammabundi	:	List of holdings cultivated by the owners or tenants.
Jamwa Mata	:	Name of a Hindu deity.
Jawar	:	A kind of millet.
Jhar Shahi	:	Jaipur coins bearing a *Jhar* or spray

		of six sprigs or branches.
Jeera	:	Chief spring or *rabi* crop.
Jhoopra	:	A cottage rate levied on artisans and others.
Kamdar	:	An administrative officer of the State/estate.
Kankut	:	Division of standing crops by appraisement.
Kanoongo	:	Revenue officer of sub-division of district.
Khalsa (land)	:	The land held or administered directly by government or the sovereign.
Kharif	:	Autumn produce/crops.
Kharita	:	A special letter generally sent in a silken bag.
Khillat	:	Robe of honour.
Khoj	:	Search
Khusra	:	Rough *Jammabundi* accounts.
Khuttuni	:	Rough *jummabundi* accounts.
Kunsari	:	A cess levied by the Raj as *nazarana.*
Kupperdwara	:	Private treasury of Jaipur king.
Kyfeeut	:	A special letter from a ruler or *Darbar.*
Lambardar	:	A village headman.
Lathies	:	Sticks.
Mahajan	:	A trader; money-lender.
Mahkma-khabar	:	A State Department under the Mughals.
Mamlaguzar	:	A land revenue official.
Mansabdar	:	An official in Mughal service; holder of a *mansab.*
Masha	:	A smaller unit of weight equivalent to 8 *ratis.*

Mohur	:	Gold currency of Jaipur State.
Motamid	:	A state official in diplomatic service.
Mukhtiar	:	An attorney; Chief Minister of a State.
Mukka	:	Chief autumn crop.
Mulba	:	A money cess levied on cultivators.
Mutka	:	An earthen pot.
Mutsudier	:	Land revenue officer sent from the *tahsil.*
Naib-Darogha	:	A deputy superintendent of police.
Naib-Nazim	:	Deputy or Assistant to *Nazim.*
Naib-Vakil	:	Deputy or Assistant to Vakil.
Nalbut	:	A cess levied by the Raj on fields irrigated by wells belonging to the State.
Nazar	:	An offering to a superior or a holy person; a tribute from a vassal.
Nazarana	:	Monetary present offered by a vassal or noble to the sovereign; succession fee.
Nazim	:	The governor of a province or *nizamat* (district).
Novisindas	:	Land revenue officer sent from the *tahsil.*
Nullah	:	A rivulet.
Ouduk	:	A rent-free religious grant made under a solemn oath.
Pae-kashts	:	Villagers taking up land in another village.
Panj-hazari	:	Rank of five thousand mansab.
Pao	:	One-fourth of a part.
Paona	:	One-fourth of a seer taken as cess by *Bhumia.*
Pargana	:	A small administrative land revenue

		unit; a tract of land consisting generally of fifty to hundred villages.
Patel	:	Headman of a village.
Patwari	:	A village revenue accountant and recorder of rights of land.
Peshcush	:	A present.
Poorbia (sepoys)	:	Sepoys from eastern belt (U.P., Bihar etc.).
Pothikhana	:	Library containing books.
Pucca bund	:	Permanent dam.
Pulla	:	Seed.
Punni	:	Grass.
Rabi	:	Spring produce/crops.
Rati	:	The smallest unit of weight
Reh	:	Gathering of the corn and binding into sheaves after reaping.
Rubakar	:	Official letter.
Ryotwari	:	A land revenue system making settlement with *ryots* or cultivators.
Sahukar	:	A banker; money-lender.
Sanad/Sunnud	:	A grant; official document; agreement.
Sardar	:	A chief; commander; noble.
Sati	:	Concremation of wife on the funeral pyre of her dead husband.
Seedha batai	:	Actual division by measuring the corn.
Shahna	:	An officer sent by *tahsildar* to make preliminary arrangement for *batai*.
Sowar	:	A horseman; rank of *mansabdar* denoting his cavalry.
Subahdar	:	Governor of a province
Tahsil	:	A small administrative unit.
Tahsildar	:	An officer in charge of a *tahsil*.

Takkavi	:	Loan given by the government to the cultivators for agricultural purposes.
Talao	:	A tank.
Taluka	:	An estate.
Talukadar	:	Holder of an estate.
Tankha	:	Salary; rent free grant made in lieu of pay.
Thagi	:	Robbery; the practice of strangling and robbing.
Thakur	:	A Rajput chief or noble.
Thanadar	:	An officer in charge of a police station or *thana*.
Thikana	:	An estate or headquarters of estate.
Thikanadar	:	Chief of a *thikana* or estate.
Tola	:	A unit of weight equivalent to 12 *mashas*.
Tupdar	:	A temporary employee to superintend the *batai* operations.
Vakil	:	An agent of the ruler or the prince; pleader; legal expert.
Vakil-i-Mutlaq	:	Tax Commissioner.
Watan	:	Country or heritage; hereditary possession.
Zamindar	:	A landlord; peasant proprietor.
Zamindari	:	A land revenue system making settlement with *zamindars* or landlords.
Zillah	:	A district.
Ziladar	:	A district officer.
Zenana (Apartment)	:	A lady; harem; female quarters in the royal palace.

Bibliography

PRIMARY SOURCES

(a) Proceedings (unpublished) of the Government of India, 1818-1905

(National Archives of India, New Delhi) under the following heads :

Foreign Department, Political Consultations.

Foreign Department, Secret Consultations.

Foreign Department Proceedings, Political, Political A, Political B, A-Political-I, A-Political-E.

Foreign Department Proceedings, Internal, Internal A, Internal B, Internal Deposit.

Foreign Department Proceedings, General, General A, General B, A-General-I.

Foreign Department Proceedings, Financial, Financial A, Financial B, A-Financial-I.

Foreign Department Proceedings, Revenue, Revenue A, Revenue B.

Foreign Department Proceedings, Judicial, Judicial A, Judicial B.

Foreign Department Proceedings, Military, Military A, Military B.

(b) Correspondence with Home Government (unpublished)

Despatches from the Government of India to the Secretary of State for India.

Despatches from the Secretary of State for India to the Government of India.

(c) Jaipur Agency/Residency Record, Part I (unpublished)

(National Archives of India, New Delhi)

The following relevant files have been consulted :

Sr. No. 105,	Currency,	File No. 4/1902-15
Sr. No. 109,	Boundary,	File No. 47/1871-74
Sr. No. 110,	"	File No. 1/1872
Sr. No. 111,	"	File No. 42/1874-76
Sr. No. 112,	"	File No. 45/1874
Sr. No. 113,	"	File No. 41/1876
Sr. No. 114,	"	File No. 45/1876-77
Sr. No. 115,	"	File No. 46/1876
Sr. No. 116,	"	File No. B-7/1/1876-84
Sr. No. 117,	"	File No. 413/B/8/1876
Sr. No. 118,	"	File No. 47/1876-77
Sr. No. 119,	"	File No. 48/1885
Sr. No. 119/E,	"	File No. 1/1884
Sr. No. 119/F,	"	File No. 2/1885
Sr. No. 119/G,	"	File No. 3/1885
Sr. No. 119/J,	"	File No. 12/1887
Sr. No. 119/K,	"	File No. 4/1887-90
Sr. No. 119/O,	"	File No. 5/1890
Sr. No. 121,	"	File No. 6/1894
Sr. No. 123,	"	File No. 7/1896
Sr. No. 124,	"	File No. 8/1896
Sr. No. 125,	"	File No. 1/1893
Sr. No. 126,	"	File No. 2/1897-1925
Sr. No. 127,	"	File No. 2/1902
Sr. No. 128,	"	File No. 11/1902
Sr. No. 134,	"	File No. 20/1869-72
Sr. No. 135,	"	File No. 21/1871-1929
Sr. No. 146,	Decoration,	File No. 27/1871
Sr. No. 153,	"	File No. I/61/1903-11
Sr. No. 154,	"	File No. I/75/1904

Sr. No. 165,	Extradition,	File No. 1/1867
Sr. No. 166,	"	File No. 2/1867-68
Sr. No. 167,	"	File No. 6/1874
Sr. No. 169,	"	File No. 16/1896
Sr. No. 170,	"	File No. 27/1898-1908
Sr. No. 171,	"	File No. 17/1901-06
Sr. No. 181,	"	File No. 587/1873-1913
Sr. No. 182,	"	File No. E/32/1882
Sr. No. 183,	"	File No. E/33/1884-1916
Sr. No. 184,	"	File No. 31/1891
Sr. No. 185,	"	File No. 280/1903
Sr. No. 206,	Indian States,	File No. 1/1866
Sr. No. 207,	"	File No. 6/1868
Sr. No. 214,	Judicial,	File No. 24/1877
Sr. No. 215,	"	File No. 10/1887
Sr. No. 217,	"	File No. 13/1891
Sr. No. 218,	"	File No. 17/1894
Sr. No. 220,	"	File No. 29/1902
Sr. No. 221,	Judicial,	File No. 32/1905
Sr. No. 229,	Jagirdars,	File No. 129/1868
Sr. No. 230,	"	File No. 2/1869
Sr. No. 231,	"	File No. 3/120/1870
Sr. No. 233,	"	File No. 8/1881
Sr. No. 234,	"	File No. 21/1882
Sr. No. 235,	"	File No. 23/1882
Sr. No. 236,	"	File No. 29/1884
Sr. No. 237,	"	File No. 418/30/1884-85
Sr. No. 241,	"	File No. 38/1886
Sr. No. 249,	"	File No. 60/1893
Sr. No. 258,	"	File No. 75/1898
Sr. No. 259,	"	File No. 76/1900
Sr. No. 266,	"	File No. 121/49/1904
Sr. No. 267,	"	File No. 122/149/1904
Sr. No. 272,	"	File No. 100/1905-1907
Sr. No. 273,	"	File No. 45/1906
Sr. No. 321,	Military,	File No. 1/1857-58
Sr. No. 326,	"	File No. 7/1876
Sr. No. 327,	Miscellaneous,	File No. 86/1876-96
Sr. No. 334,	"	File No. 72/1905
Sr. No. 341,	"	File No. 171/1864

Sr. No. 383,	Prisoners,	File No. 6/1904
Sr. No. 390,	Post and Telegraph,	File No. 12/1881-1923
Sr. No. 391,	"	File No. 15/1885
Sr. No. 392,	"	File No. 19/1887
Sr. No. 394,	"	File No. 38/1897
Sr. No. 396,	"	File No. 39/1898
Sr. No. 397,	"	File No. 40/1898
Sr. No. 398,	"	File No. 46/1899
Sr. No. 400,	"	File No. 35/1899
Sr. No. 401,	"	File No. 22/1900
Sr. No. 402,	"	File No. 52/1902
Sr. No. 403,	"	File No. 60/1904
Sr. No. 405,	"	File No. 70/1906
Sr. No. 406,	"	File No. 74/P/60/1906
Sr. No. 407,	"	File No. 78/1907
Sr. No. 409,	"	File No. 81/1908
Sr. No. 414,	"	File No. 108/1913
Sr. No. 451,	P.W.D.,	File No. 8/1874-82
Sr. No. 410,	Railway,	File No. 87/1909
Sr. No. 461,	"	File No. 1/1864-69
Sr. No. 462,	"	File No. 161/1864-73
Sr. No. 465,	Railway,	File No. 19/1873
Sr. No. 466,	"	File No. 5/1875
Sr. No. 468,	"	File No. 9/1875
Sr. No. 470,	"	File No. R/30/1879
Sr. No. 471,	"	File No. 3/1880
Sr. No. 473,	"	File No. 3/1883
Sr. No. 474,	"	File No. R/20/1884
Sr. No. 475,	"	File No. 10/1892
Sr. No. 476,	"	File No. 28/1892-94
Sr. No. 477,	"	File No. R/18/1895
Sr. No. 478,	"	File No. R/44/1896
Sr. No. 479,	"	File No. R/50/1896
Sr. No. 481,	"	File No. R/18/1898-1908
Sr. No. 482,	"	File No. R/64/1899
Sr. No. 484,	"	File No. 41/1903
Sr. No. 485,	"	File No. R/38/1903
Sr. No. 486,	"	File No. R/39/1903
Sr. No. 487,	"	File No. 5/1904-21

Sr. No. 552, Salt, File No. 1/1870-73
Sr. No. 554, Salt, File No. 4/1871
Sr. No. 555, " File No. 5/1871
Sr. No. 556, " File No. 6/1875
Sr. No. 557, " File No. 7/1876
Sr. No. 558, " File No. 8/1876
Sr. No. 559, " File No. 9/1877
Sr. No. 560, " File No. 10/1878
Sr. No. 561, " File No. 23/1878
Sr. No. 562, Salute, File No. 3/1879
Sr. No. 563, Salt, File No. 12/1879
Sr. No. 566, " File No. 4/1886
Sr. No. 572, " File No. 5/25/1901
Sr. No. 631, Shooting, File No. 1/1871
Sr. No. 637, Settlement, File No. 4/1893
Sr. No. 638, Shooting, File No. 5/14/1896
Sr. No. 650, Suttee, File No. 2/1869
Sr. No. 652, " File No. 4/1873
Sr. No. 653, " File No. 5/1877
Sr. No. 654, Suttee, File No. 6/1882
Sr. No. 655, State forces, File No. 54/1930
Sr. No. 659, " File No. 40/1931
Sr. No. 660, Tribute, File No. T/14/1867
Sr. No. 663, Treaties, File No. 1/1868
Sr. No. 664, " File No. 3/1869-70
Sr. No. 665, Treaties, File No. 4/1870-72
Sr. No. 666, " File No. 5/1886
Sr. No. 667, Titles, File No. 3/1870
Sr. No. 667, " File No. 2/1883
Sr. No. 672, Trees, File No. 4/1873
Sr. No. 685, Resident, File No. 3/1915

Besides the files enumerated above, the following files pertaining to 'Arms Act' have also been consulted : File No. 1/1878; File No. 4/1891; File No. 5/1895-1909; File No. 7/1905-1914.

(d) Private Papers of Viceroys/Secretary of State for India (unpublished)

(Microfilms, National Archives of India, New Delhi) :
Papers of John Lawrence, Viceroy, 1863-1869.

Papers of Lord (Earl of) Mayo, Viceroy, 1869-1872.
Papers of Lord Northbrook, Viceroy, 1872-1876.
Papers of Marquis (third) of Salisbury, Secretary of State, 1874-1878.
Papers of Lord (Marquis) of Lansdowne, Viceroy, 1888-1894.
Papers of Lord (Earl of) Elgin, Viceroy, 1894-1899.
Papers of Lord (Marquess) Curzon, Viceroy, 1899-1905.

(e) Published Reports and Records

Reports on the Political Administration of Rajputana States for the years from 1867-68 to 1904-05.
Annual Administration Report of the Jaipur State for the period from Ist April 1905 to the 31st August 1906.
(The above-mentioned Reports are available at Central Library, University of Rajasthan, Jaipur, Abu Collection).
Jaipur State Public Works Department Reports for the years from 1869 to 1905.
(available at Maharaja Sawai Man Singh II Museum and Library, Jaipur).
Reports on Public Instruction in Jaipur State for the relevant years.
Reports on the Administration of Inland Customs for the relevant years.
Final Report of Famine Relief Operation in Rajasthan during 1899-1900.
Jaipur Census Reports for the years 1881, 1891 and 1901.
(The afore-mentioned Reports are available at Rajasthan State Archives, Bikaner).
Jaipur Records (Rajasthan State Archives, Bikaner) under the heads: Revenue, P.W.D., General.

(f) Published Government Gazettes

Imperial Gazetteer of India, 25 Vols., London, 1908-1909.
Of these Vols. III, IV, XIII, XXI have been especially made use of in the present study.
Imperial Gazetteer of India, Provincial Series, Rajasthan, Calcutta, 1908.

(g) Collected/Selected Documents and Compilation Works

Aitchison, C.U. (Compiler), *A Collection of Treaties, Engagements and Sanads relating to India and Neighbouring Countries, 14 Vols., Calcutta, 1929-32.*

Of these Vol. III published from Calcutta in 1932 is the most relevant for the present study.

Banerjee, A.C. (Compiler), *Indian Constitutional Documents,* Vols. I, II and III, Calcutta, 1948, 1961.

Beatson, Stuart (Compiler), *A History of the Imperial Service Troops of Native States,* Calcutta, 1903.

Ilbert, Sir Courtney, *The Government of India : Being a Digest of the Statute Law Relating Thereto,* London, 1898.

Kaye, John William, *Selections from the Papers of Lord Metcalfe,* London, 1845.

Martin, Montgomery (ed.), *The Despatches, Minutes and Correspondence of Marquess Wellesley during his administration in India,* 5 Vols., London, 1836, 1837.

Owen, Sidney J., *A Selection from the Despatches, Treaties and Other Papers of the Marquess Wellesley during his Government of India.*

The Army in India and its Evolution, Government of India publication, Calcutta, 1924.

Tupper, C.L. (Compiler), *Indian Political Practice,* 3 Vols., Calcutta, 1895.

(h) Speeches of Viceroys (published)

Speeches by the Marquess of Dufferin and Ava, Calcutta, 1889.

Speeches by the Marquess of Lansdowne, Vol. II, Calcutta, 1895.

Speeches of Lord Curzon about Indian States and Princes in Raleigh, Thomas (ed.), *Lord Curzon in India : Being a Selection from his Speeches as Viceroy and Governor-General of India,* 2 Vols., London, 1906.

(i) Records (relevant) of Chamber of Princes (published)

Proceedings of the Meetings of the Chamber of Princes (Narendra Mandal), 1921-1946, New Delhi.

Proceedings of the Meetings of the Standing Committee of the Chamber of Princes, 1921-1945.

The British Crown and the Indian States : An Outline Sketch presented to the Indian States Committee on behalf of the Standing Committee of the Chamber of Princes, London, 1929.

The Indian Princes and the Paramount Power — Grievances and Inequitable Adjustments of Imperial Burdens, 4 Vols., London, n.d. (Punjab State Archives, Patiala).

(j) Contemporary Newspaper Reports (published)

Selections from the Vernacular Newspapers published (Ajmer-Merwara and Rajputana) for the years 1895 and 1896

Reports on Native Newspapers of the Punjab and North-Western Provinces for the year 1864-1905.
(available in the Library of National Archives of India, New Delhi).

SECONDARY SOURCES

(a) Books

Adams, A.D., *The Western Rajput States*, London, 1899.

Agarwal, S.C., *Sambhar Lake Salt Sources*, Delhi, 1951.

Aitchison, Charles, *Lord Lawrence*, Oxford, 1894.

Arora, A.C., *British Policy towards the Punjab States, 1858-1905*, Jalandhar, 1982.

Arora, Anju, *The Princely States : British Paramountcy and Internal Administration, 1858-1948 : A Case Study of the Kapurthala State*, New Delhi, 2001.

Ali, Refaqat, *The Kachhawas under Akbar and Jahangir*, New Delhi, 1976.

Ashton, S.R., *British Policy towards the Indian States, 1905-1939*, New Delhi, 1985.

Asopa, J.N. (ed.), *Cultural Heritage of Jaipur*, Jodhpur, 1982.

Banerjee, A.C., *The Rajput States and the East India Company*, Calcutta, 1951.

Batra, H.C., *The Relations of Jaipur State with East India Company, 1803-1858*, Delhi, 1958.

Bell, Evans, *The Annexation of the Punjab and the Maharaja Duleep Singh*, London, 1882.

Bhatia, B.M., *Famines in India*, Bombay, 1963.

Bhargava, V.S., *Rise of the Kachhawas in Dhundhar (Jaipur) from the earliest times to the death of Sawai Jai Singh (1743 AD)*, Ajmer, 1979.

Bhatnagar, V.S., *Life and Times of Sawai Jai Singh 1688-1743*, Second Edition, Delhi, 2002.

Bhattacharyya, Sukumar, *Rajput States and the East India Company from the close of 18th century to 1820*, New Delhi, 1972.

Brooke, J.C., *Political History of the State of Jaipur*, Calcutta, 1868.

Boulger, D.C., *Lord William Bentinck*, Oxford, 1892.

Chavda, V.K., *Gaekwads and the British — A Study of their Problems, 1875-1920*, Delhi, n.d.

Copland, Ian, *The Princes of India in the Endgame of Empire, 1917-1947*, Cambridge, 1997.

Coupland, R., *Indian Problem, 1833-1935*, London, 1943.

Crewe, Quentin, *The Last Maharaja : A Biography of Sawai Man Singh II of Jaipur*, London, 1985.

Dilks, David, *Curzon in India*, 2 Vols., London, 1969.

Dodwell, H.H., *The Cambridge History of India Vol. VI*, Cambridge, 1932.

Duff, James Grant, *A History of the Marhattas, Vol. III*, Calcutta, 1918.

Erskine, K.D., *Western Rajputana States Residency and the Bikaner Agency*, Allahabad, 1909.

Forbes, Rosita, *India of the Princes*, London, 1939.

Franklin William, *Military Memoirs of Mr. George Thomas*, London, 1805.

Fraser, Lovat, *India under Curzon and After*, London, 1911.

Gahlot, J.S., *History of Rajputana*, Reprint Jodhpur, 1980.

Gandhi, M.K., *Indian States Problem*, Ahmedabad, 1941.

Gopal, Sarvapalli, *British Policy in India, 1858-1905*, Cambridge, 1965.

Griffin, Lepel H., *The Rajas of the Punjab*, Reprint Patiala, 1970.

H.H., The Maharaja of Jaipur, *A History of the Indian State Forces*, Bombay, 1967.

Hendley, Thomas Holbein, *A Medico-Topographical Account of Jeypore*, Calcutta, 1895.

Hooja, Rima, *A History of Rajasthan*, New Delhi, 2006.

Hunter, W.W., *Life of Earl of Mayo, Vol. I*, London, 1875.

Jain, M.S., *Rajasthan through the Ages (A Comprehensive History of Rajasthan from 1761-1949 AD), Vol. III*, Bikaner, 1996.

Jeffrey, Robin (ed.), *People, Princes and Paramount Power : Society and Politics in the Indian Princely States*, Delhi, 1978.

Khadgawat, Nathu Ram, *Rajasthan's Role in the Struggle of 1857*, Jaipur, 1957.

Kapil, F.K., *Rajputana States, 1817-1950*, Jodhpur, 1999.

Kasturi, Malvika, *Embattled identities : Rajput lineages and the Colonial State in Nineteenth-Century North India*, Delhi, 2002.

Kaye, John William, *The Life and Correspondence of Major-General*

Sir John Malcolm, Vol. I, London, 1856.

———, *The Life and Correspondence of Charles Lord Metcalfe*, Vol. I, London, 1858.

———, *A History of the Sepoy War in India, 1857-58*, 3 Vols., London, 1870-76.

Keith, A.B. (ed.), *Speeches and Documents on Indian Policy, 1750-1921, Vol. I*, London, 1922.

Khan, Shaukat Ali, *History and Historians of Rajasthan*, Delhi, 1981.

Lee-Warner, William, *The Protected Princes of India*, London, 1894.

———, *The Native States of India*, London, 1910.

Lyall, Alfred, *Ruling Princes, Chiefs and Leading Personages in Rajputana and Ajmer*, Calcutta, 1931.

Maclagan, Michael, *Clemency Canning*, London, 1962.

Majumdar, A.K., *Chaulukyas of Gujarat : a survey of the history and culture of Gujarat from the middle of the 10th to the end of 13th century*, Bombay, 1956.

Majumdar, R.C. and others (ed.), *The History and Culture of the Indian People : British Paramountcy and Indian Renaissance*, Vol. IX, Bombay, 1963.

Majumdar, R.C., *The Sepoy Mutiny and the Revolt of 1857*, Second Edition, Calcutta, 1963.

Malcolm, Sir John, *Political History of India, 1784-1803*, Vol. I, London, 1826.

———, *Political Histoy of India, 1784-1923*, Vol. II, Reprint New Delhi, 1970.

Malleson, G.B., *A Historical Sketch of the Native States of India*, London, 1875.

Marchioness of Bath (ed.), *The Private Journal of Marquess of Hastings*, 2 Vols., London, 1858.

Mathur, R.M., *Rajput States and the East India Company*, Delhi, 1979.

Mehrotra, S.R., *The Emergence of the Indian National Congress*, New Delhi, 1971.

Mehta, Asoka, *The Great Rebellion*, Bombay, 1946.

Mehta, M.S., *Lord Hastings and the Indian States*, Bombay, 1930.

Menon, V.P., *The Story of the Integration of the Indian States*, Calcutta, 1956.

Mill, James, *History of British India, Vol. VI*, London, 1848.

Muir, Ramsay, *The Making of British India, 1756-1858*, Manchester, 1915.

Neogy, A.K., *The Paramount Power and the Princely States of India, 1858-81*, Calcutta, 1979.

Pandey, A.B., *Later Medieval India, 1526-1761 AD*, Allahabad, 1967.

Panikkar, K.M., *An Introduction to the Study of the Relations of Indian States with the Government of India*, London, 1927.

———, *Indian States and the Government of India*, London, 1932.

———, *The Indian Princes in Council*, London, 1936.

Panikkar, K.N., *British Diplomacy in North India : A Study of the Delhi Residency 1803-1857*, New Delhi, 1968.

———, (ed.), *John Malcolm : The Political History of India, 1784-1823*, Vol. II, New Delhi, 1970.

Phadnis Urmila, *Towards the Integration of Indian States, 1919-1947*, Bombay, 1968.

Prasad, Amba, *Indian Railways*, Bombay, 1960.

Prasad, Beni, *History of Jahangir*, Allahabad, 1940.

Prasad, Bisheshwar, *Bondage and Freedom, 1858-1947, Vol. II*, Delhi, 1979.

Prasad, R.N., *Raja Man Singh of Amber*, Calcutta, 1966.

Prasad, Sri Nandan, *Paramountcy under Dalhousie*, Delhi, 1964.

Prinsep, H.T., *History of Political and Military Transactions in India during the Administration of the Marquess of Hastings, 1813-1823*, 2 Vols., London, 1825.

Raikes, Charles, *Notes on the Revolt in the North-Western Provinces of India*, London, 1858.

Ramusuck, Barbara, N., *The Princes of India in the Twilight of Empire : Dissolution of a Patron-Client System, 1914-1939*, Columbus, Ohio, 1978.

Ray, Mihir Kumar, *Princely States and the Paramount Power, 1858-1876*, New Delhi, 1981.

Roberts, P.E., *History of British India*, Reprint London, 1958.

———, *India under Wellesley*, Reprint Gorakhpur, 1961.

Ronaldshay, *The Life of Lord Curzon*, New York, 1928.

Ross-of-Bladensburg, *The Marquess of Hastings (Rulers of India), Vol. III*, Oxford, 1893.

Roy, Ashim Kumar, *History of the Jaipur City*, New Delhi, 1978.

Rudolph Sussane Hoeber and Lloyd I. Rudolph, *Essays on Rajputana: Reflections on History, Culture and Administration*, New Delhi, 1984.

Saksena, B.P., *History of Shah Jahan of Dihli*, Allahabad, 1962.

Sarkar, Jadunath, *A History of Jaipur, c.1503-1938* (revised and edited

by Raghubir Sinh), Reprint New Delhi, 1994.
Sastry, K.R.R., *Indian States*, Allahabad, 1941.
Savarkar, V.D., *The Indian War of Independence 1857* (8th edition), New Delhi, 1970.
Saxena, K.S., *Political Movements and Awakening in Rajasthan, 1857-1947*, New Delhi, 1971.
Saxena, Malti, *Impact of the British Sovereignty on the Economic Conditions of Rajasthan*, Delhi, n.d.
Sharma, B.K., *Peasant Movements in Rajasthan, 1920-1949*, Jaipur, 1990.
Sharma, Dashratha, *Early Chauhan Dynasties*, Delhi, 1959.
Sharma, G.N., *Rajasthan Studies*, Agra, 1970.
———, *Rajasthan Through the Ages, Vol. II*, Bikaner, 1990.
Sharma, Hari, *Princes and Paramountcy*, New Delhi, 1978.
Sharma, M.L., *History of the Jaipur State*, Jaipur, 1969.
Sinh Ranbir, *History of Shekhawats*, Jaipur, 2001.
Smith, Bosworth, *Life of Lord Lawrence, Vol. II*, London, 1883.
Smith, V.A., *Akbar the Great Mogul*, Reprint Delhi, 1966.
———, *The Oxford History of India*, Oxford, 1920.
Srivastava, A.L., *A Short History of Akbar the Great, 1542-1605*, Agra, 1972.
Srivastava, H.S., *The History of Indian Famines, 1858-1918*, Agra, 1968.
Strachey, Sir John, *India : Its Administration and Progress*, Reprint Delhi, 1977.
Stern, Robert W., *The Cat and the Lion : Jaipur State in the British Raj*, Leiden, 1988.
Stratton, J.P., *The Jaipur-Amber Family and State*, Jaypur, 1885.
Tillotson, Giles, *Jaipur Nama, Tales from the Pink City*, London, 2006.
Tod, Colonel James, *Annals and Antiquities of Rajasthan, Vol. III*, edited by William Crooke, Reprint Delhi, 1994.
Tupper, Sir Lewis, *Our Indian Protectorate*, London, 1893.
Vashishtha, Vijay Kumar, *Rajputana Agency, 1832-1858*, Jaipur, 1978.
———, *1857 Revolt in the Princely State of Jaipur*, Jodhpur, 2008.

(b) Unpublished Ph.D. Theses

Bhargava, Vijay Lakshami, "British Policy towards the State of Rajasthan (1818-1947)", University of Rajasthan, Jaipur, 1973.
Bhatnawat, Shyam Singh, "A Study of Kachhawalia Nobility of Jaipur during 1700-1858 AD", University of Rajasthan, Jaipur, 1984.

Kaushik, Shobha, "Railways in Rajasthan", University of Rajasthan, Jaipur, 1987.

Mathur, Ram Kalyan, "Growth and Development of British Paramountcy in Rajasthan (1803-1858)", University of Rajasthan, Jaipur, 1972.

Mitra, Mallika, "Economic Impact of British Suzerainty Over Rajasthan (1818-1900)", University of Rajasthan, Jaipur, 1991.

Pawa, Saroj, "British Diplomacy in Rajasthan, 1858-1881", University of Rajasthan, Jaipur, 1982.

Soni, Moneeka, "Economic Impact of British Paramountcy in Rajputana, 1900-1947", University of Rajasthan, Jaipur, 1992.

(c) Journals and Periodicals

Bengal Past and Present, Calcutta.

Journal of Indian History, Trivandrum.

The Quarterly Review of Historical Studies, Calcutta.

Proceedings of Indian History Congress.

Proceedings of Rajasthan History Congress (Annual), 1967-2009.

Index